Baptists and the American Experience

Baptists and the American Experience

JAMES E. WOOD, JR.,
Editor

Judson Press® Valley Forge

3 1822

BAPTISTS AND THE AMERICAN EXPERIENCE

Unless otherwise indicated, Bible quotations in this volume are in accordance with the Revised Standard Version of the Bible, copyrighted 1952 and 1971 by the Division of Christian Education of the National Council of the Churches of Christ in the United States of America, and are used by permission.

Additional Bible quotations have been taken from *The New Testament in Modern English,* Rev. Ed. Copyright © J. B. Phillips 1972. Used by permission of The Macmillan Company and Geoffrey Bles, Ltd.

Library of Congress Cataloging in Publication Data
Main entry under title:

Baptists and the American experience.

Bibliography: p. 361.
Includes index.
1. Baptists—United States—Addresses, essays, lectures. I. Wood, James Edward.
BX6235.B36   286'.0973   76-22689
ISBN 0-8170-0721-0

The name JUDSON PRESS is registered as a trademark in the U.S. Patent Office.

Printed in the U.S.A. ⊕

Dedicated to

JOSEPH MARTIN DAWSON (1879-1973)
Executive Director, Baptist Joint Committee on Public Affairs
1946-1953

and

CARL EMANUEL CARLSON (1906-1976)
Executive Director, Baptist Joint Committee on Public Affairs
1954-1971

Articulate spokesmen for and ardent defenders of
religious liberty and the witness of Baptists
in public affairs

Preface

Centuries ago, the prophet Isaiah sounded forth a call to Israel, "Know whence you have come and whither you are going." In a similar vein, during the week of January 12-15, 1976, participants from across the nation, representing eight national Baptist bodies of the United States along with representation from the Baptist Federation of Canada, convened in Washington, D.C., for a National Bicentennial Convocation: Baptists and the American Experience. Planned on behalf of eight national Baptist bodies of the United States, the event was termed "convocation" because it was a calling together of Baptists to a deeper awareness of the commitments and realities of the American experience in the light of Baptist faith and practice.

Behind the planning for the Convocation was the conviction that the Bicentennial would have profound implications for the community of faith in America as well as the nation as a whole. It provided an appropriate and practical means whereby eight national Baptist bodies of the United States could join hands to review and reevaluate Baptists and the American experience. In both its breadth and focus the event was unprecedented for the Baptists of America.

The Convocation was held at the beginning of the year with the hope that critical questions would be raised and fresh insights would be gained regarding America's Bicentennial so as to challenge and enrich the role of Baptists in America. The event was planned independent of official civil observances of the Bicentennial in order that special focus could be given to the prophetic role of religion in the life of the nation.

While the Convocation was consciously planned so as to come at the beginning of the Bicentennial, the dates of the Convocation,

January 12-15, hold a special significance in American Baptist history since they come between the birthdays of two of the most influential figures Baptists have contributed to this nation. The Thursday preceding the Convocation marked the birthday of Isaac Backus, who was born January 9, 1724. No individual in America stands out so preeminently as the champion of religious liberty during the eighteenth century as does Isaac Backus. The Convocation closed the following Thursday on the birthday of Martin Luther King, Jr., who was born January 15, 1929—just a little more than two hundred years after Isaac Backus. No Baptist minister in the twentieth century has exerted more influence on the course of American history, nor more eloquently defended the cause of human rights, than Martin Luther King, Jr. Like Backus, King suffered imprisonment, Backus for religious liberty and King for his belief in the American dream of "liberty and justice for all." The legacies of Isaac Backus and Martin Luther King, Jr., may well have symbolized the Convocation's raison d'être and its hope for the future.

With but one exception, all the essays in this volume were expressly prepared for and originally presented at the Convocation. They are presented now in this volume in order to assure their wide distribution and to make more permanent their contribution toward discerning the role of Baptists in the life of the nation. The editor is particularly grateful to the contributing authors, representing six national Baptist bodies, for giving so generously of themselves in preparation of these essays for publication.

Special acknowledgment must be made to the following persons for their generous counsel and suggestions: Clarence C. Goen of Wesley Theological Seminary, Washington, D.C.; Winthrop S. Hudson of Colgate Rochester Divinity School/Bexley Hall/Crozer Theological Seminary, Rochester, New York; Lynn May, Jr., of the Southern Baptist Historical Commission, Nashville, Tennessee; W. Morgan Patterson of Golden Gate Theological Seminary, San Francisco, California; E. C. Smith of the Metropolitan Baptist Church, Washington, D.C.; Lorraine Williams of Howard University, Washington, D.C.; and Frank H. Woyke, former Executive Secretary of the North American Baptist Conference and former Associate Secretary of the Baptist World Alliance. To the Baptist Joint Committee on Public Affairs and staff the editor is deeply indebted for the preparation of this volume for publication. Two members of the staff, John W. Baker and Mrs. Fern Hamman, deserve special mention. As in all my labors, I owe an immeasurable debt of gratitude to my wife Alma. *James E. Wood, Jr.*

Contents

Introduction

JAMES E. WOOD, JR.

I

Stemming from the left-wing Puritanism of the English Reformation, Baptists emerged in seventeenth-century England out of a movement of dissent. Their emergence coincided with the beginnings of English colonization of the New World, of Jamestown in 1607 and Plymouth Rock in 1620.

During the latter part of the sixteenth century small groups of radical Puritans, known as "Separatists," became impatient with the delay of English authorities to effect a thoroughgoing reform of the Church of England. The Separatists differed from their fellow Puritans primarily in their conception of the church. There were of course differences among the Separatists themselves. Baptists came from those Separatists who envisioned the church as being comprised of persons who, "gathered" by the Holy Spirit, had covenanted with God and with one another in the formation of a congregation without any ties to a national church or to the state. They insisted that a true church should be composed of "visible saints" or believers only, that each local church should be completely autonomous, and that each believer should have equal voice in determining the affairs of the church. This, they contended, was the New Testament pattern of the church and hence the essential polity of any true church.

As Nonconformists, Separatists were persecuted as heretics of the church and traitors of the state. James I swore, "I will make them conforme themselves, or I will harrie them out of the land...."[1] Thus, religious persecution under James I forced many of the Separatists to

11

seek asylum in Holland, which welcomed Separatists from 1595 onward. Some of the Separatists settled in Leiden and some settled in Amsterdam. Eventually the Leiden congregation sailed for America and settled Plymouth Colony in 1620. An Amsterdam congregation of Separatists was formed in 1607 under the leadership of John Smyth. Here Smyth instituted the practice of believer's baptism, i.e., baptism restricted to those who made a voluntary confession of faith. From these Separatists, Smyth led approximately forty persons to organize the first Baptist church in 1609. Later, dissatisfied with Smyth's negotiations for union with Dutch Mennonites, Thomas Helwys led approximately a dozen persons to return to England in 1611 and to establish, apparently surreptitiously, the first Baptist church in England, at Spitalfield just outside London. Since this congregation held to the theology of Jacobus Arminius, that Christ had died for all, it became the first of a line of Baptist churches known as General Baptist churches.

Helwys brought with him a book he had written while in Amsterdam, *The Mistery of Iniquity,* which boldly set forth, for the first time in the English language, the right of universal religious liberty. Helwys wrote:

> Our Lord the King is but an earthly King, and he hath no authority as a King, but in earthly causes, and if the King's people be obedient and true subjects, obeying all humane laws made by the King, our Lord the King can require no more: for men's religion to God is betwixt God and themselves: the King shall not answere for it, neither may the King be jugd betwene God and Man. Let them be heretikes, Turcks, Jewes, or whatsoever, it apperteynes not to the earthly power to punish them in the least measure.[2]

The distribution of the book in England resulted in the confinement of Helwys in Newgate Prison by order of James I.

In order to distinguish themselves from the Dutch Mennonites, as well as other Separatists, this first Baptist congregation drew up a Confession of Faith. They pressed the covenant concept, beyond that of the Puritans, to mean the repudiation of infant baptism and the absolute separation of church and state. From their beginning in England, Baptists forthrightly contended for liberty of conscience and religious liberty. To Baptists, religious liberty required nothing less than the separation of church and state. The Baptist Confession of 1612, "Propositions and Conclusions concerning True Christian Religion . . . ," was signed by dissidents who had earlier fled the persecution of James I. Article 84 proclaimed:

> That the magistrate is not by virtue of his office to meddle with religion, or

matters of conscience, to force or compel men to this or that form of religion, or doctrine: but to leave the Christian religion free, to every man's conscience, and to handle only civil transgressions (Rom. xiii), injuries and wrongs of man against man, in murder, adultery, theft, etc., for Christ only is the king, and lawgiver of the church and conscience (James iv. 12).[3]

This confession has been generally accepted as "perhaps the first confession of faith of modern times to demand freedom of conscience and separation of church and state."[4]

Two years later, in 1614, Leonard Busher, apparently a member of this same Baptist congregation in England, courageously contended for full religious liberty for all, including Jews and Catholics, openly to profess and propagate their faiths. In a tractate entitled *Religious Peace or a Plea for Liberty of Conscience,* Busher advocated the separation of church and state as follows:

King and magistrates are to rule temporal affairs by the swords of their temporal kingdoms, and bishops and ministers are to rule spiritual affairs by the Word and Spirit of God, the sword of Christ's spiritual kingdom, and not to intermeddle one with another's authority, office, and function. ... It is not only unmerciful, but unnatural and abominable, yea, monstrous, for one Christian to vex and destroy another for difference and questions of religion.[5]

Busher maintained that one should be able to write, print, and publish diverse religious views freely.

A second group of English Baptists emerged in 1638, when a new congregation was formed by several members of a Congregational church in London over the question of believer's baptism. Requesting dismissal from the Congregational church, they formed the first of a line of Baptist churches known as Calvinistic or Particular Baptists, so named because of their view of limited atonement, that Christ died for the elect. Although Baptists still had no legally guaranteed civil rights, Baptist churches and membership increased and Baptist principles came to exert some influence on English life. John Milton, perhaps England's greatest poet artist and an ardent Puritan Separatist, came to accept believer's baptism. He joined with Baptists in the espousal of religious liberty. "Give me the liberty," Milton wrote, "to know, to utter, and to argue freely according to conscience, above all liberties."[6] John Bunyan embraced the Baptist faith and became one of its most illustrious preachers and leaders.

The year 1644 is profoundly significant in the history of religious liberty and Baptist witness thereto, for within that year were published Milton's *Areopagitica,* Roger Williams' masterpiece, *The Bloudy Tenent, or Persecution for the cause of Conscience,* which was actually published in London and not in America, and the

London Confession of 1644, which remains a landmark in Baptist thought as "the first publication of the doctrine of freedom of conscience, in an official document representing a body of associated churches."[7] Drawn up by the Particular (Calvinistic) Baptists in order to distinguish themselves from the General (Arminian) Baptists and the Anabaptists, the Confession was the basis of Henry C. Vedder's writing early in this century, "Baptists might fairly claim that, whatever might have been said by isolated individuals before, they were the pioneer body among modern Christian denominations to advocate the right of all men to worship God, each according to dictates of his own conscience, without let or hindrance from any earthly power."[8] Meanwhile, from this period on, the Particular Baptists steadily became the leading group among the English Baptists.

This brief résumé of Baptist beginnings in England is important in understanding the beginnings of Baptists in America, with which present-day American Baptists are all too unfamiliar. But it is also a reminder that the experience of Baptists in colonial America was largely an extension of the situation in which they found themselves back in England during the same period. What makes the account all the more relevant to this volume is that the beginnings of Baptists in England were practically contemporaneous with the beginnings of Baptists in America.

II

As in England, Baptist beginnings in America were met by harassment, intolerance, and persecution. In neither a Puritan-established Massachusetts Bay nor an Anglican-established Virginia would Baptists find any more recognition of religious liberty than in seventeenth-century England. To be sure, the powers of the episcopacy and the Crown were immeasurably weaker in America, but establishment in the New World largely followed the pattern of the Old. Nine of the thirteen colonies had established churches: in Massachusetts, Connecticut, and New Hampshire the Congregational Church was established by law, while in Maryland, Virginia, North Carolina, South Carolina, Georgia, and New York City and three neighboring counties the Anglican Church was established. The four exceptions to establishment were Rhode Island, Pennsylvania, New Jersey, and Delaware. Both of the original and most influential of the colonies, Virginia and Massachusetts, resisted religious toleration and were slow to permit religious pluralism. Except for Rhode Island and Maryland, religious toleration did not come into the colonies until the eighteenth century. The early Puritans desired freedom *for themselves,* and Puritan leaders expressly condemned democracy, which Governor John Winthrop, the real founder of the Massachusetts Colony, called "the meanest and worst of all forms of government."[9] John Cotton, who regarded even toleration as "anti-Christian," wrote, "It is better that the commonwealth be fashioned to the setting forth of Gods house, which is his church: than to accommodate the church . . . to the civil state." Of democracy, he wrote, "I do not conceyve that ever God did ordeyne it as a fitt government eyther for church or commonwealth." Like his Puritan contemporaries, Cotton held that "Theocracy" was "the best forme of government in the commonwealth, as well as in the church."[10] The pioneer Baptist leader John Clarke wrote of Massachusetts during this period: "The authority there established can not permit men, though of ever so civil, sober and peaceful a spirit and life, freely to enjoy their understandings and consciences, nor yet to live, or come among them, unless they can do as they do, say as they say, *or else say nothing,* and so may a man live at Rome also."[11]

As noted in the first two essays in this volume, prior to the American Revolution Baptists were a small and somewhat disinherited sect. While Baptists were to become by the nineteenth century the largest Protestant denomination in America, they were the most persecuted of all religious sects in colonial America. Many of the most prominent early Baptist leaders were persecuted for the propagation of their faith. Largely banished from Massachusetts Bay, where Baptists first appeared in the New World, Baptists sought refuge in Rhode Island, Pennsylvania, and the southern colonies.

Accounts of persecution of Baptists during the colonial period are numerous. Roger Williams and John Clarke, both of whom led in the founding of the first Baptist churches on American soil, Providence in 1639 and Newport in 1641 respectively, fled Massachusetts' authorities who charged them with disseminating "divers and dangerous opinions." Obadiah Holmes was arrested in Lynn and publicly whipped in Boston in 1651 for preaching against infant baptism. The minister of the first Baptist church of Boston was repeatedly imprisoned and his health undermined as a result of the harsh treatment given him on account of his preaching. Upon the completion in 1678 of the first meetinghouse for Baptists in Boston, the General Court ordered its doors closed and decreed that Baptists be "inhibited to hold any meeting therein or to open ye doors thereof." When Henry Dunster, who was the first president of

Harvard College and who held that position for twelve years, became a Baptist, he was summarily dismissed in 1654 upon the request of the General Court that the college not "continue in office any teacher unsound in faith." Three years later Dunster was prosecuted twice for refusing to have his infant daughter baptized.[12] Indeed, persecution of dissenters continued in Massachusetts until 1692 when a new charter from William and Mary granted a degree of toleration.

Harassment followed Baptists also in Virginia, which nevertheless was the scene of the greatest growth of Baptists in the South. Although persecution was less severe generally than in Massachusetts, between 1765 and 1770 in Virginia "the persecution of the Baptists," one historian has written, "may be rated as the worst and most inexcusable assault on freedom of conscience and worship, which our colonial history describes."[13]

The story of Baptists and the American experience must necessarily begin with Roger Williams. America's greatest prophet of liberty in the colonial period and founder of the colony of Rhode Island, and for a time a Baptist himself, Williams sought to maintain the religious and scriptural basis for religious liberty and the separation of church and state. Inspired by John Murton, who had become pastor of the first Baptist church on English soil upon the imprisonment of Thomas Helwys, Williams maintained with Murton that religion must be free from state interference. Williams insisted that the authority of the state is "not religious, Christian, etc., but natural, human, [and] civil," and therefore it is "improper" in proscribing conscience or religious matters. Williams laid the foundation for the secular state, which he saw as supported by scripture and Christian theology. "All lawful magistrates in the world, both before the coming of Christ Jesus and since," Williams wrote, "are but derivatives and agents . . . serving for the good of the whole.[14] Therefore, "no civil state or country can be truly called Christian, although true Christians be in it."[15]

To Williams, church and state must be separate not only for the church to be the church, but also for the state to be the state, God to be God, and for Christians to be Christians. The state can never assume that the role of God, who alone is Lord of conscience, and faith, to be genuine, must be free and voluntary. As a consequence Williams maintained that compulsory and tax-supported religion is unchristian, that Israel cannot be a model state for Christians, that the Indians held a prior right to the land, and that the democratic state requires an equality of all persons and groups before the law. It would be difficult to overstate the importance of Williams to

American and Baptist history.[16] The late Perry Miller, esteemed for his remarkably sound judgment of American colonial history, declared:

> For the subsequent history of what became the United States, Roger Williams possesses one indubitable importance, that he stands at the beginning of it. Just as some great experience in the youth of a person is ever afterward a determinant of his personality, so the American character has inevitably been molded by the fact that in the first years of colonization there arose this prophet of religious liberty. . . . as a figure and a reputation he was always there to remind Americans that no other conclusion than absolute religious freedom was feasible in this society.[17]

The significance of Williams must always include the *fact* of the "livelie experiment" of Rhode Island, the birthplace of Baptists in the New World and the first modern state which guaranteed full religious liberty and the separation of religious matters from civil authority.

John Clarke, Williams's close associate and founder of the second Baptist church on American soil at Newport, Rhode Island, was no less vigorous than Williams in advocating complete religious liberty. Clarke shared with Williams a strong belief in "soul liberty" or freedom of conscience. It was of course largely through the efforts of this Baptist, John Clarke, who remained in England from 1651 to 1664, that the charter for Rhode Island was issued in 1663. In petitioning Charles II in 1662 for a charter for Rhode Island, Clarke declared, "A most flourishing civil state may stand, yea, and best be maintained . . . with a full liberty in religious concernments." [18] When issued, this unique charter forthrightly stated that "noe person within the sayd colonie, at any time hereafter, shall bee in any wise molested, punished, disquieted, or called in question, for any differences in opinione in matters of religion. . . ." [19] Although less well known than Williams in American intellectual and political history, Clarke is hardly less significant to religious liberty in America and is today generally credited with being "Father of Rhode Island" and "Father of American Baptists."

The eighteenth century holds special significance in American Baptist history as well as in our national history. As noted in the first essay in this volume, not until then did Baptists experience any substantial growth of churches, geographically or numerically. A phenomenal growth began during the last decades of the eighteenth century—a phenomenon which has subsequently and dramatically marked the history of Baptists in the United States.[20] Aided by the great colonial awakenings, the Baptist struggle for religious liberty also reached its climax during this period, with the adoption of the First Amendment to the Constitution.

III

When viewed in retrospect, Baptist beginnings markedly underscore the changed status of Baptists in twentieth-century America. In less than two hundred years since the founding of the nation, Baptists have moved from the position of a persecuted and disinherited sect to the largest Protestant denomination in America, comprising approximately one-seventh of the total population. In many parts of the country Baptists have become socially established as the dominant and largest religious community. Far from being regarded as radicals or revolutionaries, as they were in seventeenth-century England and America, Baptists today are generally and widely regarded as politically and socially conservative, defenders of the status quo. As one perceptive Baptist historian has expressed it, "Far too easily the Baptists lost their radical stance only to become captive to a culture and too often the uncritical advocates of a folk religion that they helped to create."[21]

The essays in this volume attempt to review and interpret for today the symbiosis of Baptists and the American experience, from the beginnings of the nation up through the present. Although the essays in this volume were occasioned by the Bicentennial, they have not been written in terms of celebrating the American experience or to be self-serving of Baptist interests in America. The Bicentennial is far more than a celebration of two hundred years of America's nationhood. To be sure, there is much to celebrate in the American experience, but there is also much to lament in that experience. Like Israel of old, let it be said, America has often failed to be the nation that it has professed to be. Any honest examination of the American past, or present for that matter, should serve as a reminder of the disparity between the professed ideals of the nation's commitments and the manifest realities of the nation's history. Therein lies much of the irony of, and much of the struggle within, the American experience. Meanwhile, Baptists have been an integral part of that experience, both its manifest realities as well as its professed ideals. For Baptists to exercise the prophetic role of religion must not mean a refusal to assume some responsibility for the failures of the nation to live up to its commitments.

One of the real dangers of "celebrating the Bicentennial" has been the tendency to sanctify the American experience and to mythologize the past so as to obscure the blemishes of our national history. Disparities and inconsistencies in the American experience are thereby largely ignored. The tendency is no less descriptive of religious denominations as well. Such "celebration" of the past easily takes the form of self-congratulation and self-justification. A creative tension between the ideals and realities of the American experience is always needed. This tension is equally needed in the life of any denomination.

Particular attention is given in this volume to the role Baptists have played and/or not played in America and the influence, both good and bad, of the American experience on Baptists. The role of Baptists is viewed critically, both positively and negatively. The essays which follow are both appreciative and critical of "Baptists and the American Experience." While the essays are marked by a sense of history, their purpose is to provide a basis upon which to perceive the present and to meet the challenges of the future, not to dwell on the past.

Probing analyses of the interaction of Baptists and the making of the nation are provided in Part One. Both the influences on Baptists and the influences of Baptists in the making of the nation are scrutinized and evaluated in these first two essays. At the conclusion of his essay, Edwin S. Gaustad poses the crucial question of whether, upon reflection, "Baptists constitute a leaven in national life, or have they become the loaf?"

The essays in Part Two of this volume examine the real meaning for today of the American Revolution and the basic truths embodied in the Declaration of Independence and the Constitution, especially the Bill of Rights. The American Revolution was more than a beginning. Certainly, it does not symbolize an end, but a commitment of the nation to the future. As Benjamin Rush wrote in 1786, "A belief has arisen that the American Revolution is *over*. This is so far from being the case that we have only finished the first act of the great drama."[22] Two hundred years later, we, too, must declare that the American Revolution is not over—its agenda is still not complete. Thus, these essays attempt to underscore in more meaningful ways for today that the American Revolution remains unfinished so long as the promise of the American dream of "liberty and justice for all" remains unfulfilled. The dynamics of the American Revolution belong to each generation of Americans.

Part Three focuses on the interaction of the church and the nation at home and abroad. This theme is inextricably intertwined with Baptists and the American experience. Baptists have been profoundly influenced by American culture and have in fact often been identified as one of America's truly indigenous denominations. Nowhere else have Baptists flourished as in the United States, and their missionary or world outreach has been one of the prominent features of American Baptists. The historical juxtaposition of the world outreach of Baptists and the gradual emergence of the United States as a world power is a reality which simply cannot be ignored. Part Four is concerned with the dynamics of religious liberty and public policy. No theme is more central to Baptists and the American experience than religious liberty, which on the one hand has long been regarded as the most distinctive feature of American political and religious life, and on the other hand has been the most conspicuous principle of Baptist faith and practice. The American tradition of religious liberty and the separation of church and state, as embodied in the First Amendment, represented on behalf of the founding fathers a bold experiment unparalleled in human history. The uniqueness of this American tradition of church-state relations is of tremendous importance in understanding both the political and religious history of the United States. It was fundamental in the development of this nation and is widely regarded as America's greatest contribution to world civilization.[23] To this, it must be said, Baptists clearly made a distinct and notable contribution.[24] It is this tradition of religious liberty that has made possible the witness of the churches in public affairs, which is, in fact, the exercise by the churches of their religious liberty. Today serious threats to the First Amendment may be found in the recurring propensity of the nation's political leaders to absolutize American nationalism or "national interests" and to give preferential status and special sanctity to America in the form of a civil religion which boldly declares, "America is great, because America is good." Such a stance is incompatible with biblical faith and with the prophetic role of religion which views all nations as being under divine judgment.

The essays in Part Five provide important case studies of various Baptist bodies which have shared in the American experience and reflections on the unity and diversity of Baptists. As four of the essays in this section illustrate, the proliferation of Baptists in America has been primarily cultural—regional and ethnic—and not theological. The black Baptist experience, although sorely neglected in the historiography of both American Baptists and American Christianity, is an important part of the history of the Baptists of America as well as the history of American Christianity. These essays also highlight the pluralism of Baptists and reflect, in their own way, the pluralistic character of the nation itself. The motto on the obverse side of the Great Seal of the United States—*e pluribus unum*—testifies to an American concept that unity and diversity are not incompatible terms. It may even be suggested that unity is the product of diversity. At no point would one find Baptists more in harmony with the American character than in this regard. For, as the concluding essay suggests, unity and diversity are "mutually supportive and enriching." They go hand in hand. This interdependence of unity and diversity is urgently needed to be rediscovered by Americans generally and by Baptists in particular as the nation enters its third century.

NOTES

[1] Wilbur K. Jordan, *The Development of Religious Toleration in England (1603-1640)* (Cambridge: Harvard University Press, 1936), p. 20.

[2] Thomas Helwys, *A Short Declaration of the Mistery of Iniquity,* fac. reprint ed. (London: Kingsgate Press, 1935), p. 69.

[3] William L. Lumpkin, *Baptist Confessions of Faith,* rev. ed. (Valley Forge: Judson Press, 1969), p. 140. See also W. T. Whitley, *The Works of John Smyth,* 2 vols. (Cambridge: Cambridge University Press, 1915), vol. 2, p. 748.

[4] Lumpkin, *Baptist Confessions of Faith,* p. 124.

[5] *The Baptist Encyclopedia,* rev. ed., s.v. "Busher, Leonard"; see also Anson Phelps Stokes, *Church and State in the United States,* 3 vols. (New York: Harper & Row, Publishers, 1950), vol. 1, p. 113.

[6] John Milton, *Areopagitica* (1644); readily available in numerous collections of Milton's works and anthologies of English literature.

[7] Henry C. Vedder, *A Short History of the Baptists* (Philadelphia: The American Baptist Publication Society, 1907), p. 212. This confession has been perhaps the most influential single Baptist confession of faith. "Its immediate value to Baptist life can hardly be overstated," says Lumpkin, *Baptist Confessions of Faith,* p. 152. It was also about this time that the term "Baptist" was used to apply to those Separatists who insisted upon believer's baptism.

[8] Vedder, *A Short History of the Baptists,* p. 213.

[9] John Winthrop, *The History of New England from 1630 to 1649;* cited by Ernest Barker, *Church, State and Education* (London: Methuen and Co., Ltd., 1930), p. 121.

[10] John Cotton, *Letters to Lord Say and Seal* (1636); reprinted in Perry Miller and Thomas H. Johnson, *The Puritans* (New York: American Book Company, 1938), pp. 209-210.

[11] John Clarke, *Ill Newes from New England: Or a Narrative of New-England's Persecution, Wherein is declared That while old England is becoming new, New England is become Old* (1652); cited by John M. Mecklin, *The Story of American Dissent* (New York: Harcourt Brace Jovanovich, Inc., 1934), p. 139.

[12] See Sanford H. Cobb, *The Rise of Religious Liberty in America* (New York: Macmillan, Inc., 1902), p. 204.

[13] *Ibid.*, p. 111.

[14] *The Bloudy Tenent, of Persecution for cause of Conscience, discussed, in a Conference between Truth and Peace* (1644); see vol. 3 of *The Complete Writings of Roger Williams,* 7 vols. (New York: Russell and Russell, Inc., 1963).

[15] See James Ernst, *Roger Williams: New England Firebrand* (New York: Macmillan, Inc., 1932), p. 429. Unfortunately, the author views Williams, as did Vernon Parrington, as primarily a political philosopher rather than a theologian.

[16] See, for example, George Bancroft, *History of the United States* (New York: D. Appleton and Co., 1892), vol. 1, pp. 375-376: "The First person in modern Christendom to assert in its full plenitude the doctrine of liberty of conscience"; Oscar S. Straus, *Roger Williams: The Pioneer of Religious Liberty* (New York: Appleton-Century-Crofts, 1956), p. 15: "Perhaps much more than we have realized Roger Williams became the real founder of the New Republic. . . ."; Francesco Ruffini, *Religious Liberty* (London: Norgate Co., 1912), p. 171: "Henceforth the noble cause of religious liberty may find one who will develop it with greater vigour of reasoning and more copious erudition, but never one, however fervent a believer, who will excel Roger Williams in breadth of conception of sincerity of advocating that cause."

[17] Perry Miller, *Roger Williams: His Contribution to the American Tradition* (Indianapolis: The Bobbs-Merrill Company, Inc., 1953), p. 254.

[18] *Records of the Colony of Rhode Island and Providence Plantations;* cited by Stokes, *Church and State in the United States,* vol. 1, p. 205.

[19] *Ibid.*

[20] See Edwin Scott Gaustad, *Historical Atlas of Religion in America* (New York: Harper & Row, Publishers, 1962), pp. 10-13, 55-59.

[21] William R. Estep, "New England Dissent, 1630–1833: A Review Article," *Church History,* vol. 41 (June, 1972), p. 251.

[22] Benjamin Rush, *Essays: Literary, Moral, and Philosophical,* 2nd ed. (Philadelphia: Thomas and Wm. Bradford, 1806), p. 68.

[23] To quote from a famous case before the New York Supreme Court, the principle of complete religious liberty "has always been regarded by the American people as the very heart of its national life"; *Miami Military Institute* v. *Leff,* 129 Misc. 481, 220 N.Y.S. 799, 810. Peter Drucker has written that "the relationship between religion, the state, and society, is perhaps the most fundamental—certainly it is the most distinctive—feature of American political as well as American religious life"; cited by William Lee Miller, "Religion and the American Way of Life," *Religion and the Free Society* (New York: The Fund for the Republic, 1958), p. 18. See also Leo Pfeffer, "Freedom and Separation: America's Contribution to Civilization," *Journal of Church and State,* vol. 2 (November, 1960), pp. 100-111.

[24] See Joseph M. Dawson, *Baptists and the American Republic* (Nashville: Broadman Press, 1956); William G. McLoughlin, *New England Dissent, 1630–1833,* 2 vols. (Cambridge, Mass.: Harvard University Press, 1971); and Anson Phelps Stokes, *Church and State in the United States,* vol. 1, pp. 194-216, 306-310, 353-357, 368-375, 759-763; vol. 3, pp. 485-489.

PART ONE

Baptists:
The American Revolution,
and the Making
of a Nation

1

Baptists,
the Pilgrim Fathers,
and the
American Revolution

WINTHROP S. HUDSON

Between 1770 and 1800 Baptists emerged from relative obscurity to become the largest denomination in America.

This thirty-year period is known as the age of the American Revolution. It began in 1770 with the "Boston Massacre" and other skirmishes preceding the Declaration of Independence. It included the seven-year war that followed, the makeshift political arrangements of the Articles of Confederation, the struggle to draft and then to secure the adoption of the federal Constitution, and finally the time of testing in the last decade of the century when it was not yet clear whether or not the new nation could gain sufficient stability to survive.

These thirty years from 1770 to 1800 were a troubled time for most American churches. The Presbyterian General Assembly in 1798 echoed a common lament when it bewailed the "general dereliction of religious principle and practice among our fellow citizens" and complained of a "visible and prevailing impiety and contempt for the laws and institutions of religion." Similar views were voiced by leading Congregational and Episcopal divines. Lyman Beecher reported that "irreligion hath become in all parts of our land, alarmingly prevalent," with "the name of God . . . blasphemed, the bible . . . denounced, the sabbath . . . profaned, the public worship of God . . . neglected." So depressed had Bishop Samuel Provoost of the Episcopal Church become that in 1801 he relinquished his episcopal duties, being convinced that the church would "die out with the old colonial families."[1] Baptists, on the other hand, had little cause to express such gloomy forebodings about their prospects.

Baptist experience during the politically troubled years from 1770 to 1800 was in marked contrast to that of denominations which in 1770 had enjoyed preeminence in numbers, prestige, and influence. Unlike the denominations which were lamenting a prevailing impiety and neglect of public worship, Baptists had been and were experiencing a sweeping surge of growth. Instead of diminishing in numbers, Baptists had increased. They had increased at such an astonishing rate that by 1800 Baptists had outpaced all other religious bodies to become the largest religious group in America, with twice as many adherents as the next largest denomination.[2]

Such a startling and even disconcerting countertrend among Baptists requires some explanation. How does one account for this remarkable Baptist growth when other denominations were suffering demoralization and decline?

I

To measure the magnitude of the Baptist achievement from 1770 to 1800, it is necessary to go back to the preceding thirty years to place the period in proper perspective.

As late as 1740 Baptists in America were a small, undistinguished, and little-noted religious group. There were only a handful of churches in New England (three in Connecticut and eight in Massachusetts), a similar handful in the middle colonies (five in New Jersey and six in Pennsylvania), and a still smaller handful in the southern colonies. Even Rhode Island, which traditionally had been regarded as a center of Baptist strength, had only one "regular" Baptist church, the others being Seventh Day or Six Principle churches outside of what was to be the mainstream of Baptist life.

Thirty years later, in 1770 the number of Baptist churches was still modest. Their rate of increase, to be sure, from a very small base, was impressive. While not yet regarded as a serious rival by the major denominations, Baptists nonetheless were exhibiting unusual vigor and vitality. This was true in New England where the new vitality first manifested itself. It also was true in the South where, after 1755, the contagious enthusiasm of Baptist preachers from New England began to awaken a growing response.

In retrospect it is clear that by 1770 Baptists had several things going for them—increasing numbers, new leaders, a new spirit, and a new sense of mission, purpose, and destiny. In one way or another all these were related to the "Separate" Congregationalists of New England. Even in the South the multiplying number of Baptists was the result of the vitality introduced by New England "Separates" turned Baptist. In 1755, Sandy Creek, North Carolina, became the base from which the revivals associated with Shubal Stearns radiated throughout the North Carolina piedmont and the adjacent counties of southside Virginia. Stearns's brother-in-law, Daniel Marshall, also from New England, extended the sphere of vigorous Baptist evangelistic activity into South Carolina and Georgia. Later, John Leland, of Connecticut, was to bring a new burst of Baptist zeal to the central piedmont area of Virginia. These successes in the South and those of lesser degree in the middle colonies pointed back to New England where the shape of things to come had been fashioned.

The story of the pre-1770 shift in Baptist fortunes begins with the Great Awakening in New England and with the attempts that were made to contain the fervor generated by the Awakening. The containment efforts led to tension, conflict, division, and in the end to a steady drift of Congregationalists into the Baptist fold.

The enthusiasm spawned by the Awakening created tension primarily at two points.[3] The first was the insistence of partisans of the Awakening that church membership should be restricted to those who could testify to their own personal experience of the miracle of grace. The second was the desire of the "awakened" to have "awakening" preachers as their pastors. The pattern of conflict varied from parish to parish. Where an "awakening" preacher was firmly entrenched as pastor, there was less likelihood of overt conflict. But when a new pastor was to be called, ordained, and installed, ample opportunities existed in the political-ecclesiastical arrangements of the New England system to thwart the desires of the "awakened." This was true even when the partisans of the Awakening were able to marshal the support of the church membership. When any of these opportunities for obstruction were utilized, the eager enthusiasts of the revival were quick to assert that the spiritual energy released by the Awakening should not be subject to restraint by an unregenerate parish majority composed of nonchurch members, nor by an extra-congregational ecclesiastical authority (most commonly by ministerial associations), nor by acts of the General Court. As sturdy individualists, members of the "awakened" faction were especially scornful of the notion that God operated through an elite composed of "the learned clergy and the upper social orders." In the Awakening, so they believed, God had "demonstrated his willingness, in this New World, to by-pass these groups" and to make his will known directly to "His chosen saints of whatever order of society or learning."[4]

When "awakened" Congregationalists failed to reform their parish church and especially when they were denied the right to ordain the pastor of their choice, many proceeded to withdraw and form a "Separate" congregation of their own. Subject to constant legal and ecclesiastical harassment by representatives of the Standing Order, these "Separate" Congregationalists tended to gravitate into the ranks of the Baptists.[5] This drift to the Baptists was equally true of disenchanted Congregationalists who did not have an opportunity to take the intermediate step of forming or joining a "Separate" church.

It is not surprising that there should have been this drift to the Baptists, for the disaffected Congregationalists found the Baptist churches congenial at almost every point. Baptists were firmly committed to a church membership restricted to convinced believers. Baptist churches were democratically governed and not subject to control by any unregenerate parish majority. Baptists had long defended their right to religious liberty. Theologically, "Separates" and Baptists were of one mind, and the shift to the practice of believer's baptism was neither difficult to make nor difficult to justify on the basis of convictions which had been the occasion for the "Separates'" break with the churches of the Standing Order.

As a consequence of the drift to the Baptists, the once powerful "Separate" movement in New England withered away after 1754.[6] The former "Separate" Congregationalists constituted a new breed of Baptists. They were neither accustomed to nor ready to accept a sectarian status and the social stigma such status entailed. Many had been and were persons of some stature in their respective communities, and they were not prepared to submit easily to infractions of what they considered as their rights.

As important as the new members Baptists garnered in the years prior to 1770 were the new leaders they acquired, leaders who were brash, self-confident, and self-assertive. By 1760 the new leaders had seized the initiative. Hitherto Baptists had sought little more than "mere survival within the Puritan system."[7] The new leadership, however, was not content to maintain a defensive posture and hope that by good behavior they would be able to retain the concessions granted them by the Standing Order. The new leaders had a larger goal than mere survival in mind. Instead of seeking concessions, they were determined to reform the whole New England system. Far from being passive, they were bold and aggressive, even truculent, in their attacks on the Standing Order and in their demand that it be restructured on the basis of full and complete religious liberty.

As was true in the South, the new Baptist leaders in New England were former "Separate" Congregationalists, men who had sharpened their propagandist weapons and developed their leadership skills in the guerrilla wars they had waged both within and against the established Congregational churches. The most conspicuous of the new leaders was Isaac Backus. It was Backus more than anyone else who infused the Baptists of New England with a new sense of mission, purpose, and destiny: a sense of mission, purpose, and destiny which was first identified with the "errand into the wilderness" of the Pilgrim Fathers, and then later was linked to the mission, purpose, and destiny of the emerging nation.

During the decade prior to 1770 Backus was busy fashioning what can only be described as a propagandist coup. Far from being upstarts, he insisted, Baptists were the true heirs of the first settlers. Unlike the representatives of the Standing Order who had defected from the first principles of New England, Baptists had remained constant in their devotion to the founding fathers. In doctrine, in church government, and especially in their defense of religious liberty, Baptists were the faithful children, the loyal descendants, of those who had fled oppression in their native land to establish a haven of liberty in the American wilderness.

In tract after tract, Backus depicted New England as "the land to which our ancestors fled for religious liberty."[8] It is true, he acknowledged, that it was not long before a "warping off" from the principles of the founders began to take place. But, Backus noted, this "warping off" began quite accidentally and unintentionally. New Englanders were scarcely aware at the outset how unscripturally they were confounding church and state together, for they continued to make strenuous efforts in the early years to keep them distinct.[9] As time passed, however, those who had left England to find freedom to worship God according to their own consciences became as fond of a compulsory religious uniformity as those from whom they fled. Fortunately, Backus observed, "nothing teaches like experience." Consequently, it is much "easier now to discover the mistakes" that were made "than it was for them to do it then."[10]

The most interesting and audacious propagandist item Backus produced was his *History of New England,* a detailed account of the mistakes that had been made and of the oppressions that flowed therefrom.[11] His purpose in compiling the history, as he noted in the Preface to the first volume, was to document the fact that "oppression on religious accounts was not of the first principles of New England but was an intruder that came in afterward." This point was reiterated in the second volume, with Backus again noting that "the first planters of New England requested no more than equal liberty of conscience" and that "on this foundation was New England planted. . . ." [12] This was the basic premise Backus had sought to establish in his tracts, but he also wished to pin down a larger contention. Taken as a whole, his *History of New England* was a remarkable tour de force, for Backus had the audacity to add as a subtitle: "with Particular Reference to the Denomination of Christians Called Baptists." The clear inference was that Baptists provided the central thread, the continuing witness, the true succession in the history of New England.

The mind-set cultivated by the propagandist campaign did two very important things for Baptists. By identifying themselves with those who first came to New England, Baptists gained status and respectability. This, in turn facilitated their evangelistic efforts and made it much easier to win new recruits. It also made their attacks on the Standing Order immeasurably more effective. In the second place, it gave Baptists a larger sense of mission. They came to view themselves as instruments of a new reformation that would restore New England to its first foundation. Through the Baptists the whole political-ecclesiastical order of New England was to be remodeled and reconstituted to bring it into conformity with the original purpose of the "errand into the wilderness."

By their accounts of how the memory of the Fathers had been dishonored by past and present oppressions, Baptists sought to prick the consciences of leading representatives of the Standing Order. In even more demanding tones, Baptists reminded the Massachusetts leadership of the "charter liberties" guaranteed tender consciences by the Charter of 1691. In their demand for religious liberty, Baptists were touching the New England establishment at a vulnerable point. Ever since Massachusetts Bay had lost its original charter, New England Congregationalists had utilized carefully qualified arguments for religious liberty as a means of defending their privileges against Anglican encroachments, and this had led to some modification of their practice. Still the basic system remained unimpaired. So commonplace had the appeal to religious liberty become that in 1765, when John Adams became alarmed by the twin threats of "stamping" and "episcopizing," he felt neither hesitancy nor embarrassment in attempting to rally public opinion with the peremptory summons: "Let the pulpit resound with the doctrines and sentiments of religious liberty," for there is "direct and formal design on foot, to enslave all America." [13] The Baptist response to such rhetoric was to press the Congregationalists ever more firmly to bring their practice into accord with their profession.

The Baptist propaganda campaign was more successful in winning new members than it was in effecting change in the New England church-state system. Still it did succeed in placing the Congregational establishment on the defensive. Ezra Stiles, for example, in 1760 felt it necessary to defend the liberality of the New England way in his *Discourse on the Christian Union*. This was an indirect reply, for Stiles blandly ignored specific complaints that were being made. Instead he simply affirmed that New England's ecclesiastical arrangements were fully consonant with a profession of religious liberty. He described "the happy policy of establishing one sect without infringing on the essential rights of others" which "is peculiar to the three New England provinces where Congregationalism is the establishment." The secret of this "happy" state of affairs is two-fold. First, the congregational polity of the established churches provides its own guarantee of liberty and guard against tyranny. There can be no centralized ecclesiastical despotism, since "each congregation had an unlimited, absolute, and self-determining power in the choice of their own officers." Second, other churches are permitted to exist, and while all inhabitants are taxed for the support of religion, certified members of recognized dissenting groups can assign their taxes to the church of their choice. This latitude, Stiles concluded, makes possible "the friendly cohabitation of all."[14]

Stiles's idealized account was of small comfort to Baptists. It glossed over the disabilities and harassments which made "friendly cohabitation" difficult for those who existed on the periphery of privilege. It did serve, on the other hand, to confirm representatives of the Standing Order in their view that they were pursuing an enlightened and benevolent policy of religious liberty. Those on the periphery of privilege, however, found Stiles's description of their situation far from persuasive. Small wonder that they should have greeted with some reserve John Adams's ringing summons in 1765 to join the Congregationalists in preaching up the doctrines and sentiments of religious liberty. Whose liberty did he have in mind?

II

With this backward glance at the Baptists in the years prior to 1770, the question still remains: How does one account for the emergence of the Baptists from relative obscurity in 1770 to become by 1800 the largest religious group in America, with twice as many adherents as the next largest denomination? By 1770 Baptists were increasing in number, but the total was still modest.

One indispensable prerequisite to Baptist success was whole-hearted support of the American Revolution. In 1770 this support could not have been taken for granted. While Baptists shared the grievances of other colonists and were predisposed to join the agitation which preceded the Declaration of Independence, New England Baptists were momentarily ambivalent about breaking the ties with the mother country. They hesitated because their fight for liberty had not been with the British but with the New England Congregationalists. The Standing Order in New England was their major antagonist, circumscribing their freedom by actions of parish majorities and by regulations of the General Court. Indeed, from time to time, Baptists had been able to appeal to Britain for protection against the denial of what Baptists regarded as their "charter rights." Were Baptists prepared to sacrifice this advantage? From which direction came the greatest threat to their liberties?

In 1770 Backus noted that many New Englanders who were loudest in their "cry of LIBERTY and against oppressors are at the same time themselves violating the dearest of all rights, LIBERTY OF CONSCIENCE." [15] Three years later, writing on behalf of the Grievance Committee of the Warren Association, Backus acknowledged that "a general union" for "the preservation of our liberties" was of great importance. But, he asked, "how can such a union be expected so long as that dearest of all rights, equal liberty of conscience, is not allowed?" You who "inhabit the land to which our ancestors fled for religious liberty" complain "because you are taxed where you are not represented." May we not make the same complaint of you? "Is it not really so with us?" [16]

It did not take New England Baptists long to resolve their dilemma. They quickly concluded that the greater threat came from England and England's bishops. The answer to their dilemma was to campaign on two fronts—against Britain for civil liberty and against the Congregationalists for religious liberty. They would join their neighbors to counter the threat from abroad without relaxing their struggle to secure religious liberty at home. "While the defence of the civil rights of America appeared [to us] a matter of great importance," reported Backus in 1784, "our religious liberties were by no means to be neglected; and [among us] the contest concerning each kept a pretty even pace throughout the war." [17]

Elsewhere in the colonies, except perhaps in Virginia, Baptists had no such quandary to resolve. Even where there was an establishment of religion, the infringement of civil and religious liberties came from the same source. The government of the king and the church of the king constituted a common foe, and few Baptists entertained qualms about joining the revolutionary struggle.[18] The Anglican religious establishments, moreover, were mostly paper establishments which quickly toppled and collapsed.[19] Only in Virginia did the Church of England have any strong indigenous support, and in Virginia the Baptists adopted the two-front strategy being pursued in New England. In Virginia, John Leland provided the conspicuous leadership in the two-pronged enterprise, carrying on the struggle for religious freedom during the war years as part of the revolutionary struggle itself.[20]

A second external circumstance effectively reduced the competition for members. If identification with the Revolutionary cause was a factor favorable to Baptist growth, Anglicans and Quakers suffered from the lack of such identification. Both groups were casualties of the Revolution.

The Church of England, stigmatized as the church of the royal officials, survived the war as a dwindling denomination. Its unpopularity had been augmented by the ardent Toryism of most of its clergy, especially those sent out by the Society for the Propagation of the Gospel. Moreover, the church itself was in disarray. Some members had defected; some had gone to England; and some had joined the exodus of United Loyalists to Canada. Even more damaging was the loss of clergy, with only a small portion remaining after the war. Dwindling flocks were thus left without shepherds. Only a single Anglican clergyman remained in Pennsylvania, and this was true also in North Carolina and Georgia. New Jersey, with four, fared somewhat better. Virginia fared best of all, but even in Virginia the number of Anglican clergy declined from ninety-one to twenty-eight, and there were no new men to take the place of those who had departed.

The Quakers, who had been scattered in not insignificant numbers throughout all the colonies, were equally torn and weakened by the war. The pacifism of the Society of Friends precipitated numerous defections, and few "fighting Quakers" resumed their former religious affiliation. Furthermore, in some quarters Quakerism was suspect because of its presumed association with Toryism.[21]

The third factor which helps explain the dramatic shift in the fortunes of the Baptists was the new aggressive leadership they had acquired by 1770 from the "Separate" Congregationalists. It was a leadership sufficiently vigorous and energetic to carry on their two-front campaign for "liberty, both civil and religious," without being diverted from their evangelistic efforts. They were as busy seeking to convict people of sin and to lead them to a conversion experience as they were preaching up the war. And while they were winning converts and lending support to the struggle for independence, they also were carrying on lobbying activities in New England, in Virginia, and at the sessions of the Continental Congress to forward the cause of religious liberty. All three endeavors were viewed as interrelated and constituting but a single cause.

This seeming superabundance of energy is only a partial explanation of the success of the Baptist preachers. Even more important as an explanation of their effectiveness are two related features of Baptist clerical leadership. It was drawn directly from the ranks of the laity, and during the period from 1770 to 1800, in marked contrast to other denominations, it was never in short supply.

A fourth circumstance favorable to Baptist growth was the general climate of opinion. No other denomination was more closely in tune with the popular mood. According to Edmund Burke, a "fierce spirit of liberty" was at the bottom of the uproar in the colonies over sugar and stamps, tea and taxes.[22] During the course of the war this "fierce spirit of liberty" was further intensified. "Don't tread on me" was one slogan among many which expressed the spirit of Americans who had become chary of any infringement of their individual rights. To a people fiercely devoted to liberty and highly individualistic in temper, Baptists had a built-in appeal.

The Baptist appeal was especially self-evident in the consistency of the Baptist commitment to religious liberty, a term to which even those opposed to the elimination of all special privilege had to give at least lip service. Anglicans, at this point, were burdened with the albatross of two hundred years of history. Congregationalists also were tainted with the onus of special privilege and religious taxation. The Presbyterian clergy in Virginia were ready to settle for a "general assessment" and were called to account on this score by Presbyterian laity from "the Valley." Quakers, by the end of the Revolution, were out of contention as a possible major denomination.

In an even broader sense, the Baptist emphasis on individual rights, lay control, and local autonomy typified the American spirit. The accepted doctrine that there be "no government without the consent of the governed" placed primary stress on individual consent. Representation was necessary to accomplish certain ends, but the strength of anti-federalist sentiment made it clear that direct participation in decision making in one's own locality was much to be preferred. This was the popular mood. It was highly individualistic and highly self-assertive.

Most denominations scrambled in one way or another to adjust and adapt to the prevailing temper of the people. The prospects of a reconstituted Church of England were none too bright, and it was recognized in 1785 that, if it was to have any chance of survival, its constitution must conform to the dictates of republican sentiment. In drafting the constitution for the newly christened Protestant Episcopal Church, care was taken to safeguard the rights of local lay vestries, to provide for lay representation at all levels in the life of the church, and to delegate no powers to a General Convention which could be handled by a local congregation. The authority of bishops was circumscribed, being almost wholly limited to ceremonial and pastoral functions.

Roman Catholics were no less cognizant of the coercion imposed by the American temper in the post-war years. The effect of the pervasive American Spirit on Roman Catholics was explained by Archbishop Maréchal of Baltimore in 1818.

> The American people pursue with a most ardent love the civil liberty which they enjoy. For the principle of civil liberty is paramount with them, so that absolutely all the magistrates, from the highest to the lowest, are elected by popular vote. . . . Likewise all the Protestant sects . . . are governed by these same principles, and as a result they elect and dismiss their pastors at will. Catholics in turn, living in their midst, are evidently exposed to the danger of admitting the same principles of ecclesiastical government. [23]

Catholics not only had been exposed to the danger, but also many had succumbed to it. John Carroll, who was to be the first Roman Catholic bishop in the United States, had written in 1783 that "our religious system has undergone a revolution, if possible, more extraordinary than our political one." As part of this revolution, Carroll insisted that American Catholics had a right to choose their own bishop, one "in whose appointment Rome shall have no share." Carroll also was firm in acknowledging the right of the laity to participate in the selection of the priest who was to be their pastor.[24] Even Carroll, however, would have judged that members of the congregation at Norfolk carried the adjustment to American ways too far when they asserted that the bishop, according to the "civil liberties" guaranteed by the laws of Virginia, had no authority to interfere in the affairs of any congregation or in "any of their religious matters, whatever."[25]

Congregationalists could have made an easy adjustment to the prevailing climate of opinion. Instead they continued to profess that they found no contradiction between their practice and the popular mood, and they remained saddled with the anomalies of the Standing Order. Presbyterians, for their part, were somewhat immobilized in attempting to reconcile the authority of a General Assembly with assertions of local rights until a compromise was reached which provided a kind of localism by endowing presbyteries with certain rights not subject to appeal. The compromise had the disadvantage, in terms of adapting to the temper of the time, of sheltering the clergy within the presbytery and thus protecting them from being overridden by local congregations.

Baptists, on the other hand, needed to make no concessions to the popular mood. They typified it. Whatever centralized organization the Philadelphia Association had provided disintegrated with the rapid multiplication of churches and local associations both during and after the war. By the end of the war Baptist democracy was firmly wedded to the independence and lay control of the local church. Baptists were so closely in tune with the temper of the time that they had no difficulty in regarding themselves and being regarded by others as a truly American church. The popular mood fostered by the Revolution could not have been more favorable to Baptist growth.

How does one account for the phenomenal growth of the Baptists? They had given unqualified support to the Revolution. Competition had been reduced. They had an ample supply of aggressive leadership. They were closely in tune with the popular mood. Finally, Baptists had developed a sense of mission and destiny that was related not only to the gospel but also to the emerging nation.

Isaac Backus had carefully cultivated the conviction that the Baptists were the true heirs of the Pilgrim Fathers, called to reform the existing order in New England to bring it into accord with the founding principles of the first settlers. During the course of the war this sense of mission was broadened and deepened. Baptists began to view their fight against the Standing Order in New England and against the Anglican establishment in Virginia as the opening battle of the American Revolution. As the new nation emerged after the war, Baptists more and more came to identify their own struggle for liberty with the aspirations of the American people as a whole. Baptists had contended for a return to the founding principles of the Pilgrim Fathers, and these were the same principles which were to serve as the foundation of the new nation.

Ever since the Great Awakening, Baptists had believed themselves to be engaged in a great work of redemption, looking forward with eager anticipation to the time when righteousness would be exalted and the wolf and the lamb, the leopard and the kid, the lion and the calf would lie down together. But indispensable to this harmony with God and one another which constitutes the millennium is a free society in which equality prevails, the sources of antagonism are removed, and no restraint is placed on the spread of God's truth. This was the larger vision, an intermingling of concern for "liberty, both civil and religious," to speed the time of reconciliation and purely voluntary obedience. This vision was the ground of the Baptists' vigorous evangelistic activity, and so attuned to the Revolutionary ethos had they become that their numbers multiplied with astonishing rapidity. As the most thoroughly "American" of all religious groups, it is not surprising that by 1800 Baptists had become the largest religious denomination in America.

NOTES

[1] Leonard Woolsey Bacon, *A History of American Christianity* (London: James Clarke & Co., 1899), p. 213. Lyman Beecher, "The Practicality of Suppressing Vice" in *Lyman Beecher and the Reform of Society* (New York: Arno Press, 1972), p. 19.

[2] Edwin S. Gaustad, *Historical Atlas of Religion in America* (New York: Harper & Row, Publishers, 1962), p. 52. Baptist numerical predominance was not to be challenged until some twenty years later when the Methodist Church, organized in 1784, had accumulated a full head of steam.

[3] A third point of contention was the practice of itinerant and lay preaching.

[4] William G. McLoughlin, *New England Dissent, 1630–1833,* 2 vols. (Cambridge, Mass.: Harvard University Press, 1971), vol. 1, p. 337.

[5] A similar division among Presbyterians did not produce the same result, for neither party among the Presbyterians was legally subordinated to and harassed by the other. Neither Presbyterian group had to contend with the problem posed by a legal establishment and the intervention of governmental authority.

[6] William G. McLoughlin, *Isaac Backus and the American Pietistic Tradition,* ed. Oscar Handlin (Boston: Little, Brown and Company, 1967), p. 84.

[7] McLoughlin, *New England Dissent,* vol. 1, p. 491.

[8] Backus, *An Appeal to the Public* (1773), reprinted in William G. McLoughlin, ed., *Isaac Backus on Church, State, and Calvinism: Pamphlets 1754–1789* (Cambridge, Mass.: Harvard University Press, 1968), p. 339. Almost a quarter century earlier, Backus had initiated this theme when he wrote of "our fore Fathers who left their Pleasant Native Land for an houlling Wilderness . . . that they might have Liberty of Conscience." McLoughlin, *Isaac Backus and the American Pietistic Tradition,* p. 56. See also *ibid.,* p. 19.

[9] Isaac Backus, *A History of New England, with Particular Reference to the Denomination of Christians Called Baptists,* 2 vols. (Newton, Mass.: Backus Historical Society, 1871), vol. 1, p. 36.

[10] *Ibid.,* p. 37.

[11] Backus published the first volume of his *History of New England* in 1777.

[12] Backus, *History of New England,* vol. 1, p. viii; vol. 2, pp. 184-185.

[13] C. F. Adams, ed., *The Works of John Adams,* 10 vols. (New York: AMS Press, Inc., 1971), vol. 3, pp. 462, 464.

[14] Ezra Stiles, *A Discourse on the Christian Union* (Boston: Edes and Gill, 1761), pp. 37, 43, 97-99.

[15] McLoughlin, *Isaac Backus and the American Pietistic Tradition,* p. 122.

[16] McLoughlin, ed., *Isaac Backus on Church, State, and Calvinism,* pp. 338-339.

[17] McLoughlin, *Isaac Backus and the American Pietistic Tradition,* p. 135.

[18] Morgan Edwards in Philadelphia was a notable exception and was censured for his supposed Tory sympathies.

[19] This was true in New York, Maryland, North Carolina, South Carolina, and Georgia when the supporting prop of English authority was withdrawn. Typical was New York's speedy action in repealing all laws or acts which "may be construed to establish or maintain any particular denomination of Christians." The North Carolina Assembly anticipated the repudiation of British authority when it refused in 1773 to renew the Vestry Act. This had the practical effect of putting an end to the establishment.

[20] As early as June 12, 1776, Edmund Pendleton sought to forestall popular sentiment for religious liberty and to preserve some remnant of Virginia's religious establishment by securing the adoption of a "Declaration of Rights" which asserted that "all men are equally entitled to the free exercise of religion" but left untouched existing legislation of privilege and support. Later a "general assessment" to be distributed impartially among all Christian churches was proposed as a rear guard action in defense of the establishment. The issue was settled in 1785 with the adoption of the "Bill for Establishing Religious Freedom" which rejected any general assessment for religious purposes as well as any religious test for public office.

[21] Even Congregationalists suffered to some degree from the exodus of United Empire Loyalists.

[22] F. G. Selby, ed., *Burke's Speech on Conciliation with America* (London, 1912), pp. 17-21.

[23] John T. Ellis, ed., *Documents of American Catholic History* (Chicago: Henry Regnery Company, 1967), p. 214.

[24] James Hennesy, "Square Peg in a Round Hole," *Records of the American Catholic Historical Society of Philadelphia,* vol. 84 (December, 1973), pp. 170-171.

[25] *Documents of American Catholic History,* p. 221.

2

Baptists
and the Making
of a
New Nation

EDWIN S. GAUSTAD

Before treating the Baptists in the making of a new nation, it is necessary to consider the making of the Baptists in that land out of which a new nation was to come. Four elements in their evolution in early America will be noted.

I. THE MAKING OF THE BAPTISTS

In the beginning was a name: Rhode Island. So far as both the American scene and the Baptist denomination are concerned, the centrality of Rhode Island is difficult to exaggerate. There, as all know, Roger Williams engaged in classic conflict—one can almost say the cosmological conflict—with John Cotton. And while Williams's spiritual heirs may cling to one or another of his courageous deeds or memorable words, I find the most suggestive clue to his career in *The Bloudy Tenent of Persecution,* published in London in 1644. "Having bought truth dear, we must not sell it cheap, not the least grain of it for the whole world. . . ." But Williams was, as we also know, a Baptist only briefly and tangentially—only as a temporary shelter in his ceaseless search for spiritual peace, in his relentless quest for assurance.[1]

For John Clarke in Newport the association with Baptists was sustained and the leadership sturdy. On the Island of Aquidneck, Clarke organized the settlement of Portsmouth in 1638, and the following year he founded Newport, as a hopeful experiment in "democracy, or popular government." This effort was so daring that it needed defining:

> That is to say, It is in the Powre of the Body of Freemen orderly assembled, or the major part of them, to make or constitute Just Laws, by which they will be regulated, and to depute from among themselves such Ministers as shall see them faithfully executed between Man and Man.[2]

But this was only a brave beginning, the beginning of a struggle which can too readily be sentimentalized or drained of all its agony, betrayal, and near failure. Clarke, obliged to spend twelve bleak and frustrating years in London (1651–1663), fought against horrendous odds to make Rhode Island's position somewhat more secure by obtaining a royal charter. That charter came—gratifyingly, miraculously—on July 8, 1663. From an England which had restored its monarchy only three years before, from an England which had passed a new Act of Uniformity only the year before, came a charter of unprecedented liberality and vision. These are the "royal" words:

> And whereas, in theire humble addresse, they have ffreely declared, that it is much on their hearts (if they may be permitted), to hold forth a livelie experiment, that a most flourishing civill state may stand arid best bee maintained . . . with a full libertie in religious concernements; and that true pietye rightly grounded upon gospell principles, will give the best and greatest security to sovereignetye, and will lay in the hearts of men the strongest obligations to true loyaltye: Now know yee, that wee beinge willinge to encourage the hopefull undertakeinge of oure sayd loyall and loveinge subjects, and to secure them in the free exercise and enjoyment of all theire civill and religious rights . . . have therefore thought ffit and doe hereby publish, graunt, ordeyne and declare, That our royall will and pleasure is, that noe person within the sayd colonye, at any tyme hereafter, shall bee any wise molested, punished, disquieted, or called in question, for any differences in opinione in matters of religion, and does not actually disturb the civill peace of our sayd colony; but that all and everye person and persons, may from tyme to tyme, and at all tymes hereafter, freelye and fullye have and enjoye his and theire owne judgments and consciences. . . .

And so the New World gave birth to "the first secular state of modern times."[3]

As with Roger Williams, the denominational descendants of John Clarke have their favorite epitaphs. I would call attention to the preface to Clarke's one major work, *Ill Newes from New-England* (London, 1652), that searing account of his arrest in Massachusetts, the fining and whipping of Obadiah Holmes, the senseless persecution showing that "while old England is becoming new, New-England is becoming Old." In the preface, Clarke wrote, "I have rather chosen to bear witness to the . . . truth, which is but one, than to bear witness against the lie, which is so various, knowing that the truth once established shall discover the falsehood, and light breaking forth shall scatter the darkness."

Thus, Williams and Clarke provided a stance and a standing ground. And while we think of both men, by a kind of intellectual reflex, as preeminently champions of religious liberty, it is important to note that they were preeminently pursuers of truth. It was because truth was distorted, suppressed, or lost that consciences must be kept free. All the tiresome discussions about liberty becoming license are pointless if the steady pursuit of truth remains—as it was for Williams and Clarke— life's first priority. On Rhode Island's ground (which they secured) flourished General Baptists and Particular Baptists, Six-Principle Baptists, and Seventh Day Baptists, and of course dissenters of every stripe who found a haven there.[4] On this same ground a century later Baptists were able to erect their first center for higher education, "this Liberal & Catholic Institution" which was also concerned with the steady pursuit of truth. But the College of Rhode Island (later Brown University)[5] was neither the creation nor the possession of Rhode Island alone. Its origin owed most to another major element of early American Baptist life: the Philadelphia Association.

Organized with five churches in 1707, the Philadelphia Association, even in its earliest years, transcended the parochial limits of city and of colony. And one-half century after its founding, the Association extended its influence all the way from Nova Scotia to South Carolina—and abroad to England, Ireland, and Wales. If Rhode Island provided the eponymous heroes and enduring phrases, Philadelphia provided the discipline and the order. The Calvinist or Particular Baptists of seventeenth-century England gave to the Philadelphia Association its confession of faith along with its concern for order. Philadelphia, in turn, gave to Baptists in America a pattern of faith and of life. Those two concerns found expression in the printing in 1743 (by Benjamin Franklin) of *A Short Treatise of Church Discipline* (drawn up by Benjamin Griffith) as well as a *Confession of Faith*. These documents took seriously the "constitutional rules . . . engrosed [sic] in the archives of sacred truth" (Oliver Hart's words), outlining the standards of admission, the procedures for censure, admonition, suspension, and, if necessary, excommunication. This Association, the model for so many that followed, believed itself competent "to declare and determine the Mind of the Holy Ghost" and to "decree the Observation of Things . . . appointed in the Scripture."[6] While not setting itself above the churches, the Philadelphia Association did assume a position of authority alongside of, not subservient to, the several churches. Thus conceived, that Association gave a stability and direction to Baptist life in the critical and formative period of development in the eighteenth century.

A third major component of Baptist life prior to America's nationhood was the Great Awakening. If Rhode Island provided the stance and Philadelphia the order, that sweeping revival provided the momentum and eventually the bulk. Before the Awakening, Baptists—however dedicated to liberty of conscience and purity of faith—were a scattered and feeble few. After that wave of religious excitement, whole churches and whole communities adopted Baptist views and swelled Baptist ranks. Speaking of Protestant Christianity generally, the Great Awakening was not so much a device for recruitment as it was (in a current phrase) a mechanism of consciousness raising. Tired and traditional members, cold and formal preachers, compromised and graceless covenants now seemed unacceptable, perhaps intolerable. Those who moved to a New Side or saw a New Light frequently kept moving and looking until they gravitated toward and settled within a Baptist fold which seemed to offer the kind of church life they were seeking.

The growth from 1750 to 1800 was swift, phenomenal, and—to some—frightening. Shortly before the end of the century, a Massachusetts Congregationalist, seeing his own denomination's numerical superiority threatened, wrote *Impartial Inquiries, Respecting the Progress of the Baptist Denomination.* Hardly impartial at all, Noah Worcester betrayed his deep anxieties as well as his natural prejudices. Baptists proliferate, he wrote, among other reasons because they have an abundance of unqualified preachers.

> Many people are so ignorant as to be charmed with sound [rather] than sense. And to them, the want of knowledge in a teacher . . . may easily be made up, and overbalanced, by great zeal, an affecting tone of voice, and a perpetual motion of the tongue. If a speaker can keep his tongue running, in an unremitting manner . . . and can quote, memoriter, a large number of texts from within the covers of the Bible, it matters not, to many of his hearers, whether he speaks *sense* or *nonsense.*[7]

But Worcester also acknowledged that Baptists took advantage of revivals and "divisions in societies." Put in more positive terms, this meant that the denomination was forged in an evangelical fire that swept across young and old, rich and poor, white and black in those emotion-packed years of the mid-eighteenth century. Evangelical fervor continued to be the distinguishing mark of expanding, exploding Baptist forces far beyond the dawn of America's new nationhood.

A fourth and final historical contribution to the Baptist makeup in America was, to be sure, the sentiment and passion of revolution itself: from Rhode Island the words, from Philadelphia the form, and from the Awakening the power. From the Revolution, above all else, came the opportunity—the opportunity to move into and to help mold a society, the opportunity to be more than protester, dissenter, and nagger. Baptists became active participants, shapers as well as shakers, creating a new respect for their language and their action, both of which were formerly deemed radical or antisocial, blasphemous or treacherous. Of course, respectability could be both blessing and curse, but at the very least it opened the door of opportunity in the making of a nation and the remaking of a social order.

In the Revolutionary era's reaction to taxation without representation, Baptists chafed under the continued obligation to pay taxes to support a ministry they could not and did not attend. *This* taxation without representation was being done by Americans to fellow Americans. Baptists found the revolutionary sentiment against Parliament fully applicable against, for example, Massachusetts lawmakers whose work resulted in constant harassment, social stigma, and financial injustice. The consequence, declared Isaac Backus in 1774, was that Baptists were determined no longer to be "certificate men," no longer to pay the state's unjust tax "not only upon our principles of not being taxed where we are not represented but also" upon our principle of not rendering "that homage to any earthly power, which I and many of my brethren are fully convinced belongs only to God."[8]

In a wave of "massive civil disobedience" (to use William McLoughlin's phrase), Baptists cried "Enough!" to the fines, to the confiscation of property, to the imprisonments which followed a conscientious refusal by Baptists to grant that the state had any right to say who went to church: where, or why, or whether. Civil rulers pretend to have a right "to set up one religious sect above another," but they have no such right. Civil rulers pretend to be lawful representatives in religious matters, but they are not. Civil rulers pretend to advance the cause of religion, but, Backus pointed out, all they really advance is "envy, hypocrisy, and confusion, and so to the ruin of civil society."[9] The mood and moment of the Revolution granted to Baptists, therefore, the unique opportunity to move from sectarian isolation to national participation. Their stance seemed to fit the challenge of building a new nation.

With these four American strands woven into its British ecclesiastical and theological heritage, Baptists by 1789 were ready to play their part in creating "a more perfect union."

II. "PRESENT AT THE CREATION"

That part was most clearly played in bringing about constitutional guarantees of religious liberty. In the populous and powerful state of Virginia, Baptists organized a General Committee in the very year that the War of Independence ended. This committee, formed in October, 1783, agitated against marriage laws that worked a hardship upon dissenters even as they favored the Anglican clergy. The committee also intensified the Baptist opposition to Anglican vestries—to those boards which were in one sense authoritative only for Episcopalians but were in another sense the governmental arm which reached all in such matters as levying taxes and caring for the poor.

Baptists petitioned that vestries as *public* entities be dissolved. By the 1780s, Baptists had moved beyond pleas and memorials for mere toleration: that belonged to an earlier time. In 1772, for example, Baptists in Lunenburg County found

> themselves restricted in the exercise of their religion, their teachers imprisoned under various pretences, and the benefits of the Toleration Act denied them, although they are willing to conform to the true spirit of that act, and are loyal and quiet subjects; and therefore, praying that they may be treated with the same kind indulgence, in religious matters, as Quakers, Presbyterians, and other Protestant dissenters enjoy.[10]

But that was before the Revolution, before the wholesale rejection not only of England's Parliament and king, but also of England's "imperious bishops" and the national church. After the Revolution, Baptists sought not "the same kind indulgence" but the obliteration of every remaining link between the Episcopal Church and the State of Virginia.

Of course in the heat of revolution and after, little sentiment could be found anywhere in Virginia for enlarging the official sanction and support of the Church of England. But that this official church should be sharply diminished, or that its former high estate be completely erased and every vestige removed—this demand was not obvious either immediately or universally. Nor was it clear that the Episcopal Church must be reduced to the common level of the dissenting churches. Perhaps Baptists, Quakers, Presbyterians, Methodists, and others should be raised to the favored level of the Anglicans. So argued James and Patrick Henry, among others. Let us pass a bill in Virginia, these proponents advocated, that established not one church but all churches, a bill in behalf not of the narrowly sectarian but the broadly Christian. From 1779 to 1786 repeated attempts were made to pass a "general assessment" bill that would provide for "The Christian Religion [which] shall in all times coming be deemed and held to be the established Religion of this Commonwealth. . . ."[11] Of course, the problem was that only Christianity was to be official; and secondly, that to be "official," the state was necessarily in the business of defining precisely what was truly Christian. Baptists joined with others in bringing about the defeat of Patrick Henry's general assessment plan, though the principal credit here must go to James Madison and his eloquent *Memorial and Remonstrance.* Madison offered fifteen persuasive reasons why state support for all churches was no better than state support for one. Besides, experience and history prove "that ecclesiastical establishments, instead of maintaining the purity and efficacy of Religion, have had a contrary operation."

Concurrent with resistance to this general assessment, Baptists kept a steady pressure upon those lingering privileges mentioned earlier which were still retained by the Episcopal Church. A fair and adequate law with respect to marriages seemed so slow in coming. In 1780 "the Baptist Association met at Sandy in Charlotte" and petitioned the Virginia legislature to see that all its law accorded with the new "Republican Spirit" and the newly recognized rights of conscience. We "have with Grief observed that Religious Liberty has not made a single Advance, in this Commonwealth, without some Opposition." Traditions died hard, and privileges yielded slowly. But the right of dissenters to perform marriages anywhere was "an Affair of so tender a Nature, and of such importance" that England more than a hundred years earlier had confirmed the validity of marriages during the Protectorate. Virginia could not do less; the time had come, the Baptist petitioners concluded, to "consign to Oblivion all the Relicks of Religious Oppression, and make a public Sacrifice of Partiality at the glorious Altar of Freedom." Their petition, dated November 8, 1780, bore fruit by December 18 of that year when a bill "declaring what shall be a lawful marriage" was passed. It was not yet a perfect bill, but it was a major move against that intolerable "Partiality."[12]

Four years later, in 1784, Baptists were alarmed and annoyed when the Virginia Assembly granted incorporated status to the Church of England's successor, the "Protestant Episcopal Church"; the Assembly further conveyed "every Tract or Tracts of Glebe Land" to the sole use of this newly organized church. To the Baptists such action seemed contrary to the sentiment and letter of Virginia's own constitution and its own Bill of Rights, and even more contrary to Thomas Jefferson's Bill for Establishing Religious Freedom.

Frequently quoting Jefferson against this most recent legislative act, the Baptist General Committee in a 1786 petition declared:

> New Testament Churches, we humbly conceive, are, or should be, established by the Legislature of Heaven, and not earthly power; by the Law of God and not the Law of the State; by the Acts of the Apostles, and not by the Acts of an Assembly. . . .
>
> If truth is great, and will prevail if left to itself . . . we wish it may be so left, which is the only way to convince the gazing world, that Disciples do not follow Christ for Loaves, and that Preachers do not preach for Benefices.[13]

With these words the protracted struggle for the repeal of Virginia's incorporation act began. Petitions flowed in from many sources, urging that the freedoms won in the "late happy Revolution" not be so quickly and cavalierly discarded or diminished. Early in 1787 when the act of incorporation was finally repealed, church-state separation in Virginia seemed to be secured.

Yet the issue of property continued to irritate. The glebes, those agricultural lands granted to the Anglican Church in the days before the Revolution, looked like only another vestige of partiality and privilege. Should not these lands now, after the Revolution, belong to all the people? Presbyterians in 1787 pointed out that the "new" Protestant Episcopal Church was in no sense the same as the "old" Church of England and that the infant should not, therefore, receive or maintain title to colonial grants made to the parent. Furthermore, since all Virginians had had to pay taxes to support that old establishment, all Virginians should now reap the benefits from the sale of these lands. "To take what is common property, and designed for common benefit, and bestow upon this infant church, to the exclusion of the great majority of the community, is too glaring a piece of injustice to pass unnoticed, or be suffered to continue in a free country."[14] Baptists, joining in the plea that glebe lands, at least the vacant ones, be sold in behalf of the public, had by 1790 launched their campaign in earnest.

A full decade of petition, counter-petition, debate, and homily swirled around this property dispute. Each fall when the Assembly met, it was presented with a petition from the Baptist General Committee with a regularity, wrote one historian, like that of "an unfailing Thanksgiving turkey."[15] Finally, under these steady pressures, as well as the influential radicalism of the French Revolution, the Virginia legislature in 1802 confiscated these Episcopal properties. The story does not end there, however, for in 1815 the U.S. Supreme Court heard its first case in the area of religion. In that case, *Terrett* v. *Taylor,* the Court decided—not on First Amendment grounds but on grounds of property and corporation rights—that the Virginia legislature had erred, that the American Revolution did not demand that all property claims begin anew nor did it void the right of a religious corporation to retain its charter. Natural justice as well as constitutional law had been violated and the glebe lands were returned.

Utilizing Virginia as a single but important example of Baptist "presence at the creation" of the Republic, one sees insistent zeal for an unfettered conscience and an unfavored church; this zeal gave legal shape to a fresh idea and a sense of purpose to an expanding sect. With a vigor derived from the large influx of new members and an inspiration from the broad territorial vistas that beckoned them, Baptists were strategically positioned to discharge major social and cultural tasks in the first half of the nineteenth century. Three such tasks may be briefly noted.

III. THE MAKING OF A NATION

The first task was in the category of unfinished business: a Federal Constitution adopted in 1789, a Bill of Rights in 1791, disestablishment state by state either shortly before or shortly after those dates—yet in Connecticut and Massachusetts the church-state alliance seemed to go on and on. The petition technique, so effectively utilized in Virginia, found its application in New England as well. In Connecticut in 1804 the Danbury Association complained that Baptists still had property taken away "by force, or our bodies cast into prison, if we do not pay the preachers which we never chose, never hear, and in whom we place no confidence as our guides to heaven." All previous memorials to the legislative, the Association noted, "have been treated both with neglect and contempt. . . ." But one might question how long this neglect could continue for "Our churches do increase in numbers . . . [and] the rights of men are better understood than they formerly were. . . ."[16] Another fourteen years passed before Connecticut's new constitution would provide that "no person shall by law be compelled to join or support, nor be classed with, or associated to, any congregation, church, or religious association." In Massachusetts, establishment lingered even longer, and the forces that overthrew it were even more mixed. The Baptist John Leland, having returned in 1791 to Massachusetts after fourteen influential years in Virginia, articulated much of the evangelical resistance to "that rotten nest-egg which is always hatching vipers: I mean the principle of intruding the laws of men into the Kingdom of Christ. . . ." If rulers are determined to make laws about religion, about building churches, paying preachers, etc., Leland wrote, then they should be logically consistent and "complete the code." Everyone "who did not believe, should pay ten pounds . . . every soul who did not deny himself, and take up his cross daily, should pay fifteen pounds . . . whoever did not love God with all his heart, should be imprisoned a year—and . . . if a man did not love his neighbor as himself, he should be confined for life." [17] This was only one way of pointing to the absurdity of Massachusetts' continuing interjection of law into religion. Unitarians, Universalists, Episcopalians, and others joined in complaints and petitions that were finally heeded in 1833.

A second role concerned the grouping and solidifying of forces to meet the threats of imported French radicalism and homegrown rationalism as well as the worldwide evangelical challenges. In 1814 the General Missionary Convention of the Baptist Denomination in the United States of America for Foreign Missions was formed in Philadelphia—an altogether appropriate location in view of the Philadelphia Association's commitment and contribution to church order. This new convention (since it was to meet every three years, it was known more simply as the Triennial Convention) elected Richard Furman of Charleston, South Carolina, as its first president and responded to the unplanned presence of Baptist missionaries, the Adoniram Judsons, in Burma. The sudden responsibilities abroad did not distract Baptists from the evangelical opportunities and obligations at home. If anything, the missionary impulse, once stimulated, seemed to recognize no bounds.

At the second Triennium, John Mason Peck was authorized to begin a work in the opening West—a work so sustained and so vast as to make his name almost a synonym of western missions. Peck fought against ignorance, anarchy, and immorality—evils to which the frontier everywhere was prone. As though these enemies were not enough, Peck also found harmful and debilitating the many divisions among Christians generally and among Baptists specifically: mission and anti-mission, Calvinist and Free Will, "Primitive" and "Regular." He reported in Kentucky, for example, a typical situation where a number of Baptist preachers, divided on certain points of doctrine, were "not altogether friendly in ministerial intercourse."

> Each possessed his share of the imperfections of human character; each was more or less selfish; petty rivalries prevailed, and small differences were magnified, as each party looked at the other through the medium of prejudice. In a word, the pioneer preachers of Kentucky were very much

like the ministers of the Gospel in every age, nation, and country; no better, no worse; only a little more frank, and even blunt . . . and did not conceal their thoughts and emotions with the same ingenuity and tact as has been done in some places.[18]

Peck's realism also enabled him to minister to the frontier settlers without sentimentalizing them, yet never growing cynical concerning them. With the work of Peck and many others, male and female, America experienced a second Great Awakening, with Baptists showing no reluctance to utilize both the urban revival in the East and the camp meeting in the West.

By 1832, the western work required even more organization which resulted in the formation of the American Baptist Home Missionary Society. This society sent out missionaries, especially to "the weak and destitute," built churches, and encouraged the proper training of the clergy. In a jubilee volume published a half-century later, the Society looked back with understandable pride on a period of great growth in schools and colleges, in missions and membership. Baptists numbered only about 100,000 at the beginning of the century but had grown to nearly a million at mid-century and over two million one generation later. The Society was especially pleased to note the progress among blacks, where membership had risen sharply, despite the turbulence of war and the disruptions of everyday life.[19] And this brings us to the third notable element in the Baptist making of a nation.

The rapid entry of blacks into the Baptist fold enhanced (though it did not perfect) the active partnership between this still-being-freed people and this still-being-molded nation. Despite all the drama and sacrifices of the foreign mission effort, no story there can match the Baptist progress among America's black population. Some of that progress was through conscious missionary effort, some through gradual extension of southern "culture religion" from whites to blacks, some through clear choice of a church free from white bishops or superintendents or ruling elders. But from whatever stimulus and motivation, American Negroes throughout the nineteenth century and well into the twentieth responded to the Baptist call in a proportion vastly greater than their white counterparts. New organizations developed—missionary conventions, educational associations, Sunday School unions, publishing agencies—to meet and to minister to the burgeoning number of black Baptists, North and South, East and West. For a time these agencies cooperated with the corresponding societies of the white Baptists. But by 1895, it became necessary to create a Convention that was safe from a condescension and bias too readily seen in the white-dominated conventions. Speaking in behalf of the new National Baptist Convention, the Reverend E. K. Love of Savannah, Georgia, declared:

> I am a loyal Baptist and a loyal Negro. I will stand or fall, live or die, with my race and denomination. . . . It is just as reasonable and fair for Negroes to want [their own agencies] to themselves as it is for white people to want them to themselves. . . . It never was true anywhere, and perhaps never will be, that a Negro can enjoy every right in an institution controlled by white men that white men can enjoy. There is not as bright and glorious a future before a Negro in a white institution as there is for him in his own. . . . We can more thoroughly fill our people with race pride, denominational enthusiasm and activity, by presenting to them for their support enterprises that are wholly ours.[20]

And as the National Baptist Convention's first president, E. C. Morris, observed, the creation of this new and separate entity revealed, as only it could, "a host of intelligent, self-reliant, practical leaders among us. . . ."[21]

In at least these three ways, then, Baptists contributed a social dynamic to the nineteenth-century national scene: in continued vigilance over the tender liberties of conscience; in strengthened organization for evangelization within and beyond the nation; and in an inclusive and racially mixed constituency that ultimately became America's largest Protestant family.

IV. BAPTISTS IN THE MIDST OF A NATION

Were it not for John Mason Peck's good example, it would now be convenient to ignore the harsher realities, speaking only of contributions and achievements, of unslackened progress and unchecked charity. But to recall Peck: "Each possessed his share of the imperfections of human character. . . . " Those imperfections (on which Baptists have no monopoly but from which they are not exempt) have led to slavery, to schism, and to war; they have led to bitter rivalries and mutual recriminations, to racial prejudice and sexist practice, to anti-Catholic passions and anti-intellectual demagoguery, to cultural captivities, and to cultural irrelevancies. For most denominations in America, the twentieth century—unlike the nineteenth—has been a time of merger and reunion: northern with southern Methodists, northern with Scottish Presbyterians, northeastern Congregationalists with midwestern Evangelical and Reformed, Norwegian with German Lutherans, and so on. But not the Baptists. The great schism of 1845, North and South, and the rise of the National Baptist Convention a half century later only initiated the process of separation and fission that has gone on unabated. In 1915 another National Baptist Convention, this one unincorporated, came into being; and, in succeeding decades, there arose the American Baptist Association, the Conservative Baptist Association, the National Primitive Baptist Convention, the General Association of Regular Baptists, the North American Baptist Association, and the Progressive National Baptists. These are not tiny splinter groups or one-man bands; together they total more than six million members! And what is the impact, what is the social dynamic of these six million, or of the other twenty million Baptists—or of all of them together in contemporary America?

What, for example, is the cultural thrust of 26 million Baptists in America compared with, say, that of 6 million Jews in America; of 26 million Baptists compared with 3 million Episcopalians in America; of 26 million Baptists compared with ½ million Jehovah's Witnesses in this nation, or compared with 100,000 Quakers, or compared, even, with 14,000 Amish?

Well, one hears the rebuttal already. It is not the Baptists' duty or purpose to be a "dynamic social force," to have a cultural "impact." Their duty is to serve and fear a God who is above men and nations. True. So it was the duty of Rhode Island's Baptists in the 1650s, of Virginia's Baptists in the 1780s, of Philadelphia's Baptists in the nineteenth century. But in the course of doing their duty to God, liberal charters were secured; improper ecclesiastical privileges were cast off; a nation was born; and a young denomination strode boldly across a continent and a world.

Today, the question is: Do 26 million Baptists constitute a leaven in national life, or have they become the loaf?

NOTES

[1] For the best treatment of Williams, see Edmund S. Morgan, *Roger Williams: The Church and the State* (New York: Harcourt Brace Jovanovich, Inc., 1967); and, Perry Miller, *Roger Williams: His Contribution to the American Tradition* (New York: The Bobbs-Merrill Company, Inc., 1953).

[2] Thomas Williams Bicknell, *The Story of Dr. John Clarke* (Providence: the author, 1915), p. 140.

[3] The charter is found in *Rhode Island Colonial Records* (Providence: A. C. Greene and Brother, 1857), vol. 2, pp. 3-21; the concluding quotation is from Carl Bridenbaugh, *Fat Mutton and Liberty of Conscience Society in Rhode Island, 1636-1690.* (Providence: Brown University Press, 1974), p. 5.

⁴On the Six-Principle Baptists, see the basic history by Richard Knight, *History of the General or Six-Principle Baptists in Europe and America* (Providence: Smith and Parmenter, 1827). For one facet of the Seventh-Day Baptists in the Revolutionary era, see Jeannette D. Black and W. Greene Roelker, *A Rhode Island Chaplain in the Revolution: Letters of Ebenezer David to Nicholas Brown 1775-1778* (Port Washington, N.Y.: Kennikat Press, reprint 1971). And for colonial Baptists generally, one may still consult with much profit Isaac Backus's *A History of New England with Particular Reference to the . . . Baptists,* 2 vols. (Newton, Mass.: Backus Historical Society, 1871). Bridenbaugh (see note 3, above) argues that the heterogeneity of seventeenth-century Rhode Island has been so exaggerated as to cause historians to lose sight of the strong and successful economic structure built up by its citizens.

⁵For Brown's early years, see Reuben A. Guild, *History of Brown University . . .* (Providence: Snow and Farnham, 1867) and Walter C. Bronson, *The History of Brown University, 1764–1914* (Providence: Brown University, 1914).

⁶All quotations in this paragraph are from Robert T. Handy, "The Philadelphia Tradition," in Winthrop S. Hudson, ed., *Baptist Concepts of the Church* (Valley Forge: Judson Press, 1959), pp. 42, 46, 48.

⁷Noah Worcester, *Impartial Inquiries, Respecting the Progress of the Baptist Denomination* (Published in Worcester, Mass. in 1794), pp. 19-20, quoted in C. C. Goen, *Revivalism and Separatism in New England, 1740–1800* (New Haven: Yale University Press, 1962), p. 284. For the impact in Virginia and the development there of a radically new culture, see Rhys Isaac, "Evangelical Revolt: The Nature of the Baptists' Challenge to the Traditional Order in Virginia, 1765 to 1775," *William & Mary Quarterly,* vol. 31 (July, 1974), pp. 345-368.

⁸In Alvah Hovey, *A Memoir of the Life and Times of the Reverend Isaac Backus* (Boston: Gould and Lincoln, 1859), pp. 220f.

⁹See William G. McLoughlin's article, "Massive Civil Disobedience as a Baptist Tactic in 1773," *American Quarterly,* vol. 21 (Winter, 1969), pp. 710-727, as well as his extraordinary and definitive study, *New England Dissent, 1630–1833: The Baptists and the Separation of Church and State,* 2 vols. (Cambridge: Harvard University Press, 1971). Backus's words are from vol. 1, pp. 553-554 of the work just cited.

¹⁰W. T. Thom, *The Struggle for Religious Freedom in Virginia: The Baptists* (Baltimore: Johns Hopkins Press, 1900), vol. 18, nos. 10-12, p. 45.

¹¹For the full text, see H. J. Eckenrode, *Separation of Church and State in Virginia* (New York: Da Capo Press, 1971), pp. 58-61.

¹²*Ibid.,* pp. 67-70.

¹³*Ibid.,* p. 119.

¹⁴*Ibid.,* p. 132.

¹⁵*Ibid.,* p. 142. See all of chapters 7 and 8 for a full discussion of the glebe lands; also, see Thom, *The Struggle for Religious Freedom,* pp. 85-91.

¹⁶McLoughlin, *New England Dissent,* vol. 2, p. 999.

¹⁷See Leland's "fashionable fast day sermon" entitled "A Blow at the Root" in L. F. Greene, ed., *The Writings of John Leland* (New York: Arno Press, reprint 1969), pp. 241-242, 247.

[18] Quoted in Paul M. Harrison, ed., *Memoir of John Mason Peck* (Carbondale, Ill.: University of Southern Illinois Press, 1965), p. liii.

[19] See *Baptist Home Missions in North America* (New York: American Baptist Home Mission Society, 1883), pp. 8-9, 421.

[20] Both Love and Morris are quoted in E. S. Gaustad, *Dissent in American Religion* (Chicago: The University of Chicago Press, 1973), pp. 32-34.

[21] *Ibid.*

PART
TWO

Baptists
and Human Rights
in the
American Experience

Baptists
and
Human Rights

GARDNER TAYLOR

If vigilance is the price of liberty, then agitation, petition, and dissent are substantial parts of that vigilance which gains and maintains human rights. This would seem to make the cause of human rights a natural and inevitable part of the life-style of all Baptist people. Surely, the way of dissent, of demurrer, of filing exception to whatever may be in vogue is a part of the Baptist heritage. Some wry wit, noticing this Baptist trait of dissent, has said that wherever one sees two Baptists, one is certain to find at least three opinions.

I

This irksome quality of dissent and agitation was asserted by Baptists in the founding days of the American nation, though their dissent was not occasioned by lack of sympathy on the part of Baptists with the purposes of the American Revolution. Isaac Backus reported that

> the Baptists were so generally united with their country in the defense of their privileges, that when the General Court at Boston passed an act in October, 1778, to debar all men from returning into their government, whom they judged to be their enemies, and named three hundred and eleven men as such, there was not one Baptist among them. Yet there was scarce a Baptist member of the legislature which passed this act.[1]

The Baptists of New England, William Warren Sweet suggested, were such staunch supporters of American independence for two reasons. While Baptists had undergone severe persecution at the hands of the Congregationalists, wherever Episcopalians were in complete control of the government, Baptists were allowed no rights whatever; therefore, they had no hope of any real advantage by supporting the English cause. A second reason was that the principles upon which resistance was based were Baptist principles; therefore, they could not avoid joining with their countrymen in a cause so clearly founded on truths which Baptists strongly upheld.[2]

The agitation of Baptists during this time was based, rather, upon the failure of the American colonies to guarantee sufficiently an aspect of human rights, that is, religious liberty. "In the 1769 Minutes of the Warren Association it is stated that 'many letters from the churches mentioned grievous oppressions and persecutions from the Standing order.'" It was this situation in New England which led Baptists to send a delegation—among them President James Manning of the College of Rhode Island—to the meeting of the First Continental Congress in Philadelphia to make an appeal for religious liberty. When these Baptist representatives appeared, Samuel and John Adams of the Massachusetts delegation denied that there were any real restrictions of the rights of religious minorities.[3] This may have been one of the earliest attempts at "cover-up" in America—this time being an attempt to shield and to deny an embarrassing condition of religious persecution in the body politic.

The same irksome agitation which Baptists carried on in New England against religious proscription was carried on in Virginia, a sign that Baptists were either hypersensitive or that there actually was religious discrimination in the American colonies. As a matter of fact, from 1768 to 1774 more than thirty Baptist preachers in Virginia were arrested because of their religious teaching, though the civil authorities insisted that the arrests stemmed from the fact that the Baptists were disturbing the peace by calling unlawful assemblies and the like. The Baptists in Virginia used petition after petition to remind the Virginia Assembly that religious liberty should not be forgotten in the struggle for political liberty. A Baptist church in Prince William County, Virginia, petitioned the Virginia Assembly that while the colony was contending for the civil rights of mankind against enslavement by a powerful enemy, the petitioning church considered it their duty to petition for their religious privileges.[4]

It must be sadly recorded that apparently many Baptists, North and South, did not see the need to view religious liberty as but a part of the whole of human rights, all of which needed support by Christian people. Of course, the matter of human rights in America was seen largely as a matter of the rights of the colonists not to be politically oppressed by England. However, no one can long discuss human rights in America without coming upon the denial of these rights to the slave population. In a somewhat different sense, the same comment would have to be made in regard to the denial of rights to American Indians, but that belongs to a later part of this discussion.

That many Baptists did not join their passion for religious liberty to the whole issue of human rights is not to say that they were alone in this blind spot. Many Christians, it may be said most Christians, saw slavery as a justification for various and curious doctrines as to God's appointment and approval of that institution as part of the divine economy. Of course, it may be argued that the presence of slavery as an important part of early American history demanded and received doctrines of Christian explanation friendly to the institution of slavery and all that it entailed of superiority, inferiority, and dehumanization of both slave and slave master.

Such doctrines were not lacking among the preachments of some of early America's most honored and respected churchmen. Cotton Mather in 1689 "urged that the Christianized blacks would make more efficient slaves." He also told the masters that they need have no fear of losing their slaves on account of baptism, "since Christianity contained no law forbidding servitude." Mather urged that masters were duty bound to teach their bondsmen that "it is God who has caused them to be servants, and that they serve Jesus Christ while they are at work for their masters." Nowhere did he ever give the slave any hope of becoming a free man. Perhaps this was too much to expect of the Boston Puritan, especially since he himself owned slaves.[5]

Cotton Mather, the Puritan, did not stand alone in his embrace of the institution of slavery. Up until the eve of the Revolution, most of the prosperous Quakers in all the colonies still held slaves. William Penn, the English Quaker who founded Pennsylvania, held slaves until his death in 1718. At the same time, it must be said that by the beginning of the nineteenth century Quakers had cleansed themselves of the taint of slaveholding. John Carroll, a Roman Catholic priest and himself later to become Archbishop of Baltimore, owned several slaves. It was generally believed among Catholics that slavery did not violate the law of God as long as it was distinct from what Catholic thinkers and leaders called the "abuse" of slavery. Colonial Anglicanism, like New England Puritanism and Roman Catholicism, held that human bondage was compatible with Christianity.

Since Baptist people have seen themselves as strong partisans of liberty, then it is reasonable to wish that they would have stood, alone if necessary, for the cause of all human rights in revolutionary America. Further, one might have hoped that Baptists with their free and untrammeled reading of the Bible would have seen, even where others failed to do so, the great Hebrew-Christian biblical sweep of the unity of creation, the image of God in all men and women, the long cry in the Scriptures for justice, and the "one-blood" doctrine of the New Testament. Perhaps Baptist insistence on human rights during prerevolutionary times might have been more noticeable had their numbers been larger, since there were only sixty-five thousand Baptists in the United States as late as 1790.

In the years leading to independence, Baptists might have sensed more noticeably or more memorably that the new nation about to be born into history represented a freshness and a force which might well correspond very closely to the great principles of liberty and individual dignity which lay behind the Baptist movement. Though the Baptists who petitioned the Continental Congress about religious liberty did not extend their pleading to human rights, they must have sensed that a momentous and greatly hopeful entity in history was being born to the sound of the themes of liberty and independence which swirled through the colonies. Indeed, it is difficult for anyone to read the Declaration of Independence, even casually, without concluding that those who had to do with its authorship felt that they were dealing with something at once splendid and august. Making every allowance for a natural flair for lofty language in Thomas Jefferson and his fellows, the thought persists in the reading of the Declaration of Independence that those who composed it felt that the new American nation had before it a grand destiny and that that destiny had dimensions beyond the purely human. Abraham Lincoln, speaking at Gettysburg nearly a century later, would give expression to this idea when he set forth the noble hope that "this nation under God shall have a new birth of freedom. . . ."

II

There seems little in the disparate and loosely confederated colonies to give one the notion that the exalted language of the Declaration of Independence was rooted in any grandeur or power of the new nation. In fact, the nation was an accident, or so it seemed, of a new and painful policy of George III and his Lord of the Treasury and Chancellor of the Exchequer, George Grenville. Emerging from the long and costly Seven Years' War (1756-1763), England decided that the imperial defenses in North America needed substantial enlargement. British garrison forces in North America were to be increased "from a peacetime establishment of 3,100 men to 7,500." The plan was that after the first year, these troops would be supported by the colonies. This plan was at the root of the issues that gradually led the American colonials to seek independence.[6] The discontent was founded, considerably before the incident mentioned above, to be sure, upon the position taken by the colonists that they should have control of their local affairs.

Along with the troop expansion, Grenville issued a royal proclamation on October 7, 1763. The chief purpose was to prevent, at least temporarily, colonial expansion westward, for the principal cause of conflict with the Indians was seizure of their lands. Farmers who wanted to till the land and speculators who hoped to profit by sale of the land raised strong protests. The proclamation was frequently violated by settlers. While the measure did win some friends for the British among the Indians, it turned many farmers and speculators, who wielded strong influence in the colonies, against England.[7]

There were, to be sure, more laudable roots supporting the branch and flower of American disaffection with and resistance to Britain. The Stamp Act, passed in the spring of 1765 by the British Parliament, was a source of irritation and protest. This law provided for tax on such legal documents as legal papers, newspapers, licenses, and the like. The American colonists protested, to no avail, that these taxes were excessively burdensome and unconstitutional.

One should not overlook in a quick survey of the background of the beginning of the American experience a certain spectral shadow of what the colonists feared might become religious persecution. The Anglican Church, through its Society for the Propagation of the Gospel in Foreign Parts, established a mission church in Cambridge, Massachusetts, in 1761. As if this were not enough to arouse the suspicions and fears of the colonists in this center of Congregationalism, the archbishop of Canterbury at the time, Thomas Secker, sought to prevent the Congregationalists from sending missionaries to the Indians. Thus, the colonists were to be denied both the privilege of exploiting the Indians by cheap purchase or seizure of their lands and that of evangelizing them by missionary enterprise—an intolerable state of affairs, indeed.

Later, there would be new measures that would be seen as intolerable by the Americans. The Townshend Duties, passed in the spring of 1767, placed duties on tea, glass, lead, papers, and the like. Following bitter objections, the measures were relaxed, but in 1773 Lord North, who had become chancellor of the exchequer, pushed through the Tea Act which placed the use of tea in the colonies in the hands of the East India Company which proposed to sell the tea to merchants of its own choosing. The long and growing sense of injustice became more than the Americans could bear, and they destroyed 342 chests of tea in Boston harbor, opting, as they believed, for human rights over property rights.

Step by step, the new nation, the United States of America, came into being. It came into existence, on the one hand, through a resentment based on hunger for profits and a desire for exploitation, as represented by the colonists' reaction to Britain's decision that the lands of Indians, the original Americans, should not be seized or bought at unfair prices. It came into existence, on the other hand, because of a lofty and admirable commitment to justice and a belief that human rights are tied in with the Divine will, as represented by the opposition to oppressive taxation and a denial to the colonists of the right of participation in the decisions which affected and influenced their lives. This ambiguity has lived on in American history down to the present day.

III

Whatever ambivalence leaders like Thomas Jefferson must have felt about the nature of the nation's birth, they believed that the infant republic had a significance far beyond that to be seen in its weak and tentative beginning. John Adams saw "a parallel between 'the case of Israel' and that of America, between the conduct of Pharaoh and George III." Writing to his wife in May, 1776, Adams remarked, "'Is it not a saying of Moses, "Who am I, that I should go in and out before this great people?"' . . . Reflecting upon his role, Adams was filled with a profound sense of 'awe.'"[8] George Mason, who authored the Virginia Declaration of Rights and who but for his passion for privacy might have won the enduring remembrance of the republic, looking back on the events surrounding the Revolution, said, "Taking a retrospective view of what is passed, we seem to have been treading on enchanted ground."[9]

One can hardly read the Declaration of Independence without gaining the impression that a sense of divine presence, or at least of enormous and incalculable destiny, attended the beginning of the American undertaking. Much has been written of the religious faith of those who were the nation's spokesmen at its beginning. We have been told again and again that many of the founding fathers were disciples of English Deism with only a nominal commitment to Christian faith. No one ought to gloss over this, especially since there is more than a little evidence that this assertion represents substantial truth. In 1816, for example, John Adams wrote to Thomas Jefferson, saying, "The Ten Commandments and the Sermon on the Mount contain my religion."

At the same time, the point ought to be made, granting the Deistic beliefs of some of the founding fathers, that the English Deists are hardly to be called atheists or anti-Christian in their outlook. Unorthodox, to be sure, but hardly anti-Christian! The Deists' greatest departure from orthodox Christian views occurs in their belief that God created the world in accordance with rational laws available to human discovery. The term "Deist" as an epithet was created by the conventional churches because while the Deists made little or no assault on the Christian faith, they did launch massive intellectual attacks on the institutions of religious faith. They denied pomp and ceremony in all forms of religion and described their distaste for temples, churches, and synagogues. The ominous sound we hear in the word "Deism" is due, therefore, partly to the opprobrium which orthodox Christian apologists attached to the word when they used it. At the very least, the Deists embraced natural religion and honored and revered Jesus Christ, particularly for his ethical teachings.

It may be said that, at the very least, the founding fathers possessed large residual Christian deposits in their whole outlook. Some months ago, *Time* magazine's Bicentennial issue carried the text of the Declaration of Independence showing the numerous changes which were made in the document as it moved through the minds and deliberations of the Continental Congress. In that process, some of the fifty-six members of the Congress who at last affixed their signatures to the document saw to it that the Declaration was amended to show a relationship between the new nation and God. At the conclusion of the actual Declaration of Independence and following the withering bill of particulars indicting George III, the members of the Congress had these words inserted: "appealing to the Supreme Judge of the world for the rectitude of our intentions." At the end of the Declaration and just before the well-known phrase, "we mutually pledge to each other our Lives, our Fortunes and our sacred Honor," the members of the Congress had the following words inserted: "with a firm reliance on the protection of divine Providence." It may be argued that the phrases listed above were perfunctory gestures in the general direction of the Deity as is customary often in political statements.

Such a notion that the references to God in the Declaration were meaningless other than as expected language is greatly crippled by what must be considered the "heart-statement" of the Declaration of Independence. The linchpin of the whole document is to be found in the deathless passage, "We hold these truths to be self-evident [the phrase used originally was "We hold these truths to be sacred and undeniable"] that all men are created equal, that they are endowed by their Creator with certain unalienable Rights, that among these are Life, Liberty and the pursuit of Happiness." This assertion, influenced to be sure by John Locke and French philosophers, goes back to the wellspring of the Hebrew-Christian reading of human nature as being endowed by God for his purposes.

When one reads the "self-evident" portion of our Declaration of Independence, the assertion may also be made that it is the American political creed that no parliament or congress, however representative, enjoys the right of granting "the unalienable rights of life, liberty and the pursuit of happiness." These are rights which precede and supersede any human convocation, secular or religious. Along this line, it might be interesting to point out that the Thirteenth, the Fourteenth, and the Fifteenth Amendments, so treasured, so reverently and so wistfully quoted and repeated in the little southern schools of my childhood, do not make the claim that the crucial amendments setting the nation against its dark past of slavery are granting amendments.

The language of the amendments rises to the religious affirmation of the "self-evident" portion of the Declaration in their statements about freedom from slavery, "the privileges or immunities of citizens," and the "right of citizens of the United States to vote." The Thirteenth Amendment does not say that the government of the United States shall make men and women free; it says rather that "neither slavery nor involuntary servitude . . . shall exist within the United States"; thus government shall not deny this freedom which is inherent. The Fourteenth Amendment does not say that "privileges or immunities" of citizenship are granted by the Constitution to Americans, any Americans; it says rather that those privileges and immunities which are inherent according to the Declaration of Independence shall not be abridged. The Fifteenth Amendment contains no suggestion of government's granting the right of citizens to vote; it only states that this right, again inherent in citizenship, "shall not be denied or abridged."

I suggest that the underlying principle set forth here is part of the divine intention in the service of which the American nation was ordained in history. The doctrine of God-given rights, running back through Jean Jacques Rousseau and John Locke and the rest, has roots in biblical faith and in something which I believe God was intending in human history. Surely, the authors and subscribers of the Declaration were thinking and phrasing far beyond their own practices and even their own beliefs, and yet one finds it difficult to believe that they were deliberately setting forth ideas and convictions which were fraudulent to their own consciences and which would be so placarded before the generations.

Professor Ewart Guinier of Harvard once said in my hearing that the signers of our Declaration must have stumbled fearfully in conscience and pen before deciding not to list some "excepts" in the blazing words, "We hold these truths to be self-evident, that all men are created equal." Had they been loyal only to their own practices and beliefs, they would have had to set down a long list of "excepts." "All men are created equal," "all". . . except blacks, "all" . . . except Roman Catholics (even though the Carrolls of Carrollton were respected citizens), "all" . . . except Southern Europeans, surely "all" . . . except Indians, and "all" . . . except Jews! How long the list would have stretched had these people not been in the hands of a purpose far beyond their own power to describe or to discern! It is either an act of Divine purpose or one of the greatest frauds in all of political history that there should stand the words, "We hold these truths to be self-evident, that all men are created equal, that they are endowed by their Creator with certain unalienable rights, that among these are Life, Liberty and the pursuit of Happiness."

IV

The God by whose will the nation came into being and under whose scrutiny it lives out its tenure gave to the United States a sublime political creed whose roots lie deep in Hebrew Christian thought. With this grand commitment, he gave to the infant nation issues of racial disparity of incalculably large and formidable dimensions. The physical problem of a vast continent to be made an instrument of the new nation's existence was large. Even larger, incredibly so, was the problem of color and cultural differences as represented by the Indian and the black slave.

The presence of the American Indian on the North American continent, and particularly that portion of it which became the United States, gave to the new nation a chance and challenge to make real its profession of political faith. The Northwest Ordinance, passed in 1787, set forth what is loftiest in the nation's soul. One of its articles stated, "There shall be neither slavery nor involuntary servitude in said territory." It stated further:

> the utmost good faith shall always be observed toward the Indians, their lands and property shall never be taken from them without their consent; and in their property, rights and liberty, they shall never be invaded or disturbed, unless in just and lawful wars authorized by Congress; but laws founded in justice and humanity shall from time to time be made, for preventing wrongs being done to them and for preserving peace and friendship with them.

These words are worthy indeed of a people entrusted by the "laws of nature" and of "nature's God" with the "self-evident" passage of the Declaration of Independence.

One sees the other side of the nation's soul in the Removal Act of May 28, 1830. The act as written gave the President of the United States power to negotiate with tribes east of the Mississippi on a basis of payment for their lands. When Indians resisted such arrangements, military force was used. In ten years one hundred thousand Indians were moved westward. This was not enough as the American wagon trains rolled toward the Pacific, for the discovery of gold in 1848 in California meant that the gold would have to be gotten, no matter what happened to the Indians. That the Indians resisted violation of their lands gave legitimacy to whatever atrocities were visited upon them. This policy culminated in the slaughter by the Seventh Cavalry in December, 1890, of more than two hundred Indian men, women, and children at Wounded Knee, though the Indians had already surrendered. This nation "under God," under God's scrutiny and judgment, has yet to cleanse itself of the monstrous outrages against a people who more often than not welcomed and helped the new settlers on this continent.

It is an irony of American history that this nation has dealt most shabbily with those who occupied the nation before the colonists came, the American Indians, and with those whom the colonists brought here by force, the black Americans. Lerone Bennett describes in almost mystic terms the arrival of the first slaves in the new land aboard a Dutch ship.

> She came out of a violent storm with a story no one believed, a name no one recorded and a past no one investigated. She was manned by pirates and thieves. Her captain was a mystery man named Jope, her pilot an Englishman named Marmaduke, her cargo an assortment of Africans with sonorous Spanish names—Antony, Isabella, Pedro.
>
> What seems unusual today is that no one sensed how extraordinary she really was. Few ships, before or since, have unloaded a more momentous cargo.

From whence did this ship come?

From somewhere on the high seas where she robbed a Spanish vessel of a cargo of Africans bound for the West Indies. . . .

The captain "Ptended," John Rolfe noted, that he was in great need of food; he offered to exchange his human cargo for "victualle." The deal was arranged. Antony, Isabella, Pedro, and 17 other Africans stepped ashore in August, 1619. The history of the Negro in America began.[10]

What might have been the history of this country and what might have been the fortunes of many of its people had this event, or a similar one, never taken place? The nation's conscience would perhaps have been spared an endless scarring, though the atrocities against the Indians might have claimed their rightful pain in guilt and rationalization. There would be no American blacks with their strange cultural amalgam of Africa and Europe and an "X" they_ created which we call "soul." The nation would have missed whatever advantage it received economically in the labor of hundreds of thousands of people for 244 years. These are all imponderables, but they insist on being considered and pondered.

Looking at America's "peculiar institution," slavery, and its tragic aftermath of civil strife and a long and as yet unended harvest of guilt and resentment, we search for some clue of moral and religious meaning.

The American people are not sinners above all other sinners. Quite to the contrary, there are in the American spirit remarkably strong impulses of compassion and high purpose. Only rarely have the people of this country flocked to the standards of those who appealed to their basest passions and least worthy instincts, and then only when the appeals were cloaked in noble and acceptable terms and code phrases.

There is one great weakness in the American temper which is revealed from a reading of our past. It is the inability of the nation to sustain its energies and resources in the pursuit of a goal when that goal proves elusive and difficult to attain, when great cost, financial or psychological, is required, and when prolonged individual sacrifice is demanded.

Let the case of human rights in America be an example, though ecology or some other not easily and not quickly achieved objective could serve as an example. The nation has come to several momentous times and circumstances when events faced the republic with a chance to choose the high road. Surely, this happened at the time of the nation's independence. Again, at the end of the Civil War, the nation had paid in death and destruction until, as Abraham

Lincoln put it in his Second Inaugural Address, "The wealth piled by the bondman's two hundred and fifty years of unrequited toil" was sunk and "every drop of blood drawn with the lash" was paid by another drawn with the sword. There was a fitful start toward wiping out differences between Americans based on the accidents of birth, but the nation's moral energies were soon spent and found wanting in the chance to make a deal and to get ahead. Still again in May, 1954, the nation came to another great junction. The last sanctuary of American jurisprudence, the U.S. Supreme Court, said that segregation was, of itself, unjust and unconstitutional. The nation made another start and seemed to surge forward until the late 1960s. Then, the price seemed too high and the time demand too long in prospect. Now, so much of that thrust is gone. It has been lost in the nation's inability to make long and sustained sacrifices in the cause of truth and of God.

Who can tell what the nation's future is as we face forward from the Bicentennial? It ought not to be said that we have fallen shorter than other nations in our bigotry born of greed and in our greed born of bigotry, since no other nation in all of history has even been entrusted with so noble a political creed together with such opulent resources and at a point in time when all of that could make all of the difference. James Sanders, Auburn Professor of Old Testament at Union Theological Seminary, says in his imaginative "covenant lawsuit" concept of God against old Israel that "God alone is the judge and the redeemer."[11] Herein is our hope. Indeed, our only hope is that the Lord of history may still be intent on having the United States of America serve his purposes; and surely human rights are no minor part of those purposes.

V

Baptists have a large stake in the whole cause of human rights in America, upon which the fate of the nation may well hang. For better or for worse, Baptist people are in the majority in the regions where human rights heretofore have been most rigidly proscribed and where the ugliest forms of racism have until recently had their greatest expression.

The most desperate need of American political life today is to have within the body politic some people whose loyalty to the nation goes deep enough for them to present it with the truth of God, the mandate of the Bible, and the spirit of the New Testament.

As a people of the Bible, and with among the strongest doctrinal affirmation of human freedom before God of any of the religious denominations of America, Baptists have the opportunity to speak to the conscience and soul of the nation, if we can reinterpret who we are and why we are here in this moment of history.

To be sure, there are problems in coming to this prophetic role in the country. There must be a more searching definition of the old and favorite term among Baptists, "separation of church and state." Surely, this must not be intended to mean "renunciation" of responsibility in the communal life of government which affects us all. Of course, Baptists have never really followed this doctrine in the strictest sense, since all through the country Baptists have taken active roles in influencing government in crusades against liquor, gambling, and infringements on religious liberty. What is needed here is an understanding that Baptists have responsibility to speak to the society, to seek to influence it with all of the mandates of the gospel. It is a sad fact of history that where human rights are concerned, black Baptists (and not enough of them) have been in the forefront of the struggle in disproportionate numbers. One has only to mention the name of Martin Luther King, Jr., to summon the vision of the largest thrust made in this century in the interest of human rights.

In order to rise to a prophetic role, Baptists must come to see that the highest honor they can receive is not to be lionized, courted, praised, and patronized by political people. Reinhold Niebuhr, it is said, greatly approved the comment of James Madison which stated, "The truth is that all men having power ought to be distrusted." [12] Baptists might well serve their Lord better if they can lose their adulation for the princes of the earth and center their admiration and devotion on the Prince of glory. As P. T. Forsyth said long ago, men are not saved by flattering them; they are saved by being opposed in their natural impulses and proclivities. Though it does not realize it, the nation cries out for, and bleeds for, some participatory presence—yet in another sense detached—which confronts it and speaks to it in terms of a higher will and a higher law. Political people have claimed to recognize this reality, as in the inaugural speech of one of our presidents who said, "Here the people rule. But there is a higher power, by whatever name we call Him, who ordains not only righteousness but love, not only justice, but mercy." [13] The people of Christ need to take this seriously; indeed, it is their calling and vocation to assert and to serve this faith as they deal in the communal affairs to which all are called as Christians living in a political order. In this, we shall be faithful to our Lord about whom Forsyth said in his Beecher Lectures:

The Saviour of the world was not made or moulded by the world; and the world knew, and still knows in Him a presence that must be either obeyed or destroyed. He always looked down on the world He had to save. He always viewed it from God's side, and in God's interest. He always stood for God against the men he would save. It was indeed with divine pity he looked down, and not contempt; but it *was* with pity. . . .[14]

Who is sufficient for these things? Baptist people have the lordship of Christ, the authority of the Scriptures, and the doctrine, in rare purity, of the priesthood of the believer—the royal status of every Christian—and, therefore, the dignity of all people. Alas, we have some historical and organizational barriers which hold us back from a full and free and faithful witness of Jesus Christ to our social order. We are divided along regional and racial lines though there has been some minimal, mutual interpenetration of these borders and barriers. Baptists in the North have a noble history of identification with human rights, but they have been torn and weakened in past generations by doctrinal divisions. Southern Baptists have an illustrious history of doctrinal purity, unity, and evangelism, but they carry the stigma of having been participants for the longest time in the vile institution of slavery and its aftermath. Black Baptists have an heroic history of having, through Christ, become a people of warm and fervent discipleship, the community of faith having been fashioned out of the most total despair ever faced by a people. Sadly enough, they are divided by political concepts of denomination and carry the weight of a suspicion and resentment toward white Baptists which, if exposed, would be shocking even to themselves.

Over all of this is Christ with his pleading, insistent prayer which reaches out from the earliest Christian undertaking down to our own crucial time and circumstance, "Neither pray I for these alone, but for them also which shall believe on me through their word; that they all may be one; as thou, Father, art in me, and I in thee, that they also may be one in us: that the world may believe that thou hast sent me" (John 17:20-21, KJV). What high stakes the Lord mentions here— nothing less than the credibility of Jesus Christ before the world!

Dare any Baptist who loves the Lord not see the overriding urgency of a truly united Baptist witness to our country which now, sadly and tragically enough, is divided and confused, frightened and insecure about its future, and uncertain about its basic assumptions?

A nation met in holy love by a united Baptist witness, standing on the great historic principles of our Baptist legacy of liberty and freedom, might, by God's grace, hear and receive the answer to its pathetic and desperate wail, expressed in so many ways.

Is there no balm in Gilead
To make the wounded whole?

The united and faithful witness to the nation of Baptist people who are truly committed to their historic distinctives of liberty and freedom might send forth a glad and glorious word of deliverance ringing through the land. People beholding this could well cry:

> But then the Holy Spirit has come
> And has revived our national soul again.

NOTES

[1] Cited in William Warren Sweet, *Religion in the Development of American Culture 1765–1840* (New York: Charles Scribner's Sons, 1952), p. 33.

[2] *Ibid.*

[3] *Ibid.,* p. 34.

[4] *Ibid.,* pp. 35-36.

[5] Shelton Smith, *In His Image But . . .* (Durham, N. C.: Duke University Press, 1972), pp. 5-6.

[6] *Encyclopedia Britannica,* 1970 ed., s.v. "United States," p. 610.

[7] *Ibid.*

[8] Richard B. Morris, *Seven Who Shaped Our Destiny* (New York: Harper & Row, Publishers, 1973), p. 80.

[9] *Time,* Special 1776 Issue: Independence, p. 5.

[10] Lerone Bennett, *Before the Mayflower* (Baltimore: Penguin Books, first published by Johnson Publishing Company, 1962), pp. 29-30.

[11] James A. Sanders, *Torah and Canon* (Philadelphia: Fortress Press, 1972), p. 74.

[12] Arthur Schlesinger, Jr., *The Politics of Hope* (Boston: Houghton Mifflin Company, 1962), p. 109.

[13] The Inaugural Address of President Gerald R. Ford, August 9, 1974.

[14] P. T. Forsyth, *Positive Preaching and the Modern Mind* (London: Independent Press, 1907), p. 83.

Certain
Unalienable
Rights

WILLIAM F. KEUCHER

This essay attempts to provide a brief review concerning the historical streams and antecedents which fed the ever-widening confluence of colonial independence, to offer a general overview of those unalienable rights which are implicit in the context of colonial thought and action, and to identify the erosion of some important contemporary freedoms. In reawakening the spirit of 1776, we may recover for ourselves and extend to our posterity the blessings of liberty and justice for all.

I. THE CONTEXT OF IDEAS AND ACTIONS BEHIND
THE DECLARATION OF INDEPENDENCE

On June 7, 1776, having been earlier instructed by the Virginia Convention on May 15, 1776, Richard Henry Lee obtained the floor of the Continental Congress meeting in Philadelphia and offered this resolution: "these United Colonies are, and of right ought to be, free and independent States, that they are absolved from all allegiance to the British Crown, and that all political connection between them and the State of Great Britain is, and ought to be, totally dissolved." [1]

By June 10, three days later, the Congress authorized the appointment of a committee to "prepare a Declaration to the effect of the said First Resolution." This committee, headed by Thomas Jefferson and assisted by John Adams, Roger Sherman, Robert R. Livingstone, and Benjamin Franklin, reported to the Congress on June 28 its draft of a Declaration which was adopted on July 2, 1776, and duly signed by John Hancock, as president of the Congress, on July 4. The Declaration begins:

> When in the course of human events, it becomes necessary for one people to dissolve the political bands, which have connected them with another, and to assume, among the powers of the earth, the separate and equal station, to which the Laws of Nature and of Nature's God entitle them, a decent respect to the opinions of mankind requires that they should declare the causes which impel them to the separation.[2]

To understand these causes, one must do more than examine the immediate context of Parliament's Intolerable Acts against the colonies, or the attitude of tyranny expressed by the British Crown. Michael Kammen cautions us against what he calls "an immaculate conception" view of history which becomes oblivious to the decades and centuries of fertilization, germination, and gestation.[3] He is of the opinion that to understand the colonial period of history, we must also be acquainted with the origins of its past both in event and in thought. He reminds us, "Sir Thomas More's *Utopia*, . . . preceded by more than a century the utopian schemes of Puritan Boston or Pilgrim Plymouth. . . . Americans, from the outset, . . . had a mythology before they even had a country."[4]

John Adams later wrote to Thomas Jefferson in 1815:

> What do we mean by the Revolution? The war? That was no part of the Revolution; it was only an effect and consequence of it. The Revolution was in the minds of the people, and this was effected, from 1760 to 1775, in the course of fifteen years before a drop of blood was shed at Lexington. The records of thirteen legislatures, the pamphlets, newspapers in all the colonies, ought to be consulted during that period to ascertain the steps by which the public opinion was enlightened and informed concerning the authority of Parliament over the colonies.[5]

Three years later, in a letter to Hezekiah Niles, Adams echoed similar sentiments, "The Revolution was in the minds and hearts of the people; a change in their religious sentiments of their duties and obligations. . . . *This radical change in the principles, opinions, sentiments, and affections of the people was the real American Revolution.*"[6]

During that fifteen-year span, the French and Indian Wars had come to an end with France ceding all territorial claims on Canada to Britain, as well as the Louisiana Territories east of the Mississippi River. However, despite the victorious conclusion of the war, Britain had added an estimated 100 million pounds to its national debt.

On March 22, 1765, the British Parliament, hoping to raise additional revenues from the colonies, passed a resolution known as the Stamp Act, which required payment for revenue stamps on newspapers, pamphlets, playing cards and dice, and legal documents. In response, protest was voiced leading to delegates from nine colonies, which met in New York City, to protest the principle of being taxed without adequate representation. This body, known as the Stamp Act Congress, also resolved not to import any goods which required the payment of duty. Within a year Parliament repealed the Stamp Act. On June 29, 1767, another series of actions were taken requiring the colonists to pay import duties on tea, glass, paints, oil, lead, and paper. These decisions, known as The Townshend Revenue Act, provoked protests in the colonies similar to those raised against the Stamp Act. The Massachusetts legislature asked other colonies to join them in resisting these new duties. Although the Virginia governor dissolved the House of Burgesses, members met privately to declare their boycott on imports subject to duty. On March 5, 1770, a confrontation between Boston patriots and British soldiers resulted in bloodshed and a wave of sympathy which spread across the colonies because of "The Boston Massacre."

On April 12, 1770, Parliament repealed The Townshend Act; except to dramatize their right to impose taxes, they let the tax on tea stand. After a two-year lull, the British Crown took further action authorizing the reimbursement of English duty paid on the tea shipments of the East India Company to America, thereby allowing the American tea merchants to be undersold. In retaliation, on December 16, the celebrated Boston Tea Party took place. In March, 1774, King George approved the first of a series of Parliamentary reprisals which came to be known as the Intolerable Acts. The port of Boston was ordered closed until the colonial authorities would reimburse eighteen thousand pounds for the tea which had been destroyed. Other measures to follow included the ban on public meetings without the governor's approval and the presence of British troops and the necessity to house and quarter them in private dwellings, wherever necessary and expedient.

On September 5, 1774, the First Continental Congress met in Philadelphia and issued its important Declaration of Ten Rights, including life, liberty, and property, together with the affirmation that this right had never been ceded to any foreign power whatever to be disposed of without consent. They also resolved that they were entitled to all the rights, liberties, and immunities of free and natural born subjects as if they were within the realm of England. They further established, based on the foundation of English liberty and all free government, the right of the people to participate in their legislative councils. Because they were not and could not be represented in

Parliament, they claimed the right to a free and exclusive power of legislation in their several provincial legislatures, where the right of representation could be preserved. They further claimed the right to all the attributes of English common law together with its protection. Such rights included trial by a jury of their peers, together with the right to assemble peaceably, together with the right to petition for the redress of grievances. They protested against the keeping of a standing army in times of peace without the consent of their legislatures, as contrary to the law. They further protested the action of the British Crown in contravening the independence of their legislatures as acting against the English Constitution. Their actions concluded that the "following acts of Parliament are infringements in violations of the rights of the colonists; and that the repeal of them is essentially necessary, in order to restore harmony between Great-Britain and the American colonies."[7]

In 1775 hostilities broke out in Concord and Lexington; and on May 10, the Second Continental Congress met in Philadelphia; on July 6, 1775, the Congress issued its Declaration setting forth the causes and necessity of the colonists' taking up arms: "Bound by obligations of respect to the rest of the world, to make known the justice of our cause," the Declaration set forth the particulars to which Parliament had failed to give satisfactory redress. The original hopes of finding a residence "for civil and religious freedom" seemed now seriously threatened by the despotism of the British Crown and Parliament.[8] Following the appointment of George Washington as commander of the Continental Troops, George III proclaimed that Americans were guilty of open and avowed rebellion.

On January 10, 1776, Thomas Paine published his work under the title, *Common Sense,* which advocated complete independence for the colonies. Paine wrote:

Everything that is right or natural pleads for separation. The blood of the slain, the weeping voice of nature cries, *"'Tis time to part."* . . . The Reformation was preceded by the discovery of America—as if the Almighty graciously meant to open a sanctuary to the persecuted in future years, when home should afford neither friendship nor safety.[9]

Replying to those who asked where the king would be in relationship to America, Paine responded that "he reigns above, and does not make havoc of mankind like the royal brute of Britain." Then pointing out that in order to appear undefective in earthly honors, he suggested a day set apart for the proclaiming of the charter to be placed "on the divine law, the word of God" and then placed upon the charter, a crown, so that the world may know that "in

America *the law is king.* For as in absolute governments the king is law, so in free countries the law *ought* to be king; and there ought to be no other. . . . A government of our own is our natural right." [10] Symbolical of the authority vested in the people, he suggested the crown be demolished and scattered among the people, whose right it is.

This brief chronology offers the immediate context of leading events and responses representative of the discussions and actions taken by patriots in the colonies. The sources of their discussions and actions are based on a liberty which they saw emerging from the original Colonial Charters, from the English unwritten Constitution of long-established practice, together with the English Common Law dating back to the Magna Charta, and to the concept of natural rights which existed prior to life together in society. During the decade preceding the Declaration of Independence itself, more than four hundred pamphlets and publications were published dealing with various issues of colonial freedom. In the words of Gordon S. Wood:

> It seemed indeed to be a peculiar moment in history when all knowledge coincided, when classical antiquity, Christian theology, English empiricism, and European rationalism could all be linked. Thus Josiah Quincy, like other Americans, could without any sense of incongruity cite Rousseau, Plutarch, Blackstone, and a seventeenth-century Puritan all on the same page.
> . . . To most of the Revolutionaries there was no sense of incompatibility in their blending of history, rationalism, and scripture; all were mutually reinforcing ways of arriving at precepts about human and social behavior, ways of discovering those fundamentals "applicable to every Sort of Government, and not contrary to the common Understanding of Mankind." [11]

It was in such a context that John Adams made the following appeal:

> "Let us study the law of nature, search into the spirit of the British constitution: read the histories of ancient ages; contemplate the great examples of Greece and Rome; set before us the conduct of our own British ancestors, who have defended for us the inherent rights of mankind against foreign and domestic tyrants and usurpers." [12]

When, therefore, we hear colonial patriots in a Boston town meeting resolving that it is

> the indefeasible right of subjects to be *consulted* and to give their *free consent in person* or by representatives of their own free election to the raising and keeping a standing army among them; and the inhabitants of this town, being free subjects, have the same right derived from nature and confirmed by the British constitution as well as the said royal charter; and therefore the raising or keeping a standing army without their consent in person or by representatives of their own free election would be an

infringement of their natural, constitutional, and charter rights; and the employing such army for the enforcing of laws made without the consent of the people, in person or by their representatives, would be a grievance,[13]

we are seeing a further example of the historic streams which fed their sentiment and spirit of rebellion.

The American Revolution with its Declaration of Independence is the completion of seventeenth-century political struggles in England which had demolished the doctrine of the Divine Right of Kings and vested a growing sovereignty in the British Parliament. In 1689, the British Bill of Rights had upset the right of the king to dispense with laws, while at the same moment prohibiting the maintenance of a standing army without the consent of Parliament. The Mutiny Act of 1689 decreed that the king must call Parliament into session each year; while the Toleration Act, in that same year, offered new protection for the religious liberties of English Protestants. In 1694, the Triennial Act deprived the king of his earlier right to dispense with parliamentary elections.

The growth of English democratic ideas which came into such prominent visibility in the seventeenth century have been traced by others, such as G. P. Gooch.[14] He found in the Protestant reformers a tendency which moves toward the growth of popular rights. Human rights are the fruits of such a reformation based on two basic intellectual principles: the right and duty of free inquiry and the priesthood of all believers. Free inquiry, which meant at the beginning the right of each person to read the Bible for himself or herself, "led straight from theological to political criticism." The theory of a universal priesthood led to a desire for political participation and equality.

In the same fashion, Andrew C. McLaughlin[15] has demonstrated the relationship between the covenant societies and the new political ideas and reality involving popular government and the doctrine of individual liberty and association. It was not long before the same people who discovered that they possessed the power to form a church realized that they also possessed the power to participate in and to create the structures of government.

Standing behind the Declaration of Independence of 1776 was the Declaration and Resolves of the First Continental Congress of 1774, which had preceded the Declaration with the causes and necessity of taking up arms, issued by the Continental Congress in 1775. Behind the actions of the Continental Congress were individual actions taken by the town of Boston, sponsored by Samuel Adams, and by the Virginia House of Burgesses, introduced by Patrick Henry. The

Virginia Declaration asserted that the first settlers brought with them all the liberties, privileges, franchises, and immunities of British subjects, and that this principle had been declared and sustained by two of the charters issued for Virginia, and that under the British Constitution and its protection, taxes could be levied only by the people or their representatives. The right of the people, therefore, to be governed by laws made by their own chosen representatives had never been surrendered.[16] Three further resolutions which were not adopted continued to be published as a part of the action of the Virginia House, so that the general impression contributed to an even deeper feeling of independence. Whereupon, in response to the Massachusetts House, nine colonies responded to the invitation and took action to be known as the Stamp Act Congress, urging that the abuses of a free trade and highhanded judicial acts, together with the Stamp Act itself, be repealed absolutely, totally, and immediately.[17]

Although Parliament acceded to the request of the Congress in repealing the Stamp Act, it did not accept the validity of the principles which had been argued by the colonists. Accompanying the repeal of the Stamp Act was the Declaratory Act of Parliament, which stated

> that the said colonies and plantations in *America* have been, are, and of right ought to be, subordinate unto, and dependent upon the imperial crown and parliament of *Great Britain;* and that the King's majesty, by and with the advice and consent of the lords, spiritual and temporal, and commons of *Great Britain,* in parliament assembled, had, hath, and of right ought to have, full power and authority to make laws and statutes of sufficient force and validity to bind the colonies and people of America, subject of the crown of *Great Britain,* in all cases whatsoever.... That all resolutions, votes, orders, and proceedings, in any of the said colonies or plantations, whereby the power and authority of the parliament of Great Britain, to make laws and statutes as aforesaid, is denied, or drawn into question, are, and are hereby declared to be, utterly null and void to all intents and purposes whatsoever.[18]

But, standing behind these specific actions were the long-term gains related to the development of British Common Law expressed in its Bill of Rights of 1689, dating from the Magna Charta of 1215. Richard L. Perry has done an admirable job of assembling English and American documents which spell out the sources of our liberties. Such were the tributaries which formed the continental watershed for the growth of ideas and insights, decisions and deeds which led to July 4, 1776.

II. CERTAIN UNALIENABLE RIGHTS

Vital streams of history flowed from ancient Greece and Rome to overrun and flood the banks and lowlands of feudal society. Functioning as a seedbed for the twin forces of the Enlightenment and Reformation, the rise of a new watershed produced new political feelings and institutions. Neither England nor the New World could escape the inundation. Standing behind all of the political records and documents and the growing experience of a participating society, there were the natural rights which were defined as existing antecedents to human life in society and were viewed as a gift of nature or of nature's God. In such an understanding, human rights were not regarded as the creation of the political documents like the Magna Charta, the Bill of Rights, or the Declaration of Independence. Such documents, at the most, could only be a witness and an expression to the essential rights which had always existed prior to government, prior to society, and prior to legislation.

John Dickinson, the Philadelphia farmer, attacked the idea that rights are a matter of sovereign grace or parliamentary favor. He said, "Liberties are founded on the acknowledged rights of human nature." Declaring that neither kings nor parliament can give rights essential to happiness, he asserted:

> We claim them from a higher source—from the King of kings, and Lord of all the earth. They are not annexed to us by parchments and seals. They are created in us by the decrees of Providence, which establish the laws of our nature. They are born with us; exist with us; and cannot be taken from us by any human power without taking our lives. In short, they are founded on the immutable maxims of reason and justice.[19]

Alexander Hamilton had written in similar fashion, stating that "the sacred rights of mankind are not to be rummaged for among old parchments or musty records. They are written, as with a sunbeam, in the whole *volume* of human nature, by the hand of divinity itself, and can never be erased or obscured by mortal power."[20] "Such rights," another argued, "are legal whether or not they are confirmed by some statute law." Existing independently, the rights stand by themselves as the measure of legitimacy. The Declaration of Independence was the flood tide receiving and holding the rising sentiments of colonists in behalf of three main issues which had been under discussion in serious detail and depth for more than a decade. These issues focused around the nature of representation and consent, around the nature of the Constitution and the guarantees of colonial rights, and around the issue of sovereignty.

In the Declaration and in the American Revolution one sees the completion of the struggle fought earlier in Britain. First, the Crown was recognized as an inlimited and an undivided sovereignty. That sovereignty was then distributed from the Crown to Parliament and would find its ultimate expression in being distributed in the power of the people's own participation in self-government. What was uniquely new in the American political philosophy and experience was the discovery of the distribution of sovereignty among the citizenry and the distribution of powers in the government, thereby insuring its limitation in a principle of federalism.

Henry Steele Commager observed that in the creation of a nation the colonial Congress "solved, almost overnight, two of the most intractable problems in the history of government: colonialism and federalism. . . . by the simple device of transforming 'colonies' into states, and admitting these states into the union on the basis of absolute equality . . . the Founding Fathers taught the world a lesson which it has learned only slowly and painfully. . . ."[21] Declaring that "all government derives its power from the consent of the governed," they "invented the constitutional convention as the appropriate instrument for making, altering, abolishing, and remaking government; that is, they legalized revolution."[22] In the familiar words of the Declaration, they said:

> We hold these truths to be self-evident: that all men are created equal; that they are endowed, by their Creator, with certain unalienable rights; that among these are life, liberty, and the pursuit of happiness:—That to secure these rights, governments are instituted among men, deriving their just powers from the consent of the governed; that whenever any form of government becomes destructive of these ends, it is the right of the people to alter or to abolish it, and to institute a new government, laying its foundation on such principles, and organizing its powers in such form, as to them shall seem most likely to effect their safety and happiness.[23]

In reading the Declaration, it is well to note that there is elaborate enunciation of its many rights as we have seen spelled out in the Boston Declaration of 1772, or the Congressional Declaration of 1774. It also becomes apparent that there are striking similarities between the Declaration of Independence and the Bill of Rights which had been reported to the Virginia Convention on May 27, 1776, and subsequently adopted June 12, 1776. Correspondence indicates that copies of the Virginia Bill were being circulated among members of the Continental Congress in Philadelphia, whose committee had been chosen on June 11, but did not make its report until June 28.

"Endowed by their Creator with certain unalienable rights"—these rights are specified in terms of life, liberty, and the pursuit of happiness. Nearly all of the earlier versions of these familiar words substitute the word "property" for "happiness." Sir William

Blackstone, in elaborating on what he considered to be the primary rights of Englishmen, specified "the rights to life, liberty and property." [24] Subordinate rights which serve to protect these primary rights were five in number: the right of self-defense, the right of petition, the right to one's day in court, the right to impose limits on the discretionary power of kings, and the right to representative government. Arthur M. Schlesinger, Jr., has made a case from his reading of contemporary colonial literature that the pursuit of happiness meant not its chase but its practice. [25]

The self-evident truths could be identified as axioms of a free society that needed no proof. Jefferson's first draft read, "We hold these truths to be sacred and undeniable." It is thought that perhaps the insertion of "self-evident" as a better rendering reflects the hand of Benjamin Franklin, while also reflecting his scientific bent.

Affirming the self-evident truth that men having been created equal and endowed by their Creator with certain unalienable rights, the Declaration does not specify in traditional social contract theory those rights that may have been surrendered in behalf of the social contract. "Unalienable rights of property" might mean that a person must give consent for the surrender of property, but if the unalienable rights refer to that which cannot be traded or surrendered, we are led into the area of conscience. Francis Hutcheson has stated that liberty of conscience "is not only an essential, but an unalienable branch of natural liberty. This right appears from the very constitution of the rational mind which can assent or dissent solely according to the evidence presented, and naturally desires knowledge. ... It cannot be subject to the will of another." [26] In this sense, "unalienable" means that their nature makes them untransferable. Later in the debate on the New Hampshire constitution in 1784, an alternative formulation read:

> When men enter into a state of society, they surrender up some of their natural rights to that society, in order to insure the protection of others; and, without such an equivalent, the surrender is void. Among the natural rights, some are in their very nature unalienable, because no equivalent can be given or received for them. Of this kind are the RIGHTS of CONSCIENCE. [27]

However, if one reads the full text of the Declaration of Independence, it becomes apparent that although the inalienable rights of the colonists have not been spelled out in explicit statement, they are, nonetheless, implicitly present both in terms of the assumptions behind the Declaration and in terms of the grievances stated against the British Crown. In effect, each grievance could be regarded as a negative statement of specified rights which have been violated by the tyranny of the Crown. In such a reading,[28] (1) "he has refused his assent to laws the most wholesome and necessary for the public good" becomes the right to be free of an oppressive tyranny. (2) "He has forbidden his governors to pass laws of immediate and pressing importance" becomes the right to a government of law rather than the capriciousness of an absolute sovereign. (3) "He has refused to pass other laws for the accommodation of large districts of people, unless those people would relinquish the right of representation in the Legislature. . . ." becomes the right to be represented in the legislature by a person of your own choosing. (4) "He has called together legislative bodies at places unusual, uncomfortable, and distant from the depository of their public records. . . ." becomes the right of access to public records. (5) "He has dissolved representative houses repeatedly. . . ." becomes the right to the election franchise. (6) "He has refused for a long time . . . to cause others to be elected . . . the state remaining . . . exposed to all the dangers of invasion from without and convulsions within" becomes the right to domestic tranquillity. (7) "He has endeavored to prevent the population of these states; for that purpose obstructing the laws for naturalization of foreigners, refusing to pass others to encourage their migrations. . . ." becomes the right to freedom of movement and emigration. (8) "He has obstructed the administration of justice. . . ." becomes the right for due process of law. (9) "He has made judges dependent on his will alone for their tenure of their offices. . . ." becomes the right to equity under the judicial process. (10) "He has erected a multitude of new offices and sent hither swarms of officers to harass our people. . . ." becomes the right to be secure and uncoerced. (11) "He has kept among us in times of peace standing armies, without the consent of our Legislatures. . . ." becomes, together with (12), the right of civil power to be free from military subjection and domination. (13) "He has combined with others to subject us to a jurisdiction foreign to our Constitution. . . ." becomes the right to be protected by the Constitution from an unjust tyranny.

A close examination of the list of grievances specified in the Declaration of Independence offers a clear enunciation of the rights and liberties to which the colonists felt themselves protected under their charters, under the protection of English common law, and the development of their American system of representation. The Declaration therefore concludes that, under the kind of tyranny they have been facing, they have the right to alter and dissolve established political ties and the right to form a new national sovereignty independent of either the British Crown or the British Parliament. The right of their consent also construes their right to act upon their dissent. Such a right cannot be justified in any of their written documents inasmuch as they do not yet have a national Constitution. However, their Preamble states the basis of such a right:

> When in the course of human events, it becomes necessary for one people to dissolve the political bands, which have connected them with another, and to assume, among the powers of the earth, the separate and equal station, to which the Laws of Nature and of Nature's God entitle them, a decent respect to the opinions of mankind requires that they should declare the causes which impel them to the separation.

Their right to choose to decide to be free comes from no other source than the laws of nature and of nature's God. They conclude with a solemn affirmation:

> "We therefore the representatives of the united States of America in general Congress assembled appealing to the supreme judge of the world for the rectitude of our intentions do in the name and by authority of the good people of these colonies solemnly publish and declare— That these united colonies are and of right ought to be free and independent States; that they are absolved from all allegience to the british Crown, and that all political connection between them and the state of great Britain is & ought to be totally dissolved. . . . And for the support of this declaration, with a firm reliance on the protection of divine providence, we mutually pledge to each other our lives, our fortunes & our sacred honor." [29]

The pledge and guarantee of unalienable rights is the mutual commitment and dedication of life, fortune, and sacred honor.

III. THE EROSION OF CIVIL AND RELIGIOUS LIBERTIES

The freedom and independence claimed for the colonies under the Declaration of Independence were neither universal nor unlimited. This is but another way of saying that the American Revolution was incomplete for many persons living in the new Republic. It would require another hundred years before slaves would receive their emancipation and another hundred years before the related institutions of slavery could be more fully dismantled, allowing minority groups to begin receiving what the Declaration aspired to and what the Constitution of 1787, with its further amendments, presumed to guarantee. The election franchise for women would take another 150 years, and after 200 years the validity of the Equal Rights Amendment for women is still being vigorously debated. Our national experience tells us that many of our equal liberties have been unequally experienced.

But if the American Revolution is meant to be a continuing

experience to extend the blessings of liberty to those disenfranchised, we should also note that many of the liberties, both civil and religious, secured for us in the Declaration and in the Constitution, have suffered erosion with the passing of time. For example, twenty-five years ago, a daily newspaper sent out two reporters asking people interviewed at random to sign a petition saying that they believed in the Declaration of Independence. Out of 112 persons interviewed, in one metropolitan city, all but one refused to sign. People were afraid that the Declaration voiced or made some kind of subversive demand. Another paper in another urban area tried the same experiment and encountered the same spirit of suspicion and distrust.[30]

We can be sure that in the past twenty-five years more people in America have been disconnected from their heritage of freedom. If the Bill of Rights were up for adoption today, the pervading climate might easily jeopardize adoption of this significant portion of our American Constitution. The erosion of our democratic options sees a little bit of freedom dying with each passing generation, while we continue in our failure to renew the foundations of freedom and to stitch up its torn fabric.

The erosion of freedom may be seen at many points where the dikes created by our political institutions and our constitutional safeguards have been breached and broken. An examination here of three representative losses vital to a free society may be helpful.

1. *The erosion of liberty itself.* The Declaration of Independence speaks of "life, liberty and the pursuit of happiness." It appears today that Americans have become increasingly willing to barter many of their precious civil liberties for the promise and hope of increased security. In the face of rising lawlessness, crime in the streets, murder and mayhem, kidnaping and hijacking, bombing and terrorism, necessity suggests or compels increased security measures. But in the process, freedom of movement in an open society must give way to the more narrow limits of a repressed closed society. Despite our vaunted democratic philosophy and principles, in actual practice we find ourselves tending toward the practices of a totalitarian society. If there are places where the American citizen cannot travel for security reasons outside the country, if there are an increasing number of areas inside the country off limits—like airports and other public buildings—at what point will life in free America differ from life in a closed society behind some iron or bamboo curtain?

I wish that I could be more prescriptive as to how we can balance on the one hand the precarious risk of freedom and on the other hand our overwhelming propensity for safety and security. I can only suggest the beginning of an answer. What has happened is that Americans have lost touch with the formative sources of their founding principles and events. From the normative, social theory of an open society, we have been building, stone by stone, the restrictive prison cell of a closed society. And much of what we have done has seemed wise, right, and justifiable in response to the pressures and threats of contemporary events.

In World War II individual and social freedoms had to be edged out of a clear focus as the primary agenda became the winning of a war. Later there was the Korean War which was accompanied by an era of fear and defensiveness symbolized by "McCarthyism." Mixed with that spirit was the developing cold war, as our nation attempted to deal with the ever-widening expansion of Communist aims and the uncertain political developments of the Third World. Interspersed with a cold war on all fronts, the United States faced a continuing series of international incidents in Asia, Africa, the Middle East, and Latin America. Since 1940, Americans have known thirty-five years of persistent pressures on their democratic institutions and on their civil liberties and personal freedom. The people's right to know has been steadily diminished. The right to participate in the affairs of government has decreased as the distance between the citizens and their elected and appointed officials has increased. The increased complexity of international problems, coupled with the growth of distance, has made citizens less competent to function as an electorate and to discharge the sovereignty vested in them as the people, rather than in the government which was created to express and institutionalize their purposes.

During the decade of the sixties, the social protest and unrest in the urban ghettos, on the college campuses, and among minority groups (who had not yet been admitted either to the freedom of the earlier American open society or to the security and safety of the closed society) pushed us further away from our liberties, as we opted for either repressive measures or the security of a closed society, fearing the risks of an open society.

What is the remedy? How can America restore and guarantee its people the essential rights of life, liberty, and the pursuit of happiness? Some voices are heard telling us that it is too late and that in our kind of world the problem of order and security must lead us closer to George Orwell's *1984* with increased measures of governmental authority, security, and control.

Hopefully, the sentiments spoken by the late Justice Hugo L. Black in 1960 might once again capture the American imagination. Justice Black said:

> Since the earliest days philosophers have dreamed of a country where the mind and the spirit of man would be free; where there would be no limits to inquiry; where men would be free to explore the unknown and to challenge the most deeply rooted beliefs and principles. Our First Amendment was a bold effort to adopt this principle—to establish a country with no legal restriction of any kind upon the subjects people could investigate, discuss and deny. The framers knew better, perhaps, than we do today, the risks they were taking. They knew that free speech might be the friend of change and revolution. But they also knew that it is always the deadliest enemy of tyranny. With this knowledge, they still believed that the ultimate happiness and security of a nation lies in its ability to explore, to change, to grow and ceaselessly to adapt itself to a new knowledge born of inquiry free from any kind of governmental control over the mind and spirit of man.[31]

Can we regain that spirit? We can be sure that a society does not automatically pass from being a closed society to an open one merely by broadening the strictures. Two radically divergent social theories cannot be successfully mixed. We must abandon the one and we must choose the other. A high priority for the American system and its citizens must be the rediscovery of the principles of freedom which created the lively experiment of American liberty and launched its pursuit of freedom with justice for all.

2. *The erosion of a free conscience.* Our secular society must recover the lost qualities of its life and of its openness. The Bicentennial challenge to the religious community of America, including Baptists, is to renew and rediscover the meaning of religious liberty which has been eroded in the search for conformity to replace diversity and dissent.

To understand the history of nonconformity is to resist the pressures encouraging us to stereotype our faith. No single creed is big enough to exhaust the full meaning of faith. No single verbalization or religious formulation can be accepted as final or infallible. Each statement of truth by any human being is at best provisional, rather than permanent. A free conscience stems out of the claim of an undivided sovereignty which persons hear in the voice of God. Believing that God has promised a living guide, a free conscience resists the closed mind with its fear and its suspicions and remains open and receptive to further light and clearer knowledge. A free conscience will not hide in false shelters, nor seek to shield itself from the purest light by the idolatries which intervene between God's call and our response. A free conscience understands that it is better to help make people safe for ideas, rather than to seek to make ideas safe for people.

To be true to our Baptist heritage, we must be prepared to fight for the right of those who hold a view different from ours—not only to hold it passively, but also to propagate it as persuasively as they can. Shortly before his death, the late Pope John XXIII gave religious freedom a fresh start among Roman Catholics by taking sides with religious leaders who had rejected the idea that error has no rights. Error is an abstract idea; it is living, breathing, mortal people who err and make mistakes; and people (despite their fallibility) do have rights. It was a sad irony that, at the very moment when Roman Catholics were coming into a new understanding of religious freedom, many Baptists in America were turning their backs upon their past heritage and witness, seeking in the debate and discussion of the so-called "Prayer Amendment" to the Constitution to harness the power and the prestige of the state as an engine of religious persuasion.

It is the freedom of a free conscience which provides us the right not only to be Baptists, but also for Methodists to be Methodists, for Jews to be Jews, for Mormons to be Mormons, for agnostics to be agnostics, and for atheists to be atheists. It is the liberty of a free conscience which understands that our diversity as Baptists cannot be unmolested until a climate of freedom prevails which safeguards the right of all other groups to live and work side by side unmolested despite their diversities. Such a profound conviction is the watermark of our Baptist experience which runs through all of history from Thomas Helwys, who in 1612 published the first plea in England advocating full religious liberty for all. As Helwys wrote, "Let them be heretics, Turks, Jews or whatsoever."[32] Standing behind these essential convictions is the awareness that God not only has a way of taking care of his own, but also that he has a way of taking care of himself! The Truth forever established in heaven cannot be forever defeated on earth. To free the human mind from its chains and to liberate the conscience from its bonds is to enable a person to think God's thoughts after him, to seek his face, and to follow in his ways. If Baptists could learn how to trust God with his freedom and to trust the free conscience of fellow human beings, they would go a long way toward remedying the erosion of a free conscience and religious liberty.

3. *The erosion of the free exercise of religion.* Life, liberty, and the pursuit of happiness led from the Declaration of Independence of 1776 to the adoption of the American Constitution in 1787, with its guarantees against the establishment of religion or any prohibition against the free exercise of religion. Thomas Jefferson voiced the

convictions destined to prevail in the new nation when he said:

> I do not believe it is for the interest of religion to invite the civil magistrate to direct its exercises, its discipline, or its doctrines; nor of the religious societies, that the General Government should be invested with the power of effecting any uniformity of time or matter among them. . . . Every religious society has a right to determine for itself the times for these exercises, and the objects proper for them, according to their own particular tenets; and this right can never be safer than in their own hands, where the Constitution has deposited it.[33]

These sentiments of Thomas Jefferson had been expressed vocally and persistently by colonial Baptist leaders. John Leland, in Virginia, Isaac Backus—functioning as perhaps the first lobbyist for religious liberty in behalf of the Warren Baptist Association—and others, pressed home the inconsistency of those colonists who were protesting the injustice of a British tax on tea, while continuing to tax colonial Baptists for the support of a religious establishment.[34]

But if the First Amendment guarantee still stands on paper, it has become a paper tiger which benign neglect has allowed to erode. Government decrees and decisions have limited the free exercise of religion among American churches. For example, Congress in 1934 passed legislation denying tax exemption to religious and other charitable organizations found guilty of devoting a "substantial part" of their activities to "carrying on propaganda or otherwise attempting to influence legislation." The Internal Revenue Service has defined "substantial" to mean expenditures of more than 5 percent of an organization's total budget. The effect of this tax policy is to invade the freedom of the church and to divide the sovereignty of Jesus Christ as Lord of the conscience and head of the church. The effect of this tax policy is to violate the guarantee of the First Amendment that no law can be passed by Congress or by a federal agency exercising a legislative capacity of Congress to prevent the free exercise of religion in America. The effect of this tax policy is a coercive penalty which enables governmental power to infringe upon the involvement of the churches in the life of the nation, while allowing possible punitive action against those churches or religious organizations which are deemed "unacceptable." The effect of the policy is to tell the church of Jesus Christ what its gospel allows or permits and how far the nature of its Christian mission extends. The guarantee of the First Amendment includes the full and free exercise of religion, but we are facing the erosion of this right by the encroachment of a federal agency acting beyond its competency in the field of religious definition.

The free exercise of religion is an empty shibboleth if it does not provide freedom for churches and denominations to define the meaning and extent, the depth and scope of their Christian mission. For many Christians and various denominations this mission must mean more than private meetings where people gather to say prayers, to sing hymns, and to conduct religious devotions and exercises. The imperative of the Christian mission calls us to witness and to work in the public realm on behalf of our Christian faith. One cannot read colonial history without sensing the presence of Christian leaders and churches in the public realm; nothing has changed in the formal guarantees of the Constitution to deny that continued right of religion in public affairs.

The mission of the church, under the right of the Constitution in the free exercise clause, must allow freedom for prophetic witness when the plumb line of God's justice may be laid against social and political as well as ecclesiastical institutions and practices. Faithfulness to this Christian mission may mean acting in a national interest, but faithfulness to that mission may also lead against Caesar's interest. The church in America must be free to define its mission and to be unadjusted to customs of a passing age because of a higher adjustment to the permanence of a new age. The mission of the church and the free exercise guarantee must provide the right, on occasions, when out of good conscience Christians and corporate church actions may appear to be un-American, just as Moses was un-Egyptian, Isaiah was un-Babylonian, Jesus was un-Jewish, Paul was un-Roman, Dietrich Bonhoeffer was un-Aryan, and Boris Pasternak was un-Russian.

In 1944, in one of the earliest official statements taken by the Baptist Joint Committee, it was affirmed: "We believe that religious liberty is the ultimate ground of democratic institutions, and that wherever this liberty is questioned, restricted, or denied by any group—political, religious, or philosophical—all other human rights are imperiled."[35] In commenting on that action, James E. Wood, Jr., Executive Director of the Baptist Joint Committee declared, "It has been this integral relation of religious liberty to Baptist faith and the need of Baptists to exercise their religious liberty on matters affecting public policy that has resulted in the corporate witness of Baptists in public affairs."[36]

If America is to be a nation under God, we must not isolate or insulate our political institutions from the criticism of religious ideals in which God's truth may reach us in providence and judgment. In the words of the early apostolic testimony, "There is another king and his name is Jesus" (see Acts 17:7). That may be good news for the world, but it is bad news to the despotisms and false rulers of every age. As Lord of history, God is working everywhere to achieve his eternal purposes that his will may be done on earth and in the affairs of people and nations, even as it is done in heaven. Everyone and everything, what we do privately, what we do socially, and what we do in the public realm—everything stands under the judgment of his truth and justice.

We must recapture this full freedom to define the mission of the church if the erosion of the free exercise guarantee is to be repaired.

CONCLUSION

We need to probe deeply into the historic roots and origins of our nation's life and liberty. Hopefully, to be in touch once again with the formative sources, the founding events, and the documentary experience of our Revolutionary history may reawaken or strengthen our moribund institutions or some sleeping sentiments lodged in the dormitory of our minds. If the Bicentennial celebration helps our age to claim the unfulfilled promise of an unfinished democracy, the past can hearten and inspire a rededication to the aims spoken of in the Declaration of Independence as "life, liberty and the pursuit of happiness."

But let us take to heart an insight about freedom which Kyle Haselden saw before his untimely death. "The free man," he wrote, "is not our ultimate objective. Freedom . . . is for us a means to an end, not an end in itself. We seek, not a free man, but a full man. . . ."[37]

For the Christian faith, this means we seek the uncoerced freedom whereby we can choose to follow Christ's way, whose bondage is perfect freedom and whose self-emptying sacrifice fulfills and enriches the whole world. The happiness of that pursuit remains inexhaustibly alluring. Whether on Main Street or in metropolis, affairs are soul-sized and need the Mind of God![38]

NOTES

[1] Carl Becker, *The Declaration of Independence* (New York: Alfred A. Knopf, 1942), p. 3.

[2] *Ibid.,* p. 5.

[3] Michael Kammen, *People of Paradox* (New York: Alfred A. Knopf, 1973), p. 7.

[4] *Ibid.,* p. 9.

[5] Cited in Bernard Bailyn, *The Ideological Origins of the American Revolution* (Cambridge: The Belknap Press of Harvard University Press, 1967), p. 1.

[6] *Ibid.,* p. 160.

[7] Richard L. Perry, *Sources of Our Liberties* (New York: American Bar Foundation, 1959), p. 288. Resolves of the First Continental Congress, October 14, 1774. Reprinted by permission of New York University Press.

[8] *Ibid.,* pp. 295-300.

[9] Thomas Paine, *Common Sense and Other Political Writings* (New York: The Bobbs-Merrill Company, Inc., 1953), p. 23.

[10] *Ibid.,* p. 32.

[11] Gordon S. Wood, *The Creation of the American Republic, 1776-1787* (Chapel Hill: University of North Carolina Press, Institute of Early American History and Culture, 1969), pp. 7-8.

[12] Cited in *ibid.,* p. 6.

[13] Bailyn, *The Ideological Origins of the American Revolution,* p. 113.

[14] Cf. G. P. Gooch, *English Democratic Ideas in the Seventeenth Century* (New York: Harper & Row, Publishers, 1959).

[15] Andrew C. McLaughlin, *The Foundations of American Constitutionalism* (New York: New York University Press, 1932), pp. 3-29.

[16] S. E. Morison, ed., *Sources and Documents Illustrating the American Revolution, 1764–1788,* 2nd ed. (Oxford: Clarendon Press, 1923), p. 17.

[17] Perry, *Sources of Our Liberties,* pp. 270-271.

[18] *Ibid.,* p. 269.

[19] Bailyn, *The Ideological Origins of the American Revolution,* p. 187.

[20] *Ibid.,* p. 188.

[21] Henry Steele Commager, "The Revolution as a World Ideal," *Saturday Review* (December 13, 1975), p. 14.

[22] *Ibid.*

[23] Declaration of Independence, cited in Perry, *Sources of Our Liberties,* p. 319.

[24] Arthur N. Holcombe, *Securing the Blessings of Liberty* (Chicago: Scott-Foresman American Government Series, 1964), pp. 26-27.

[25] Arthur M. Schlesinger, Jr., *A Case Book on the Declaration of Independence* (New York: Thomas Y. Crowell Company, 1967), pp. 216-218.

[26] Cited in Staughton Lynd, *Intellectual Origins of American Radicalism* (New York: Pantheon Books, A Division of Random House, Inc., 1968), p. 45.

[27] Cited in *ibid.,* p. 54.

[28] Cited in Becker, *The Declaration of Independence,* pp. 10-14.

[29] Cited in *ibid.,* pp. 16-17.

[30] See Irving Brant, *The Bill of Rights* (New York: The Bobbs-Merrill Company, Inc., 1965), p. 5.

[31] Hugo L. Black, "Address to New York University on 17 February 1960."

[32] Cited in the *Baptist World,* vol. 6 (October, 1959), p. 2.

[33] Cited in Norman Cousins, ed., *"In God We Trust"* (New York: Harper & Row, Publishers, 1958), p. 137.

[34] See William G. McLoughlin, ed., *Isaac Backus on Church, State, and Calvinism: Pamphlets, 1754-1789* (Cambridge, Mass.: Harvard University Press, 1968).

[35] Baptist Joint Committee on Public Affairs Statement, adopted in 1944; cited by James E. Wood, Jr., in "Executive Director's Report," October, 1975.

[36] James E. Wood, Jr., "Executive Director's Report," October, 1975, p. 2.

[37] Kyle Haselden, "Baptists and Religious Freedom," *Missions,* vol. 158 (May, 1960), p. 25.

[38] William F. Keucher, *Main Street and the Mind of God* (Valley Forge: Judson Press, 1974), pp. 93-94.

Liberty
and Justice
for All

WALFRED H. PETERSON

LIBERTY

American Religious Liberty and Baptists

The dramatic development of religious liberty on this side of the Atlantic from the founding of Rhode Island through the drafting of the Bill of Rights and the constitutional and legal changes in the several new states was remarkable in at least two ways. First, it involved a radical change in law in spite of the fact that in a general way the American Revolution was not radical. Our revolutionaries changed the seat of government from London to fourteen locations over here. They did not change the common law very quickly or very much, and most of the new Bills of Rights rested on solid British precedent. But concerning the exercise and establishment of religion, they were radical.

Second, the development of religious liberty here was remarkable, because it occurred when, for many of the ruling class, religion was still important or, at least, still hotly controversial. Later, John Stuart Mill was to observe in Britain that religious freedom flourished when religion lacked vitality.[1] But that insight was not appropriate to such as Roger Williams, John Clarke, Isaac Backus, and John Leland, or to their opponents or supporters in the fight for freedom. The ideas and forces that moved America to religious liberty operated when religion was a potent and divisive factor in the nation's life.[2]

Certainly, Baptists helped promote this good radicalism. The names in the previous paragraph remind us of that. And non-

Baptist authorities on the history of religious liberty give Baptists strong praise.[3] The praise implies that Baptist leaders enjoyed much enthusiastic support on this issue from the rank and file in their churches.

Certainly, also, Baptists benefited from the freedoms won. Statistics of their growth testify to that, and if something bad happened to quality over the years, I reject as unfounded the idea that liberty was responsible for it. If more proof of benefit is needed, may I add the testimony of my Swedish Baptist immigrant parents? They knew beyond doubt that American freedoms were better for the gospel and their churches than the old country's practices. They only regretted that with all this freedom people insisted on using a markedly inferior language.

Did Baptists Keep the Faith?

From the time of the state disestablishment battles, ending in 1833, until the 1940s, the name "Baptist" is all but lost in commonly available reference works on religious liberty. True, this may be a problem of historiography. The issues of religious freedom were almost exclusively related to the individual states during that period. State history has a way of getting lost and is difficult to research even where it exists.

Perhaps, however, Baptists rested too much on the great victories of the past which insured their religious freedom. After all, in spite of the fact that Baptist histories always say Baptist churches were populated by members of the working classes in the nineteenth century, Baptists were becoming part of mainline American religion. No more were Baptists threatened by government for their religious expressions. But others were.

To start with the always forgettable, blacks under slavery had only the barest autonomy and freedom for their religious life. For example, in Alabama slave law did permit more than five slaves to assemble for public worship with the consent of the owner, whereas more than five slaves could not assemble for other purposes. But it forbade preaching by a slave ". . . without a license . . . from some religious society of the neighborhood," and without "the presence of five slaveholders." The same rules applied to free blacks.[4] Apparently, there was no effort by Baptists who accepted slavery to alter such limits in dramatic ways. There also seems to be no evidence that Baptists tried to seek freedom-oriented solutions to the problems and persecutions of the Mormons.

If these references to ancient history and peculiar institutions seem irrelevant today, the struggle of Jehovah's Witnesses is a bit more up-to-date. In the sad but triumphant record of Jehovah's Witnesses' cases, running from *Lovell* v. *Griffin* (1938) to *Niemotko* v. *Maryland* (1951), the American Civil Liberties Union (ACLU) came to the Witnesses' aid several times—and once even the American Bar Association did so—but not any local, state, or national Baptist agency.[5] In the very middle of that period, the newly organized Baptist Joint Committee on Public Affairs filed two amicus curiae briefs in Supreme Court cases on religious establishment issues, so the Committee's neglect of the Witnesses seems odd.[6] Also in 1951, the Reverend Carl Kunz, who called himself a Baptist, fought the City of New York for the right to preach on its sidewalks. He went through all levels of judicial hearings from the police commission to the U.S. Supreme Court with apparently only ACLU assistance.[7]

Unquestionably, if by the middle of this century a knowledgeable person felt her or his religious freedom was being denied, she or he would *not* hasten to the First Baptist Church to find support. Worse yet, the First Baptist Church would *not* be very likely to seek out such a person to offer aid. (At least in the states of Minnesota and Washington where I was and am most acquainted, I know of no cases where Baptists became the champions of some party claiming oppression for their religious exercise.) The ACLU has done so with victorious results in both states and that includes victories as late as 1974.

To be sure, there are successes to recount. The organization of the Baptist Joint Committee in 1939 was one of them, and it came shortly before the Supreme Court in *Cantwell* v. *Connecticut* (1940) held that the Fourteenth Amendment makes the religion clauses of the First Amendment applicable to the states. There was a growing feeling that it was essential that there be a united Baptist witness in public affairs in the nation's capital. Since then activities of the Baptist Joint Committee have been important on many occasions to the nation, to Baptists, and to religious freedom. Its good work on the prayer cases and the prayer amendments alone merits special notice. And there has been much more than that. But it is the one clear exception to the rule that Baptists are not widely recognized today as the stout champions of freedom. (Notice, Baptists give the BJCPA about the same financial support as that received by *one* active *state* chapter of the ACLU. That can scarcely be called a strong commitment.)

Did Baptists Renew the Faith?

Any success or failure in "keeping the faith" should not preoccupy us. We must attend more to the quality of our faith. Times change, and the modes of expressing our belief in religious freedom should change with them. Further, our ideas on how that freedom is achieved or denied must change. Have we adapted to the new?

When Baptists helped lead this nation to religious liberty in its early years, they did so against the reality of church establishments. Therefore, religious liberty and the separation of church and state tended to be synonymous. They needed to stress "the wall of separation" then, and we need to do so today, but with qualification.

While affirming "separation of church and state," Baptists practiced not a little of "cooperation of church and state." Baptists did so in the military, hospital, and prison chaplaincies. On foreign mission fields Baptists often did so in marked ways, accepting church-state relations there that would have moved them to fight at the barricades at home.

Why did Baptists practice such cooperation? Because in some matters freedom of religion required it. The chaplain and the missionary could not have functioned freely without cooperation with the state. So, Baptists substituted cooperation for separation. It was a mark of wisdom.

Clearly, religious freedom was and is the highest *end* respecting relations with the state. A clean separation of church and state is necessary as a *means* to that end for many purposes. But a wise cooperation of church and state is also necessary to that end. And recently, we have been reminded by Alexander Solzhenitsyn that an outright opposition of church and state may also be necessary in some circumstances.[8] These circumstances are not only found in the bitter lands of dictators. In the United States head-on opposition to the state is needed when it promotes civil religion, as it and its leaders so commonly do.

Unless Baptists know the difference between the essential *end* (religious liberty) and the less-than-essential *means* (some form of church-state relations), they may find themselves worshiping a slogan even when it hurts the cause of religious liberty. Baptists cannot avoid substantial cooperation with the state in many endeavors. Besides those already mentioned, slum clearance projects, use of radio and television, and aid to some of the impoverished come immediately to mind.

Are Baptist Public Positions Supported by the Members?

A poll taken several years ago by the Christian Life Commission of the Southern Baptist Convention indicated that the person in the pew was not much different from the average American in the support given to fundamental human rights.[9] Alas, the showing of the average American is miserable on such polls. And John L. Eighmy's *Churches in Cultural Captivity*[10] and Rufus B. Spain's *At Ease in Zion*[11] join in finding many Baptists contented middle-of-the-roaders in relationship to their culture. All this and more remind us that it is very difficult for large religious denominations to be the champions of anything controversial. Regretfully, almost any religious liberty case is apt to be controversial.

For example, in 1948 the Baptist Joint Committee filed an amicus curiae brief in *McCollum* v. *Board of Education*.[12] It supported the case of a humanist, Vashti McCollum, who objected to voluntary religious education courses taught by appointees of churches in the public schools of Champaign, Illinois. The appeal, which was won before the Supreme Court with an 8 to 1 decision, asserted that religious education programs in the public schools violated the establishment clause. The Committee thereby helped win a landmark case in U.S. church-state relations.

When news of the amicus brief reached the papers, however, some Baptist leaders of the Northern and Southern Baptist Conventions attacked the Committee for making an error. The thrust of their criticism was that while the Baptist Joint Committee brief might be good law and even good church-state theory, the rank and file would never understand its wisdom.[13] It would offend "our people."

A more celebrated example came when the Baptist Joint Committee and Baptist leadership had to deal with the problem of school prayer amendment resolutions. In Atlantic City, where both the American and Southern Baptist Conventions met in 1964 in several joint sessions, a skillfully worded resolution supporting the First Amendment as written in the Constitution was submitted to each Convention. Both Conventions passed the resolution overwhelmingly, but there is little doubt that the resolution as passed was not by any means supported by all Baptists.[14]

What does this mean for our denominations? It means this: More effort and money must be spent on the education of Baptists on religious liberty and related issues. That is, Baptist leadership must try harder, for freedoms have always been promoted on important issues by a special kind of leadership. It took a John Adams, a Thomas Paine, and a Thomas Jefferson in the 1770s to rivet the people's attention on the cause of freedom and independence. And in an age when Baptists are ever more subject to institutional guidance, it will take articulate and persuasive denominational leaders to raise the people's consciousness of freedom's concerns. Eternal leadership is the price of freedom!

JUSTICE

American Justice and Baptists

There is in the history of political thought no assurance that a champion of liberty will also be a champion of justice. When political thought is overlaid with religious thought, the likelihood of a positive correlation between the two becomes less certain. Therefore, it is not surprising that while one can find references to "Baptists" in the indexes of many general works on religious liberty, one is not very likely to find such references in general works on, for example, the Progressive Era, labor reform, or social welfare movements.

There are, of course, many reasons for this difference. Many of them quite properly work to make the observation less than earthshaking. But not all of them work in that way. Two may be of special interest to note here.

Religious Liberty Versus Justice

A passage from Robert G. Torbet's *A History of Baptists* is striking. It makes Baptist championship of religious freedom a cause for the relative lack of Baptist interest in the issue of slavery.

> Although Mennonites, Quakers, German pietists in Pennsylvania, and Congregationalists in New England had gone on record as opposing slavery in the late eighteenth and early nineteenth centuries, Baptists seem to have been absorbed too greatly in their own struggle for religious liberty to have occupied themselves much with this issue which was still in its infancy.[15]

The sentence almost shocks the reader today. Yet many good movements have had a political specialty that left them short of energy and resources to spend on other worthy battles. In some circumstances, specialization can be the prudent course of action.

Perhaps, this was the case with our Baptist forebears. Religious liberty was certainly an issue of great moment in the Revolutionary period. Could Baptists have left religious liberty to the traditionally established churches, the Deists, other small religious sects, or those who based the claim of liberty wrongly from the Baptist perspective? No. It is scarcely surprising that Baptists spent their primary efforts on religious freedom possibly to the neglect of efforts on other matters that very well might have merited their special attention.

Yet, if Baptist devotion to religious liberty formerly lessened the involvement of Baptists in causes of social justice, that does not justify a Baptist preoccupation with religious liberty today. Why not? Because, while religious liberty's definition will always concern the believer, in this land a very large measure of religious freedom has been assured. Even if religious liberty is our highest political priority, it need not be our highest priority in dollars or energy spent on political matters. We must adjust to the American experience. Both 1776 and 1791 were long ago. New battles on other fronts summon us. For example, some Baptists would devote enormous effort to fight against state aid for busing children to parochial schools, while they would not spend a dime to fight for busing that would achieve better education for blacks. We must learn to rearrange priorities in relation to the nation's needs today.

Another point must be made respecting the idea that religious liberty might be opposed to justice in the way life really runs. Some Baptists have so tied religious liberty to a distorted notion of separation of church and state that they demand that churches not involve themselves in civil affairs. This, Torbet observed, has been one reason for Baptists' lack of commitment respecting the abolition of slavery in the early nineteenth century. They were, he says, hesitant ". . . to violate the principle of noninterference of the church in civil affairs." [16]

That thinking still exists today. When the author worked for the Baptist Joint Committee in the 1960s, people continually asked the question, "How can you say church and state should be separate, if your office lobbies in Washington?" Indeed, a recent book on religious lobbying begins by asking that question in a tone that sounds hostile to church activity in political matters. [17]

Certainly, if religious liberty is to be realized by the individual and the group, it cannot be tied to any church-state relations theory that prohibits religiously inspired, collective action on problems of social justice. Biblical faith is not concerned only with purely spiritual matters. It is also concerned with matters temporal, including a wide range of civil or public affairs. The Old Testament prophets attest to that in ample degree.

Religion Versus Justice

The contrast between the spiritual and temporal reminds us that religion, including Baptist variants, has been the practical opponent of justice. Not a few Baptists, past and present, have so centered their religious thought and action on a simplistic, personal evangelism and/or quiet piety that they have all but ignored or even flatly opposed interest by their churches and fellow believers in social and political activity, let alone reform. The author's own religious heritage was of this quality, and his decision to become a political scientist could only be understood by some friends when they were told that a person could teach, as well as practice, the stuff. Somehow teaching was thought to have a bit of a spiritual dimension.

Pushed to an extreme, this otherworldly branch of Christianity would make even religious liberty unimportant. Alyoshka, the Russian Baptist semi-hero in Alexander Solzhenitsyn's *One Day in the Life of Ivan Denisovich,* might hold such a position.[18] His faith told him that God's will was being done, whatever the tragedy. Perhaps his faith is appropriate for a person in an Arctic prison camp without earthly hope. Only an inner peace with God and the hope of eternal bliss might ease the pain he knew. A "coming-for-to-carry-me-home" religion has probably always found a hearing among slaves.

In contrast, at first thought a free American Christian might be expected to be a religious-political activist. Why? Because here in the United States there have been, relatively speaking, material abundance, advanced technology, and highly developed organizational skills that led many to suppose that a better world for all could be created readily. Further, many Christians, including Baptists, have experimented with the available political machinery during both the Revolutionary era and the prohibition period and have found they could make it work for their goals.

Yet, in spite of the resources and power available, in spite of political successes, in spite of the forceful leadership of Walter Rauschenbusch and others, and in spite of the good work of many denominational agencies and commissions, Baptists have always had among them a great many people, leaders included, who at best have given only lip service to working on the problems of social justice. To them religion as practiced lacked a prophetic dimension in the Old Testament sense.[19]

One hopes that this position has been eroded over the years. While the appearance and emphasis of the Jesus' People movement pointed in the other way, the trend for those who were once proudly "evangelical" in the traditional sense has been to increase their social concern as a part of their religious calling. A recent sign of this trend was the 1973 "Declaration of Evangelical Social Concern." It found many "evangelical" leaders raising the banner of social justice in a deliberate effort to follow their religious mandate and to repudiate "evangelical" failures on this point in the past.[20]

But one year after their "Declaration" these people found themselves in trouble. Their trouble reminds us of one more way in which our religion can work against a deep concern for justice. When the "Declaration" was drafted in 1973, those who were at the conference had a wonderful time. For them there was joy in beginning a new battle. But the 1974 conference was different. Disputes over planks in the social justice platform erupted. The clear focus made possible by the generalities of their earlier work was lost. They felt frustrated. Why?[21]

While Christians must demand justice as a part of the exercise of their faith, that very faith does not detail what justice is or how it can be achieved. The Bible gives no blueprint, only a command to do justice and create a better society. Thus, Christians have scarcely any more unity on the issues of what a just social system is and how to develop it than the public around them. There is no surprise, then, that one can find sincere Baptists and other Christian anarchists, laissez faire-ists, welfare state-ists, and socialists. Baptists reflect the American political experience and spectrum because there is no Baptist political-economic-social position, except for the call for religious freedom. And that call does not help Baptists on matters such as economic distribution or war and peace.

But how does this lack of a specific program mean that religion opposes justice? Since the original unity of Baptists stems from a religion that stresses the centrality of the spiritual well-being of the individual, and since it is hard to develop a unity based on political and economic programs, there is hesitation to jeopardize the former by giving particular emphasis to the latter. While Baptists give emphasis to social justice at conferences far from home and in the sessions and work of agencies well insulated from the rank and file, Baptists generally do not give special emphasis to social problems in most local Baptist churches. Denominational agencies often deal with controversial matters. American Baptist and Southern Baptist agencies can speak boldly. They do so, and well. They lead as well as speak, but they may frequently lead only a select few within their respective denominations.

Within certain segments of Baptist denominations and within many local Baptist churches, one can claim some degree of unity on individualistic and purely religious grounds. Baptists can claim little or no unity on matters of political and social structures except a unity with regard to the concepts of justice, fairness, and humaneness. That unity breaks down as soon as implementation of a specific welfare program is considered. And no one can say authoritatively that this or that scheme is a moral necessity. Therefore, to maintain religious unity, Baptists tend toward silence or generalities on social issues.

The Advantage of a Deprived Minority

While members of social classes who are relatively well off find it hard to agree on programs of social justice designed to improve the lot of the poor, members of deprived classes may have less trouble in reaching general agreement. Having less to lose and more to gain from most reasonable efforts at promoting equality and economic reforms, they can very well unite behind a leader who gives voice to their claims and grievances. Deprivation, if not too severe, can be the cement that unites.

Baptists with a sense of history should understand this. They were the deprived minority in the late eighteenth century. Baptists then united so firmly that their impact was enhanced.

Therefore, it should be no suprise that the greatest champion of social justice that Baptists can claim in the twentieth century arose out of a black Baptist church. Martin Luther King, Jr., spoke eloquently for a deprived minority and for a time rallied them and others around the civil rights movement.

In a special way, King was a product of the American experience. His ability to capitalize on that fact was an important part of the source of his success in the society at large. The American experience had by the 1960s still not overcome its traditional racism and much that went with it. But many of America's religious denominations, the nation's political philosophy, and American law demanded equality of treatment regardless of race. The contrast was too glaring not to produce a movement and a leader.

Martin Luther King, Jr., spoke the language of religious Americans, using their idiom to point out their racial sins. He also spoke the natural law philosophy of the Declaration of Independence, using its words and logic to call the nation back to its pure, first purposes. Further, he used the legal terms of the Fourteenth Amendment, thereby forcing the nation to admit its legal wrongs. King set the powers that be reeling, because he knew the language of their ideals and pretensions so well. His "Letter from Birmingham City Jail" was unanswerable, for it was a letter the nation had written in its best moments of the past two hundred years.[22]

How fortunate it was that King gave the United States an opportunity to stride toward freedom in terms that were appropriate to its truest heritage! And how fortunate that he added the element of nonviolence to the nation's consciousness! A glance at our past and its evils and at such terrible scenes as North Ireland and Lebanon today should make us all the more aware of our debt as Baptists and

Americans to this man. We must promote his ideals for justice and for domestic tranquillity. Unfortunately, we have not done so very effectively to this hour.

CONCLUSION

Baptists helped give America its great measure of religious freedom. True, there is still much work to do on this matter, for eternal vigilance is the price of liberty. America has reaffirmed this constitutionally guaranteed freedom. Religious liberty in America is relatively secure. Watch its implementation, we must, but we need not place our highest political priority there any longer.

Today, we must shift our highest priority concern to social justice. More difficult to define and more difficult to achieve than religious freedom, it, nevertheless, ought to occupy the attention of the free movement of Baptists in its diverse groupings for the next two hundred years.

NOTES

[1] John Stuart Mill, *On Liberty* (New York: Bobbs-Merrill Co., Inc., 1956), pp. 10-11.

[2] Admittedly, this point must be qualified by the thesis of Franklin H. Littell which correctly asserts that church membership was very low in the eighteenth century. See *From State Church to Pluralism,* rev. ed. (New York: Macmillan Publishing Co., Inc., 1971), pp. 29-32.

[3] A good, relatively thorough but brief description of the work of these men for freedom by a non-Baptist source is Anson Phelps Stokes, *Church and State in the United States,* 3 vols. (New York: Harper & Row, Publishers, 1950). This is also available in an updated one-volume edition. Anson Phelps Stokes and Leo Pfeffer, *Church and State in the United States,* 2nd. ed. rev. (New York: Harper & Row, Publishers, 1964).

[4] "Slave Code of Alabama," cited in Richard Bardolph, ed., *The Civil Rights Record* (New York: Thomas Y. Crowell Company, 1970), pp. 6-10.

[5] For the best treatment of these cases, see David R. Manwaring, *Render unto Caesar* (Chicago: The University of Chicago Press, 1962).

[6] For an account of these briefs see Walfred H. Peterson, "Religious Lobbying: Some Problems and Practices," *Foundations,* October—December, 1976.

[7] *Kunz* v. *New York,* 340 U.S. 290 (1951).

[8] See a record of correspondence between Alexander Solzhenitsyn and Sergii Zheludkow in "A Russian Challenges the Kremlin," *The Christian Reader,* September—October, 1974, pp. 34-40.

[9] Floyd A. Craig, "Poll Shows Many Southern Baptists Would Limit Traditional Rights," *Report from the Capital,* vol. 27 (February, 1972), p. 8.

[10] John L. Eighmy, *Churches in Cultural Captivity* (Knoxville: The University of Tennessee Press, 1972).

[11] Rufus B. Spain, *At Ease in Zion* (Nashville: Vanderbilt University Press, 1961).

[12] 333 U.S. 203 (1948).

[13] For an account of this, see Stanley L. Hastey, "A History of the Baptist Joint Committee on Public Affairs" (Th.D. diss., Southern Baptist Theological Seminary, 1973).

[14] "Baptist Groups Oppose Prayer Amendments," *Report from the Capital,* vol. 19 (June–September, 1964), pp. 8, 3.

[15] Robert G. Torbet, *A History of the Baptists,* rev. ed. (Valley Forge: Judson Press, 1963), p. 282.

[16] *Ibid.,* p. 284.

[17] James L. Adams, *The Growing Church Lobby in Washington* (Grand Rapids: William B. Eerdmans Publishing Company, 1970), p. xi. Elsewhere, I have attempted a fuller answer to this contention. See Peterson, "Religious Lobbying: Some Problems and Practices."

[18] Alexander Solzhenitsyn, *One Day in the Life of Ivan Denisovich* (New York: Frederick A. Praeger, Publisher, 1963).

[19] I think this is well supported by Robert G. Torbet's assertion, "It has generally been true of Baptists that they have subordinated their social interest to their evangelical concern." See Torbet, *A History of the Baptists,* pp. 452-453.

[20] See "Evangelicals on Justice, Socially Speaking," *Christianity Today,* vol. 18 (December 21, 1973), p. 370.

[21] See "Doing the Declaration," *Christianity Today,* vol. 19 (December 20, 1974), pp. 312-313.

[22] Martin Luther King, Jr., "Letter from Birmingham City Jail," in Hugo Adam Bedau, *Civil Disobedience: Theory and Practice* (New York: Pegasus, affiliated with Bobbs-Merrill Co., Inc., 1969), pp. 72-89.

Equality
Under
the Law

CHARLES G. ADAMS

Thomas Jefferson, principal author of the Declaration of Independence, said in 1776, "We hold these truths to be self-evident, that all men are created equal, that they are endowed by their Creator with certain unalienable Rights, that among these are Life, Liberty and the pursuit of Happiness. That to secure these rights, Governments are instituted among Men, deriving their just powers from the consent of the governed." With these words a new nation was born, throwing off the prenatal shackles of the authority mechanisms of Tudor-Stuart England to embrace the experience of self-government and self-determination. In terms of the question "Who shall rule America?" the American Revolution was over before the fighting began. One writer observed:

> It proved impossible for the British to cope with the colonists because the Redcoats were confronted not by a few malcontents, but by a thoroughly integrated society resting on a foundation of responsible self-goverment. To win the Revolution a few battlefield victories would not suffice: His Majesty's forces had to crack and destroy a whole social system.[1]

Yet that strong social system founded on the principles of liberty and equality had at its inception certain internal contradictions. Thomas Jefferson's "all" was arbitrarily limited, circumscribed, and qualified. Had the founding fathers been literally truthful concerning their actual beliefs and practices, they would have said, "All men are created equal with the following exceptions: slaves, Negroes, Catholics, Asians, atheists, women, Jews, nonproprietors, Indians, heretics, etc." Gardner Taylor has observed that "it is either an act of divine purpose or one of the largest frauds in mankind's political history" that the words in Jefferson's Declaration appeared and still stand without explicit exceptions.[2]

The founding fathers declared truths which were transcendent to their own attainments. While Jefferson wrote his brilliant proclamation of human equality based on divine creation, he owned slaves who had no guarantee or protection of life, no liberty, and were restrained from any protracted pursuit of happiness. Abraham Lincoln, who echoed Jefferson's exalted language at Gettysburg, had a wife who could not vote or run for public office. America has never lived up to the principle of human equality declared in and by her birth. There has always been tension between the lofty ideal and the actual practice.

American history is the story of the agony and ecstasy of the contraction and expansion of the principle of equality in the political and social experience of the New World. We see the principle expanding with the passage of the Thirteenth, Fourteenth, and Fifteenth Amendments to the Constitution—expanded in the Civil Rights Act of 1866—expanded during Reconstruction—contracted in 1876 when federal forces no longer guarded equal protection in the South—contracted in 1896 with the legalization of Jim Crow laws—expanded in 1920 when women's right to vote was recognized and constitutionalized—contracted in the witch hunt of the early 1950s, symbolized by the late Senator Joseph McCarthy—expanded in 1954 in *Brown* v. *Board of Education* (347 U.S. 483) wherein the Supreme Court mandated universal, integrated quality education—expanded in 1964 with civil rights legislation—contracted in 1973 in *San Antonio Independent School District* v. *Rodriguez* (411 U.S. 1) wherein the status quo in the conventional method of financing schools was upheld—contracted in 1974 in *Milliken* v. *Bradley* (418 U.S. 717) which disallowed a metropolitan area plan for the desegregation of Detroit Public Schools—contracted in 1975–1976 as public opinion continued to swing toward the right in fear and reaction.

The current conservative trend is taking place on all levels of human interaction and expression. All age groups of the American white majority are becoming less tolerant of racial minorities—especially if such toleration is accompanied with increasing expenditures of tax dollars and/or traumas over busing. The current situation is reminiscent of the post-Civil War era when the number of white advocates of civil rights declined greatly. "As the old radicals—Charles Sumner, Wendell Phillips, George W. Julian, William Lloyd

Garrison—died, there were no replacements."[3] Are there any current replacements for John F. Kennedy, Lyndon B. Johnson, Martin Luther King, Jr., or retired Supreme Court Justice William O. Douglas?

The principle of equality before the law is currently under attack. One way of attacking it is to make it absurd and then reject it vehemently. What is meant by the words "All men are created equal"? Antagonists to human equality define it as follows: "All social inequalities are unnecessary, and unjustifiable, and ought to be eliminated."[4] By "social inequality" the author refers not only to class or status but also to any political, legal, or economic differences among people, "irrespective of whether the inequality results from one's own choice and effort or that of another."[5] Even rewards, awards, and punishments are counted as social inequalities. In such a definition the idea of reward based on merit which is in turn based on performance is rejected. Such rejection is absurd, thus totally unacceptable. To define equality along these lines is one method of opposing it. Obviously all are not created equal in physical or psychological nature. There are human diversities of sizes, shapes, colors, and aptitudes. "Regardless of training, some men can never run a 4-minute mile; and, regardless of motivation and quality of teaching, some youngsters can never learn calculus."[6] These genetic or aptitudinal differences are not distributed according to nationality, religion, sex, or race. There are wide variations within each group. There are some normal white children who will never succeed as philosophers, and there are some black children who will become skilled in manipulating abstract symbols.

Race is no determinant of ability and aptitude. Environmental opportunities, however, will determine whether or not inherited gifts will ever be developed and expressed. If an individual is born with such a magnificent physique as would make him an Olympic champion but grows up in such poverty that he is given only a deficient diet, lacking essential nutrients, and matures in the slum environment of a crowded tenement building where there is no room for play and exercise, he will never develop and express his championship potential. A child may be born with the latent ability to be a mathematician or a physicist; but if her primary and secondary educational experiences are inadequate and incomplete she will never attain the promise of her inherited gifts.

All are not created equal in terms of gifts and abilities; but all are created equal in genus, species, and the right to opportunities to develop what abilities and gifts they have. It is criminal and unjust for government or society to intercept or interdict one's God-given equality of opportunity. The purpose of government is to restrain itself and others from the arbitrary, authoritarian, or majoritarian interception of equality of opportunity. "The Thirteenth Amendment does not say that the Government of the United States shall make men free, it says rather that 'neither slavery nor involuntary servitude . . . shall exist within the United States'—thus Government shall not deny this freedom which is inherent."[7] The Fourteenth Amendment does not grant equal protection of the law; it restrains government from abridging or denying to any person the equal protection of the laws. The Constitution has stood and will stand the test of time and change because it makes no false claims. It does not purport to give anybody anything. Our freedoms and our gifts are given us by our Creator. We are divinely endowed. The Constitution was ratified and a new nation was born to affirm and guard those endowments lest any tyrant trample on the God-given rights of humankind.

The right to equal, quality educational opportunity is implicit in the creation, and therefore implicitly guarded by the Constitution. "This view had received eloquent sanction from many of the founding fathers, from the constitutions of all the states, and from the declarations of the Supreme Court."[8] Before 1973, the Supreme Court had always affirmed and protected the idea and practice of universal, free, quality education as "the very foundation of good citizenship"; education was placed "at the very apex of the function of the state"; it was heralded as "necessary to prepare citizens effectively and intelligently in our open political system"; it was affirmed that it "prepares individuals to be self-reliant and self-participants in society." The Supreme Court proclaimed, "Americans regard the public schools as a most vital civic institution for the preservation of a democratic system of government."[9]

We are currently witnessing an entirely new Supreme Court attitude toward public education. In *San Antonio Independent School District* v. *Rodriguez* (1973), five justices announced that educational opportunity was not a fundamental interest or a fundamental right. Similarly in *Milliken* v. *Bradley* (1974) the Court held that the political community that governs the dispensing of educational opportunity is not the state, but the school district. Thus we see a denial of the principle and the retreat of federal and state responsibility for the equitable distribution of educational resources, which constitute the poor's only instrument of upward mobility.

These recent decisions on public education represent a reversal of *Brown* v. *Board of Education* (1954) wherein racial and economic discrimination in public education was outlawed and the basic human right to equal educational opportunity was announced in no uncertain terms: "Such an opportunity, where the state has undertaken to provide it [public education], must be made available to all on equal terms." Free and equal education is the nourishment that feeds and sustains all other basic human freedoms guaranteed in the Constitution. The freedoms of speech and assembly mean nothing if people cannot express themselves or understand the statements of others. The right to vote is a cruel mockery if a person cannot read the ballot. The right to privacy is a curse if it isolates hordes of people in the darkness of ignorance and deprivation. The right to self-determination is automatically surrendered if a person lacks the knowledge to control his or her environment and shape his or her destiny. The right to buy and sell is a travesty if a person cannot count money and make intelligent choices. The right to life is a hoax if one cannot make a living. We wait upon some future court to reaffirm and declare a person's fundamental and divine right to educational opportunity.

Facing backwards is a strange way to go forward; yet we are backing into the future by attempting to recreate the situation that existed before *Plessy* v. *Ferguson* in 1896, (163 U.S. 537) wherein segregated public facilities and services were allowed provided they were made equal in quality. Before 1896 public services were segregated and inferior. In 1896 the law was "separate and equal." In 1954 the law became "separate is inherently inferior." In 1973 we saw the legitimation of inferior educational facilities, and in 1974 we witnessed the legalization of racially separate educational resources thus reinstituting the nineteenth-century practice of separate and inferior.

When the Supreme Court upheld the San Antonio Independent School District in adhering to the practice of using property taxes as the principal source of funding for public education, it supported the legal toleration and sanction of unequal public schools inequitably funded due to variations in property values between poor districts and wealthy districts. For example, the poorest district in Michigan has a property value of $2,230 per child while the richest Michigan district has a property value of $66,951 per child.

Some school districts in a state have ten thousand times the fiscal capacity of others and that even within a single metropolitan area there are variations of ten or fifteen to one. In Texas, local services per pupil ranged from $610 in the richest districts to sixty-three dollars in the poorest. With state funds added, the range was $815 to $306. In California, the citizens of

West Covina were paying twice the tax rate of Beverly Hills and getting about half the amount for the schools that Beverly Hills obtained.[10]

Obviously such wide differences in the amounts of monies used to provide educational resources make a tremendous difference in the quality of education a district can offer. John Coons is quoted as saying, "If money is inadequate to improve education, the residents of poor districts should at least have an equal opportunity to be disappointed at its failure."[11] The inevitable result of funding schools from property taxes is that the poorer districts will be able to spend much less for educational facilities and salaries than wealthier districts. No matter how you define educational opportunity, a poorer district cannot offer as substantial and adequate quality of educational experience as a district able to spend much more for each child. Unless public funds are used to subsidize poorer districts, closing the gap between education for the rich and education for the poor, we shall see poor children continually denied the right to qualitative educational experience. Dissenting in *San Antonio Independent School District* v. *Rodriguez* (1973), Justice Thurgood Marshall said:

> The majority's decision represents an abrupt departure from the mainstream of recent state and federal court decisions concerning the unconstitutionality of state educational financing schemes dependent upon taxable local wealth. More unfortunately, though, the majority's holding can only be seen as a retreat from our historic commitment to equality of educational opportunity and as unsupportable acquiescence in a system which deprives children in their earliest years of the chance to reach their full potential as citizens. The Court does this despite the absence of any substantial justification for a scheme which arbitrarily channels educational resources in accordance with the fortuity of the amount of taxable wealth within each district.
>
> In my judgment, the right of every American to an equal start in life, so far as the provision of a state service as important as education is concerned, is far too vital to permit state discrimination on grounds as tenuous as those presented by this record.[12]

In *Milliken* v. *Bradley* the Supreme Court acquiesced in the realization that by ordering a "Detroit only" integration plan the Detroit system would remain racially segregated with many schools 75 to 90 percent black. The Chief Justice said that "there is no constitutional power in the courts"[13] to remedy this complaint. Segregation in American society is not a thing to be desired. It means ostracism, stigmatism, and exclusion. It amounts to banishment from public favor and privilege. *Milliken* v. *Bradley* violates the principles set forth in *Brown* v. *Board of Education*. We observe here the narrowing of the responsible community, the atomization of the body politic into arbitrary districts which are held sacrosanct even if they do violate the "equal protection" clause of the Fourteenth Amendment. This amounts to a new federalism of local autonomy within state entities. The state, which is responsible, is absolved and the Constitution is made to govern each district separately. This neo-intrastate federalism effectively freezes local districts into conventional racial patterns with no chance for change or reformation. Dissenting, Justice Byron White said that the Court had fashioned out of whole cloth an arbitrary rule. He added, "I am even more mystified how the Court can ignore the legal reality that the constitutional violations . . . were committed by governmental entities for which the state is responsible and that it is the state that must respond to the command of the Fourteenth Amendment." [14] The state's failure to desegregate the schools by means of redistricting or cross-district communication is an injury against the disadvantaged which the Supreme Court refused to remedy. Again we await some future tribunal to reverse and correct the current judicial retrogression. Justice Marshall in a dissenting opinion said that the decision in *Milliken* v. *Bradley* is "a giant step backward. . . . [It] is more a reflection of a perceived public mood that we have gone far enough in enforcing the Constitution's guarantee of equal justice than it is a product of neutral principles of law." [15]

The notion that the principle of equality has been stretched far enough dominates the contemporary mood. There is a premature tiredness in the American spirit, a lack of resolve to pay any price necessary to secure basic human rights. The Bicentennial, like the centennial, found America unwilling quickly to secure for every citizen equality before the law. Gardner Taylor says:

> There is one great weakness in the American temper which is revealed from a reading of our past. It is the inability of the nation to sustain its energies and resources in the pursuit of a goal when that goal proves elusive and difficult to attain and when great cost, financial or psychological, is required and when prolonged individual sacrifice is demanded. [16]

A great case in point is the current status of affirmative action advances as perceived by those who represent the majoritarian Establishment in the United States. The white war against affirmative action is picking up speed and gaining judicial and scholarly respectability. Our wealthy vice-president said recently that too much has been done for the poor. There is needed a strong rationale to explain and to defend affirmative action as a corrective measure intended to reverse long-standing customs and procedures of unjust racial exclusion. It is not discrimination *in* reverse. It is discrimination *to* reverse a racially discriminatory system of power distribution.

Corrective justice demands that institutions and corporations which have been "color struck" for generations must not all of a sudden become so "color blind" that they will fail to make special provisions and exceptions to the rules, policies, and procedures in order to help the long-excluded segment catch up to an equal position at the starting line. The mere existence of civil rights laws and requirements that institutions no longer discriminate against blacks, as they once did, are necessary but not sufficient to correct the entrenched wrong. Whereas institutions have discriminated against blacks for hundreds of years, they must now discriminate in favor of blacks for at least the next twenty-five years in order to give them a chance to catch up. Equal opportunity is not the mere absence of discrimination but the presence of special inducements and provisions designed to close the gap between black and white. The concrete reality of equal opportunity depends not only upon an open road but also upon an equal start. This means that there will be whites who must be bypassed for promotion while blacks will be allowed to go higher. This means that the white applicant will be denied while blacks, who are deemed to be less qualified, will be admitted. This procedure must be understood to be a remedial measure to correct an old, time-honored system of injustice.

If a race is systematically locked out of the labor pool by deliberate denial of opportunities in training and experience, how in heaven's name will they ever garner the necessary training or accumulate sufficient experience to compete for jobs? The vicious cycle of racial discrimination has three points: deprive, disqualify, deny. The deprivation of opportunity leads automatically to disqualification and that in turn gives the rationale for denial which in turn brings about continued and repeated deprivation. The cycle continues until broken by affirmative action. The late Whitney Young argued with passionate pen and skilled tongue that those who had been systematically and habitually excluded by race would require special inducements of inclusion and redoubled encouragements in order to narrow the gap that exists in economics between black and white. I heard him give a graphic illustration to score the point. He called upon his audience to visualize two men running the mile in a track meet. One is well equipped, wears track shoes, and runs on cinders. The other is barefoot and runs in the sand. It is no surprise that one runner is far ahead of the other who seemingly has no chance to catch up. The fellow who is behind is given track shoes and placed on the cinder track. Naturally it takes time to get his feet on the track.

Seconds later it should surprise no one that the newly equipped and relocated runner is still yards behind and will never catch up unless something special is done to even the contest. That "something special" is what scoffers refer to as "reverse discrimination." Such designation is but the term "affirmative action" twisted by knaves to make a trap for fools.

The remedy to racial segregation and color discrimination calls for sustained and intensive therapy to restore black victims to an equitable place within the life race whose objective is the pursuit of happiness, i.e., self-fulfillment. The individual rights of whites must not be allowed to take precedence over the remedial rights of a whole racial group which is struggling against the majority to throw off the shackles and chains of the cruel past.

To change the image, the black person is, as it were, a patient in the hospital of corrective justice who receives the controlled, therapeutic conditions and treatments of institutional favoritism in order that he or she might be strengthened and restored. To throw a sick person into abrupt interaction and competition with well people in the name of nondiscrimination would be as unrealistic as it is cruel. Sick folk need special treatment in order that they can be healed and made equal to well people. Afterwards, they will be treated equally in this competitive society dedicated to equality and excellence. In airplane boarding procedures, the halt and maimed are allowed to enter first. Similarly, as black people and other minorities board the escalator of upward mobility, these sick and exploited passengers must be admitted and promoted first until, over a period of time, they become equal competitors.

Affirmative action does not lead to the loss of quality or the surrender of excellence. The attrition rates for blacks who were admitted via affirmative action to the University of Michigan were reportedly lower than the white drop-out rate. Similarly, among those blacks who are presently enrolled in Harvard Divinity School, there is not one who has lower than a grade B average, while there are some whites who fall below grade B. These two examples are sufficient to challenge Paul Seabury's assumption that affirmative action recipients are ipso facto unqualified and will forever exhibit serious deficiencies in performance. Seabury says that the effects of affirmative action "may well constitute the single greatest threat to the quality of our lives today." [17] We reply that a black student may be admitted to college by virtue of her previous disadvantagement, but she will not be graduated unless she makes the grade. A black suspect may be given his "day in court", but he will not be acquitted unless he is proven innocent. A black athlete may be admitted to compete in the Olympic contest, but she will not become a champion unless she wins the contest. A black may be hired to fulfill a quota, but he will not be sustained on the job unless he can do the work and earn his daily bread with quantitative and qualitative distinction. The external gates of entrance must be opened wider to accommodate the once systematically excluded, but the internal standards need not be lowered nor the goal post moved closer in. America can by special remedies achieve equality as well as efficiency.

Our great nation has not yet lived up to the lofty declaration that "all men are created equal." There is still much painful tension between the exalted principle and everyday practice. As we face a new century of progress and a new world wherein arbitrary barriers must give way to the broadest possible national and international inclusion, it is hoped we will experience a "new birth of freedom" characterized by a rededication to the principle of human equality and a complete reformation of all our social and political practices.

NOTES

[1] William W. Wattenburg, ed., *"All Men Are Created Equal"* (Detroit: Wayne State University Press, 1966), p. 18.

[2] Gardner Taylor, "Some Musings on a Nation 'Under God,'" *Interpretation,* vol. 30 (January, 1976), p. 40.

[3] Wattenburg, *"All Men Are Created Equal,"* p. 39.

[4] J. Roland Pennock and John W. Chapman, *Equality* (New York: Atherton Press, 1967), p. 13.

[5] *Ibid.,* p. 14.

[6] Wattenburg, *"All Men Are Created Equal,"* p. 88.

[7] Taylor, "Some Musings on a Nation 'Under God,'" pp. 39, 40.

[8] Robert M. Hutchins, "Two Fateful Decisions," *Center Magazine,* vol. 8 (January—February, 1975), p. 7.

[9] *Ibid,* p. 7. All of the above Supreme Court declarations concerning universal, free public education are quoted in this source.

[10] *Ibid.,* p. 11.

[11] *Ibid.*

[12] *San Antonio School District* v. *Rodriguez,* 411 U.S. 1 (1973), pp. 70-71.

[13] *Ibid.*, p. 10.

[14] *Ibid.*

[15] *Ibid.*

[16] Taylor, "Some Musings on a Nation 'Under God,'" p. 42.

[17] Paul Seabury, "The Idea of Merit," *Commentary,* vol. 54, no. 6 (December, 1972), p. 45. See also Irving Kristol, "About Equality," *Commentary,* vol 54, no. 5 (November, 1972), pp. 41-47.

One
Nation
Under
God

C. WELTON GADDY

Each time a citizen recites the pledge of allegiance to the American flag, a theistic confession of personal faith is uttered and a religious understanding of the national state is propagated. The words are familiar ones: "I pledge allegiance to the flag of the United States of America and to the republic for which it stands, *one nation under God,* indivisible, with liberty and justice for all."

The general idea of government as an institution extant under the Providence of God is at least as old as the biblical writings. Founders of this nation seemed to conceive of their new democratic experiment in some sense as being "under God." Specific references regarding the United States' status under God began to appear with frequency in the speeches of Abraham Lincoln.

When the pledge of allegiance to the American flag was penned, the author, who was a minister, did not make use of the phrase "one nation under God." However, amidst the religious boom of the 1950s a secular Congress injected these words into the popular national statement. As a result, terms which had historically symbolized profound religious truths (from the awesome sense of special destiny which characterized the self-identity of many of the early colonists to the preoccupation with the dialectical themes of covenant and judgment which marked the thought of Lincoln) were now reduced to a civil creed which could be repeated perfunctorily.[1]

What is the contemporary meaning of "one nation under God"? Is this a basic tenet of American political thought or a bold statement of religious conviction? Does the phrase promise national security by implying our government has special favor with God or does it warn of divine judgment by emphasizing our government's moral accountability to God? Must the statement be considered an impetus to international involvement in the sense of religious mission or a mandate to function with civil responsibility at home and abroad in accord with the true nature of government?

A serious grappling with these questions plunges one into the morass of contemporary discussions on civil religion. Answers do not come easily. Though civil religion is apparently an indisputable aspect of our national life and, some would say, an inevitable phenomenon in any nation, defining civil religion, understanding its role, and evaluating its influence are burdensome tasks. Here, however, are the components of an agenda aimed at understanding the contemporary meaning of "one nation under God" and the context in which that meaning must be discussed.

DEFINITION

Definitions of civil religion are almost as numerous as are those people who have written on the subject. Fundamental, however, is the insight of Robert Bellah. Little had been said concerning civil religion in contemporary society until this sociologist published a landmark article in the Winter, 1967, issue of *Daedalus*. Most of the material on civil religion now in print was precipitated by Bellah's thoughts as recorded in that periodical.

According to Bellah, a civil religion, distinct from the religion of the churches, does exist in this nation. Simply stated, it is "an understanding of the American experience in the light of ultimate and universal reality."[2] Bellah found the dogmas of this civil faith to be identical with the dogmas of the civil religion described in Rousseau's *The Social Contract*—existence of God, a life to come, reward of virtue and punishment of vice, and exclusion of religious intolerance.[3]

Six years after the publication of the *Daedalus* article, Bellah once again affirmed the existence of civil religion in the United States. In his own words, this phenomenon is "the religious dimension of American political life that has characterized our republic since its foundation . . . whose most central tenet is that the nation is not an ultimate end in itself but stands under transcendent judgment and only has value insofar as it realizes, partially and fragmentarily at best, a 'higher law.'"[4] For Bellah, this religion is the child of continuous intercourse between Judeo-Christian theology and the American political experience.

Another important perspective on civil religion has been elaborated by Will Herberg. Having written on the general subject even prior to Bellah's first article, Herberg's recent work has defined the precise content of American civil faith. "It is an organic structure of ideas, values, and beliefs that constitutes a faith common to Americans as Americans, and is genuinely operative in their lives; a faith that markedly influences, and is influenced by, the professed religions of Americans."[5]

Unlike Bellah, Herberg has found little evidence of a transcendent dimension in the civil religion of this nation. It is a "religion of democracy."[6] Any spiritual elements which may relate to the civil faith have been thoroughly secularized. Culture is the parent of this popular system of belief. "The American Way of Life is the operative religion of the American people."[7]

The thoughts of Bellah and Herberg represent the two basic approaches to defining civil religion. Obviously, Bellah has placed more emphasis on the religious dimension of the civil faith noting its derivation from the historic religious faiths of Judaism and Christianity while Herberg has stressed the social-political dimension of civil religion and noted its indebtedness to culture. Other definitions of civil religion can be charted on a continuum between these two perspectives. Those who speak of "the religion of the Republic"[8] and a "Protestant civic piety"[9] rely heavily upon the religious foundations of civil faith. Conversely, some draw their meanings from culture as they write of a "democratic faith" and "religious nationalism."[10]

Grammatical marriage of the two terms "civil" and "religion" fails to reflect the dynamic tendencies toward divorce extant between the social-cultural realm and the spiritual realm which they represent. Though the two realms are inevitably related, they are radically distinct and are at times almost mutually exclusive. "Civil" connotes the arena where strong, competing social forces make decisions by means of balance and compromise. "Religion" refers to that system of beliefs and practices to which persons assign final significance in confrontation with the ultimate problems of life.[11] A proliferation of definitions of civil religion will persist because there can be no unanimity on whether this phenomenon is cultural or spiritual.

A second reason why so many definitions of civil religion will continue to exist with such a great diversity of meanings between them is that civil religion is more a matter of personal interpretation than a systematic statement of doctrines. As Bellah has pointed out, "There is no orthodox interpreter, no government-supported school of civil theology, no censor with power to forbid what does not conform."[12] The specific meaning of civil religion is left to the private interpreter. The term may embrace a variety of symbols, myths, attitudes, and rituals which are of importance to significant numbers of people.[13] Larry McSwain was right when he wrote: "There is no one civil religion. There are endless varieties of accommodation, legitimation and resistance between the institutional embodiments of faith and the civil practices of the nation."[14]

For this writer, civil religion represents a fusion of religious principles, cultural mores, and democratic ideals. American civil religion has skillfully and selectively borrowed from the documents of democracy, the aspirations of the citizenry, and the traditions of various faith groups. Normative principles have been established and then applied to emerging issues in various situations so that new emphases are always developing. The result is a concept dynamic rather than static in nature.

Sociologically, civil faith may be identified with an idealized view of the American way of life, though this is quite different at points from the way life in America really is. From the other perspective, civil faith may be functionally defined as religion though it cannot theologically be identified with Christianity (or any other particularistic faith).

FUNCTION

Civil religion has been a factor in the American experience ever since the first English settlers came to this land. The concept of nationhood embraced by these people was shaped by their preoccupation with the teachings and images of the Bible—the book they knew best.[15] Thus, before ever disembarking from the ship in Boston Harbor, John Winthrop could speak of New England as a "Citty upon a Hill" and pledge "soe shall wee keepe the unitie of the sipirit in the bond of peace, the Lord will be our God and delight to dwell among us as his owne people and will commaund a blessing upon us in all our wayes. . . ."[16]

Victory in the Revolutionary War further entrenched civil religion in the national psyche and enhanced the colonists' belief that they were God's chosen people. In his first inaugural address, President George Washington stated, "Every step by which we have advanced to the character of an independent nation seems to have been distinguished by some token of providential agency. . . ."[17] The new nation came to be equated with the new Israel.

Individually, the early leaders of the nation represented a cross section of religious and nonreligious beliefs. Corporately, they committed themselves to the universal truths which are common to many religious traditions. These they synthesized with various precepts of English political thought in writing the basic documents of our government. The words and acts of the founders during the early days of the republic molded the form and set the tone of the civil religion which has endured to this day. According to Sidney Mead, there was at the end of the eighteenth century "for the first time in the history of Christendom a genuinely *religious* alternative to orthodox Christianity. . . ." [18]

Crises in the life of the nation have been the occasions for expanding the content of civil religion. New situations invited or demanded new emphases. The Civil War was a case in point.

During the agonizing days of the Civil War serious questions arose regarding the meaning of nationhood. Many of those answers which were found to be most satisfactory came cloaked in religious garb. President Lincoln viewed the divided nation in light of a covenant relationship with God and the certainty of judgment under God. He understood his own leadership as benefiting from God's assistance and standing under God's judgment. [19] As a result of the tragedy of this dark period, the themes of death, sacrifice, and rebirth became permanent elements in American civil religion. [20]

Frequently, in times of stability as well as of crisis, the president of the nation has had more influence than anyone else on the form and content of civil religion. In addition to the mood of the citizenry and the international balance of power as substantive factors in the development of civil faith, the quality of religion exemplified by the president directly affects the civil religion of the time. [21] The office of the president is where the symbols, beliefs, and attitudes of the citizens meet and interact. Those who occupy the oval office at the White House "play their parts, acting out their priestly and prophetic functions, piecing together those constellations of meaning which become the precarious vision of their various constituencies." [22]

Will Herberg has helpfully described the ethos of civil faith: "The American Way is dynamic; optimistic; pragmatic; individualistic; egalitarian . . . and pluralistic." [23] Great value is placed upon the capitalistic free enterprise system, education, and sanitation. Coupled with principles, such as idealism, individualism, and unity, is a belief in some Supreme Being.

Celebrative rituals and various expressions of worship are found among committed civil religionists. National heroes, like George Washington and Abraham Lincoln, have been elevated to the status of civil heroes and appropriately honored. Government holidays, such as Memorial Day, Independence Day, and Labor Day, have been treated as holy days and their emphases observed by both ecclesiastical and secular organizations. The Lincoln Memorial and Arlington National Cemetery have become shrines which attract mass pilgrimages. The United States' flag has been made a national symbol meriting statements of personal commitment to it. Allegiance to government policies has sometimes been made the test of patriotic orthodoxy even as verbal affirmations of national leadership have occasionally been considered the proper litanies of national loyalty.

Civil religion has inspired in this nation a sense of identity and a concept of mission which are extremely important and potentially dangerous. Though both merit critical examination and a healthy suspicion, both continue to receive some public support.

As national values, history, and ideals were religionized, the citizens of this government came to view themselves as members of the new Israel. Americans were believed to be God's chosen people. Indicative of this mind-set was the utilization of religious terms and symbols on government property and in civil affairs.

During the Civil War the proposal was made that references to God be imprinted on the nation's currency. The rationale was that such an act "would relieve us of the ignominy of heathenism" and "place us openly under the divine protection we have personally claimed." [24] Even today, United States' dollar bills bear the mottoes *Annuit Coeptis*—"He [God] has smiled upon our beginnings" and *Novus Ordo Seclorum*—"A New Order of the Ages." From a religious perspective, symbols of faith were replacing faith.

Various presidents have nurtured the idea of a religious nation, though none has openly advocated a Christian nation. Such was the spirit of President Dwight Eisenhower's often-quoted remark: "Our government makes no sense unless it is founded in a deeply felt religious faith—and I don't care what it is." [25] Propagation of a religious identity is one important means of gaining support for national policies. The adjective "religious" placed before "America or "nation" grants to the noun an ultimacy which it does not otherwise possess. This is why long ago Alexis de Tocqueville could refer to religion in America as "a *political institution* which powerfully contributes to the maintenance of a democratic republic among the Americans." [26]

Conviction of a special national identity provoked the related concept of a special national mission. Nowhere is the consciousness of American messianism more vividly stated than in a passage from the noted author Herman Melville: "Long enough have we been skeptics with regard to ourselves and doubted whether, indeed, the political Messiah had come. But he has come in us, if we would but give utterance to his promptings."[27]

Like Israel of old, America was to serve the world as a witness and a missionary. Both the late nineteenth-century thought of "manifest destiny" and the early twentieth-century ideology of the "war to end all wars" were based on such a conviction regarding the nation's special role in the world. Woodrow Wilson could speak of the nation's military effort in World War I as a "righteous cause" in which all of humanity was served.[28] In like manner, President Harry Truman declared, "God has created us and brought us to our present position of power and strength for some great purpose."[29] Even more boldly, President Richard Nixon vowed, "America is the hope of the world, and I know that in the quality and wisdom of leadership America gives lies the only hope for millions of people all over the world, that they can live their lives in peace and freedom."[30]

Today civil religion is alive and influential in America. Seldom has it experienced celebration such as that which it enjoyed in the Nixon administration prior to Watergate. White House worship services and religiously garnished rhetoric strongly affirmed the national convictions of a religious identity and a special sense of mission. Apart from blatant religious rituals, President Gerald Ford has contributed to the civil religion consciousness through his approach to his two most controversial decisions. Regarding both the pardon of Richard Nixon and the announcement of a limited amnesty, Ford appealed to "a power higher than the people" and confessed his belief that "The Constitution is the supreme law of our land and it governs our actions as citizens. Only the laws of God, which govern our consciences, are superior to it."[31]

The Bicentennial year may be seen in retrospect as an occasion for one of the grandest and gaudiest festivals of civil faith ever held. Public media devoted almost constant attention to leaders of the Revolution, songs of patriotism, and documents of democracy. A red, white, and blue draped marketplace peddled an almost infinite variety of Bicentennial wares. Churches, synagogues, and civic organizations all alike programmed numerous nationalistic emphases.

Now is the opportune moment for a reassessment of civil religion. More critical evaluation is in order. The values of civil faith must be defined and its dangers publicized. As Christians, we dare not nurture through celebration a phenomenon which can compromise authentic faith and destroy the integrity of democracy, while claiming to support both.

By both definition and function civil religion is a social-political and religious phenomenon. Thus, an honest evaluation of its influence must be bifocaled. The following critique is an attempt to view the benefits and dangers of civil religion from a social-political perspective and from a religious perspective.

SOCIAL-POLITICAL CRITIQUE

Positive

Civil religion unites the beliefs, values, and symbols of people so as to contribute to the possibility of a social order. Bellah pointed out that "any coherent and viable society rests on a common set of moral understandings about good and bad, right and wrong, in the realm of individual and social action."[32] Since order is mandatory for a society to persist, some form of civil religion is essential.

Civil religion legitimates political action. Politics is the means by which decisions get made in a democracy. Civil religion does not disparage this fact but encourages the political process and supplies moral principles by which it can be evaluated. Citizens are sensitized to the importance of doing politics, not as games-playing for selfish interests but as responsible workmanship for the building up of the nation. By affirming an analogy between political categories and religious ones, tendencies to misuse political power and engage in political absolutism are brought under moral judgment.[33]

Civil religion contributes substantially to the development of community. In America diverse strains of people have found common ideals and principles around which they could build a life together. Individual identity could be retained while community was experienced. The key has been a "constellation of ideas and standards that bind . . . people together—what Abraham Lincoln . . . referred to as the 'bonds of affection; the mystic chords of memory' that constitute the score for 'the chorus of the Union.'"[34]

Devoid of identity and community, persons succumb to depression. Freedom must allow self-realization as well as social interaction. Both personal identity and social community were encouraged by the covenant concept in civil religion. It has produced "colorful and creative persons who do not seem to have been stifled so much as . . . strengthened by the social character of their faith."[35] The ties of civil religion have served as "'bonds of affection' which bind all the heterogeneous people together in . . . a union . . . more cosmopolitan, more universal, more general, than the bonds of affection which bind a particular group of these people together in a particular voluntary association, even though it be called a church."[36]

Negative

Civil religion elevates the nation and its leaders to unjustifiable places of supremacy. Corporately, national piety tends to divide the world into "us—the good guys" and "them—the bad guys." Suspicion is cast on all efforts at international cooperation and on any person who fails to fit into "the American way" of life. Entire nations may be labeled "the enemy" and military action against them understood as "moral." The realistic danger of such a radical nationalism developing out of civil religion was demonstrated in Nazi Germany.

A narrow commitment to this nation alone, such as may be fostered by civil religion, threatens contemporary efforts at detente and renders the concept of interdependence virtually unattainable. James Armstrong has stated the issue correctly: "If the United States has the right to think of itself before thinking of the well being of others, it follows that every other nation has the same inherent right. The 'survival of the fittest,' then, becomes the acceptable law of the jungle."[37]

Individually, civil religionists place leaders of government on pedestals which stand too high. Victory in an election does not assure administrative and legislative infallibility. The trappings of a government office fail to protect the occupants from mistakes and sin. Political leadership should be respected and supported but not at the expense of one's moral integrity. Leaders must be held accountable to the public for whom they work.

Civil religion dogmatizes political policies and threatens dissent. Conviction regarding the rightness of a particular policy sometimes causes a civil leader to use religion as a kind of glue to bind together the national will behind the policy or as a kind of emotional catchword to elicit support for the policy. That leader's position is then identified with "right," and all opposition to it is labeled as "wrong." Such action and belief abort the political process and threaten the existence of democracy.

Dissent is a basic right of the American citizen. Civil religion seeks to compromise this right by allowing dissent only if the majority is willing to permit it. The only other alternative is for the dissenters to persuade the majority that they no longer represent dissent.[38] Since some of this nation's most progressive actions have been precipitated by the positive tension created by dissent, the right of citizens to disagree with a policy through protest must be protected.

Civil religion embraces a racial bias. Most accounts of American civil religion, like this one, begin with the English invasion of the New World. Little or no attention has been devoted to native Americans, blacks, and other minorities as well as to the contributions which they have made to life in this land. The sacred narratives of culture faith have been constructed primarily around "the mighty deeds of the white conquerors."[39] At this point civil religion is historically inaccurate and morally insensitive.

A "melting pot" concept of the United States sought to force all immigrants into a common mold. As C. Eric Lincoln has observed, "The slave block and the Statue of Liberty alike presupposed that those who came to America would accept the niche already cut for them in the existing social order by pre-existent forces operating for the preservation of established prerogatives."[40] Any perpetuation of the "melting pot" metaphor of the nation and support for such a method of entrance into the nation must be challenged. Persons inhabiting America have every right to be as diverse as the varying terrains of land on which they live.

Non-acceptable in contemporary society is an ideology (especially one bearing the title "religious") which ignores major segments of the population. All of our citizens have a heritage to be celebrated, a dignity to be respected, and a potential to be affirmed.

RELIGIOUS CRITIQUE

Positive

Civil religion has bequeathed to the nation a heritage of moral concern. A minimal morality continues to dominate national thought. In the form of a communal ethic, basic moral principles enter into the decisions of economic organizations, professional associations, family groups, and political structures. Major critical problems are resolved in interaction with the moral insights of the Declaration of Independence, the Constitution, Supreme Court decisions, and presidential proclamations. Though the basic norms for behavior may be more humanitarian than Christian, attention to some form of ethics is far better than no moral consciousness at all.

Civil religion has emphasized a transcendent dimension to life. At its best, civil religion has perpetuated an understanding of nationhood which views government from the perspective of ultimate reality. Belief in God is the basic dogma of virtually every definition of civil religion. Thus, recognition is given to an order of truth which transcends our national life.

Robert Benne and Philip Hefner have rightly understood the significance of a belief in transcendence. "At crucial moments the civil religion grounds the aspirations of the human spirit that are inherent in the American myth. At other crucial moments it also holds the American reality—the faulty piety itself—up to the ideals of the American myth and points out the incongruity between real and ideal."[41] Thus, civil religion stands in judgment over the very culture of which it is a part. "It judges and criticizes our life as well as affirms it."[42]

In few places has the impact of the transcendent been more noticeable than in the realm of politics. Government leaders have appealed to transcendence both to warn of the likelihood of judgment on certain popular trends and to summon forth the people toward some bold new social initiative. Sovereignty of the citizenry has been subjected to the sovereignty of God. The rights of persons have been understood as residing in a religious realm which stands above the political process. Exemplary was President Kennedy's reminder to the nation that personal rights are more basic than political structures and the "point of revolutionary leverage from which any state structure may be radically altered."[43]

The element of transcendence is that which may sensitize the nonsectarian religionist to social ills which need correcting and motivate involvement in just causes which need support. Such a phenomenon has postitive value and merits affirmation.

Civil religion has created a climate conducive to religious pluralism. In most instances the general faith of the nation does not seek to eradicate particularistic faiths. Churches and synagogues are free to propagate their own systems of beliefs. Paradoxically, while specific religious groups must criticize the religion-in-general stance of the nation in light of their standards of orthodoxy, they must at the same time lend support to civil religion because of its anti-establishment approach to sectarian organizations. The content of the civil faith leaves much to be desired, but its liberal spirit of openness is appreciated.

Negative

Civil religion proclaims a false theology. Many words and phrases from Christian theology are present in civil religion. However, their meanings are radically different.

The deity of civil religion is not the God revealed in Jesus Christ.

Confessors of a culture faith worship some vague providence composed of American pluralism, devoid of personal characteristics, and unknown in historical revelation. This small deity appears to be the possession of Americans rather than the ruler of the universe.

Since the God of Christianity is a jealous God, biblical faith cannot allow any other person, system, or claim to be identified with ultimacy and to demand absolute allegiance. The authority of all rivals to the one true God should be held up to and ultimately dissolved by the penetrating light of the revelation available in Jesus Christ.

The faith of civil religionists is devoid of radical content, impersonal in orientation, and a matter of human achievement. More emphasis is placed upon the sincerity of belief and faith than upon the object or person to which commitment is devoted. President Eisenhower demonstrated the point when he said, "I am the most intensely religious man I know. Nobody goes through six years of war without a faith. That does not mean that I adhere to any sect."[44] Major distinctives separate general religious beliefs from authentic Christian faith, and the two must never be confused.

Likewise, salvation as a doctrine of civil religion does not square with Christian truth. Because of the importance of the nation in civil faith, good citizenship is sometimes mistaken for real righteousness. While revealed religion offers salvation to all who will accept it, civil religion offers salvation only to those within the American national community.[45] Noticeably absent from civil religion are the elements of repentance and forgiveness which are so crucial to Christian redemption.

Hope for the civil religionist resides in the strength of political institutions and the legitimacy of the American dream. Deep in the national psyche has been implanted the promise that any person can shake free of the past, struggle ascendingly into the present, and be greeted by a gracious, open future.[46] Thus, hope is tied to upward social mobility, economic success, and obvious personal accomplishments. Almost antithetical to the myth of the dream, Christian hope finds significance in unspectacular tasks and pleasure apart from affluence while offering a meaningful life to all. The major distinction between the two hopes resides in their sources—one of which is personal potential and the other of which is the power of God.

Civil religion confuses loyalty to the nation with faithfulness to Jesus Christ. Many Americans regard political loyalty more highly than other loyalties. They behave as if the ultimate questions of life were being decided by government alone. Though such a posture conforms to the nature of ancient pagan religions, it is foreign to the Christian faith. Politics is important for Christians but not ultimately so.

In Christianity, *ecclesia* takes the place of *civitas* "as the prime model of ultimate reality; and communion with Christ . . . displaces 'civil happiness' as the highest end of human life."[47] Christians must never "render to Caesar" that which belongs to God alone—worship, absolute obedience, and faith.

The difference between loyalty to the nation and faithfulness to Christ is the difference between the transitory and the permanent, the penultimate and the ultimate, what is human from what is of God. To recognize the "scandal of the qualitative difference, it is enough to gaze upon the cross of Christ which separates as well as binds."[48] Jesus is not merely a heavenly King whose authority is superior to earthly kings. He is the Savior of the world and the Lord of the universe as well as my personal Savior and Lord!

Civil religion obscures church-state relations. Sidney Mead's major thesis concerning civil religion is worthy of notation. He has claimed that an unresolved tension will always exist between the theology which legitimates the constitutional structure of the Republic and the theology of religious denominations.[49] A theology of generalities can be longer sustained and more widely supported apart from a theology of particulars. Related to this point, Robert Alley has sounded a warning that civil religion toys with the First Amendment. According to Alley, "Various trends in the national life suggest that a civil religion of the majority might find religious liberty something it did not care to preserve."[50] Recent efforts of some religious groups to impose their practices upon others by means of national legislation document the validity of the warning and the reality of the danger.

Civil religion silences or attempts to silence authentic prophecy. Conformity, not prophecy, is the goal of civil religion. In the face of the prophetic challenge, the nation reacts negatively, crying "divisive," so as to avoid reformation and positive change. Without a word of authentic prophecy, the nation can uncritically maintain things as they are and justify its actions by pious preachments. However, the silence of true prophets is a quiet prelude to doom for both the nation and the church.

CONCLUSION

Depending upon the nature of the civil religion in question, "one nation under God" may refer to the nation as God's servant, the nation as specially blessed by God, the nation as god, or the nation's accountability to God. One thing is certain, Christianity employs the phrase in relation to the latter meaning. Christians embrace a realistic assessment of the nation and an honest recognition that improvements are still needed in America's governmental policy and moral character.

The Christian citizen takes seriously the concept of a nation under God and seeks to nurture patriotism shaped by a healthy interpretation of that idea. Civil religion is cautiously affirmed but carefully distinguished from authentic Christianity. The Christian citizen's hope for "the nation under God" coincides with a prayer for personal growth, both of which are informed by the apostle Paul's wise words to the Romans: "Don't let the world around you squeeze you into its own mould, but let God re-make you so that your whole attitude of mind is changed. Thus you will prove in practice that the will of God is good, acceptable to him and perfect" (Romans 12:2, Phillips).

NOTES

[1] Robert Bellah has observed that the inclusion of "under God" in the pledge of allegiance was indicative of the fact that what had been taken for granted for generations was not in need of explicit recognition. The religious understanding of America was being eroded. Robert N. Bellah, "New Religious Consciousness," *The New Republic*, vol. 171 (November 23, 1974), p. 34.

[2] Robert N. Bellah, "Civil Religion in America," *Daedalus*, vol. 96 (Winter, 1967), p. 18.

[3] *Ibid.*, p. 5.

[4] Robert N. Bellah, "American Civil Religion in the 1970's," *Anglican Theological Review*, Supplementary Series (July, 1973), p. 8.

[5] Will Herberg, "America's Civil Religion: What It Is and Whence It Comes," in *American Civil Religion*, edited by Russell E. Richey and Donald G. Jones (New York: Harper & Row, Publishers, 1974), pp. 77-78.

[6] *Ibid.*, p. 79.

[7] *Ibid.*, p. 77.

[8] This is the term popularized by Sidney E. Mead. See *The Nation with the Soul of a Church* (New York: Harper & Row, Publishers, 1975) for a collection of writings in which this thought appears.

[8] One of the five meanings of civil religion discussed by Richey and Jones in "The Civil Religion Debate," *American Civil Religion*, ed. Richey and Jones, p. 17.

[10] *Ibid.*, pp. 16-17.

[11] Exemplary of functional definitions of religion are those from Martin Marty and Milton Yinger from which this statement was drawn. See Martin E. Marty, *The Pro & Con Book of Religious America: A Bicentennial Argument* (Waco, Texas: Word Books, 1975), Pro, p. 20, and J. Milton Yinger, *Religion, Society and the Individual: An Introduction to the Sociology of Religion* (New York: The Macmillan Company, 1965), p. 9.

[12] Robert N. Bellah, *The Broken Covenant: American Civil Religion in Time of Trial* (New York: The Seabury Press, Inc., 1975), p. 46.

[13] Charles P. Henderson, Jr., "Civil Religion and the American Presidency," *Religious Education*, vol. 70 (September–October, 1975), p. 476.

[14] Larry McSwain, "The Positive Values of Civil Religion in a Secular Age." This is an extremely perceptive paper which is presently unpublished.

[15] Bellah, *The Broken Covenant*, pp. 12 and 21.

[16] Bellah, "American Civil Religion in the 1970's," p. 17.

[17] Bellah, "Civil Religion in America," p. 7.

[18] Mead, *The Nation with the Soul of a Church*, p. 119.

[19] Elton Trueblood, *Abraham Lincoln: Theologian of American Anguish* (New York: Harper & Row, Publishers, 1973), pp. 31-32.

[20] Bellah, "Civil Religion in America," p. 10.

[21] Robert S. Alley, *So Help Me God: Religion and the Presidency, Wilson to Nixon* (Richmond, Va.: John Knox Press, 1972), pp. 18 and 24.

[22] Henderson, "Civil Religion and the American Presidency," p. 484.

[23] Herberg, "America's Civil Religion: What It Is and Whence It Comes," p. 79.

[24] Francis Stuart Harmon, *Religious Freedom in America* (New York: Friendship Press, 1973), p. 33.

[25] Will Herberg, "Religion in the U.S.—Where It's Headed," *U.S. News and World Report*, June 4, 1973, p. 58.

[26] Alexis de Tocqueville, *Democracy in America*, rev. ed. (New York: Vintage Books, 1945), p. 310. The italics in the quote are mine.

[27] Herman Melville, *White Jacket;* cited in Paul S. Minear, *I Pledge Allegiance: Patriotism and the Bible* (Philadelphia: The Geneva Press, 1975), p. 27.

[28] Alley, *So Help Me God*, p. 33.

[29] *Ibid.*, p. 80.

[30] Cited in James M. Wall, "On Seeing the Presidency as Sacred," *The Christian Century,* vol. 90 (May 16, 1973), p. 555.

[31] Henderson, "Civil Religion and the American Presidency," pp. 483-484.

[32] Bellah, *The Broken Covenant,* p. ix.

[33] Herbert Richardson, "Civil Religion in Theological Perspective," *American Civil Religion,* ed. Richey and Jones, p. 164.

[34] Mead, *The Nation with the Soul of a Church,* p. 39.

[35] Marty, *The Pro & Con Book of Religious America,* Pro. p. 43.

[36] Mead, *The Nation with the Soul of a Church,* p. 39.

[37] James Armstrong, *The Nation Yet to Be: Christian Mission and the New Patriotism* (New York: Friendship Press, 1975), p. 104.

[38] McSwain, "The Positive Values of Civil Religion in a Secular Age," p. 7.

[39] Charles H. Long, "A New Look at American Religion," *Anglican Theological Review,* Supplementary Series (July, 1973), p. 120.

[40] C. Eric Lincoln, "Americanity: The Third Force in American Pluralism," *Religious Education,* vol. 70 (September–October, 1975), p. 488.

[41] Robert Benne and Philip Hefner, *Defining America: A Christian Critique of the American Dream* (Philadelphia: Fortress Press, 1974), pp. 26-27.

[42] *Ibid.,* p. 27.

[43] Bellah, "Civil Religion in America," p. 4.

[44] Mead, *The Nation with the Soul of a Church,* p. 25.

[45] Charles H. Long, "Civil Rights—Civil Religion: Visible People and Invisible Religion, *American Civil Religion,* ed. Richey and Jones, p. 211.

[46] See Benne and Hefner, *Defining America,* pp. 1-55.

[47] Richardson, "Civil Religion in Theological Perspective," p. 178.

[48] Jurgen Moltmann, "The Cross and Civil Religion," *Religion and Political Society,* ed. and trans. The Institute of Christian Thought (New York: Harper & Row, Publishers, 1974). p. 21.

[49] Mead, *The Nation with the Soul of a Church,* p. vi.

[50] Alley, *So Help Me God,* pp. 145-146.

PART THREE

The Interaction
of Church and Nation
at Home and Abroad

The
Americanization
of
Baptists

W. MORGAN PATTERSON

I. THE ISSUE OF AMERICANIZATION IN PERSPECTIVE

Literature dealing with the allied subjects of Americanization and immigration appears to have mushroomed into a voluminous corpus earlier in this century before and after World War I.[1] This development coincided with or closely followed the peak years of the flood of immigrants into the United States. The basic questions raised were whether the millions of new residents could or should be assimilated into a new land and culture; and if that were possible and desirable, how and to what extent should assimilation take place? Should immigrants be urged to forsake every vestige of their European heritage? If not, to what extent and in what ways should they be Americanized? What is Americanization, and how could its goals be achieved in a pluralistic, democratic society? It soon became clear that Americanization was viewed narrowly and chauvinistically by some and therefore was an unattractive concept and goal for many writers and thinkers.

The term "Americanization" began to come into wide use in the opening decades of this century to refer to the problem of assimilation of the immigrant. Besides a growing literary output dealing with the theme, concrete efforts were also put forth by organized Americanization groups to muster popular support for their objectives.

A major factor in the heightened interest of many Americans in the subject was the possible effect of the war in Europe upon America. The presence in the United States of millions of residents who were of foreign origin, especially of German and Austrian birth, and who retained the use of their mother tongue and national customs was a source of genuine concern and even suspicion for many native Americans. To exacerbate a delicate situation, the agitation in behalf of foreign causes by propagandizers among the immigrants in this country led some Americans to conclude that the situation was volatile.

On the other hand, in many instances there was an admirable humanitarian desire to welcome the immigrants, to get to know them and their problems, and to join with them in a national expression of patriotism. As a result of these two sentiments (chauvinist and humanitarian), several new initiatives were proposed for concerted action which would assist in and hasten the process of assimilation of immigrants into American life. Various agencies and national committees worked together to implement this objective.

The National Americanization Day Committee, made up of fifty-nine prominent citizens from all sections of the United States, proposed July 4, 1915, as Americanization Day. The support and endorsement of much of the country was secured, including that of President Woodrow Wilson. This special celebration was reported to have had unusual success with more than 150 cities participating. Even more important was the apparent human impact it had.[2] The effects included a somewhat better understanding of the immigrant's plight, improved community relations with the "new" Americans, and the launching of programs for a more complete Americanization of the newcomers.[3]

This event symbolizes the widespread interest in America in the issue of Americanization. Writers, scholars, and public figures joined in debate on the desirability, values, methods, and definition of Americanization of the immigrant. Its meaning was usually understood to include

> the union of the many peoples of the country into one nation and the use of the English language throughout the nation, the establishment of American standards of living in every community of the country, a common interpretation of American citizenship, and a recognition of foreign-born men and women in the human, social, and civic as well as the industrial aspects of American life.[4]

Although a worthy egalitarianism is implicit in such a definition, Americanization was also seen by many to be unduly nationalistic and essentially indifferent to the rich traditions the immigrants brought with them. The immigrants were to extirpate all vestiges of their Old World origins and to become part of a new America.

II. THE CONCEPT OF AMERICANIZATION IN RELATION TO BAPTISTS

In applying the term "Americanization" to the Baptists, several problems immediately appear. The normal use of the word has been primarily to designate the slow and often difficult process by which aliens have adapted to their new homeland and its customs. This adaptation or assimilation has usually meant the learning of English, understanding and accepting the fundamentals of citizenship, and relating in a positive way to new institutions, new values, and new expectations. Thus, the term is not ordinarily employed with reference to groups whose basic identity is denominational, doctrinal, and religious. Rather, its thrust has been to sift out ethnic, cultural, and linguistic differences, not ecclesiastical or theological distinctions.

Secondly, the context of the term's use is the nineteenth and twentieth centuries—after a national identity has been established. Americanization can be meaningful in a precise way only after the goals and characteristics of the new nation became explicit, or at least apparent. A fundamental question then can be raised: In what sense can one speak of the Americanization of Baptists in the colonial period of the seventeenth and eighteenth centuries?

A third problem is related to the fact that although Baptists were planted in the colonies as early as the 1640s, it is quite true that ethnic Baptist groups later made their appearance in America with the surge of "new" immigrants in the latter part of the nineteenth century and the early part of the twentieth. In his standard work on the history of Baptists, Robert G. Torbet takes note of the founding of more than a dozen "foreign-speaking Baptist bodies" in the United States between 1865 and 1928.[5] Among them were Swedish, German, Hungarian, Italian, Mexican, and Russian-Ukrainian groups, to name a few.

The diversity of Baptists in America creates difficulty in any assessment of their Americanization. With about thirty-five groups comprising the Baptist family, generalization becomes a precarious venture. Besides the ethnic Baptist bodies, the special circumstances of black Baptist development must be taken into account. Other smaller Baptist groups are often characterized by isolation, lack of general organization, and absence of up-to-date information on them. Even within the larger Baptist conventions the range of viewpoint and outlook is significantly varied. How does one generalize amidst such diversity?

The issue of Americanization is even more complicated and elusive in the case of Baptists than it might be with certain other religious groups with strong European ties and a tradition of church-state connections. It is clear that such groups of the latter description might have undergone a more radical adjustment in a new country free of a church-state alignment and thereby be a more suitable object of study. However, for Baptists there was nothing to unlearn on this subject. Liberty of conscience had been at the center of their witness and doctrine from their beginnings both in England and America, and the goal of separation of church and state was a part of their heritage.

Furthermore, Baptists might be considered as indigenous to the American scene as any denominational group. Through their agitation for religious freedom to be safeguarded by effective constitutional guarantees, Baptists themselves contributed significantly to the emerging national character. In this respect one might even probe the contribution of Baptists to the content of what is called Americanism.

Historically, Americanization must be understood to mean different things in different periods of American development. In the seventeenth century, Americanization perhaps meant little more than cultivation of the capacity to survive and adapt to a new land fraught with all of the rigors and dangers of a wilderness. Nevertheless, from the outset life in America revealed a fundamental religious dimension in its inhabitants. Although the reasons for seeking these shores were obviously not always altruistic or religious, a great many persons did come because of their defiance of ecclesiastical authority and their rejection of traditional liturgical practices. Many came looking for a place of freedom to implement their own religious ideas. Thus, the fabric of Americanism in its earliest stage was woven in part with the threads of religious conviction, personal determination and courage, a desire to innovate, and freedom from oppressive church authority. (Parenthetically one might add, to Americanize someone or some group in a later century should be to make clear the religious foundations of the earliest American settlement and culture.) Baptists of that period could easily identify with these qualities. In fact, Baptists exemplified them in a remarkable degree.

The eighteenth century in America is marked by continuing settlement and stabilization, by the creation of civilizing institutions, and by a crusade for freedom—political, personal, and religious. Dominating the latter part of the century was the establishment of a national identity and the emergence of an American spirit. In a remarkable way the phrases of the First Amendment of the Constitution of the United States epitomize these unique characteristics: "Congress shall make no law respecting an establishment of religion, or prohibiting the free exercise thereof; or abridging the freedom of speech, or of the press; or the right of the people peaceably to assemble, and to petition the government for a redress of grievances."

Those words differentiated the character of life and government in America from that of every other nation and in a profound and far-reaching sense provided a basis of Americanism. To these guarantees not only did eighteenth-century Baptists subscribe with gratitude and enthusiasm, but many historians have identified and documented a Baptist role in securing them.

III. BAPTISTS AND THE NATIONAL EXPERIENCE

The remainder of this chapter will focus on the symbiosis of Baptists and the nation in the nineteenth and twentieth centuries. What is of special interest is the interaction of Baptists with national events, movements, moods, and characteristics. In what ways have Baptists been influenced or shaped by their participation in the American experience? To what extent have Baptists, consciously or unconsciously, come to reflect what may be termed the American character or style of life? What attitudes, methods, and emphases of Baptists have perhaps been drawn in some measure from American culture? It is in this sense that the issue of Americanization must now be considered.

But these questions are most difficult to answer and invariably provoke different responses. Much depends on one's definition of terms and one's recourse to generalization. What *is* the "American experience" or "American character" or "American spirit"? The issues are complex and, to a great extent, subjectively viewed.

It is axiomatic to observe that Baptists in America have been profoundly influenced by the American experience, which presumably refers to those singular developments of United States history, especially in the last two hundred years. In an authentic sense, Baptists and the nation have grown up together, and that implies reciprocal influence. On the one hand, Baptists have had their input into American life, and on the other, they have felt the impact of the broader features of the American heritage of which Baptists were only a part.

Westward Migration, the Frontier and Baptists

After the successful conclusion of the Revolutionary War and the creation of the infant nation, the beginning of an immense population shift got under way. Tens of thousands of people moved from the eastern seaboard into the valleys west of the Allegheny Mountains. Contemporary accounts tell of dozens of wagons and hundreds of people passing through towns every day, going West. Typical of the rapidity with which many towns sprang up was the settlement of Vevay, Indiana, on the Ohio River. It was laid out in 1813, and by 1816 it was "a county seat with a courthouse, schoolhouse, public library, stores, taverns, and seventy-five dwellings." It also received three mails a week and supported a weekly newspaper.[6]

Illustrative of the national proportions of the westward trek are the following census figures. The first census (1790) revealed a population of approximately four million with 94 percent living in the thirteen states. The census of 1820 reported a population of nearly ten million with 25 percent living west of the seaboard states. By 1850 about half of the population of twenty-three million was to be found west of the Appalachians.[7]

In this torrent of people moving westward Baptists participated. Their migrations into frontier areas resulted in new configurations of Baptist settlement and concentration. Nowhere were the shifts more conspicuous than in Kentucky. where new settlers and frontier revivals combined to produce some impressive statistics.[8]

Date	Associations	Churches	Members
1790	3	42	3,105
1800	6	106	5,119
1803	10	219	15,495
1810	15	286	16,650
1820	25	491	31,639
1830	34	574	39,957
1840	50	711	49,308

Frederick Jackson Turner in his famous essay, "The Significance of the Frontier in American History," has magnified the role of the frontier in the American experience. Not all historians have accepted his thesis, but there is no doubt that the frontier was an important factor in American development. Turner, in fact, spoke of a distinctive American character forged in the frontier setting. He described it as composed of

that coarseness and strength combined with acuteness and inquisitive-ness; that practical inventive turn of mind, quick to find expedients; that masterful grasp of material things, lacking in the artistic but powerful to effect great ends; that restless, nervous energy; that dominant individualism, working for good and for evil, and withal that buoyancy and exuberance which comes with freedom. . . .[9]

The reading of minutes of Baptist churches situated on the frontier might well lead one to use some (not all) of the same phrases to describe the efforts and aspirations, the outlook and deeds of Baptists.

The frontier's influence on Baptists can be seen in their use of methods designed to cope with problems created by the frontier. For example, it has been demonstrated that Baptist churches as well as others served as moral courts on the frontier in seeking to inculcate an ethical conscience in those communities where they were located.[10] Because salaried, educated ministers were few on the frontier, Baptists turned to preachers who farmed during the week and served the churches on Sunday. Nevertheless, Baptists generally recognized the importance of a trained ministry, and they began to establish colleges for that purpose.

Life on the frontier served to accent the Baptist sense of independence and democracy found in their church polity. Frontier conditions were compatible with the Baptist preference for simplicity in worship and rejection of elaborate forms. No doubt, too, the isolation and lack of formal education on the frontier tended to reinforce their inclinations toward exclusivism.

The frontier was the symbol of American expansion, vitality, and growth. It encouraged new visions, new ventures, and a new optimism. For Baptists new churches were founded, new converts were made, new associations and societies were established, and new beginnings were launched. The frontier thus stimulated new efforts and new hopes among Baptists.

Slavery and Racial Segregation

The most divisive issue of nation and church in the nineteenth century was slavery. It shattered the peace and unity of the country as it divided families, disrupted communities, and eventually pitted South against North. Its ultimate resolution, alas, lay in a decimating fratricidal war.

In the national controversy over slavery and secession it is revealing to note its impact on the churches. Along with the Methodists and Presbyterians, Baptists were split into factions opposing and favoring slavery. The effects of their secular surroundings on them are virtually unmistakable.

In tracing the attitudes of Baptists in America toward slavery, it is possible to observe several stages of development. In the eighteenth century a number of Baptist churches and leaders were on record as opposing slavery. As the nineteenth century began and slavery became more common, many churches and associations strove for a position of neutrality. Then, by the 1830s and 1840s sermons were preached and essays written to rationalize and defend slavery.[11]

These shifts seemed to correspond to the growing importance of cotton and cheap labor in the agricultural economy of the South. As cotton became king and plantation culture became dominant, slaves became increasingly valuable and indispensable. Those who owned slaves had an economic investment not to be given up easily. It is reported that in South Carolina one-third of the Baptist laymen and two-fifths of the ministers were slaveholders.[12]

Also, the concentration of abolitionist sentiment in the North and its vigorous attack on the South served to provoke bitter sectional feelings. The divorce of the two sections was symbolized by the secession of the Southern states from the Union and the formation of the Confederacy.

The effects of the tensions and acrimony over slavery finally brought schism to Baptists in 1845. The oldest national organization of Baptists had been the Triennial Convention,[13] founded in Philadelphia in 1814. Although created to support foreign missions, the body also engaged for several years in home missions and education. Then, in 1832 a similar national body was organized—The American Baptist Home Mission Society—to take over the work of home missions. With both of these agencies Baptists from the North and the South cooperated until the break in 1845.

The primary cause of separation was slavery. When the Home Mission Society declined to appoint as a missionary one who was known to be a slaveholder, Baptists in the South decided further cooperation was impossible. This decision was confirmed when in December, 1844, the board of the Triennial Convention spoke to the same issue: "If . . . any one should offer himself as a Missionary, having slaves, and should insist on retaining them as his property, we could not appoint him. One thing is certain; we can never be a party to any arrangement which would imply approbation of slavery."[14]

The upshot of these developments was the formation of the Southern Baptist Convention in Augusta, Georgia, in May, 1845.[15] Thus, the division of Baptists foreshadowed the national calamity which occurred sixteen years later.

Although the Union armies successfully concluded the Civil War, and the Thirteenth Amendment outlawing slavery became the law of the land, many social problems relating to the races were still to be faced. For another ninety years the black and white races coexisted with their separate but not equal facilities, institutions, and spheres of living. In 1954 the Supreme Court introduced a major alteration into the nation's life by declaring racial segregation to be unconstitutional. Since that momentous decision many changes have occurred on the national scene.

Not all Baptist congregations were pleased with the decision. However, the Southern Baptist Convention, the largest white Baptist body in the South, shortly after the Court's action, approved a resolution stating that the decision "is in harmony with the constitutional guarantee of equal freedom to all citizens, and with the Christian principles of equal justice and love for all men."[16] In almost all cases Baptist institutions have removed racial barriers, but integration of church membership (dependent on the action of local churches) has been minimal. Racial prejudice is still a major problem confronting Baptists. As a result of the migration of many Southern blacks to the large urban centers of the North, the problem is also no longer one faced only in the South.

Urbanization, Big Business, and Baptists

In what Winthrop Hudson styles the "years of midpassage"[17] in United States history, from the Civil War to World War I, a prominent feature of American development was the rise of the cities. Their growth was due both to industrialization and immigration. Offices and factories attracted people from the villages and rural areas, and immigrants with limited means usually settled in the cities near where they had landed.

These new masses of people were faced with frustration, poverty, crime, and the other vices of city life. Baptists sought to develop new strategies to minister to such people through the programs of their home mission organizations, rescue missions, and institutional churches. Their effectiveness was not uniform, and Baptists had to acknowledge the difficulty and the challenge of an urban ministry.

Walter Rauschenbusch, for eleven years a Baptist pastor on the edge of notorious Hell's Kitchen in New York City, and later a professor of church history at Rochester Theological Seminary, urged that the principles of the gospel message be applied to the social problems of the cities. Regarded as "the real founder of social Christianity in this country,"[18] Rauschenbusch pinpointed the ills and cataloged the shortcomings of American society and recommended the prescription of Christian socialism.[19]

In the latter part of the nineteenth century, American capitalism flourished as new fortunes were amassed in steel, oil, railroads, banking, and textiles. In this area of American development some businessmen who were Baptists benefited and subsequently bestowed generous gifts upon Baptist causes. Brothers James and Samuel Colgate, sons of the soap manufacturer, William Colgate, were devoted Baptists who gave liberally to Colgate University. The family of John P. Crozer founded and endowed the Crozer Theological Seminary in Upland, Pennsylvania, in 1868. One of the wealthiest of all American tycoons was John D. Rockefeller, Sr. His philanthropies were many, but he favored Baptist enterprises. Perhaps his sizable gifts to the University of Chicago were the most notable.

Evidence of the big-business syndrome perhaps can be traced to the churches. In the twentieth century, congregations with memberships in the thousands began to appear. For example, among Southern Baptists in 1926 there were 246 churches with memberships in excess of 1000.[20] By 1950 the number had increased to 1019,[21] and by 1975 there were 2303 churches with over 1000 members.[22] Of the latter figure 488 churches have a membership of over 2000 persons.

To explain this phenomenon, one must certainly take several factors into account: an aggressive evangelism, industrious pastors, large concentrations of people in urban and suburban areas, and other favorable conditions. However, the development of such large churches was attended by an expanded staff of ministers and other workers, multiple internal organizations and programs, elaborate and costly facilities, complex budgets and fund-raising drives, and a business manager and the techniques of big business. Of course, not many churches possessed all of these features, but the trend seemed to be set toward the adoption of as many as possible.

Some congregations and pastors have expressed a certain concern over the liability of bigness. A few have challenged members to join new mission churches or to strengthen smaller churches already in existence. However, this attitude is not widely in evidence.

Commensurate with the general rise in the educational level of the population, due in part to urbanization and the availability of greater educational opportunities, there has been an increasing emphasis on a prepared ministry among Baptists. In this century Baptists have founded numerous institutions of academic quality and strengthened others to provide theological training, and more and more young men and women have taken advantage of them. Nevertheless, a majority of pastors and other full-time church workers still do not have the advantage of seminary training or advanced education.

War and Peace

Baptists have usually condemned war in principle and coveted peace for their country and for themselves. However, they have generally accepted with a sense of obligation their responsibility to take up arms for what they deemed to be right and just. They have believed it right to defend their country and to fight for human rights and liberties. Nevertheless, their perception of the legitimacy of the cause has often come through the spectacles of national interest. Historically, loyalty to their country and its leaders has been a significant factor in the willingness of Baptists to accept the nation's decision to go to war. Baptists have usually responded favorably to the call of country when it was sounded.

In the eighteenth century there was almost unanimous Baptist support for the Revolutionary War. They believed independence from England to be the best way to rectify various injustices and the only way to secure liberty of conscience. They were therefore energetic in behalf of the colonial cause.

In the Civil War each side believed God to be on its side. To Baptists in the North, the War was just because its aim was to abolish the evil of slavery and preserve the Union. To Baptists in the South, it was just because they were defending their homes and rights. These rationales corresponded to the sectional outlook of the divided nation.

In this century as World War I approached, Baptists reiterated their abhorrence of war and their hope for world peace. However, when it was clear that war was unavoidable, Baptists chose to support their country in what was widely regarded as a crusade against the "Anti-Christ."[23] The Northern Baptist Convention in 1917 approved a resolution pledging "to the President and government of the United States our whole-hearted allegiance and support." The preamble to the resolution observed: "Whereas, Our country is at war in defense of humanity, liberty and democracy; and, whereas, we were forced into this conflict despite the exhaustion of every honorable means by our peace-loving President to save non-combatant life and to stop savagery without resort to arms. . . ."[24]

During the years intervening between the two World Wars, and consonant with the peace movement in the United States, Baptists expressed their opposition to war, supported disarmament, favored arbitration of international disputes, and urged American participation in the Court of International Justice. However, with the attack on Pearl Harbor in December, 1941, Baptists with reluctance approved the country's entry into World War II as a "grim necessity."[25]

When compared to their reaction to earlier wars, Baptists in the Vietnam era showed less unanimity on the rightness of the conflict and the wisdom of their country's participation in it. Debate revealed both opposition to it and support for it. Those who favored the war usually justified it as an effort to contain communism. This polarity of views was indicative of the division of sentiment in the nation as a whole.

Baptists and Political Action[26]

Although Baptists might not have been as active as certain other religious bodies in organizing direct lobbying groups, they nevertheless have usually had a keen interest in proposed legislation, judicial proceedings, and government decisions at local, state, and federal levels. That interest can be seen in a number of ways. For example, Baptist editors often have exposed issues of religious import and urged their readers to write their elected representatives about them.

Also, such interest is reflected in the leadership given by Baptist pastors in referendums dealing with the sale of alcoholic beverages, gambling, and similar community problems with moral or religious implications. Baptist concern over matters relating to church and state and a desire to make Baptist views on such issues known resulted in the formation in 1939 of the Baptist Joint Committee on Public Affairs.[27]

Furthermore, with a preponderance of Baptists in the South they have often had men and women of their number to serve as legislators, judges, and government officials in county courthouses, state capitals, and Washington. Thus, Baptists have not been reluctant to participate in the American political process. Rather, they have been willing for their views to be known and their influence to be felt on issues of moral and religious significance.

The heritage of Baptists on liberty of conscience has led them to be sensitive to violations of church-state separation, and their readiness to participate in the American experience has led them to keep before their elected representatives and the public the necessity of adhering strictly to the provisions and prohibitions of the First Amendment. Once having secured religious freedom, Baptists have sought to prevent its erosion. It was this which led Baptists in the 1940s to oppose an American envoy to the Vatican. Baptists have also been vigorous in their opposition to public funds to private schools and religious institutions.

Any chronicle of social and political action in the United States must take note of the major impact of the civil rights movement on American life. In the epochal years of the 1950s and 1960s black Baptists played the dominant role in the cause of civil rights. Through the remarkable leadership of a Baptist preacher, Martin Luther King, Jr., national attention was focused on the need for civil rights legislation.

In the campaign for civil rights King was ably assisted by numerous black Baptist pastors, and meetings and rallies were usually held in black Baptist churches. Perhaps the most dramatic event of the movement was the gathering of 250,000 people in Washington in 1964 when King delivered his moving sermon, "I Have a Dream." As a result of the influence and political pressure generated by the civil rights crusade, the conscience of many Americans was touched and a Civil Rights Law (1964) was enacted.

CONCLUSION

There are several obvious channels through which Baptists have absorbed some of the characteristics of American culture and have participated in the American experience. Naturally, one's residence within *any* cultural setting results in an exposure to and some assimilation of its values and forms. Seldom does even a cloistered existence effectively prevent some cultural penetration.

Secondly, participation in community life as a responsible citizen further confronts the individual with cultural peculiarities and expectations. For example, the campaign of Baptists for liberty of conscience through constitutional safeguards and the recourse of Baptists to law and the courts to protect their rights as citizens meant that they interacted with cultural institutions and had some hope of reshaping them.

Thirdly, patriotic commitment to their country or region provided the means by which cultural influences might be further mediated to individual Baptists as well as to Baptist congregations and other organizations. For example, most Baptists were active partisans of the Revolutionary cause and rejoiced in the victory over the British. A similar expression of regional loyalty is clearly reflected in the events leading to the Civil War. Sectional loyalties and stereotypes have not altogether disappeared a century after the end of that conflict.

Inevitably, the economic aspect of living life in community creates opportunities for profound cultural influence as both church member and congregation have some stake in the prevailing economic climate. Lastly, the mere acknowledgment of cultural realities necessarily presupposes some degree of influence of those realities upon individuals and denominations. Then, when one accepts the Christian mandate to confront culture with a gospel of redemption and judgment, it is inevitable that interaction with culture would result. Thus, the church's goal must be to offer an effective witness for the Christian faith through culture but to declare at the same time that culture is under the judgment of God. However, too often the church, acting initially upon good impulses, has become enamored of culture and lost sight of its spiritual objectives.

There is much in the American experience which Baptists can affirm happily and with integrity, since the national pilgrimage has been one of movement toward maximum personal freedom and securing personal rights. Baptists also share with their country its diversity and pluralistic nature. Baptist variety stems not only from their cultivation of freedom and individual qualities, but also from the ethnic character of the nation.

No doubt Baptists with their congregational democracies have flourished in part because they were set in a larger political democracy. The democratic values of the nation have often been congruent with the democratic features of Baptist churches.

Finally, in reflection upon the interaction of Baptists with the American experience, it is appropriate to suggest several dangers of which they should be aware:

1. That Baptists will enunciate the ideal of freedom and not be consistent in applying it in practice.
2. That to the degree in which they participate in American affluence, they will lose the spiritual vigor which characterizes their heritage.
3. That in their cultural enhancement and educational sophistication, they will overlook lessons to be learned from their modest origins.
4. That in their participation in the political process, they will misuse their influence for denominational advantage or misguided ends.
5. That they will fail to keep in balance and actively develop the personal and social dimensions of the gospel.
6. That in the interest of unity and peace within the denominational unit, they will fail to speak prophetically to the urgent social and moral issues of the day.
7. That they will let their noble and vital heritage become meaningless or unknown by failing to teach it to their children.

NOTES

[1] In addition to numerous others, the subject of Americanization and immigration is treated in the following works: Francis J. Brown and Joseph S. Roucek, eds., *One America,* reprint ed. (Westport Conn.: Negro Universities Press, 1954); Robert A. Carlson, *The Quest for Conformity: Americanization Through Education* (New York: John Wiley and Sons, Inc., 1975); Marcus Lee Hansen, *The Atlantic Migration, 1607–1860,* reprint ed. (New York: Harper & Row, Publishers, 1961); Edward G. Hartmann, *The Movement to Americanize the Immigrant,* reprint ed. (New York: AMS Press, Inc., 1948); Maldwyn A. Jones, *American Immigration* (Chicago: The University of Chicago Press, 1960).

[2] Edward G. Hartmann, *The Movement to Americanize the Immigrant,* pp. 112-121.

[3] Frances Kellor, "By-Products of Americanization Day," *Immigrants in America Review* (September, 1915), p. 3.

[4] Hartmann, *The Movement to Americanize the Immigrant,* pp. 124-125.

[5] Robert G. Torbet, *A History of the Baptists,* rev. ed. (Valley Forge: Judson Press, 1973), pp. 543-544.

[6] William Warren Sweet, *Revivalism in America* (New York: Charles Scribner's Sons, 1944), p. 113.

[7] *Ibid.,* p. 114. For an invaluable treatment of religious statistics, consult Edwin S. Gaustad, *Historical Atlas of Religion in America* (New York: Harper & Row, Publishers, 1976).

[8] These figures are taken mainly from J. H. Spencer, *A History of Kentucky Baptists* (Cincinnati: J. R. Baumes, 1886), vol. 1, *passim.*

[9] Frederick Jackson Turner, "The Significance of the Frontier in American History" in *The Turner Thesis,* ed. George Rogers Taylor (Boston: D. C. Heath and Company, 1949), p. 17.

[10] Cf. William Warren Sweet, "The Churches as Moral Courts of the Frontier," *Church History,* vol. 2, no. 1 (March, 1933), pp. 3-21; and Harold W. Brown, "Baptist Churches as Moral Courts," *The Chronicle,* vol. 5, no. 1 (April, 1942), pp. 82-90.

[11] These stages are documented by John Lee Eighmy, *Churches in Cultural Captivity* (Knoxville: The University of Tennessee Press, 1972), chapter 1.

[12] Torbet, *A History of the Baptists,* p. 283.

[13] The proper name for this body is "The General Missionary Convention of the Baptist Denomination in the United States for Foreign Missions."

[14] Robert A. Baker, *A Baptist Source Book: With Particular Reference to Southern Baptists* (Nashville: Broadman Press, 1966), p. 109.

[15] Cf. Robert A. Baker, *The Southern Baptist Convention and Its People, 1607–1972* (Nashville: Broadman Press, 1974), p. 161.

[16] *Southern Baptist Convention Annual, 1954,* p. 56.

[17] Winthrop S. Hudson, *Religion in America* (New York: Charles Scribner's Sons, 1965), Part 3.

[18] Reinhold Niebuhr, *An Interpretation of Christian Ethics* (New York: Harper & Row, Publishers, 1935), Preface.

[19] Walter Rauschenbusch, *Christianizing the Social Order* (New York: The Macmillan Company, 1912).

[20] *Southern Baptist Handbook, 1926,* p. 163.

[21] *Southern Baptist Handbook, 1951,* p. 91.

[22] *The Quarterly Review,* vol. 25 (July–September, 1975), p. 11.

[23] See George D. Kelsey, *Social Ethics Among Southern Baptists, 1917–1969* (Metuchen, N.J.: The Scarecrow Press, Inc., and the American Theological Library Association, 1973), pp. 106ff.

[24] Eldon G. Ernst, "Twentieth-Century Issues of War and Peace," *Foundations,* vol. 15, no. 4 (October–December, 1972), p. 308.

[25] *Ibid.,* p. 300. See also "War and Peace," *Encyclopedia of Southern Baptists,* 2 vols. (Nashville: Broadman Press, 1958), vol. 2, p. 1476.

[26] For other dimensions of this subject, note C. Welton Gaddy, "Significant Influences of Baptists on Politics in America," *Baptist History and Heritage,* vol. 11, no. 1 (January, 1976), pp. 27-38, 62.

[27] Cf. *Southern Baptist Convention Annual, 1946,* pp. 117-119; James E. Wood, Jr., "The Work of the Baptist Joint Committee on Public Affairs," *The Quarterly Review,* vol. 25 (October-December, 1974), pp. 16-25, 84.

9

Baptist
World Outreach
and U.S.
Foreign Affairs

GLENN T. MILLER

The Baptist churches, as we know them today, were deeply influenced by three broad movements in our early national history: revivalistic pietism, the enlightenment, and foreign missions. In the eighteenth century, the area that was to become the United States was swept by a great revival that made Evangelical Calvinism a major element in American thought.[1] After the Revolution had ended, revivalism gained new power as clergy and laity united in a drive to make America a Christian nation. Enlightenment ideas also began to make an impact in the eighteenth century. Independence was justified in part on the grounds of the political philosophy of the new thought, and the New England theology of Jonathan Edwards and his successors, which deeply influenced such Baptist leaders as Isaac Backus, was indebted to both John Locke and Isaac Newton for many of its characteristic insights. The constitution of the new nation itself was the product of an attempt to apply the new insights to the problem of government.[2] Even the idea of scientific progress, a mark of enlightenment thought, was in the process of becoming an assumption shared by many Americans. The missionary movement, although in its infancy in the eighteenth century, was beginning to capture the minds and hearts of America. Early in the eighteenth century, Cotton Mather had envisioned a Christian India and was familiar with the work of the Moravians.[3] At least part of the reason for the growth of Baptists in the nineteenth century was the extent to which Baptist distinctives could be presented in terms of these broader movements.

The harmony between Baptist thought and the cultural bases of the new nation was not necessarily the result of a conscious intellectual synthesis. In some areas, such as the separation of church and state, the new nation gradually came to accept positions that were related to Baptist teaching. In other areas, Baptist distinctives gained a new self-evidence from their cultural milieu. The belief in soul liberty, for example, was reenforced by the enlightenment stress on autonomy, by the revivalistic emphasis on personal conversion, and by the spread of democratic ideals of government. That each individual was able to interpret Scripture for himself was no longer a radical position: it was part of a larger climate of opinion that made it seem to many to be simply common sense or traditional Protestantism. The harmony between Baptist beliefs and the forces shaping American religious life as a whole made Baptists part of the mainstream of American Protestant opinion.

The movements that were shaping Baptist life in the early nineteenth century had a dualistic view of the relationship between the nation and the outside world. On the one hand, each of these movements tended to view the world in terms of an internationalism that stressed the equality of individuals and the freedom of nations; on the other hand, each also contained a strongly nationalistic element that tended to exalt the new nation and its goals. Thomas Jefferson and Benjamin Franklin, the purest examples of the enlightenment type of man in America, saw no conflict between their fervent patriotism and their appreciation of international culture. Both believed that democracy would triumph around the world, but both also believed that it would be the American example that would bring about the transformation. If anything, the dualism was even more pronounced among the revivalists. They could envision a day, as the Edwardsians did, in which great divines and religious presses would arise in Africa while—in almost the same breath—predicting that America would be the harbinger of this millennial transformation. In their view, America was destined to be a redeemer nation which would be instrumental in the establishment of the kingdom of God by virtue of its unique place in God's plan for the ages.[4] Missionaries, no matter how sensitive they were to the native cultures in which they worked, often saw their work as two-fold: to preach the message of Christ and to bring the blessings of civilization and American idealism. The dualism present in these formative movements tended to pass into the Baptist understanding of the relationship between the United States and the rest of the world. Throughout Baptist history, the churches have combined—

sometimes critically, sometimes uncritically—both the internationalism and the nationalism present in the movements that shaped their early nineteenth-century development.

The historian must be cautious in making generalizations about Baptist views of foreign affairs for two reasons. First, American Protestants as a whole have not held a common perspective on the nation's role in the world. John E. Smylie in his dissertation, "Protestant Clergymen and America's World Role," concluded that "the clerical ideas of America's world role must be viewed as a complex rather than a uniform or simple doctrine. There seemed to be a uniform feeling that America had a special work to do in history. But there was difference of opinion as to what history meant and the part nations played in its fulfillment."[5] Second, one must be cautious because of the nature of Baptist faith itself. Theologically, no organization of Baptists—from the local congregations to the national conventions—can present a point of view that is binding on the membership. Baptists have agreed to disagree and often have advocated diametrically opposing points of view. Russell Conwell (1842–1925) of Philadelphia, for example, built his reputation on a sermon, "Acres of Diamonds," which praised the opportunities present in the capitalist order, while his younger contemporary, Walter Rauschenbusch (1861–1918), advocated socialism as the true fulfillment of the Christian ideal. The goal of Baptist churches has not been to create institutions through which the church presents its perspectives over and against the state but to bring into being institutions and individuals who can function democratically in a democratic state. No matter how badly the churches have failed at times, their goal has been support of responsible citizenship rather than official positions, more the functioning of democratic institutions than the uniformity of positions. There are risks in this understanding of the nature and the goal of the church—as Landmarkists and other confessionally inclined Baptists have pointed out—but Baptists, by and large, have been willing to take those risks. All histories of Baptist positions on world affairs, consequently, are histories of how some Baptist individuals and institutions understood the place of the United States among the nations.

I. THE IMPACT OF MISSIONS

Historians of missions have pointed out that the nineteenth century saw both a transformation of missions and an expansion of missionary activity.[6] Although generalizations in this area are dangerous, one can argue that the change was one in which missions moved from being primarily an official matter of state policy to being primarily a popular movement.[7] The symbol of this transformation was the rise of the various missionary societies that would serve as the sponsors of the work abroad. In England, the Baptist Missionary Society was founded in 1792, followed by the London Missionary Society in 1795, the Church Missionary Society in 1799, the British and Foreign Bible Society in 1804, and the Wesleyan Missionary Society in 1817–1818. Americans were not far behind. State organizations for missions began to be organized in 1787, and a student prayer meeting at Williams College provided the impetus for the establishment of the American Board of Commissioners for Foreign Missions in 1810. The nineteenth century would see a further expansion in the number of American sending agencies, including the development of the American system of denominational boards.

There were many factors leading to this expansion of missionary activity in the nineteenth century, but two stand out as having particular significance: the rise of evangelicalism and the popularity of millennialism. Evangelicalism continued the older Puritan emphasis on conversion. Even those who were born into a Christian society were believed to need to pass through an experience of radical personal transformation. To be saved was to be born again into a new life in Christ. This helped to bridge the gap between the pagan world and Christendom, at least theoretically, by putting all nonconverted individuals on the same level. If it was the task of the Christian to win others to Christ in London or Boston, then it was likewise the task of the Christian to win others in India and China. Moreover, evangelicalism was the sponsor of a number of reform movements that sought to transform society. Prison reform, antislavery, temperance, the education of women, and the better care of orphans were just a few of the causes which the Evangelicals advocated. Foreign missions were part of this program of active faith. Just as earthly conditions would be improved at home by social reform, so the world at large would be brought closer to the kingdom of God by the extension of the blessings of Christian society to others. To Christianize was to civilize as well as to convert. J. A. deJong in his excellent study, *As the Waters Cover the Sea,* has shown how the development of millennial thought in the seventeenth and eighteenth centuries prepared the way for nineteenth-century missionary expansion.[8] The new eschatology was not a complete revision of the older patterns of thought. Traditional ideas of hell, heaven, and the last judgment were retained, and one of the principal motivations for missionary activity was the desire to save the heathen from the wrath to come. What was changed was the interpretation of the events preceding the Last Judgment. Where traditional theology had either identified the millennial reign of Christ with the church or had seen the judgment breaking suddenly into history, the new millennialism foresaw an almost infinite period of earthly prosperity before the end of time. During this glorious period, Christ would reign on earth through the moral obedience of men to his government or kingdom. Believing that this millennium was near, missionaries went out confident of success. It was not hard for such nineteenth-century Americans as Samuel Francis Smith, Baptist editor and missionary enthusiast, to hear "sweet freedom's song" both in the national aspirations of Americans and in the work done in India.[9]

From the beginning of William Carey's famous mission to India in 1793, Baptists in the United States were interested in the world outreach of their denomination. The Philadelphia Association corresponded regularly with the London-based society, and William Staughton, the English-born pastor of the First Baptist Church of Philadelphia, wrote *The Baptist Mission in India* to help raise funds for the enterprise. By 1802, the Massachusetts Baptist Missionary Society had been organized and was sponsoring preaching tours in North America.[10] The growing interest in missions, however, revealed a weakness in Baptist polity; the churches were too separated from each other to be able to act effectively abroad. When Luther Rice and Adoniram Judson became Baptists and decided to continue their missionary labors, it was clear that Baptists needed to act. Perhaps Baptists in the United States would have developed a national organization by the slow process of joining associations together into state conventions, as occurred in South Carolina in 1821,[11] and state conventions into national bodies, but the missionary imperative sparked the organization of the first national body and sustained interest in it. Interest in foreign lands led to unity at home and the development of new structures by Baptists to enable them to meet the needs that they saw in other lands.

Although slavery must be seen as the principal factor that led to the division of Baptists into sectional organizations in 1845, it was not the only issue in the controversy. Baptists in the South were concerned with the organizational structure of the missionary enterprise. To them—as to the Old School Presbyterians—missions were not something apart from the life of the churches which could safely be entrusted to voluntary associations but were a part of the very essence of the church itself. The command to preach the gospel to all nations applied both to individuals and to churches. Consequently, they reasoned, it was necessary for the churches to take concerted action to fulfill the divine commandment. Just as each local church was to be missionary minded, so the associations and their logical extensions, the conventions, were to be missionary minded. Interestingly enough, Baptists in the North adopted a more convention-centered polity in 1907—in the midst of another period of missionary excitement.[12] For good or ill, the basic national structures of Baptist life have been related to the churches' involvement with the wider world.

Missionary activity also served to bring Baptists together spiritually. Luther Rice, who toured the eastern and southern states securing support for Judson, carried with him news of what Baptists were doing in other parts of the nation. *The Latter Day Luminator,* published in Philadelphia from 1818 to 1825, was founded to carry the news of the Baptist mission to Burma, but from the beginning it also carried articles on theology, lists of ordinations, news of various evangelical enterprises, and reports of the funds on hand. In these and other ways, the missionary movement helped to start and sustain other ministries. It is doubtful if any other Baptist enterprises, with the possible exception of some of the colleges, would have expanded at the rate that they did without the ties between them and the world missionary outreach.

Any evaluation of the impact of Baptist missionary ties on Baptist understanding of foreign affairs is of course difficult. John K. Fairbank in his presidential address to the American Historical Association in 1968, "Assignment for the '70s," wrote:

> The missionary in foreign parts seems to be the invisible man in American history. His influence at home, his reports and circular letters, his visits on furlough, his symbolic value for his home constituency seem not to have interested academic historians. . . . Mission history is a great and underused research laboratory. . . .[13]

If the general impact of missionaries on American life has been neglected, their role in foreign affairs has been, if anything, even more obscure. Joseph L. Grabill argues convincingly that historians have only begun to open up this topic, seldom going beyond the obvious statements about the economic significance of the outreach.[14] It is clear that more research is needed in this area. Nevertheless, some tentative generalizations can be made.

One of the effects of Baptist missionary activity was to create a favorable picture of the British empire in the minds of post-Revolutionary Baptists. Most early Baptist missions were located within the Empire, and Baptists from the United States cooperated with English Baptists in the establishment of missionary stations. The earliest examples of such cooperation antedate the Judson mission. The British East India Company was opposed to sending missionaries to India, because it believed that they might disrupt trade with the area and upset the people. In order to implement this policy, they refused to allow missionaries to sail on their ships which had a virtual monopoly on the England to India run. The British Baptists discovered that they could get around this restriction by sailing to the United States and taking passage there for their destination. Naturally, while in the United States, the new missionaries visited churches and presented their concerns.

The kind reception which Americans received from British Baptists also created a mood of goodwill. In the midst of the War of 1812, for example, William Carey promised to take the Americans under the protection of British Baptists so as not to interrupt their work.[15] Baptist relations with Britain also involved the very real protection which British military power provided for the missionaries and their converts. Robert G. Torbet has pointed out that "the successful spread of British rule and protection to missionaries was hailed as a boon in Burma, South India, Assam, and Bengal-Orissa."[16] Anyone familiar with the difficulties that the mission in Burma faced from the hostile local government and, in particular, from the persecution of the Karen converts can easily understand this rejoicing. British power seemed to be paving the way for the expected conversion of Asia.

Other factors were involved in the growing Baptist appreciation of the British empire. Deeply embedded in both American and British culture was a belief in the superiority of "Anglo-Saxon" institutions, laws, culture, and language.[17] To Alexander Campbell, "'No event in the future, next to the anticipated millennial triumph, appears more natural, more probable, more practicable or more morally certain and desirable, than this Anglo-Saxon triumph in the great work of human civilization and redemption.'"[18] Anglo-Saxonism was a complex phenomenon. Although it contained even in its most sensitive proponents, elements of racism, it was also a belief in the reign of law, human equality, and religious freedom. At times, it was almost a code for those elements in British and American life that the churches believed were worthy of export. In addition, Anglo-Saxonism contained prophetic elements. In looking back to the almost mythical Germanic conquest of England, many people were able to find precedents for further democratic reforms in the present. Both the Puritan and American revolutionaries had used Anglo-Saxonism in this way as part of their ideological justification for changing the structure of government. The links between this tradition and the Christianity of the Progressive Era, including the Social Gospel movement, are close. English may or may not have been "'by eminence the *religious* language'"[19] but Anglo-Saxonism helped to make it the missionary language. Wherever nineteenth-century British or American missionaries went, they brought their language with them. By the end of the nineteenth century, English was the most widely spoken language on earth.

If nothing else, the close relationship between Baptist missions and the British Empire contributed to the widespread sympathy for Britain that became evident after the settlement of the Alabama claims. Although this sympathy was partially the result of the influence of such neonativists as the Adamses and Lodges of Massachusetts, it cannot be completely understood without some understanding of the importance of missions in shaping the American mind. By the time of the First World War, the *Religious Herald,* the state Baptist paper of Virginia, could confidently state that "the sympathies of ninety-nine out of a hundred citizens of this country—not German born or of German extraction—are with the allies."[20] Respect for Britain's role in the missionary enterprise continued to shape Baptist opinion through the Second World War. In a sharp editorial on October 10, 1940, "We Must Face the Facts," the *Watchman-Examiner* called for American support of British missions, a religious equivalent to the aid policies of the government:

> The only sending country not impaired by war is the United States. American churches face an unprecedented challenge. The full weight of responsibility for the world missionary enterprise rests on the Christians of this country. *Great Britain was proportionately the greatest missionary sending country in the world before the war broke out. Her vast interests in the gospel call for outside support. . . .*[21]

The cooperation between missionary and empire, begun in the days of Carey, was a powerful influence on Baptist and other Protestant public opinion. The missionaries may have been the real architects of Anglo-American cooperation or they may have been only one factor in shaping public opinion to accept that cooperation, but it is difficult to imagine the course of events without them.

The importance of missionaries in foreign affairs, of course, was not simply a matter of public opinion. Although most missionary societies and boards attempted to follow the wise advice of Rufus Anderson—an influential secretary of the American Board of

Commissioners for Foreign Missions—to keep "the missionary and political currents of the world as distinct as possible," this was easier said than done.[22] The missionary was on the field, often the only Westerner with knowledge of the local language, customs, and laws. He or she was the natural choice as an intermediary between the local population and merchants and diplomats who had business to conduct. William A. Reid, the negotiator of the Treaty of Tientsin, in 1858, claimed, "Without them as interpreters, the public business could not be transacted. . . . There is not an American merchant in China . . . who can write or read a single sentence of Chinese. . . ."[23] In addition to their service as unofficial envoys, missionaries and their supporters at home exerted pressure on diplomats and their governments to secure the privileges which they needed for the expansion of their work. The Reverend Samuel Wells Williams, for example, was credited with securing the "religious toleration" classes of the Treaty of Tientsin which provided protection for both the missionaries and the converts in China.

American missionaries to the Near East, one of the earliest areas of American endeavor, have exerted a continuing influence on American thinking about that region.[24] Hertzel Fishman believes that the "intrusion of American missionaries, along with their Anglican and Lutheran (German) counterparts, into the Near East undoubtedly contributed to involving their respective governments in the region's problems."[25] Supporters of these missions were influential in the government following the First World War and helped to shape American policy in that troubled region. Although Baptist commitments in the area were minimal, they shared the widespread Protestant concern with the area and its problems. On March 4, 1920, the *Watchman-Examiner* challenged Baptists:

> American sentiment should not be slower [than English] in expressing itself [on the Middle East], even though we are at present deprived of a vote by the unpardonable delay in ratifying the Treaty. To leave the Turk in Constantinople, no matter how stripped of actual power there, would be to lose one of the strongest moral effects and greatest points of vantage which the world at large has looked for as a result of the world catastrophe.[26]

Fishman believes that the impact of missionary impact in the Near East still influences American Protestant thinking about the area and that it has contributed to pro-Arab sympathies in the State Department.[27]

Kenneth Scott Latourette, the great Baptist historian of missions, has argued that the nineteenth century saw a progressive separation of colonialism and missions.[28] In part, this separation reflected a change in the general nature of Western expansion. The Western imperialism of the seventeenth and eighteenth centuries had been directed primarily toward areas, like the Americas, that could be settled by Europeans. With some exceptions, the nineteenth-century version of European expansion was directed toward areas where Europeans could never hope to displace the native populations. The goal was more to civilize these regions than it was to colonize them. As a result, Baptists and other Americans felt that they could engage in what the Reverend Alexander Blackburn, a Philadelphia Baptist, called the "Imperialism of Righteousness."[29] This imperialism was based on cultural domination and was backed by the full authority of Western science and technology. Given the nineteenth-century understanding of their task, Baptist missionaries could not avoid being agents of this more subtle form of conquest. In establishing schools, hospitals, libraries, and printing presses, they helped to tear down traditional patterns of thought and authority. In being agents of Christ, they were agents of enlightenment as well.

The type of Christianity that Baptists sought to export was the enlightened pietism of the United States. But—both for financial and theological reasons—Baptist missionaries were also involved in the task of establishing self-supporting and self-governing congregations abroad. Elisha L. Abbott, a Baptist missionary to the Karens of Burma, was one of the earliest advocates of indigenous churches as the national product of missions. On January 8, 1843, he led a council in examining two of his assistants, Myat Kyaw and Tway Poh for ordination at the Magyibin church. They subsequently became strong leaders of the Karen churches. In May, 1845, the Karen Theological Seminary was opened at Moulmein, and the Karens organized their own Home Missionary Society in 1851. The policy of enabling local churches and local societies and conventions to conduct their own business proved to be very successful, especially in Burma. *Re-thinking Missions: A Laymen's Inquiry After One Hundred Years,* published in 1932, stated that "the highest percentage of self-support in East Asia, if not in the world, has been attained by the Karen [Baptist] churches in Burma, but all the churches in Burma rank high, the Baptists reporting eighty per cent and the Methodist fifty."[30] The organization of the Baptist World Alliance in 1905 reflected in part the gradual triumph of the Baptist belief in local autonomy, even on the mission fields. In the Alliance, despite the fact that the finances are largely provided by Baptists from the English-speaking countries, all constituent bodies are equal, and an attempt is made to involve all of them in decision making.

The drive for local autonomy and indigenous churches was a counterweight to the work of the missionaries as apostles of Western culture. If, on the one hand, the missionaries believed in the superiority of Western culture, they were forced to believe in the ability of non-Western peoples to assume responsibility for their own churches and missionary programs as well. American missionaries, hence, could export both sides of the contradictory view of the world implicit in their own position. Like the missionary, the faith that was exported was both nationalistic and internationalistic at the same time. In exporting this type of faith, the missionary movement also awoke the spirit of nationalism among non-Western peoples.

The missionary movement could also serve as a point of reference from which the policies of the home country could be called into question. William O. Carver, the most influential Southern Baptist missiologist during the first half of the twentieth century, realized that missions were among the factors that were creating a new world situation in Asia. In 1945, he warned Baptists that the Second World War could not be turned into yet another Western drive for expanded empire: ". . . the course which Great Britain and the United States seemed to be plotting with a view to giving a new era of extended white [Anglo-Saxon] domination leads inevitably to the speedy revolt of all Asiatic—and African—peoples. Unless radical change is quickly made in British-American policy this war will not end." [31] Other Baptists were equally perceptive. The *Religious Herald* saw great value in the reawakening of Asia:

> Ancient cultures in Asia have been suppressed and partly submerged by the aggressive impact of the West for nearly two hundred years. Late developments in the Orient indicate that the multitudes are becoming restless and resentful to the extent that they are ready to make an effort to restore part of what they have lost. Neither the people of Asia nor of Africa show any disposition to turn back. Their face is towards a future which will be defined in terms of modern understanding. . . .[32]

Most Baptists probably did not share such advanced views of the Third World situation, and developing an approach to those countries, adequate to today's situation, is still a problem confronting both Baptists and the American government. But the fact that such opinions could be expressed by Baptist spokesmen indicates that the missionary enterprise was capable of stimulating creative thinking about world affairs.

The primary influence of missions on foreign policy was probably indirect. Many Baptists learned about the world from the missionary activities of their churches, and this knowledge helped them to play a more responsible role as citizens. Kenneth Scott Latourette wrote:

> The missionary enterprise has been an important agency in educating Americans in world-mindedness. Through planning in terms of the "evangelization of the world in this generation," it has taught thousands to think in global terms. By its very nature, it has been anti-isolationist. It has helped to familiarize thousands of Americans with country after country and people after people with whom they would otherwise have had little or no direct contact. Even more significantly, the missionary enterprise has contributed a particular kind of world mindedness. It has encouraged thousands of Americans to think of the rest of the world not as a field for political or commercial empire but as an opportunity for brotherhood.[33]

In short, the missionary enterprise has been a great educational institution. It has opened the eyes of Baptists to the world around them, and—however imperfectly—has suggested the possibility of a better world order.

Baptist involvement in foreign missions, then, has been one way in which the churches have influenced the nation's conduct of foreign affairs. The missionary movement helped to cement relationships with other nations, especially Britain, which were also involved in the task; it helped to create a worldwide Baptist fellowship of free and autonomous churches; at times, it was directly involved in the making or interpretation of American foreign policy; and it stimulated thought about the wider world situation among Baptists. Like the other movements which stimulated Baptist growth, the missionary movement was frequently affected by the belief in America's special role in the world as the redeemer nation.

People, nations, societies, and churches are always products of their own times and to some extent, at least, reflections of broader cultural patterns. What is surprising is the extent to which the missionary movement enabled many Americans to escape their provincialism and narrow understandings of American self-interest. In addition, missions have had a profound effect on extra-congregational Baptist structures. Baptists owe their organization into conventions and societies in large measure to the missionary enterprise and its need for financial and spiritual support. Baptist concern with missions has been one of the dominant marks of their denominational life for two centuries, and this concern has helped them to mature as a denomination. In looking abroad, the Baptists of the United States discovered themselves at home and became united in spirit. If one goal of Baptist churches in the public area has been to create responsible citizens in a democratic state, then missions have moved Baptists as a denomination closer to that goal. Its results have not been seen in the form of dramatic church proclamations or confrontations between the churches and the state, but they have been influential as Baptist people have participated in the social, political, and cultural life of the American nation.

II. BAPTISTS AND GREAT POWER ISSUES

Although foreign missions, as was noted in the preceding section, have continued to exert an influence on Baptist thinking about foreign affairs down to the present, the twentieth century has seen a wide variety of Baptist responses to world events. The reasons for this expanded interest in foreign affairs are almost self-evident. First, the place of the United States in the world community has changed, both psychologically and actually. For good or ill, the United States has become a world power with interests throughout the world. Baptists, as well as other Americans, have had to search for new ethical categories that might guide the nation in making difficult decisions. Second, the twentieth century has been a period in which American foreign policy decisions were of crucial importance to the average American. We have fought two world wars, exerted police action in Korea, engaged in an undeclared war in Vietnam, and intervened militarily in various other countries. Both Asia and Africa have awakened to a sense of their own relative importance in the world and of their relative economic poverty. The world has become more interdependent than it was in the past. In addition, the nineteenth century's optimism about the eventual triumph of religious liberty, always an important concern for Baptists, has eroded. Despite the fact that religious liberty is now enshrined in the constitutions of most governments, it has been negated in country after country in the twentieth century. Our century ranks with the period of the Reformation and Counter-Reformation as one of the great ages of religious persecution and intolerance. In short, the times themselves have called for vigorous thought and action in defense of religious liberty and human rights.

All of the responses that Baptists have made to this rapidly changing scene cannot be examined here. However, an attempt will be made to deal with representative events and institutions that illustrate Baptist patterns of thought and action.

For Baptists in the United States, the event that began to move them toward a deeper concern with foreign affairs was the Spanish-American War. The struggle was important for two reasons: it marked a turn away from the traditional American preoccupation with North America as well as the acquisition of an overseas empire, and it symbolized America's emergence as a world power. In struggling to understand the conflict, Baptists were attempting to come to terms with the issues that were transforming America's role in the world.

As one might expect, the event did not produce a unified Baptist perspective. Prominent clergymen and laity supported intervention in Cuba; prominent clergy and laity opposed it. Some, such as R. S. Gifford Nelson, a Philadelphia Baptist, came close to the truth when they claimed that the war was the product of "base persons who disgrace journalism" by their engagement "in a display of their reckless mendacity and constitutional depravity."[34] The media, especially the newspapers, were becoming increasingly important in foreign affairs, and the churches were having difficulty understanding the media's role. Most Protestant leaders in America agreed with Charles Sheldon, the author of *In His Steps,* who believed that newspapers could be purified, if they would only remove such evident evils as sports reporting, liquor and tobacco advertising, and—that great inducement to sin—the Sunday edition. Only a crisis, such as war, led some leaders to take a more serious look at the forces shaping public opinion.

Likewise, there were prominent Baptists on both sides of the debate over the annexation of foreign territory, especially the Philippine Islands. Winthrop Hudson has argued that many of the clergy who supported annexation had to learn to do ideological somersaults in order to find moral justification for the new conquests. After all, many of these new imperialists had originally favored the war as an anti-imperialist measure designed to free Cuba from Spanish oppression. In Hudson's view, the debate was almost a classic case of a nation that had never learned to do wrong knowingly searching for supports for its actions.[35] Yet, one wonders if all Americans felt themselves on the horns of such a dilemma. Some Baptists were clearly expansionists from the beginning. On July 13, 1898, before the war had ended, the missionary leaders of various denominations met in New York to divide up the Philippines. The meeting was chaired by S. W. Duncan, the secretary of the American Baptist Missionary Union, who took an active role in the discussions. It is quite clear that the individuals present at this meeting and the institutions which they represented were prepared to act as soon as conditions permitted the sending of American personnel abroad.[36] Some of those present may not have envisioned actual annexation, but it is clear that they all anticipated a settlement of the question that would be favorable to the interests of the United States. If some Americans had never learned to do wrong knowingly, other

Americans were seemingly completely unaware of the moral issues involved and, hence, had no need for theological or ideological justifications.

Interestingly enough, two of the most important Baptist papers, the *Baptist Standard* and the *Watchman-Examiner,* maintained a basically anti-imperialist stance.[37] To the editor of *The Watchman,* George Horr, American imperialism was clearly in violation of the Declaration of Independence and the Constitution. Any war, such as the action taken against the Filipino revolutionaries, that was fought to secure foreign possessions, consequently, was clearly unjust. Horr did not believe that there was any difference between American conduct in the Islands and the conduct of other imperialist powers in their possessions. In a biting editorial, he compared the American war in the Islands with the British war in South Africa:

> Both Great Britain and the United States find themselves engaged in wars that are becoming repugnant to the moral sense of these great peoples. In both instances the forecasts of military men as to their probable duration have been ludicrously untrustworthy. . . . In both cases, the principal obstacle to a cessation of hostilities is the pride of the English speaking nation.[38]

The most that the two papers would concede to imperialist sentiment was the demand that if the Islands were annexed, which seemed to be the most probable result, the United States should hold them more as trustees than as imperial overlords.

The long-drawn-out struggle in the Islands, Winthrop Hudson has argued, tended to return Americans to their traditional anti-colonial policy, at least for a generation.[39] But this was only part of the significance of the debate and its aftermath. Just as the war showed America that it was a great power, so the debate revealed how little understanding of that status was present among Baptists in the United States. The ideological anxiety which Hudson discussed in terms of Americans' unwillingness to do wrong knowingly was partially the result of a lack of theological and political categories with which to understand the issues involved in the reality and use of power. Both sides in the debate, whether they changed part of their positions to justify annexation or not, tended to appeal to what they felt were self-evident moral axioms. In retrospect, the discussion seems to have been almost incredibly naive and shortsighted. The only lesson learned was that things had changed. Walter Rauschenbusch, the Social Gospel theologian, put this lesson in his customarily vivid language:

> We may look back regretfully at the long period of history during which we

lived in the safe isolation of ocean walls. . . . But now the growth of our youth at home is ended; the life work of manhood lies before us. The pillar of fire has lifted and moved. We must break camp and follow, though none of us have traveled the trackless future to tell whither we are going. As a nation we must learn to walk by faith and not by sight. And if we have needed the help and light of God in the past, how much more will we need him in the future.[40]

Unfortunately, the new reality did not call forth the creative thinking that would have enabled Americans to meet the next crisis more maturely.

If the Spanish-American War and the subsequent imperial expansion of the United States caught the churches off guard, the First World War found them little or no better prepared. E. T. Clark, the pastor of First Baptist Church, Winchester, Virginia, looking back at the catastrophe, claimed:

In 1917 the church was less prepared for war than was the nation. It was taken off guard, and thus being caught in the maelstrom of so terrific a force it became, in a larger sense than we realize, a part of the destructive machine of war. Our pulpits became agencies of propaganda, a large part of which we have since learned was based upon lies and falsehood.[41]

It is not hard to find statements that support Clark's reading of events.[42] In its "Report on the World Crisis," the Southern Baptist Convention of 1918 declared, "The issues at stake are not primarily personal or political. They are in essence religious. They are concerned with fundamental human rights and liberties. They touch the very foundations of moral law."[43] W. I. Hargis in the *Baptist Record* of November 8, 1917, went even further in his support of the war: "We are fighting for a principle that is dearer than life. We are fighting to establish in every land the things that Jesus brought to the world and for which he laid down his life. . . ."[44] Even the normally mild-mannered *Religious Herald* saw the war as a great religious crusade. "The great objective of the war," it declared, ". . . is nothing less than the firm establishment of our own Baptist organizing principles in the political life of the world."[45] Such strong statements, however, did not go far enough to satisfy the more war-minded in the churches. Richard H. Edmonds, a Virginia Baptist layman and newspaper editor, objected to the mild tone of the clergy.

The failure of the minister of the Gospel to cry against the barbarism of Germany, the immorality of its war and the immorality of its warfare, has done infinite harm to the cause of Christ. It has made millions of people feel that in a great emergency . . . the Church of God failed to measure up to its responsibilities and was neutral in the time of the world's most fearful immorality . . . [when] neutrality becomes immoral.[46]

Despite some reservations about the way in which religion was handled in the camps, Baptists tended to see the war as a struggle for righteousness and democracy. There was little real analysis of the underlying causes of the conflict. The war was a millennial clash between the forces of darkness and the forces of light, and those on the Lord's side were clearly visible.

Yet, in the midst of all the patriotic rhetoric, there was some uneasiness about the situation. The *Watchman-Examiner* felt that it was important to remind Baptists as follows: ". . . let us not glorify war, for war is hateful, cruel, malignant, fiendish. . . . War is a necessity in the selfishness and wickedness of our present civilization, a grim, awful, terrible necessity, but no more to be glorified than a hangman's noose which is also necessary."[47] Baptist leaders also expressed some concern that the war would brutalize both victor and vanquished. The usual justification for the conflict was a modification of the just war tradition. The churches were behind the war, because they believed that the war was the only means by which the international order could be reestablished and justice attained. In a situation of anarchy, each nation had to act as judge and jury in its own and humanity's cause. Consequently, although hatred was a natural temptation, Baptists should seek to overcome it or their belief in a juridical war would be compromised. Americans, church leaders argued, had no quarrel with the German people, only with their government. Preachers and laity were exhorted to ". . . avoid in ourselves and discourage in others . . . such highly-wrought and extravagant speech as would tend to stir up passion and wrath. . . ."[48]

There was also a sense, much stronger before America entered the conflict, that the war was a disaster. Walter Rauschenbusch had appealed to his fellow denominationalists in 1914 to wear a piece of crepe on their coat lapels,[49] and he continued to be deeply bothered by the war until his death in 1918. At least part of the problem was that many Baptists were not able to put the war into perspective. E. Y. Mullins, the president of Southern Baptist Seminary, was particularly concerned with this issue in his article, "The Vision of the Preacher Against the Background of the World War." In addition to the usual warnings against hatred, he argued: "Wars deceive us by their nearness. They are like punctuation marks in a sentence, but never the sentence or history that God is writing."[50] The need for such insights would grow as the war progressed and the period of anxiety that followed began, but few were around who sensed the need.

In the main, Baptists did not encourage conscientious objection to the First World War. In part, this was because of the heavy emphasis on the justice of the Allied cause. If justice was in fact the issue, many Baptists believed, then—no matter how distasteful war might be—it was the duty of Christians to do their part in securing victory. The belief that the war was being fought to protect Western civilization, democracy, and Christianity also influenced Baptist thinking. To refuse to serve seemed to many to be a repudiation of the deepest values on which American society was based. But, despite these feelings and the war hysteria that intensified them, there were some who argued for full respect for individual conscience. In words that echoed the theological foundations of the Baptist doctrine of soul liberty, J. E. White, a pastor in Anderson, South Carolina, reminded his fellow Baptists:

> Our consciences do not belong to our country and certainly our consciences do not belong to our government. The Christian citizen should sharply discriminate between his country and its government, and if his conscience acknowledges God only as its master, not even allowing his country supreme authority over it, he should feel free to maintain his conscience whenever his conscience puts his country wrong with his conscience.[51]

The post-war world was not the utopia that many Baptists had envisioned during the conflict. Almost as soon as the firing had stopped, the idealistic goals which Baptists had supported as part of their justification of the conflict began to be abandoned by the victorious powers. The tendency to return to older ways of doing things, based on narrow definitions of national self-interest, was too great to resist. The disappointment that resulted from this return to normalcy affected some of those Baptists who had supported the war deeply. Using language usually reserved for the advocates of the liquor trade, the *Religious Herald* declared:

> The other nations will take us on our own terms, for without us, their league is a wreck and all their gains from a victorious peace are imperilled.
> We venture to assert that in no public document ever drawn by men of our own country, can be found an utterance so cynically indifferent to all that is noble and lofty in national policy, so sordid, so vile, so contemptible as this, quoted from Senator Lodge's report to the Senate on the League of Nations. No wonder that Senator McCumber denounced that report as "selfish and immoral."[52]

In retrospect, then, E. T. Clark was right; the churches had been taken off guard by the course of events. The war and the peace that followed it were far from what had been anticipated by either leadership or people. Edward B. Pollard, of Crozer Theological

Seminary, had exposed a raw nerve in 1917 when he called on Baptists "for a concerted effort to strike intelligently and effectively for religious liberty" at the end of the conflict.[53] His was a noble call and a worthy goal for the denomination, but the churches were not structurally prepared to respond to it. The Baptist response to the First World War dramatically illustrates the fact that Baptists did not have either sufficient research agencies or lobbying organizations to do more than have a sporadic effect on the course of world events. Unfortunately, little would be done to change this state of affairs until the widespread attack on religious liberty in the 1930s forced Baptists to become active in defense of their principles.

By 1934, when the Baptist World Alliance met in Berlin, it was clear that serious trouble was brewing in Europe. The *Religious Herald,* responding to events abroad and at home, warned Baptists that anti-Semitism was an "un-Christian temper."[54] Although the pre-meeting publicity for the Alliance made it clear that "expressions of international Baptist opinion cannot be expected to be in line with those of the *Deutsche Christen . . . ,"*[55] Baptists do not appear to have been fully aware of the dangers inherent in the Nazi position. In retrospect, the fact that the meeting was held in Berlin with the cooperation of the German government must be seen as one of Hitler's early triumphs in the area of public relations. The meeting of the Alliance, if nothing more, was excellent training for the later success of the Olympic Games in 1936. Significantly, the meeting directed its strongest protest against Russia which, then as now, persecuted Baptist believers. "This World Congress of Baptists representing sixty countries makes its strong protest against the increasingly severe repression of religion in Russia. We express our deep sympathy with all those who are suffering for their faith, and especially with our Baptist brethren. . . ."[56]

The greatest threat to worldwide religious liberty in the period was the worldwide revival of anti-Semitism. Even in the United States, there was a revival of this ancient prejudice in the hands of such groups as the Ku Klux Klan, the Silver Shirts, and the followers of Father Charles E. Coughlin's broadcasts from the Shrine of the Little Flower. Although this revival did not threaten the American tradition of religious liberty, it was a symptom of the extent of the problem. As early as 1920, the *Watchman-Examiner* had supported a Jewish homeland in Palestine,[57] but the growth of the problem in the thirties moved it in a more decidedly "Zionist" direction. In 1938, it declared:

All this [the revival of anti-Semitism] means that the Jews need a National

Home all the more. They need it for purposes of solidarity in order to meet the spreading attack. They need it to influence the democracies not to be so superior and offhand in the matter of dealing with oppressed Jews. They need it for political, economic and religious imperatives, which neither Great Britain nor any of the other democracies can deny them. And just as the partitioning of Palestine idea is dead, so are the plans to emigrate suffering Jews to the uncivilized parts of the earth.[58]

The prospect of a reborn Israel led the editor to prophesy that "soon the highways of the world will be filled with Jews returning to their native home. No temporizing on the part of Great Britain will be able to hinder the movement now definitely in action. . . ."[59] Unfortunately, the editor had a greater grasp of what ought to have occurred than he did of what could or would be done.

Baptist fascination with the return of the Jews was part of a larger pattern of American interest in the Holy Land. In the nineteenth century, Americans had been leaders in the study of Palestinian geography, and accounts of the Holy Land, written by travelers, were popular reading among all levels of the population. But, even more important, the land of Israel had theological significance. The return of the Jews to Israel was widely believed by both pre- and postmillennialists to be a sign of the coming of the kingdom. In 1948, the *Watchman-Examiner* was confident that the return of the Jews was a literal fulfillment of biblical prophecy.

> But, whether we understand all phases of the situation or not, there is before us an evident fulfillment of prophecy which enables the Bible student to know the line events of the immediate future will take. Israel cannot be restored except in the divine plan and purpose. If Israel is now being restored, then, as we interpret the Bible, history is rapidly approaching its climax.[60]

The millennial tradition, which was so influential in the missionary movement, also helped to shape attitudes on other world problems.

Events abroad were moving too fast for the Baptist structures of the time to function effectively. There was a need for communication with both the American and foreign governments that went beyond either resolutions passed by conventions or the ability of editors and other Baptist leaders to mobilize public opinion. The process of creating these new organizational forms, considering the gravity of the situation in Europe, was painfully slow. In 1936, the Southern Baptist Convention moved to reconstitute its Committee on Chaplains as a Committee on Public Relations. The duty of the new committee was

> . . . as situations arise, in which agencies of this Convention are compelled to confer, to negotiate, to demand just rights that are being threatened or

have other inescapable dealings with the American or other Governments, this Committee shall function, when so requested by any existing board or agency of this body, as the representative of Southern Baptists and shall report in detail to the Southern Baptist Convention the results of such conferences and negotiations.[61]

In 1937, American Baptists took a similar action. The link between the two committees was originally the person of Rufus W. Weaver, a member of both Committees and the Executive Secretary of the District of Columbia Baptist Convention. In 1939, the National Baptist Convention also authorized the creation of a Public Relations Committee. Although the process of creating a Joint Committee out of these three institutionally separate organizations was long and drawn out, the committees began to work together shortly after their formation.

The crisis that initially brought the committees together was the Roumanian attack on religious liberty. The Roumanian Ministry of Cults and Arts issued a decree, which was to go into effect October 12, 1937, that would have had the effect of closing almost all the Baptist churches in that country. The decree outlawed certain cults, such as the Millerites and Russelites, demanded that every church have one hundred male members, prohibited religious "proselytism" and the distribution of religious literature, and placed restrictions on the locations of church buildings. The Public Relations Committees of both Northern and Southern Conventions protested the act to the U.S. State Department which received assurances that the Baptist churches would be exempted by a new decree. These assurances were to prove worthless, and the Committees continued to protest to the Roumanian ambassador, Radu Irimescu, that Baptists in the United States considered the decree to be "unjust and repressive."[62] In response to this continuing crisis, the American and Southern Baptist Committees on Public Relations met together for the first time, September 15-16, 1938. The committees jointly appealed again to the ambassador to urge his government to repeal the law and—at the same time—authorized Rufus W. Weaver, A. L. Burton, and William Abernethy to draft a pamphlet to present the Baptist position to the public. This pamphlet, *The Roumanian Crisis*,[63] contained the text of the decree after its initial modification, the Associated Committees' appeal to the Roumanian government, a demand for religious toleration from the Federal Council of Churches, recommendations from the Baptist World Alliance, and an appeal by George W. Truett calling for prayer by Baptists around the world. After a brief period of persecution, the Baptist churches of Roumania were given permission to reopen. Rufus W. Weaver, who had been one of the leaders of the protest, attributed this result to the worldwide outcry against the law and to pressure from the U.S. State Department.

> Many factors have played a part in the change of attitude by the Rumanian Government—the world-wide protest sponsored by the Baptist World Alliance, the co-operation of other Christian bodies, the delicate international situation in which Rumania found itself and not least, but probably the greatest, the pressure of our own Government through the Department of State.[64]

The Associated Committees, however, should be given at least most of the credit. By acting together, the committees were able to help mobilize public and church opinion and to secure the cooperation of other institutions in attaining a common objective.

The Associated Committees, joined by the National Baptists in 1939, continued to be concerned with the worldwide threat to religious liberty and with ways to make Baptists and other Americans aware of the seriousness of the situation. One product of this emphasis was the adoption of the American Baptist Bill of Rights by the three Conventions in their annual meetings in 1939. Although the document quite properly dealt with both domestic and foreign issues, its preamble made it clear that it was largely a response to the deteriorating conditions abroad.

> No issue in modern life is more urgent or more complicated than the relation of organized religion to organized society. The sudden rise of the European dictators to power has changed fundamentally the organic law of the governments through which they exercise sovereignty, and as a result, the institutions of religion are either suppressed or made subservient to the ambitious national programs of these new totalitarian states.[65]

The American Baptist Bill of Rights was primarily a declaration of principles and beliefs, a confession of faith. It stressed the Baptist ideal of free churches in a free state and corporate responsibility of Baptists to work to make this ideal a reality. It is difficult for the historian to appraise the significance of such declarations. They do not immediately result in new policies or in programs of concerned action, but in a democratic state, their significance may be far-reaching. They serve as part of that matrix of ideas, social forces, and political actions that shape public opinion on a wide variety of issues. In terms of Baptist opinion, the American Baptist Bill of Rights can be seen as part of a maturing process through which Baptists have increasingly come to an awareness of the issues that evangelical faith faces in a ruthless and undemocratic world.

The Far East also occupied Baptist attention in this period. China had long had a romance about it in the eyes of American Christians, perhaps stemming from the days of the clipper ships or even from the medieval legends of Prester John, and America supplied a large percentage of the missionaries to that nation.[66] The Japanese invasion of China, consequently, aroused deep concern among American Baptists, particularly when the Japanese seized the University of Shanghai, a Baptist institution. Pressure was brought on Japan to return the property to Baptist control, but—aside from an unkept promise—the effort was in vain. Many missionaries were further angered by what they believed was American complacency in the China War. J. Hundley Wiley, a Baptist missionary in China, wrote home: "One of the things that has given trouble to the conscience of the missionary has been the unofficial aid rendered by America to Japan. In the last seventeen months the Pacific Ocean has been dotted with ships filled to the gunwales with material which Japan has used in her conquest."[67] Perhaps the policy of mobilizing public opinion and influencing the State Department to put pressure on Japan would have been successful in more normal times, but in the context of worsening relations with Japan, it was futile.

One other major issue on which Baptists failed to influence American policy was the appointment of Myron C. Taylor as President Franklin Roosevelt's personal representative to the Vatican with the rank of ambassador in 1939. This was both a domestic and a foreign issue. Rufus W. Weaver expressed the most commonly held Baptist position in these words: "The distinctive theory, upon which this government has been founded, is the absolute separation of church and State, and any recognition, implied or otherwise, of the political status of any ecclesiastical organization constitutes, in our judgment, an assault upon this principle."[68] The issue was debated throughout Taylor's tenure. When he resigned in 1949, Baptists, acting through their Baptist Joint Committee—as the Associated Committees were now called— expressed concern over the appointment of a successor and attempted to get their case before the public. Although many felt that these fears were unrealistic at the time, the attempt to appoint General Mark Clark as a full ambassador in 1951, possibly with a view to influencing the Catholic vote in the 1952 elections, proved that the fears were well grounded. The proposed appointment was defeated in the House of Representatives when the budget line for the mission to the Vatican was deleted.

The individual who led the fight against the embassy in Rome was Joseph M. Dawson, Executive Director of the Baptist Joint Committee on Public Affairs, a position which had been created in

1946. Dawson himself was an extraordinary leader and an ideal choice to lead the committee. He had been pastor of the First Baptist Church of Waco, "Texas's mother church," and had been noted for his controversial stands on social issues. It is difficult to classify Dawson theologically, politically, or socially. A warm evangelical, he reminds the historian most of Walter Rauschenbusch in the breadth and depth of his concerns, but with more of a practical knowledge of politics—perhaps learned in the rough and tumble struggles among Texas Baptists—than Weaver had possessed.

Dawson's great strength was as a publicist. His *Battle for America: An Ambassador to the Vatican* and his contributions to the *Report from the Capital,* which he founded, on the issue of representation in Rome were clear, hard-hitting statements of Baptist thinking on church-state problems. Although Dawson did try to influence the executive branch of the government—at one point, Truman refused to meet with him because of his persistence on the issue—Dawson realized that American policy was the product of the interaction of many factors. By presenting his case to the people, Dawson was able to help shape the congressional thinking that finally defeated the obnoxious measure. The final result, of course, was not simply the result of Baptist actions. Other evangelical denominations brought pressure on Congress, and many Americans who were not Baptists were suspicious of the issue, but one cannot underemphasize the effects of Dawson's carefully mounted campaign of public pressure on the issue.

Thanks in part to the earlier work of the Associated Committees and to general changes in American Protestant opinion, Baptists faced the Second World War with more sophistication than they had faced the earlier world crisis. Although there was a wide variety of Baptist positions on the conflict, including the pacifism of such prominent Baptists as Harry Emerson Fosdick, most Baptist leaders took the position that the war was a horrible necessity. There was little of the crusading or quick moralistic judgments that had characterized the earlier struggle. The major attention of Baptists was on the peace that would emerge from the war.

Joseph M. Dawson was a convinced supporter of the United Nations and one of many Baptists who worked to see that the new world organization got a fair hearing and reasonable public support. Like many Baptists, he hoped that the United Nations would be a powerful advocate of religious liberty throughout the world, but his thought on the subject was tempered by realism. In an address to the Baptist World Alliance, he stated:

Under the searchlight of Christianity, candor compels us to admit that [the] UN is not perfect, but sincerity insists that we accept it as being the nearest practical answer to the Christian demands. We know now that no one nation has enough wisdom and virtue and resources to resuscitate, rebuild and redirect our poor devastated world. We know that no nation can any longer live to itself. All nations must, as best they can, draw together, and live and struggle onward and upward together. [69]

Dawson's attitude may not have been representative of all Baptists, but it was probably shared by the leadership of the various Baptist groups. It symbolizes an increasingly realistic search for means to obtain limited goals. One might dream of worldwide religious liberty, but one supported the United Nations, despite its imperfections.

The post-war period also saw the Baptist Joint Committee protesting the denial of religious liberty around the world. Fascist Spain was a major offender as were Colombia, Russia, and the other Communist nations. The Baptist position was that any denial of religious rights was a support for tyranny, and the committee hoped that the United States would consider human rights in making its foreign policy and aid agreements. Unfortunately, the type of ideological purity in international relations that such consideration would entail was becoming increasingly difficult for the nation. The United States was a great power, engaged in periodic conflict and constant competition with the Soviet Union. In the light of this situation, the nation felt that it had to take its allies where they could be found and not impose the American system on other countries. The need for bases in Spain, for example, was more important to the nation's military position than was the denial of civil liberties to a segment of the Spanish population. Present-day American questioning of such great power politics, which has served to ally the United States with some of the most autocratic regimes in the world, however, may open the way for a reevaluation of American policy.

Stanley L. Hastey, in his dissertation, "A History of the Baptist Joint Committee on Public Affairs, 1946–1971," believes that the focus of the Baptist Joint Committee changed during the period in which C. Emmanuel Carlson headed the agency, 1954–1971.[70] The Committee moved to assume more of the posture of a research and information bureau than of an agency of political action. In part, this was because of the difference in temperament between Joseph M. Dawson, the first Executive Director (1946-1953), and his successor. Dawson was a former pastor and activist; in contrast, Carlson came to the position from a career in academic life and brought to it the concerns of an educator. He had a fear of quick and easy answers to complex questions and believed that the agency could best serve its people by careful analysis of major questions, the progressive education of the churches, and the development of a Baptist consensus. In order to attain these goals, he led the agency to undertake a thorough study of its philosophy and organization and brought together leading Baptists to help investigate the theological meaning of historical positions.

Carlson's program should be evaluated in the light of the history of Baptist responses to foreign affairs. As we have seen, the churches and their leaders were often unprepared to act on many of the most important issues on the international stage. As a result, some Baptist leaders were tempted simply to repeat platitudes that sounded right but which did not deal adequately with the problem at hand. Carlson's approach, although perhaps too academic for some Baptists, was an attempt to meet this serious problem. The impact of Carlson's leadership is hard to determine. *Report from the Capital* did not become required reading for either pastors or laity, although Carlson himself was a popular speaker, and the more theological projects which he encouraged appear to have reached only a small number. His great influence was probably on the leadership of the churches—influential pastors, state Baptist editors, convention executives, and theological instructors—in short, on the makers of Baptist opinion. It was through them that he reached the average church members and helped them to understand the issues facing the nation.

The advantages of Carlson's style of leadership are identical with its disadvantages. Unfortunately, the scholar is seldom a charismatic leader, and the rapid mobilization of public opinion— unfortunately—depends on individuals who can exert an immediate influence on the media and on other individuals and institutions that shape that opinion. If Baptists needed the type of scholarly leadership in the public area that Carlson provided, they also needed a prophetic voice that could rally them around the issues that confronted the nation in the nineteen fifties and sixties. In this period, it was far too easy for Baptists and other Americans to rely on the nation's military and economic power to solve the problems of a troubled world. But, noting the need for such a charismatic voice, paradoxically, affirms the basic soundness of Carlson's insight. Baptists have, by and large, been fortunate in the quality of their leadership. They have never lacked persons who were charismatic or who had the ability to take prophetic stands. The need has been for these resources to be developed to the point where they were able to make the maximum impact on the society as a whole.

The tendency to concentrate responsibility for foreign concerns, apart from missions, in the Baptist Joint Committee has been both good and bad. On the positive side, it reflects a realization on the part of Baptists that ad hoc committees, church papers, and even individual convention agencies cannot deal with world problems without the broader Baptist cooperation in research and action provided by the Committee structure. In today's world, the churches must be represented in the nation's capital where their representatives can monitor events and where they can make their opinions known to those who hold and exercise power. In a democratic state, it is the obligation of every group that is concerned with the nation's welfare to make its positions known and to see that its perspectives receive a fair hearing. To refuse to act as a group is to refuse to exercise one's rights. It is particularly important that Baptists do this collectively. The different Baptist conventions have been divided by historical forces, such as racial prejudice, sectionalism, and minor differences in theological interpretation, that obscure the deeper bonds that hold them together. United, the Baptist movement is a more powerful force for righteousness than any convention taken by itself could possibly be. In working on national and international problems, perhaps Baptists can also form some perspective on the issues that divide their communions. Baptist concern with foreign missions helped to unite Baptists at the beginning of the nineteenth century, and one can only hope that Baptist concern with the nation's problems will have a similar effect today.

On the negative side, despite the broad representation on the committee, the structure has had to rely on a limited staff with a limited budget. Although this essay has tended to concentrate on the role of the Joint Committee in foreign affairs, it should be remembered that the committee is also concerned with domestic matters, including the important area of church-state relations. The result has been that the Executive Director has had to be very selective in the choice of issues to be researched and on which action is to be urged. That Baptists have been unusually fortunate in the quality of men who have provided leadership in this role should not be an excuse to ignore the problem. In part, the limitations of the Joint Committee are rooted in a Baptist theological difficulty. As a denomination, despite the presence of prophetic leaders, Baptists have not developed a theology of social action and political responsibility that takes seriously the need for collective action on the part of the churches. The tendency has been to interpret belief in liberty in overly individualistic terms that lose sight of its political implications. One of the key insights that has come from the Joint Committee's work is the necessity of doing well that theological homework.

III. SUMMARY

This essay has attempted to give an overview of how Baptists have thought about America's world role and how they have influenced the nation's conduct of its foreign affairs. The interpretation has not sought to be exhaustive. Not only could other individuals and institutions have been chosen for emphasis, but also this study has not dealt with the long history of resolutions passed by Baptist conventions—state, local, or national—nor has it attempted to appraise the significance of those resolutions. Two elements in Baptist history have been stressed: the missionary movement that was crucial and remains crucial for Baptist thinking about foreign affairs and the responses of representative individuals and institutions to the issues raised by America's status as a great power. The analysis of these two strains hopefully will provide the reader with some insights into how Baptists have struggled with the question of how to be responsible citizens in a democratic state.

NOTES

[1]Since the publication of Alan Heimert, *Religion and the American Mind: From the Great Awakening to the Revolution* (Cambridge: Harvard University Press, 1966), there has been a lively debate over the role of Evangelical Calvinism in the nation's early history. Although many areas need further investigation, it is clear that the perspective of the Awakeners had political and social implications.

[2]See Bernard Bailyn, *The Ideological Origins of the American Revolution* (Cambridge: The Belknap Press of Harvard University Press, 1967); Caroline Robbins, *The Eighteenth Century Commonwealth Men* (Cambridge: Harvard University Press, 1959).

[3]J. A. de Jong, *As the Waters Cover the Sea: Millennial Expectations in the Rise of Anglo-American Missions, 1640–1810.* (Amsterdam: Kampen, Kok, 1970).

[4]C. C. Goen, "Jonathan Edwards: A New Departure in Eschatology," *Church History,* vol. 28 (March, 1959), pp. 25-40. G. T. Miller, "Images of the Future in Eighteenth-Century American Theology, *"Amerikastudien,* vol. 20 (Spring, 1972), pp. 25-40. Ernest Lee Tuveson, *Redeemer Nation: The Idea of America's Millenial Role* (Chicago: The University of Chicago Press, 1974).

[5]John Edwin Smylie, "Protestant Clergymen and America's World Role" (Th.D. diss., Princeton Theological Seminary, 1959), p. 560.

⁶ See Kenneth Scott Latourette, *A History of the Expansion of Christianity,* 7 vols. (New York: Harper & Row, Publishers, 1939–1945), especially vol. 4, *The Great Century: In Europe and the United States of America;* vol. 5, *The Great Century: In the Americas, Australasia, and Africa,* and vol. 6, *The Great Century: In Northern Africa and Asia.* Also his "Colonialism and Missions: Progressive Separation," *Journal of Church and State,* vol. 7 (Autumn, 1965), pp. 330-349.

⁷ Latourette, "Colonialism and Missions," pp. 348-349.

⁸ de Jong, *As the Waters Cover the Sea.*

⁹ Smith was the author of both "My Country, 'Tis of Thee!" and "The Lone Star," a poem that encouraged Baptists to continue their outreach in India, even when finances were very low.

¹⁰ Robert G. Torbet, *Venture of Faith: The Story of the American Baptist Foreign Mission Society and the Woman's American Baptist Foreign Mission Society, 1814–1954* (Philadelphia: Judson Press, 1955), pp. 8-13.

¹¹ Robert Baker, *The Southern Baptist Convention and Its People, 1607–1972* (Nashville: Broadman Press, 1974), p. 130. The author takes the view that the convention system was implicit in early Baptist associationalism.

¹² See Paul A. Varg, "Motives in Protestant Missions, 1890–1917," *Church History,* vol. 23 (March, 1954), pp. 68ff.

¹³ Cited in Joseph L. Grabill, "The 'Invisible' Missionary: A Study in American Foreign Relations," *Journal of Church and State,* vol. 14 (Winter, 1972), pp. 93-105.

¹⁴ *Ibid.* See also Joseph L. Grabill, *Protestant Diplomacy and the Near East: Missionary Influence on American Policy, 1810–1927* (Minneapolis: University of Minnesota Press, 1971); Clifton J. Phillips, *Protestant America and the Pagan World: The First Half Century of the American Board of Commissioners for Foreign Missions, 1815–1860* (Cambridge: Harvard University Press, 1969); Valentin H. Rabe, "The American Foreign Mission Movement, 1880–1890" (Ph.D. diss., Harvard University, 1965); Smylie, "Protestant Clergymen and America's World Role."

¹⁵ Robert Baker, *A Baptist Source Book: With Particular Reference to Southern Baptists* (Nashville: Broadman Press, 1966), p. 59. Baker dates the letter December 20, 1812.

¹⁶ Torbet, *Venture of Faith,* p. 121.

¹⁷ James E. Wood, Jr., "Anglo-Saxon Supremacy and Protestant Missions in the Nineteenth Century," in *The Teacher's Yoke: Studies in Memory of Henry Trantham* (Waco: Baylor University Press, 1964), pp. 215-231.

¹⁸ Cited in *ibid.,* p. 225.

¹⁹ Cited in *ibid.* p. 226.

²⁰ *Religious Herald* (September, 1914).

²¹ *Watchman-Examiner,* October 10, 1940, p. 1072, italics added.

[22] Cited in Arthur Schlesinger, Jr., "The Missionary Enterprise and Imperialism," in John K. Fairbank, ed., *The Missionary Enterprise in China and America* (Cambridge: Harvard University Press, 1974), pp. 351-352.

[23] Cited in Schlesinger, "The Missionary Enterprise and Imperialism," p. 348.

[24] Grabill, *Protestant Diplomacy.*

[25] Hertzel Fishman, *American Protestantism and a Jewish State* (Detroit: Wayne State University Press, 1973), p. 23.

[26] *Watchman-Examiner,* March 4, 1920, p. 304.

[27] Fishman, *American Protestantism and a Jewish State,* pp. 178-183.

[28] Latourette, "Colonialism and Missions: Progressive Separation."

[29] Schlesinger, "The Missionary Enterprise and Imperialism," p. 356.

[30] William Ernest Hocking, Chrm., The Commission of Appraisal, *Re-thinking Missions: A Laymen's Inquiry After One Hundred Years* (New York: Harper & Row, Publishers, 1932), p. 88.

[31] W. O. Carver, "America and Russia," *Baptist Standard,* July 26, 1941.

[32] *Religious Herald,* April 14, 1955.

[33] Kenneth Scott Latourette, *Missions and the American Mind* (Indianapolis: National Foundation Press. 1948), pp. 35-36.

[34] Cited in Smylie, "Protestant Clergymen and America's World Role," p. 395.

[35] Winthrop S. Hudson, "Protestant Clergy Debate the Nation's Vocation, 1898–1899," *Church History,* vol 42 (Winter, 1973), pp. 110-118.

[36] Torbet, *Venture of Faith,* p. 351.

[37] Ivor B. Thomas, "A Baptist Anti-Imperialist Voice: George Horr and *The Watchman,*" *Foundations,* vol. 18 (October–December, 1975), pp. 340-357.

[38] *Ibid.,* p. 355.

[39] Hudson, "Protestant Clergy," pp. 116-118.

[40] *Ibid.,* p. 118.

[41] E. T. Clark, letter in *Religious Herald,* November 16, 1939, p. 10.

[42] Ray H. Abrams, *Preachers Present Arms,* reprint ed. (Scottdale, Pa.: Herald Press, 1969).

[43] *Southern Baptist Convention Annual, 1918,* "Report on the World Crisis."

[44] Cited in George P. Kelsey, *Social Ethics Among Southern Baptists, 1917–1969* (Metuchen, N. J.: Scarecrow Press, 1973), p. 107.

[45] *Ibid.*

[46] Richard H. Edmonds, in reply to remarks by E. Y. Mullins, *Religious Herald,* August 8, 1918.

[47] *Watchman-Examiner,* April 19, 1917, p. 494.

[48] *Watchman-Examiner,* April 12, 1917, p. 454.

[49] *Religious Herald,* October 8, 1914.

[50] *Religious Herald,* July 4, 1918.

[51] *Religious Herald,* February 28, 1918.

[52] *Religious Herald,* September 25, 1919.

[53] *Watchman-Examiner,* September 20, 1917, p. 1211.

[54] *Religious Herald,* September 20, 1934, p. 11.

[55] Press release cited in *Religious Herald,* June 28, 1934, p. 9.

[56] Cited in *Religious Herald,* September 13, 1934, p. 16.

[57] *Watchman-Examiner,* March 4, 1920, p. 304.

[58] *Watchman-Examiner,* December 22, 1938, p. 1348.

[59] *Watchman-Examiner,* October 27, 1938, p. 1148.

[60] *Watchman-Examiner,* June 3, 1948, p. 567.

[61] Stanley LeRoy Hastey, "A History of the Baptist Joint Committee on Public Affairs, 1946–1971" (Th.D. diss., Southern Baptist Theological Seminary, 1973), pp. 17-18.

[62] *Ibid.,* p. 27.

[63] Rufus Washington Weaver, *The Roumanian Crisis* (Washington D.C.: American Baptist Survey Commission, 1938).

[64] Hastey, "A History of the Baptist Joint Committee," p. 32.

[65] *The American Baptist Bill of Rights* (Washington, D.C.: Associated Committees on Public Relations, 1940), p. 2.

[66] See M. Searle Bates, "The Theology of American Missionaries in China, 1900–1950," in Fairbank, ed., *The Missionary Enterprise in China and America,* pp. 135-137.

[67] *Religious Herald,* January 26, 1939, p. 9.

[68] Cited in Hastey, "A History of the Baptist Joint Committee," p. 35. See also Anson Phelps Stokes, *Church and State in the United States,* 2 vols. (New York: Harper & Row, Publishers, 1950), vol. 2, p. 101. For a discussion of the response of all Protestants, see vol. 2, pp. 96-112.

[69] Cited in *Religious Herald,* August 28, 1947, p. 20.

[70] Hastey, "A History of the Baptist Joint Committee," pp. 103-180. My evaluation of Dawson is deeply indebted to Hastey who gives an excellent description of the man and his work.

PART
FOUR

Religious Liberty
and
Public Policy

Religious Liberty
and
Public Policy

JAMES RALPH SCALES

On the steps of the Capitol in 1920 George W. Truett proclaimed the distinctives of Baptist faith and practice. Like Pericles summoning the Athenians to recall the sources of their greatness, Truett provided a synthesis of the very best in our tradition, and none of us expects to improve on it fifty-six years later. It was, of course, an unapologetic, self-congratulatory review of our polity from a pulpit genius at the height of his powers. My own father was among those present, giving witness throughout his life to the lifting force of a great vision as enunciated by the most famous Southern preacher of his day. Truett's was a legendary presence. When he claimed for the Baptist people a preferred status in the pantheon of Christian heroes, he created and embodied our self-image. Multitudes felt ennobled by his preaching and lived out their lives in undeviating agreement with the beliefs he expressed that day. Such was the scope of his influence, the grandeur of George Truett's character, the exalted theme of his discourse, the majesty of his rhetoric. Outside the sacred canon, there are few masterpieces which all of us can claim with pride as our common possession. Here is one. The heart of the Truett message has been widely quoted:

> Baptists have one consistent record concerning liberty throughout all their long and eventful history. They have never been a party to oppression of conscience. They have forever been the unwavering champions of liberty, both religious and civil. Their contention now is, and has been, and, please God, must ever be, that it is the natural and fundamental and indefeasible right of every human being to worship God or not, according to the

dictates of his conscience, and, as long as he does not infringe upon the rights of others, he is to be held accountable alone to God for all religious beliefs and practices. Our contention is not for mere toleration, but for absolute liberty. There is a wide difference between toleration and liberty. Toleration implies that somebody falsely claims the right to tolerate. Toleration is a concession, while liberty is a right. Toleration is a matter of expediency, while liberty is a matter of principle. Toleration is a gift from man, while liberty is a gift from God. It is the consistent and insistent contention of our Baptist people, always and everywhere, that religion must be forever voluntary and uncoerced, and that it is not the prerogative of any power, whether civil or ecclesiastical, to compel men to conform to any religious creed or form of worship, or to pay taxes for the support of a religious organisation to which they do not belong and in whose creed they do not believe. God wants free worshippers and no other kind.[1]

We still need to hear Truett's words. Our world is in disarray, the people distracted, and the national purpose confused. We pray for miracles of leadership that will recapture the dream, renew our consensus, and reawaken our sense of destiny. But in spite of fervent appeals for national rededication, we risk a response of massive boredom. That happened in the Civil War centennial years, 1961 to 1965, when we grew not inspired but restless and then indifferent. Let me suggest that one of the reasons for our apathy is that in two hundred years—more accurately, 185 years—we have come to take the Bill of Rights for granted. We have come to agree with E. Y. Mullins, the scholar, and George Truett, the orator, who proclaimed that religious liberty was as nearly absolute as any safeguarded by constitutions or practiced as a natural right without protection of law.[2]

This liberty is not absolute, as we shall see: many a vigilant citizen has found occasion, with increasing frequency in recent years, to ring the alarm bells. But a dispassionate observer must say that religious freedom has been enlarged these two hundred years despite the unconcern of the mass of the population. The wall against establishment has not been breached. The constitutional limitations have restrained governments more powerful than any complained of in 1776 or any that might have been prophesied in 1791, when the Bill of Rights was adopted. Nor has the Church, in A. C. Reid's compelling phrase, "permitted itself to be joined in unholy wedlock with the State."[3]

Despite the widespread indifference we have noted, and despite the inroads of irrationalism and skepticism, the First Amendment freedoms are, without exception, more firmly entrenched than when Truett spoke in Washington, D.C., in 1920. The world of ideas has been opened up by what Dean Rusk called "the aspiration explosion of our time." Our own people are better educated. The number of seminary graduates in our pulpits has grown exponentially in the last two generations. The remarkable influence of fourscore Baptist colleges cannot be ignored. Such watchdogs as the Baptist Joint Committee on Public Affairs have alerted those seriously concerned about constitutional issues. Our example of religious liberty has become worldwide in its force. Even in the most stultifying societies, we have seen some relaxation of dogma. We would be well advised not to give all the credit to the American example. I traveled most of the past month in Latin America and saw some evidence of John XXIII and felt the fresh air of reform in the Roman Catholic Church. There are still sharp contrasts between city and rural parishes, but in nearly all communions, many changes have been adopted, nearly all of them in the direction of freedom.

I accept as historically correct the views we have been hearing about our origins and the greatness of our ancestors. The scholar's big word for that worshipful attitude is filiopietistic. How did it happen that such genius was concentrated in a few colonies, with results so providential to humanity? How did it happen that the eighteenth-century rationalists provided the greatest shelter and safeguard for religious faith? It is ironic, perhaps, that the ideas of Thomas Jefferson and James Madison have been sustained and strengthened in the twentieth century by the constitutional challenges of an especially contentious group known as Jehovah's Witnesses.

The pulpit and the lectern must speak to a very different world from that of Jefferson and Madison, or even Mullins and Truett. It is not the same world in which the concept of religious freedom was given its political beginnings.

The choices we are called upon to make for conscience's sake in today's world are not so dramatic as in other days. We are not likely to mount the scaffold, protesting as did Sir Thomas More that we are "the King's good servant, but God's first." We do not risk exile if we address an eloquent remonstrance to the patriarchs of the Orthodox Church, as Alexander Solzhenitsyn did.[4] Not for a hundred years has the wrong church membership disqualified a person from voting or officeholding in any of our states.

There is nonetheless an urgency to put our own welfare in jeopardy for the sake of those who have no advocates. Some of my friends wear the hair shirt, not only at the cost of considerable discomfort but also with remarkable ineffectiveness. They scorn those of us who are conspicuously comfortable, affluent, or influential in this society.

I own the truth of their hard impeachment. I do not have many occasions to risk something to preserve my own freedom. But I am surrounded by situations where, if I will, I may risk something for another man's opportunity to gain his freedom. (I should add that, at practically no risk, we can do a great deal more than we have done to expand the freedom of women.)

What I do risk is my good name, my acceptance by the Establishment, my standing in the eyes of the political and economic and academic rulers who do not like prophets or agitators or mere nuisances.

We should eternally guard ourselves against the kind of discrimination that can be only too easily implied from this. We are guilty of dividing the world between "Us" and "Them"—Us, the enlightened, the prophetic, the compassionate; Them, the benighted, the fanatical, the selfish. In the stridency of those who disagree with us, we see proof of their wrongheadedness. In our stance of dispassionate scholarship, we of course represent sweet reason. William Butler Yeats's famous lines from "The Second Coming" are recalled:

> The best lack all conviction, while the worst
> Are full of passionate intensity.[5]

Percy Bysshe Shelley observed the same human dissatisfaction in Fury's lines:

> The good want power, but to weep barren tears.
> The powerful goodness want: worse need for them.
> The wise want love; and those who love want wisdom;
> And all best things are thus confused with ill.[6]

Many will recall the remark of Justice Charles Evans Hughes in a Bar Association address at Elmira, New York, in 1907: *"We are under a Constitution, but the Constitution is what the judges say it is."*[7] The chief justice-to-be did not intend to be cynical. It does happen that a single clause in the First Amendment has been enormously expanded by judicial interpretation, as well as by assumptions of people who never read constitutions, so that religious freedom is widely accepted, in fact, as a *positive* right. Did you note in the long quotation from Truett that claim of *absolute liberty?* Tell that to the citizens of Utah who could not win admission to the Union until the Mormons made the proper legal adjustment and forbade the practice of polygamy. Tell that to the West Virginia parents whose religious ideas are contradicted by the textbooks their children must use in the public schools. Tell that to the Jehovah's Witnesses harassed by local ordinances regulating the distribution of literature and restricting meetings and electronic amplifiers in the streets and parks of our cities. Tell that to snake handlers in East Tennessee who test their faith by poison. Tell it to the administrators of church schools which must modify traditional behavior standards if their students are to share in general programs of financial assistance through the Department of Health, Education and Welfare. Tell that to all the physicians and social workers and planners who interfere with deeply held religious beliefs in such areas as abortion, euthanasia, and overpopulation. Tell that to the inmates of jails and nursing homes who have no defense from the intrusions of hymn singing and altar calls. Both bond and free can invoke the Constitution. The well-meaning participants can claim their free exercise of religion threatened; their captive audience can sometimes cite the cruel and unusual punishment clause!

These are extreme situations, you say, not serious limitations on the freedom of worship or belief or practice. Certainly none of the public policies indicated herein threatens mainstream religions. This is, of course, the constitutional point. Majorities can take care of themselves. It is the minorities, the nonconformists, and the extremists in belief and practice who need the protection of Bills of Rights.

The libertarians of 1776 and 1791 anticipated this. They were not omniscient, these ancestors we invoke. There is no evidence they were aware of any discrimination against women, and there is plenty of evidence they were unwilling to accord to blacks the rights implicit in that ringing phrase, "All men are created equal." Both John Hope Franklin, premier American historian, who happens to be black, and James E. Cheek, the president of Howard University, have written with some exasperation of the romantic view of our ancestors as moral titans.[8] It is important to remember that the men of 1776 were not setting to right all the world's ills; they were stating their own grievances in vivid language to win the good opinion of others. The founding fathers look good by contrast with European statesmen of the eighteenth century. George Cruikshank calls it a time when statesmen were without ideals, the church without vision, the Crown without honor, the common people without hope.[9] The American experience therefore presented a new dawn, and the bugle voice of Jefferson, in the great Declaration, resonated in the hearts of oppressed people around the earth.

Some of us have not wholly accepted the Fourteenth Amendment, which by judicial interpretation we thought settled, and which broadened the applicability of First Amendment principles to prohibit state as well as federal encroachment.[10] Some of us even regret the strict constructionist's success in securing an interpretation that prevents our doing things that, in a simpler and more homogeneous society, were almost universally applauded: for example, prayer and Bible reading in the schools; laws requiring the observance of Sunday as a day of rest; automatic exemption from taxation of any enterprise remotely related to religion. One negative aspect of constitutional separation may be illustrated by our inability to do the kind of thing I saw in British elementary schools: young children storing up the great truths of religious literature, memorizing lengthy passages from the Bible and the Book of Common Prayer—a wonderful regimen of memory work. This is not to give aid and comfort to unreasoning critics of the Supreme Court. Public opinion, and particularly Bible-Belt opinion of an alarmist nature, has transcended the actual decision of courts on the emotional subject of prayer in the public schools, with mischievous political effect.

We talk about affirmative action these days. It may be time for us to consider what religious freedom means positively as well as negatively. In the resolution passed by the Baptist World Congress at Stockholm in July, 1975,[11] we were enjoined to use our freedom to become more effective Christians, to become officeholders of integrity, to work for the enactment of laws and the enforcement of policies to make communities better places in which to live and to rear our children. These aspirations have properly become international in their dimension. Fifty-six years after Truett, religious freedom demands that discipleship become positive. The 1975 resolution, stronger than anything the Baptist World Alliance has ever adopted, asserts both the positive and the negative: the powers of Christian freedom as well as the limitations against state invasion; and most importantly, corporate as well as individual responsibility for the future of the human race. Good motives and good hearts are not enough to solve massive public problems. Some of the subjects identified in the Stockholm resolution are the inhumanity of the social order, aggressive nationalism, betrayals of justice, public immorality, misuse of the land and air and water, and the threat of nuclear destruction. It is a mild statement; yet most of the subjects in it were until only recently avoided by our conventions as well as by many of our congregations. Such concerns were rejected as "politics" and therefore outside the legitimate concern of Christians protected by the "wall of separation."

I think it is fair commentary that it was not fear of breaching the wall, as much as fear of arousing unpleasantness, that prevented action in these areas. The most conspicuous historical example was the silence of many in the churches regarding slavery. Most of us will acknowledge the generally poor and late response of organized Christianity to that challenge. We have been equally timid, since Reconstruction, to contend with controversial issues classified as "outside the church." Too long have we headed off discussion in our churches and in our official deliberative bodies out of fear of the irascible element among us.

No idea ought to be out-of-bounds to the Christian. The Christian ought to be the most unshockable of people. We have not been given "the spirit of fear, but of power, and of love, and of a sound mind" (2 Timothy 1:7). Timid minds dominate our proceedings in convention and congregational business conferences. As our justification for doing nothing significant in the public sector, we appeal to the separation doctrines of Jefferson and Madison almost with the reverence of medievalists appealing to Aristotle. I am concerned by the fact that the citizen and the church member do dwell in the same body. I am concerned that legalistic considerations for the Constitution sometimes, and eccentric theological objections at other times, prevent our doing what we must do to teach the young, to care for the sick, to house the homeless, to give work to the jobless, to take care of the old, and to feed the hungry.

We do not have the time here to speak to every topic on the lengthening agenda of Christian concerns. One, which may not be cosmic, but certainly timely, is the alleged deterioration of public education and all the vexing problems rapid change has brought in this sector. Who among us has not despaired in support of the public schools? Who has not personally felt the trauma and dislocation of busing? Who has not felt the shame of burgeoning segregation academies, often located in our church basements? Surely the "public policy" in our theme embraces education. As Brooks Hays has written, this is "a complex and delicate problem but not one that is beyond solution, and the alternatives to finding that solution are unthinkable."[12]

Let it be conceded, with appreciation for the devotional contribution of the nonactivist Christian, that there is a decent historical case for noninvolvement. It is usually not history, but timidity, that keeps us out of the arena of blood, sweat, and tears. It was said of Theodore Roosevelt that he made every public question a moral issue, and thought his opponent either a fool or a knave. I find that attitude prevalent in contemporary circles. Good men and women grow partisan, then doctrinaire, then humorless—and they are likely to be intolerant of the noninvolved.

Cortez Stubblefield was a cowboy preacher from the Texas Panhandle who strongly influenced Baptist pioneer missionary efforts in the Southwest. One of his comments was, "Ain't no law in Oklahoma City or Washington that says a man can't mind his own business." There is a heavy strain of isolationism in the national mood today, whether we are talking about Angola, which some of my friends on both sides can make a moral issue; or the ugly business of FBI surveillance of the private lives of citizens; or even, to use a current example that is said to have shocked President Ford, the CIA's spending six million American dollars to influence the recent Italian elections. These very well may be issues to avoid. At the very least, we can differ and not make our own view a test of Christian fellowship.

I think there is another explanation for our stance of noninvolvement. In 1976, almost as heartily as 1776, we proclaim our belief in limited government. The menace of big government is real. When Justice Louis Brandeis coined the phrase "the curse of bigness,"[13] he struck a responsive chord in our distrust of power—whether that of big government, big labor, or big business. We hate to pay taxes. We properly resent the growth of the imperial presidency and the great dukedoms and earldoms of Congress and cities and states; and we show a nostalgia for simple republicanism when we suggest the president get rid of Air Force One and ride Allegheny or the Metroliner.

Much of the criticism of government is absurd. There is no other instrument available to organized communities to accomplish those tasks that demand any degree of coercion. A good many loud persons in Congress and in the pulpit continue to do mischief by attacking the machinery of our complex society. If they continue, they may generate an unreasoning hatred of government at all levels. One recalls the Luddite riots in England of the early nineteenth century when frustrated people smashed the new machines they blamed for unemployment. Government as an instrument of good must be defended, even while government as oppressor is rebuked and cleansed.

One need not be a Tory or a sycophant to defend the institution of government. Certainly there is a response more productive than constant complaint. Those of us who are custodians of educational institutions must think sometimes we have educated just enough to earn the accusation of Caliban in *The Tempest,* "You taught me language, and my profit on't is, I know how to curse." [14] At least since 1776, our people have known how to curse! It is that right most often practiced by the descendants of revolutionists—practiced even in the Oval Office. Somehow we must find the intelligence to do creative and constructive work without losing that critical faculty necessary for eternal vigilance.

"Staying out of politics" has seemed to be the safe formula for many church people as well as educators. It was not safe, ultimately, for the German churches and universities that failed to speak up against Nazism, and it has not proved a safe policy for any of us who hope to earn the respect of the young. How poignantly we recall young Gordon Strachan in the Senate Committee hearings after recounting his misadventures in the politics of dirty tricks, and being invited to advise other young people: "Stay out!" Watergate seemed to illustrate the danger of overinvolvement. In fact, it was the reward of massive citizen indifference.

Some of our friends are "hipped" on some issues and try to get the rest of us "hyped" from our apathy. Then we find all too often that our cause was Tweedledum and the vicious enemy at least no worse than Tweedledee. Exhaustive campaigns have been conducted in my lifetime for such "moral issues" as these: the location of the county seat; water skiing on the lake that supplies the city water; getting a representative of a particular group (women, blacks, Chicanos, Indians, college faculty members) on the local school board, the City Council, or the Planning Committee; strip zoning for a quick food concession. When we trivialize our politics, or our religion, we risk alienating the people whom we need and who need us for the really significant tasks of our common humanity.

The problems of government are not simple! In states with long ballots and sophisticated initiative and referendum questions, none of us ever votes with anything like full information. I am sympathetic toward those who say that "getting out the vote" is no virtue, and multiplying the votes of the ill-informed is not worth the candle. Still and all, we are several additional millions better informed than were our precursors. When Woodrow Wilson wrote nearly a century ago of the difficulty of getting at the sources of power, he said that it must be hunted down in out-of-the-way places. [15] My problems are big, but I have John Chancellor, Walter Cronkite, and Harry Reasoner to guide me! Investigative reporting has come a long way. The press, the radio, and the television people are disliked precisely because they have been effective in uncovering so much that is wrong.

In the next quarter century I expect to see a greater concern for those articles of the Bill of Rights that do not immediately concern religious freedom. There is a seamless web that makes all our liberties one. If E. Y. Mullins was right and "religious freedom is the nursing mother of all freedom," [16] then we must care about freedom of the press, about unreasonable search and seizure. Yes! even the Fifth Amendment. Nor can we be insensitive to attempts to suppress reporters and editorialists, even those whose opinions we hate.

It occurs to me that the real dropouts from responsible Christianity and responsible citizenship are the religious mystics. They glory in their noninvolvement in the making of public policy. Some of my best friends have taken up Transcendental Meditation, and others have become mildly or militantly charismatic. Like Charles Reich and Gordon Strachan, they have given up on institutions. One prayer cell in my locality has made a worldly university an object of special petition. While I may not like the unflattering reflection on the incumbent administration, I am in no position to reject the effectual fervent prayers of the righteous, even the trendy folks who a few years ago were trying to set me up for their encounter groups.

I rejoice that we have such freedom in pluralism that people can enjoy a life of mystic contemplation amidst stubborn and scabrous social problems. That is one of the benefits of a benign society, and while I never expect to avail myself of the joys of the psychic phenomena, I will defend anyone's right to one's own seance. No doubt because of spiritual delinquency, I do not hear voices. I have never heard voices. God speaks to me in the conditions I see and hear and in the events, the crises, the analyses, and the prophecies of the scholars with whom I work.

No one can be untouched by the recent sight I had of thousands of begging children in Latin America. No one can see the neglected old, the mistreated young, and the casualties of body and soul and fortune without feeling some compulsion to act, here and now.

When I was in India thirty years ago, I lost some of my native American optimism. I felt helpless before the ultimate dilemma: the human population explosion. President Dwight Eisenhower said in 1958 that he could not imagine a subject of less concern to governments than birth control. He changed his mind, of course, and surely even our most otherworldly Christians can see the prospect that we are breeding ourselves into a new barbarism. Has that any implication for the Christian in the exercise of his freedom? Or is human life to be even cheaper than the assessment constantly made by those who distort the argument on gun control?

The Great Apostle summons us in a cryptic phrase: "You were called to freedom!" (Galatians 5:13). We know from what evils we were liberated by the men of the eighteenth century. We are still seeking, as every generation must seek, the affirmative uses of our liberty.

Earlier I used Dean Rusk's phrase, the "aspiration explosion of our time." Perhaps we started it all in 1776. Perhaps we should start something else. Across the centuries, scholars and statesmen have kept alive human hopes for a world without war. For 450 years the nation-state system has been nourished by war. Arnold Toynbee sees militarism as the chief cause for the disintegration of civilization in the last three to four millennia. It is surely time for the concept of national sovereignty to be reexamined by Christian leaders who are concerned about the preservation of life on this planet.

Call the roll of those who have dreamed dreams and seen visions of the ideal society—Plato, Augustine, Sir Thomas More, James Harrington, Campanella, Sir Frances Bacon, the Duke of Sully, Woodrow Wilson—they tried without success to fashion a shield of world law to save humanity from destruction. Neither cynicism nor despair at past failures nor complacency with the present uneasy peace must deter us, standing on the shoulders of these giants, from our urgent task. Surely in our day the scourge of mass incineration is a threat and challenge to the ingenuity, to the lifeblood, and to the very last brain cell of every one of us.

We, too, may fail, but we fail in the divine call of the Prince of Peace. It is part of the business of Christian leaders to wage peace just as tirelessly as we have waged war, remembering that peace is the reward of justice, that it requires magnanimity of mind and gallantry of spirit. Christians do care about the world, and they count no life cheap for whom also Christ died.

NOTES

[1] George W. Truett, "Baptist and Religious Liberty," in *God's Call to America* (Valley Forge: Judson Press, 1923), pp. 32-33. This address was delivered May 16, 1920.

[2] Edgar Young Mullins, *The Axioms of Religion* (Philadelphia: American Baptist Publication Society, 1908), pp. 185-200.

[3] Albert Clayton Reid, *Christ of Confusion* (Winston-Salem: Wake Forest University Press, 1974), p. 11.

[4] Alexander Solzhenitsyn, *A Lenten Letter to Pimen Patriarch of All Russia* (Minneapolis: Burgess Publishing Company, 1972), pp. 5-8.

[5] Morton Irving Seidan, ed., *William Butler Yeats* (East Lansing: Michigan State University Press, 1962), p. 34.

[6] C. H. Herford, ed., *The Dramatic Poems of Shelley* (London: Florence Press, 1922), p. 43.

[7] Samuel Hendel, *Charles Evans Hughes and the Supreme Court* (New York: King's Crown Press, 1951), p. 11.

[8] John Hope Franklin, "The Moral Legacy of the Founding Fathers," *University of Chicago Magazine* (July, 1975), pp. 24ff.; James E. Cheek, "Through a Glass Darkly; the American Idea in the Post-Modern World," speech reprinted in *Congressional Record,* December 1, 1975, p. E6347.

[9] George L. Patten, *George Cruikshank* (Princeton: Princeton University Press, 1974), p. 175.

[10] Typical of the constitutional objections to the *Engel* v. *Vitale* decision is James M. Bulman's *It Is Their Right* (Greensboro: Gateway Publications, 1975), pp. 88-91.

[11] "Resolution on Religious Liberty, Human Rights, World Peace, and Public Morality," adopted by the 13th Baptist World Congress, Stockholm, Sweden, July 12, 1975; reprinted in *Report from the Capital,* vol. 30 (September, 1975), pp. 4-5.

[12] Brooks Hays, *This World: A Christian's Workshop* (Nashville: Broadman Press, 1958), p. 115.

[13] Louis D. Brandeis, *The Curse of Bigness* (Port Washington, N.Y.: Kennikat Press, Inc., 1965). The phrase was actually used in a Bar Association speech three decades earlier.

[14] William Shakespeare, *The Tempest,* act 1, sc. 2, line 364.

[15] Woodrow Wilson, *Congressional Government* (Boston: Houghton, Mifflin and Company, 1885), p. 92.

[16] Mullins, *The Axioms of Religion,* p. 268.

11

The Meaning
of
Religious Liberty

C. EMANUEL CARLSON

As the late Mark DeWolfe Howe, then a law professor at Harvard, began his lectures on "Religion and Government in American Constitutional History," he summarized the difference between Roger Williams and Thomas Jefferson in these words: "The principle of separation epitomized in Williams' metaphor was predominantly theological. The principle summarized in the same figure when used by Jefferson was primarily political." [1]

Both Williams and Jefferson used the analogy of "a wall" as a simile of what they considered to be the proper relationships of these institutions. We can easily assume that the two men had the same general goals in mind, but "the wall" may not have had the same functions in both minds. They were separated from each other by more than a century and a half, so the conditions of life were much changed. Furthermore, Williams was a minister of the church, anxious to purify the church of the "world," while Jefferson was a politician seeking to put together a winning party. In addition, Williams knew walls as they were in New England and Jefferson knew them in Virginia. This last difference could be the continental divide which gives rise to divergent streams of thought in Baptist life. The stone walls of Virginia have always seemed to me to be a kind of fence, the functions of which are to mark a boundary and to prevent the movement of the larger animals. It was the New England setting that first introduced me to the retaining walls that lift the elevation of the garden that surrounds the home above the level of the wilderness beyond.

DIVERSE OBJECTIVES

Whatever the differences of experiential meanings Roger Williams and Thomas Jefferson may have had as to the functions of a wall, it is still true, then and now, that "the wall of separation" arises out of an assortment of goals and aspirations, be they well or poorly defined. The mentality of a majority-religious group is unavoidably different from that of a minority group that creates awareness by emphasizing more or less divergent social characteristics or religious tenets. The latter normally sees more need of freedom. Hence many see pluralism as the major force for freedom. In some minds freedom from government is important at the federal level of government but does not apply to local rulers such as school boards. They fear the former but not the latter. Some strive for the secularization of the society and its culture while others want to evangelize through all possible means. Legislation of devotional exercises is necessary to those concerned with group rituals but is repulsive to those who think of religion as highly personal. From personal experiences, I have observed any and all of these objectives among our Baptist people. Is a consensus regarding the nature and scope of freedom really possible among us?

FREEDOM OF CONSCIENCE

Authoritarian religious movements have floundered most often on the rock called "conscience." Yet there is that in human beings which sets a course of conviction and of thought with such assurance that neither pressures, arguments, nor suffering can bend the conscience. Unfortunately, some philosophers have found in this a kind of natural religion, which for them is a substitute for the Christian revelation that we have in Christ and in the Bible. While Baptists have been influenced by many social forces, the effort has been to "obey God rather than men" (see Acts 5:29).

The only limitations placed on government that stand up through national crises are the limitations that are rooted in personal religious experiences which have a more dominant control of our behavior than the pressures of convenience, of conformity, or of political alignments. Therefore, it has been my hope that our Baptist roots may grow constantly deeper and that religious liberty as a result may be even more secure to all.

The elements or activities which are included in the concept of freedom of conscience can serve as a checklist against which to test various policies and practices. No complete list is possible, but a dozen elements rank very high. Persons who enjoy freedom of conscience must in actual practice be free (1) to decide whether to worship or not to worship; (2) to join the church of their own choice, choosing their own creed and tenets; (3) to change their ecclesiastical allegiance without hindrance; (4) to nurture the faith of the children for whom they carry responsibility; (5) to choose the religious instruction for their children; (6) to express their faith and convictions personally and in group activities; (7) to travel for the advancement of their faith; (8) to associate themselves with others for corporate religious interests; (9) to use their homes and property for religious purposes; (10) to determine the causes and the amounts of their religious stewardship; (11) to make their own best judgments on moral and public issues, and express them; and (12) to have free access to information from various sources.

While these may be viewed as elements in the practical operations of a free conscience, none of them can be viewed as absolute or as being in isolation. In using these concepts, they must also be held in balance with the elements that constitute the freedom of the church as a body.

FREEDOM OF THE CHURCH

The independence of the church can also be used as a kind of lodestone for the discernment of the boundaries of religious liberty. If the churches are not free, then the people are not religiously free. Much religious experience is in community with people of kindred spirit. The life of the group is vitally related to the evangelizing of the individual and to personal expressions of life and faith.

Many who are not committed to "separation" of church and state, nonetheless, do believe in the independence of the church. In fact, some formulation of this idea is a necessary concomitant of the idea of the Lordship of Christ and of religious commitment. This has been recognized all through Roman Catholic, Orthodox, and Protestant theologies in spite of the wide diversity of working relationships between church and state that have existed in the history of Christianity.

The theme of independence could be pushed to such extremes as to make the existence of the church as a social institution in the community very dubious. For instance, if our churches should insist on their independence of sanitary and public health laws, of community law and order, of civic standards for education, of zoning laws, and of scores of other actions by political authorities which are designed for human well-being in community life, the churches might compromise rather than strengthen their Christian witness.

On the other hand, the pursuit of specific objectives by church agencies and institutions may advance by opportunism, step by step, until independence is reduced to theory or theology. Institutional relationships can move realistically into binding interdependence while the vocabulary and the theology of independence remain. This has often been the situation of churches in various places historically and has, in many situations, gone so far as to make the church the servant of the state and of society, theology notwithstanding.

We may not be prepared to renounce all agreement between government agencies and church agencies, for some contracts or agreements may be necessary or unavoidable. Yet, there must be proper limits upon this process. Otherwise, freedom is obviously in danger. Where are the proper boundaries of political collaboration of churches with local and national politicians?

Financial independence is equally important. This means shunning government sources of revenue which can dry up by fiat or legislative change. But does it not also mean avoiding dependence upon private sources of revenue which accrue because of political leanings or because of government policies? The latter is as destructive of independence as the former.

Preferential treatment in tax policy or tax credit allowed to people or corporations which support church agencies gives us a kind of gray independence, and it probably should be examined very closely. Similarly, the church's independence under the Lordship of Christ can easily be eroded by the political interests of private financial or other private interests. In fact, the private corporations are a very convenient meeting place for widely varied interests. Corporation law needs our attention badly.

From the functional viewpoint, the two areas in modern American society in which the work of the governments (taking all levels together) and the church agencies overlap most are social welfare and education. Neither the church nor the state can turn away from these interests without compromising its own insights and ideals.

Elements of freedom which the church needs in order to carry out its functions require the freedom (1) to order its own public worship; (2) to make its own formulations of doctrinal positions; (3) to determine its own organization and government; (4) to set standards and qualifications for membership and for the clergy; (5) to provide and control programs for training leadership; (6) to plan and provide for the religious instruction of its members and its youth; (7) to plan and carry out various forms of Christian service or charity; (8) to plan and carry out programs of missionary outreach; (9) to own and operate business activities which are related to its objectives; (10) to have equal status with all other religious groups before the law of the land; (11) to formulate its own moral positions insofar as these do not deprive others of similar freedom or endanger the life of the community; and (12) to interpret to the public the meaning of its insights and its principles for the institutions of society, including government. Here again we have a formulation that in the late 1950s and the early 1960s had a remarkably high level of agreement. Each item rests on its relatedness to the church's reason for being. And here, also, the erosion of changing times presents new issues that were not then on the horizon. The problem of morality in government and in society at large places before us problems that need to be considered. "Traditional" behavior may not be "Christian" behavior. In the light of all that sociologists and anthropologists have learned about the mores of society, churches must find their way to a refined Christian approach. Obviously, the church cannot be disinterested in the economic-political-social forces that fuse themselves into a nation's ethical principles.

SEPARATION OF CHURCH AND STATE

It is in defense of freedom of conscience and freedom of the church that Baptists have advocated separation of church and state. In some areas one emphasis has overshadowed the other. In this connection it should be noted that in the United States, ever since disestablishment, free churches have been largely taken for granted and most practical positions have since been based on freedom of conscience, i.e., the voluntary tradition.

God never intended church and state to be separated in history. The two institutions must exist and work out their programs in the same chronology, the same localities, with more or less the same people, experiencing the impact of the same current events. Out of this unavoidable fact arise many of the problems in church-state relations. Public education and church education must somehow share the pupil's time. "Sunday laws" are a recurring problem in religious liberty. Church building programs and city zoning laws must somehow be brought into harmonious relationship. The civic role of ecclesiastical leadership—such as ministers, priests, and nuns in public educational or political life—and the religious role of political or civic leaders give much cause for debate.

Whatever the purposes of God may be for the future age, at present we must recognize the importance of coexistence. In this necessary coexistence, however, numerous problematic interrelationships arise which call for considerate, if not for cooperative, efforts toward solutions. The proper handling of these problems is important both to the spiritual well-being of people and to the proper functioning of social organization.

Problems involved in a proper distribution of time. Many church-state tensions of our day arise out of the coexistence of these institutions and their agencies in time. They need to live by the same calendar and the same clocks, and each needs a time assignment in which to carry out these programs. Some of the expressions of this may be seen in the division of pupil time between church and public instructional efforts, including length of the school day, released time, etc.; legislation regarding religious holidays, for example, Christmas, Good Friday, Easter, Rosh Hashanah, Yom Kippur, and the like; and sabbath or Sunday legislation, including a wide diversity of approaches to the need for an "open road" for church programs.

Problems growing out of geographic coexistence. The unity of the globe like the unit of time imposes need for working relationships between the church and its agencies and the state and its agencies. Numerous problems may be identified. The selection of sites for churches in planned communities is often limited by zoning laws and other legal restrictions. The provision of land areas for churches or their agencies in urban districts being redeveloped has become a large problem, and it will become larger as more urban tracts become obsolescent and subject to redevelopment. The provision of a religious ministry to armed service personnel confronts the churches with a geographic problem (as well as other problems) because these people become highly mobile, both at home and abroad. Public lands are frequently made available to church institutions which are deemed beneficial to the community and the surrounding area.

Problems growing out of the unity of human personalities. It is neither possible nor desirable to split human personalities on the basis of institutional principles or insights. The church member should be a good citizen. Conversely, efforts are made to win citizens as church members. Here, also problems of coexistence of church and state present themselves. The role of the clergy in political life is not easily portrayed. Some nations, notably those where clericalism and anticlericalism exist, have imposed separation in principle and therefore have denied the clergy the right to hold public office or to teach in public schools. Likewise the role of the politician in the religious life of the community presents problems of example, of exploitation, and of alignments. For the ordinary church members who are also ordinary citizens there are difficult problems of transfer, motivation, and interests between the two aspects of their lives.

Neither the churches nor the governments can ignore the fact of the other set of agencies.

Problems growing out of the unity of culture. The unity of the culture of a given area also poses problems of coexistence in church-state relations. Much has been glibly said about "Christian cultures" with all too little understanding of the scriptural insights regarding the spiritual penetration of culture. Similarly, the nontheological factors in church life have been much discussed without adequate clarity on the nature of spiritual group experience. To deal with church-state relations without dealing with the church-culture relationships is to engage in superficial study or unrealistic debate without coming to terms with some vital issues.

The answers to church-state relations in this area are more likely to be of a functional nature than structural separation. An evaluation of community traditions and practices is needed. The past constantly tends to reach forward to bestow its blessings and protection on social or political traits which may have both questionable history and dubious value for human well-being but may enjoy the sanctions of law. Churches are constantly tempted to offer a complete culture pattern and to make their spiritual community self-contained if not isolated as a community within the community, e.g., Baptist schools, Baptist labor unions, Baptist insurance companies, Baptist political parties, and many more.

In many instances the churches have accepted the culture which they have found, making it their own without radical application of religious insights, and then have become staunch supporters or advocates of that culture. Such churches have become the conservative core in resistance to cultural change and have tended to become the stewards of the intangible elements of the culture itself.

In all of these problems which arise out of the necessary coexistence of church and state in history, working relationships are called for. We cannot lean on legal separation as the full solution to these problems. In fact, these are not solvable problems in the sense of resolving the tension in a permanent manner. Rather, the tensions involved must be viewed as normal and continuing. We cannot expect to Christianize fully the social, political, and cultural life of a people so it can be equated with the life of the churches. Neither should we expect churches in which Christ is honored as Lord to adjust themselves to the life of the world in which they exist. When we face the problems of coexistence, we neither deny nor minimize our emphasis on separation. On the contrary, it is this recognition of coexistence which calls for separation.

THE MEANING OF SEPARATION

While all of the above compels us to improve our vocabulary in defining church-state relations, there are aspects of the two sets of institutions which can and must be separate if they are to perform their functions within the limits imposed by religious liberty. The most significant and obvious areas of necessary separation are probably these, which were favorably received by both Southern and American Baptist Conventions in 1959:[2]

Separate reasons for being. Separation means that the church has its own "reasons for being" and that these reasons are distinct from those of the state.

Separate publics. A person is born into the state. Citizenship normally includes all the people. The New Testament church, however, is composed of regenerate people, and its fellowship is voluntary.

Distinct methods. While the state uses methods of law which are appropriate to its purposes, the church must use spiritual methods which can nurture true Christian experience and character.

Separate administration. The church cannot be a "department of ecclesiastical affairs" of the state. Each must govern its own affairs.

Separate sources of support. The state derives its revenue from the power of taxation, while the church is supported by voluntary stewardship.

Separate educational programs. The churches cannot delegate the education of their members to the state; neither should the churches become educational tools for the established political and economic order. The educational programs of the two institutions must be kept separate.

NOTES

[1] Mark DeWolfe Howe, *The Garden and the Wilderness* (Chicago: The University of Chicago Press, 1965), pp 6-7.

[2] See *Year Book of the American Baptist Convention, 1959,* pp. 127-128, and *Southern Baptist Convention Annual, 1959,* p. 421.

The Exercise
of
Religious Freedom

O. CARROLL ARNOLD

Our preoccupation in recent years has been with the establishment clause of the First Amendment. That is to say, we have been chiefly concerned with the establishment of religion. And the concern with establishment has tended to overshadow concern about the free exercise clause. The two religion clauses of the First Amendment were originally intended to be limitations on Congress. "Congress shall make no law respecting an establishment of religion or prohibiting the free exercise thereof." In the first 150 years of this Republic the matter of religious freedom, insofar as it had any contact with the law, was, in the main, left to state and local governments, and it was the business of the federal government to leave religion alone.

THREATS TO RELIGIOUS FREEDOM

The "free exercise of religion" is not an academic matter to be taken for granted. One is inclined to say in the face of the persecution of Christians, Jews, and other religious groups throughout the world, that "it can't happen here." So much attention has been given to the "establishment clause" and the separation of church and state aspect of religious freedom that the real threat to religious freedom has been forgotten—namely, exercise of religion may be, and in fact has been, prohibited.

All citizens should have been enraged at the revelations which have been issued through congressional investigations of the violations of basic First Amendment rights by the FBI and CIA. Martin Luther

King, Jr., a prominent religious leader whose phone wires were tapped, was allegedly advised to commit suicide rather than have his dossier exposed, a clear case of blackmail. This ought not to come as any great surprise to anyone, however. One remembers how in the early 1950s, during the McCarthy era, Bishop G. Bromley Oxnam in the city of Washington, D.C., was subjected to the most enormous pressure by the FBI and the House Un-American Activities Committee—pressure which can only be described as religious persecution.

The very first principle of religious liberty and its free exercise is never to take such a right for granted. No matter how benign and friendly a government may be in its outward appearance, as long as the state is the state, even though it is said to be "under God," it will on occasion push God aside and regard the right of religious freedom merely as a privilege to be withdrawn if in the opinion of the state "national security" requires it. This is not paranoid, for the United States is probably as supportive and tolerant of religious freedom as any nation in the world, but it is a reminder of the need to be vigilant. Nobody prizes religious liberty half so much as those who have lost it.

A second preliminary consideration, which is related to the first, is to keep our thinking straight about the relationship of religious freedom to the two clauses—establishment and free exercise—of the First Amendment. In recent years a great emphasis has been put upon the establishment clause. But separation is only instrumental to the larger doctrine of religious freedom. An undue emphasis on the establishment clause advances freedom very little, if any. Nobody wants an established church, and there seems very little danger of getting one. But is it generous and just of Protestants, and especially Baptists who have had a decent and respectable history of dissent, to complain about the dangers to religious freedom of an establishment of religion if they accept a de facto establishment of Protestantism?

PIETISM AND "THE WALL"

The First Amendment was designed to establish freedom and put religion and its affairs out of the reach of the state. Separation has never been absolute. The affairs of the government and the interests of the church are inextricably intertwined together, and it is the business of separation to enable the church and the state to work together in the interests of religious freedom and not to make government a restrictive or punitive agent. The government of the United States has not been and is not now neutral with respect to religious freedom, any more than it is neutral toward other First

Amendment rights—freedom of speech, press, assembly, etc. It is the avowed protector of these rights, and the chief protection should be from the incursion of government itself.

There is a viewpoint which is very common among religious and irreligious people alike that separation means religion and the state should have nothing whatsoever to do with each other; that the church should be a small enclave of pietistic interests which pursues its worship and its rituals, teaches its rather recondite doctrines, and keeps its nose out of important affairs, such as politics, business, and education. Religion in this manner is effectively fenced off from culture and public life, pledged to silence about public affairs, made docile and domesticated. "Politics and religion don't mix," it is asserted, and "that's what separation of church and state means."

There is some evidence that even the great Jefferson entertained precisely these kinds of sectarian and pietistic notions about the place of religion in public affairs. He wrote to his friend Thomas Cooper, a British scientist, whom he was trying to bring to the faculty of the University of Virginia:

> I must explain to you the state of religious parties with us, about 1/3 of our state is Baptist, 1/3 Methodist, and of the remaining third two parts may be Presbyterian and one part Anglican. The Baptists are sound republicans and zealous supporters of their government. The Methodists are republican mostly, satisfied with their government, medling [sic] with nothing but the concerns of their own calling and opposing nothing. These two sects are entirely friendly to our university. The Anglicans are the same. The Presbyterian *clergy* alone (not their followers) remain bitterly federal and malcontent with their government. They are violent, ambitious of power, and intolerant in politics as in religion and want nothing but license from the laws to kindle again the fires of their leader John Knox, and to give us a 2d blast from his trumpet. Having a little more monkish learning than the clergy of the other sects, they are jealous of the general diffusion of science, and therefore hostile to our Seminary lest it should qualify their antagonists of the other sects to meet them in equal combat. Not daring to attack the institution with the avowal of their real motives, they peck at you, at me, and every feather they can spy out. But in this they have no weight, even with their own followers, excepting a few old men among them who may still be federal & Anglomen, their main body are good citizens, friends to their government, anxious for reputation, and therefore friendly to the University.[1]

Many people believe that Jefferson's metaphor about "the wall of separation" is in the Constitution and that it has all the sanction and force of law, and that such a wall precludes the church and religion from raising its voice in criticism of the government on moral grounds or any other grounds, for that matter. And that attitude is one of the chief barriers, not to say walls, prohibiting the free exercise of religion.

If one is inclined to doubt this assumption or be defensive at this point about the doctrine of separation, then consider what freedom of the press, a companion right to freedom of religion, means. Does it mean that the press should never say a discouraging word to the government, never criticize it, never challenge it? The idea is absurd. Suppose it had taken such a supine view in the recent Watergate scandal. Suppose it had taken such a view of the CIA or the aforementioned scandalous activities of the FBI with respect to Martin Luther King, Jr.? No, the press is free to criticize and to ferret out every morsel of truth, be it good, bad, or merely dull, and the government cannot do a thing about it. In fact, it is bound by the Constitution not to interfere with the freedom of the press.

It is precisely Jefferson's wall, and the undue attention we have paid it, which has brought us to the place where all content has often been drained out of religious freedom as a positive force. We have been so preoccupied with our watch upon the wall, so paranoid about some supposed establishment of religion which somebody or other was trying to erect, that we have forgotten that the purpose of religion and the purpose of Christ for his church is that we should be free. But free for what? Free to do what?

There have been many encroachments upon the church and religion in recent years, but with a few exceptions they are trivial. Our approach to religious freedom has been to emphasize the negative. In our efforts to see to it that Jefferson's wall was tight and strong, we have allowed a wall to be erected to keep the church out of the world and we have called that normal. One is reminded of T. S. Eliot's *The Family Reunion.* Harry, the tormented hero, asks the rest of the family:

> You've been holding a meeting—the usual family inquest
> On the characters of all the junior members?
> Or engaged in predicting the minor event.
> Or engaged in foreseeing the minor disaster?
> You go on trying to think of each thing separately,
> Making small things important, so that everything
> May be unimportant, a slight deviation
> From some imaginary course that life ought to take,
> That you call normal. What you call the normal
> Is merely the unreal and the unimportant.[2]

Normalcy for us, as it was for Warren Harding, was to return to quietness, domesticity, worshiping, praying in our churches, and keeping the institution running in a well-oiled manner. But freedom is not like that. Freedom has the sound of trumpets in it, a call to battle. And there is another wall which has more to do with us and our heritage than the anticlericalism of Thomas Jefferson. It comes from the pen of that old warrior Roger Williams: ". . . when they have opened a gap in the hedge or wall of separation between the garden of the church and the wilderness of the world, God hath ever broke down the wall itself, removed the candlestick, and made His garden a wilderness, as at this day."[3] And we have forgotten the words of another old warrior who is a part of our heritage, too; his name was Martin Luther, and his definition of the freedom of the Christian man is still a classic: "The Christian man is the Master of all and the servant of all."

A CAPTIVE CHURCH

More religious freedom is enjoyed in this country than anywhere else in the world. We are not held in bondage by the government or threatened by it. But that does not mean we are free. We are held captive in Babylon. We are captive to our culture, imprisoned in the American way of life, and slaves of a "brooding secularism." We are worldly. The world has broken down the wall of separation, of which Roger Williams spoke, and has entered God's garden, and the result is total wilderness. The candlestick has not only gone out, but also its light and warmth are not even missed.

We are captive to comfort, to status and prestige, to institutional wheeling and dealing. We are infiltrated by business and its methods, by government and its bigness, by television, by football, by every facet of our culture. And we love it. We are worshipers of what William James called "the bitch goddess of success." Our values are the same as society's values—to be big, to be rich, to be powerful, and above all to win! The religious enterprise resembles nothing so much as a mirror, and like Narcissus we look in the pool and what we see we like. And we say, "You're beautiful with your modern merchandizing techniques, your advertising gimmickry, your fads and trendiness, your bureaucracies, your mergers, your million dollar budgets, your tax exempt status, and your 10 percent deductions from the IRS."

Sometimes we get a signal from the mirror, no larger than the twitching of an eyebrow, "Are you real? Are you just? Are you free? Do you love? Whatever happened to Jesus Christ?" And we want out, but how? How do you get out of Babylon when you love it so? Or to be more biblical, "How do you sing the Lord's song in a strange land?" (See Psalm 137:4.)

➤ We must begin with ourselves. We must *want* to break out and sing the Lord's song. We must return to the Protestant principle and to our Baptist tradition of nonconformity. "The Protestant principle," Paul Tillich wrote, ". . . contains the divine and human protest against any absolute claim made for a relative reality, even if this claim is made by a Protestant church. The Protestant principle is the judge of every religious and cultural reality, including the religion and culture which calls itself 'Protestant.'"[4] We know what Baptist dissent has been in the past. What it is now and what it will be in the future depends on us. Let us begin by expanding our view of what it means to be religious; let us expand our ideas of freedom, and let us resolve to expand our action for religion and for freedom.

EXPAND OUR VIEW OF RELIGION AND OF FREEDOM

We are free to exercise religion, but is the exercise of it important? We may pray and worship in our churches, operate our Sunday schools, preach for the most part from free pulpits, but what is the issue of all that? One could not possibly object to most of what comes from our pulpits. But our free pulpits are born of indifference, not freedom. We are free to be prophets, but we are very polite prophets. We are free to evangelize, but suppose all of the people on earth were Baptists like us? Would it make any difference? They would all pray and sing and read the same Bible. But the Russians would still be Russians, and we would still be Americans looking down our missiles at each other. And the blacks would still be blacks; the whites would still be whites; the poor would still be poor; and the rich would still be rich. Half the world would still be starving and the other half profligate. Would our respective governments say of us what Thomas Jefferson said of his Virginia Baptists: "They are all good republicans . . . and satisfied with their government"? Would we have any cohesive and healing message of unity in Christ? No, the southern part of Russia would be Southern Russian Baptists, and the northern half would be American Russian Baptists. (I am sure the Southern Baptists would still have the best of it, for the American Russian Baptists would have to change their name!)

The Protestant principle of self-criticism is, and I quote Pogo, "We have met the enemy and they is us." How can we talk sensibly of religious truth when we are so divided? And how can we talk sensibly to the rest of the world about freedom when we are not free with each other? For it is the truth of Christ and discipleship in his truth which sets us free. Meanwhile, we have at least fifty-seven varieties of that truth in our Baptist ranks.

Perhaps the first step we must take toward a new grasp and meaningful expression of religious liberty is to make tracks toward Baptist unity. We may say that the truth we have in Christ transcends our disunity, but it is hard for the world which is not well versed in our subtleties and gnosticisms to see that. We really ought to start expanding our religious conscience to include each other, and to feel the shame that what we have for each other has more to do with toleration than it has with liberty, that we are as separate Baptist communions more cousins than brothers, more acquaintances than lovers.

A second step is to attempt to rescue religion and religious truth from utility to which it has been prostituted in our society. There was a time in Baptist history when religion and the realm of faith was considered a road to truth in its own right and that road was respected. Modern science has eroded that mountain of faith almost to a valley. Religious truth is still tolerated but only for its utility. It is true if it works. Or, as the Supreme Court says, it is true if it serves a secular purpose or performs some social function. It is not only true, but it is also good for those same reasons. It is no help to feel sorry for ourselves on this account, for we share this embarrassing role with all manner of disciplines and institutions. Sociology, psychology, and science itself are in the same boat. They have relevance (and relevance to some is the modern substitute for truth) only insofar as they have pragmatic value.

Our problem as religionists is different, however, for we are caught in this pragmatic world with a gospel which claims to be absolutely true and ultimate. It transcends all utilitarian and pragmatic reference. But this only makes our shame more bitter for we have been meretricious like all the rest. See how we do it in the personal presentation of the gospel: "Be a Christian and tithe and you will make a lot of money. Be a Christian and find peace of mind." And notice how we have followed the major trends of history. In the nineteenth century, we followed the flag in foreign missions, fitting into imperialism and colonialism. During the two great wars of the twentieth century we were enlisted in the cause of patriotism. During the fifties we were holding the fort against communism. In the sixties the cry went up, "Be a Christian and join the revolution!"

The modern trend is quietism, inwardness, and mysticism, growing out of the disillusionment with all causes. Until we take our faith straight, as an ultimate concern quite unalloyed and unmixed with the various utilitarian goals of our society, we are not free. Until we begin to write our own agenda, quite apart from the various and fleeting agendas of the world about us, we have nothing much to say about religious freedom. When we begin to buck the system and swim upstream, we shall find out what religious freedom is and whether we have any or not.

We must expand our conscience and update it in the interest of the free exercise of religion. John Bunyan and Roger Williams had clear convictions about religious freedom and conscience, but each generation must develop its own conscience, nurture it, and express it. As James McCord, president of Princeton Theological Seminary, said recently, "Each generation has its new Caesar and his new Rubicon to cross." The worship of God is not our issue, as it was to John Bunyan and Roger Williams, but should not religious freedom be expanded to include moral conscience quite apart from belief in God? This was the decision in *Seeger* v. *United States*.[5] But why should the Supreme Court be the conscience of a nation? Is it not the role of religion to be the moral catalyst, to raise the standard of conscience? Should not the modern religious conscience include ecology? "The earth is the Lord's and the fulness thereof." And to whom does the air belong? Is it not a religious concern that we mutilate the earth and pollute the air and water? Is it not a matter of religious conscience that, in this land of the free and home of the brave, people starve while others live lavishly and wastefully? Is it not a concern for religious freedom that a third of the world faces eventual, if not immediate, starvation? Is it not a matter of religious concern that world population is growing at a rate so fast as to put the whole earth in jeopardy? Does this not all contribute to a general cheapening of human life? Is the abortion problem a cause or an effect in this new cheapness? It is obvious that religious liberty must be expanded to take in the whole idea of a free society. For unless we can all have some increased measure of political, social, and economic freedom, there will be no freedom for anybody.

OUR CONTROVERSY WITH THE STATE

Freedom is exercised only in tension. In this country the tension is not so much a tension of hostility as it is of creativity. Religion or faith proceeds and prospers only by persuasion. The state possesses and may use the power of coercion. Generally in this nation, the state and religion have been friends, even partners, but the relationship is an uneven and unequal one. There are points at which religion must refuse to put its approval upon the deeds of the state. There is a propensity for the state to protect its own security, or other interests not always benign, and to attempt to use religion for its own ends. In our pledge of allegiance to the flag, it is solemnly declared that we are a nation, "under God," but this in the final analysis may be mere rhetoric. If the state is threatened by religion, it may use its coercive power.

The state will always tend to use religion for its own purposes; and if religion enters willingly into such a meretricious arrangement, it has no right to expect to keep its independence or its self-respect. A flagrant example of a state attempting to prostitute religion occurred in the Second World War when the Soviet Union enlisted the church in the war against Germany to invoke the innate religious impulses of the people on the side of holy Russia. Any state will attempt to use religion to elicit patriotism and devotion to country during a time of war. Certainly the United States had little difficulty in doing this during both of the World Wars of this century. The First World War was called a holy war by invoking the slogan, "Make the world safe for democracy," and little dissent was heard or allowed. In the Second World War, although much of the idealism of the first encounter with Germany had been dissipated, little serious opposition to the war was mounted by organized religion. The danger of Adolf Hitler was so pressing and so malevolent and the attack by the Japanese so infamous as to raise no serious question in the United States as to the justice of its cause. "Praise the Lord and pass the ammunition" was a hymn and a religious symbol of the war. There was little serious opposition to the global conflict from the mainline denominations, although the traditional peace churches—Quakers, Mennonites, Brethren, and the like, maintained their witness of nonviolence and the rights of conscientious objectors. The military had no problem in securing chaplains. The war was not regarded as holy, but it was viewed as necessary.

The Korean War was not as popular as the two larger wars, but it transpired without serious opposition from organized religion. The Vietnam War was another story, and serious opposition to it developed early. Clergy and Laymen Concerned About Vietnam (CALCAV) seriously challenged the rationale of the war. Campus ministers throughout the nation organized students against the war. Not only was the war opposed by demonstrations, debates, "teach-ins," and much violence, but the very institution of the draft was challenged. Draft-counseling centers existed on many campuses and in some churches. Counselors and students became expert at avoiding the draft in a strictly legal manner. In fact, so faulty was the Selective Service Law that few young men who were in college and received good counseling really had to go to Vietnam. One of the many tragedies of the war was that the wealthy and the well educated could escape it. The war was fought largely by the poor and the blacks. Opposition to the war was on grounds of conscience and morality as well as expediency. The combined force of religion, conscience, and morality was powerful in showing the fatuous foreign policy upon which the war was based. The massive civil disobedience which surrounded the issue of the war came from religious or moral convictions of a "higher law" which must take precedence over the law of the state. It is a time-honored position dating back to the Hebrew prophets, affirmed by our Lord, reaffirmed by Peter and the other apostles, and restated time and time again by theologians and prophets throughout all of church history. It is clear that in our time, this voice of religion, of conscience, and of moral outrage expressed in terms of civil disobedience was largely responsible for President Lyndon B. Johnson's fall from power, and in fact, it played a considerable part in bringing an end to the Vietnam conflict and the draft. The strongest support for civil disobedience and a "higher law" comes from its religious reference, be it the Declaration of Independence's resting its case for rebellion on Nature and Nature's God, or Peter in his skirmish with government saying, "We must obey God rather than men" (Acts 5:29).

It is now well and painfully known to Americans how disastrous the Vietnam War was for the United States and for the world; we still suffer the malaise of it which expresses itself in widespread cynicism and mistrust of government. We are aware of the connection between that war and Watergate and the demise of the Nixon presidency. Recently we have been made aware of efforts exerted by various government agencies, especially the president, the FBI, and the CIA, to silence all protesters. It was to a considerable extent the exercise of religious freedom and freedom of conscience expressed in civil disobedience which mounted that protest which saved this nation from disaster. Given the inevitable growth of national power and the increased dangers of international conflict in the world, the future will afford, as the present does now afford, ample justification and need for the exercise of religious freedom in public affairs. To maintain the creative tension between government and religion in the matter of war is one of the chief functions of organized religion, certainly of Baptists, in these tumultuous times. Nothing is lacking in the equation but the courage to be what we profess to be.

In fact, there is an immediate challenge which calls for that response of courage. During the late and lamented Vietnam War, many young men were draft dodgers. In fact, that group included all kinds of people. Some evaded (or avoided) the draft by going to college, some by filing as conscientious objectors and some by many other stratagems, all legal; some were more honest than others. Some took another tack; they fled the country to Europe and Canada, mostly the latter. They were following in a tradition, no doubt, that began in the immigrations of the nineteenth century, by which thousands of young men came to this country to escape the conscriptions of Europe. The refugees from the Vietnam War are still exiles from their native land. A rather abortive attempt was made by President Gerald Ford to bring them back if they would admit they were wrong and accept the prescribed punishment. This did not appeal to most of the exiles. A man having the courage to flee in the first place was not apt to accept such a humiliating return.

The exiles left the country for a variety of reasons and motives, but many of them left for reasons of religious conviction or conscience. It is generally conceded now that the protesters against the war were right and their detractors were wrong. The latter have been very generous in forgiving themselves for being wrong, but quite slow in forgiving the protesters for being right, and especially those who fled the country. Now is the time for Baptists in the exercise of religious freedom to petition the government to give full amnesty to the exiled men in Canada and other countries. It is ungracious of this nation, not to say petulant, when we are calling for the release of political prisoners throughout the world, to ignore our own political prisoners in Canada. All of us, if we believe the gospel, are "amnestees" of God in Jesus Christ. How can we as Christians hold out for punishment against amnesty when we have so bountifully participated in the amnesty of God?

RELIGIOUS LIBERTY AND CIVIL RIGHTS

Another immediate and continuing area of our concern must be the subject of civil rights, which, as we have seen, cannot be separated from religious rights and freedom. In fact, to make any attempt to separate them seems like studied hypocrisy. Our Lord, in beginning his ministry, quoted the famous lines from Isaiah, "The Spirit of the Lord is upon me, because he hath anointed me to preach the gospel to the poor . . . to heal the brokenhearted, to preach deliverance to the captives, and recovering of sight to the blind, to set at liberty them that are bruised" (Luke 4:18, KJV).

We are all aware of the titanic struggle which our black brothers and sisters have made in recent years to secure a place of equal opportunity, equal rights, equal jobs, and equal education. And the battle goes on apace, resisted still at almost every barricade by the white majority. What we lack here is not courage so much as insight into our own prejudices and liberation from them. This is a religious problem which only the Liberator of all men and women can solve.

It is especially pertinent for Baptists to take a fresh look at the civil rights of black people especially; they are our Baptist brothers and sisters in Christ; and their cries for justice ought to reach our ears first of all. An early and eloquent expression of that cry, delivered in 1852 in a speech by Frederick Douglass entitled "The Meaning of July Fourth for the American Negro," still needs to be heard.

> What, to the American slave, is your 4th of July? I answer: a day that reveals to him, more than all other days in the year, the gross injustice and cruelty to which he is the constant victim. To him, your celebration is a sham; your boasted liberty, an unholy license; your national greatness, swelling vanity; your sounds of rejoicing are empty and heartless; your denunciation of tyrants, brass fronted impudence; your shouts of liberty and equality, hollow mockery; your prayers and hymns, your sermons and thanksgivings, with all your religious parade and solemnity, are, to him mere bombast, fraud, deception, impiety, and hypocrisy—a thin veil to cover up crimes which would disgrace a nation of savages. There is not a nation on the earth guilty of practices more shocking and bloody than are the people of the United States, at this very hour.
>
> Go where you may, search where you will, roam through all the monarchies and despotisms of the Old World, travel through South America, search out every abuse, and when you have found the last, lay your facts by the side of the everyday practices of this nation, and you will say with me, that, for revolting barbarity and shameless hypocrisy, America reigns without a rival.[6]

With few exceptions, every line of that speech has application for our day. Despite the passage of 125 years, the condition of blacks has changed very little since that speech was made. If you doubt that, read it to your black Baptist brother and see what he says. Ask him how he celebrated the Bicentennial.

This is a vast area crying for the exercise of religious liberty, for it is a religious problem. If white society is largely captive of our American culture, as it is, think how that condition of captivity is deepened, lengthened, and heightened in the black community. The problem will not be finally solved by legislation. It can only ultimately be solved in the hearts of men, particularly in those hearts which have been touched by the Liberator. Baptists have a peculiar responsibility here, more than any other denomination, and more to black people than to any other minority group. As Judah said to Joseph as they bargained over the return of Benjamin, "How can I go back to my father if my brother is not with me?" (See Genesis 44:34.)

A second concern is the religious rights of women. This is not a problem which can be resolved through the judicial processes or in courts of law. It, too, is essentially a religious problem. It is doubtful that the courts will ever try to settle a case involving the ordination of women, any more than they would try to settle the matter of the Aaronic priesthood in the Mormon church being denied to blacks. The courts have no jurisdiction over these matters. These are matters to be determined by the churches themselves. Baptists have always been quick to reply rather self-righteously to Episcopalians and others that we have been ordaining women for years. But there is more rhetoric than substance in such a reply. The truth is that our ordination of women is mere tokenism. Most churches are pastored and administrated by males, and women are relegated to lesser roles than men. There is little question, even after you have explained away all the biblical admonitions about a woman's silence and subservience, but that the nub of the issue is discrimination. We are bound by our culture, as Paul was, and only as we are freed by the Liberator, can we begin to exercise religious freedom with respect to women.

RELIGIOUS FREEDOM IN EDUCATION

Education in America is very close to the heart of the nation and perhaps has more influence on the life of the nation than any other social institution. Our compulsory system of elementary and secondary education began in the early part of the nineteenth century and was an integral part of the Protestant Establishment. The educational system consists also of a complex system of private and public higher education, including religious and secular colleges, all of which are voluntary. Some private colleges are supported in part by public tax funds; others are not. Some religious schools, or schools which have their origins and roots in religion, have access to some limited public funds; others do not.

Protestantism traditionally has felt content with the public school system of elementary and secondary education, because in its early days the system allowed some religious coloration at least. School prayers and Bible reading exercises were permitted, as were Christmas celebrations and observances of Jewish holidays. In recent cases before the Supreme Court, the former practices have been declared unconstitutional and forbidden by the no-establishment clause.

Alongside the public school, a system of parochial schools, mostly Roman Catholic, has existed for many years. The parochial schools have served as a means by which parents who wish their children to have a religiously oriented education may fulfill the requirements of compulsory education. In *Pierce* v. *Society of Sisters* ,[7] this right for parents to send their children to parochial schools, so long as the schools meet the requirements and standards which the state may properly impose, was established. It is an important right.

The public school is a cherished symbol of our democracy, but the parochial school also has an important constitutional status. The latter is also a part of our democratic and pluralistic culture and performs a valuable service.

Much controversy has focused on whether or not parochial schools, since they perform a public service in meeting the state-imposed requirement of compulsory education, and especially since federal aid to local public schools has been instituted throughout the nation, should receive some aid from tax funds. In *Board of Education v. Allen*.[8] it was ruled that state approved textbooks on secular subjects could be loaned by state or local authorities to parochial schools without violation of the Constitution. In the famous *Everson* case,[9] it was ruled that public funds could be used to furnish busing to parochial school students. Generally, state constitutions are quite strict in prohibiting any aid whatsoever to parochial schools. Some states, as in Pennsylvania, are more generous in supplying some auxiliary support. In *Meek* v. *Pittenger*[10] the U.S. Supreme Court struck down all auxiliary aid to parochial schools, except textbook loans and certain instructional materials. The Pennsylvania law had provided extensive auxiliary services including counseling, testing, psychological services, speech and hearing therapy, and related services for exceptional, remedial, or educationally disadvantaged students. All of this was ruled unconstitutional.

The government is not obliged to provide aid to parochial schools out of public funds under the establishment clause of the First Amendment. However, the Supreme Court has also held that the state must not inhibit religion nor seek to advance it. If children of public schools under federally financed programs get hot lunches, medical and nursing care, and many other auxiliary services, children in parochial schools should not be penalized and proscribed from these benefits because of their religion. Indeed, it may well be required under the free exercise clause that they not be so discriminated against and penalized.

Religious education at the college level is more confusing, but equally grave. Because a college education involves young people at a higher level of maturity and therefore able to make up their own minds about religion, colleges have been allowed more freedom with respect to the teaching of religion. Money does flow by loans and grants from public funds for buildings and some programs on church-related campuses.[11] Religion departments do exist, though marginally, in state schools throughout the nation. The Department of Religion at the University of Iowa is a notable case in point. Religion is usually greeted with great suspicion on most college campuses, but the very suspicion should be a challenge and the open door a goad to action.

The question Baptists ought to ask in these days with respect to higher education and the free exercise of religion is simple: Can a person be educated without a knowledge of religion? How can a young man or woman understand our Western world and its culture without a study in depth of the religious forces which played upon it, for ill at times to be sure, but also for good, and in either case molding and structuring the very fabric of our civilization?

If that approach is too academic, we ought to ask: "How can a young person find direction, meaning, and life without faith?" Nathan Pusey, former president of Harvard University, was not afraid to give a clear answer:

> What every young person seeks in college, from liberal education—whether or not he has articulated this—is self-discovery. What he wants most to know is what it means to be a human being, what is expected of him as such, what the world is, and what are the options in it that lie before him, and how he is to get on with others. In short, the really burning question that faces someone trying to live through his mind is what is he to do with his life? What such a person wants—what we all want—is a meaning that becomes a motivating force in our lives. And when we ask this question, whether we are conscious of it or not, we have begun to think religiously, and have begun to ask of God. I see no reason not to admit that this is so.[12]

Many avenues are open for an expanded exercise of religious freedom in the whole field of education, both at the elementary and secondary levels and at the college and university level. Where public funds are involved, the issues are volatile and complex, and they should be debated freely and honestly in legislative halls, in religious precincts, and in courts of law. But the guidelines will have to be based on what is right and just for people and the free exercise of their religion. It is obvious that where government funds are involved, there is the likelihood of government control.

Baptists have a long tradition and history of freedom and dissent, but with the necessity and the incentive gone, we have more the history of it than the present reality. How can we possess our possessions? How can we recover what we already have? How do we "exercise" the muscles we have had little occasion to use in recent years? How do we stand fast in the liberty wherewith Christ has made us free? More important, how do we stop standing fast and move on?

One thing is sure: freedom cannot be created or conferred either by legislators or judges. The Thirteenth, Fourteenth, and Fifteenth Amendments to the Constitution were designed presumably to guarantee the civil rights of freedmen. One hundred years later black people still fight for and sometimes get justice under the law. That should forever convince us of the inadequacy of legislation and the entire legal system to assure justice and freedom. Not that it would be easier to get freedom without the law. Mere anarchy and irresponsibility are as severe tyrants as legalisms. For as Justice Learned Hand once said, "Freedom is a matter of the heart."[13] It must be a passion rather than a statute upon which we depend to secure religious and civil liberty for ourselves and for those of other religious persuasions and cultural differences, even though they may appear to be quite strange, not to say odious, to us.

In the pursuit of and the passion for freedom, we must stick to our last. We must be true to the gospel, for it is its truth and the continued discipline of it which makes all people free. That does not mean withdrawal to a stained glass, monkish view of our role. We are citizens of the world. Our message is a religious message, but, as the Old Testament prophets remind us, it brings all of life into its purview. We who are not economists must call the economists into judgment on the basis of conscience. We who are not politicians must hold the politicians' feet to the fire of justice and morality. We who are not psychologists or sociologists must hold both of those disciplines to account in terms of a transcendent vision. Above all, we must reserve the sharpest and most delicate calipers to measure ourselves. Remembering our past sins against liberty, we must constantly employ the admonition of Oliver Cromwell, "I beseech you in the bowels of Christ, think it possible you may be mistaken."[14]

NOTES

[1] Adrienne Koch and William Peden, eds., *Life and Selected Writings of Thomas Jefferson* (New York: Random House, Inc., 1944), p. 697.

[2] Thomas S. Eliot, "The Family Reunion" in *T. S. Eliot, The Complete Poems and Plays* (New York: Harcourt Brace Jovanovich, Inc., 1950), p. 268.

[3] Cited by Mark DeWolfe Howe, *The Garden and the Wilderness* (Chicago: The University of Chicago Press, 1965), pp. 5-6.

[4] Paul Tillich, *The Protestant Era* (Chicago: The University of Chicago Press, 1953), p. 163.

[5] *United States* v. *Seeger,* 380 U.S. 163 (1965).

[6] *New York Times,* July 4, 1975, p. L 23.

[7] *Pierce* v. *Society of Sisters,* 268 U.S. 510 (1925).

[8] *Board of Education* v. *Allen,* 392 U.S. 236 (1968).

[9] *Everson* v. *Board of Education of the Township of Ewing,* 330 U.S. 1 (1947).

[10] *Meek* v. *Pittenger,* 421 U.S. 349 (1975).

[11] *Tilton* v. *Richardson,* 403 U.S. 672 (1971).

[12] Nathan Pusey, "Religion's Role in Liberal Education," in *Religion and Freedom of Thought* (New York: Doubleday & Company, Inc., 1954). Copyright 1954 by the Union Theological Seminary.

[13] Learned Hand, *The Spirit of Liberty,* 3rd rev. ed. (New York: Alfred Knopf and Co., 1960), p. 190.

[14] "Letter to the General Assembly of the Church of Scotland, 3 August 1650" in *The Oxford Dictionary of Quotations.*

Nationalism
and
Christian Allegiance

WILLIAM M. PINSON, JR.

During the Vietnam War a Baptist college invited me to address the student body and faculty on the Christian's response to the conflict. At that time it was open season on doves; hawks were attacking every chicken in sight; and pacifist conscientious objectors were viciously crucifying everyone who did not agree with them. The atmosphere was not ideal for objective discussion, but I went anyway, spoke, and received a civil hearing.

After the assembly a free-for-all discussion erupted in the student center. Each side went to its corner and came out fighting—with words. One Baptist student said, "If my country calls on me to fight, I must go because the Bible says I'm to obey the powers that be." Another interrupted, "I'm not going anywhere unless I feel it is God's will. We are to obey God, not men." A girl declared, "If you don't go, you don't love your country." A preacher-student intoned, "Godless communism must be stopped and God has chosen the United States as his instrument to do this. God's will *is* that we fight."

Then an ROTC officer, back from Vietnam, suggested, "As a Christian, you shouldn't blindly follow the orders of government. Some wars may be wrong and should be resisted. Simply because it is a war against communism doesn't make it right. Hitler was supported by many German Baptists because he was anti-Communist and nationalistic. But he was not doing what was right. You shouldn't put the flag above the cross." An older student, red with rage, exploded, "The cross and the flag are the same in this country!" As is often the case, the discussion was more interesting and informative than the speech. It revealed the many different positions Baptists hold concerning the Christian's relation to our nation and to national policy and action.

When nationalism and Christian allegiance are in apparent conflict, which way should the Christian go? In the antiseptic isolation of academic discussion shut off from the nasty realities of the world, the answer to the question comes easily: God's way. That is correct, of course, but outside of the ivory tower in the pits of daily life the application of that answer does not come easily. The various biblical emphases on God and government from various passages, such as Daniel 6; Matthew 22:15-22; Acts 5:29; Romans 13; 1 Timothy 2:1-4; 1 Peter 2:13-14; and Revelation 13, provide insight but no systematic solution. What is God's way? Who determines or discovers it? The state? The church? The individual? What if there are conflicting reports from each on what God wants? Which are we to believe? A careful examination of nationalism, Christian allegiance, and the proper relation between them ought to be required of us all. This brief sketch merely points the way for more extensive investigation.

NATIONALISM

Nationalism is an elusive concept. It normally goes beyond obedience and loyalty to government, exceeding patriotism. Nationalism exalts one nation over all others. It places primary emphasis on the promotion of its culture and interests over other nations. Nationalism in its extreme form calls on citizens to advance the cause of the nation at personal sacrifice, renouncing primary loyalty to any other person or group.

Where nationalism thrives, the nation assumes an exalted position, sometimes approaching deity. The people see their nation with its form of government, economy, and culture as best and therefore deserving of supremacy in the world of nations. Nationalism often leads to conquest, aggression, imperialism, and colonialism.

The ingredients of nationalism are the stuff of which religion is made. The late historian Carlton J. H. Hayes wrote a book called *Nationalism: A Religion.*[1] He traced how the modern world tends to connect God and nation or even to make the nation into a kind of God. It is not surprising, therefore, that many nations develop a civil religion in which the state displays the various components identified with religion.

History supplies many examples of nationalism wrapped in the trappings of religion. The Old Testament records that in ancient

Israel God was considered King and Leader of his people. National policy and religious ceremony, politics and piety were intertwined. In popular attitude, loyalty to Jehovah called for loyalty to Israel, and loyalty to Israel meant loyalty to Jehovah. This type of religion-government relation became the model for many nations in Europe in the Middle Ages. The concept also pervaded early rhetoric about the United States—the New Israel in the Promised Land acting under Manifest Destiny. Modern prophets, like their counterparts in ancient Israel, warned against making God and government synonymous.

Centuries later Rome developed a civil religion. Claims of divinity for Caesar and demands for citizens to acknowledge him as such posed a life-death dilemma for early believers. Nationalism and Christian allegiance met head-on in the first few centuries and called for decision. The various ways Christians decided to relate their Christian faith to nationalistic interests of Rome became the basic options for Christians in later centuries. These options will be examined later.

In more recent times also nationalism has developed the characteristics of religion. Under Adolf Hitler, for example, the Nazi movement whipped German nationalism into a religious frenzy. With pomp and pageantry never excelled by Catholicism, with fiery oratory never matched by the hottest sawdust-trail evangelist, with millenarian talk about a Third Reich lasting a thousand years, with appeals to sacrifice and ultimate loyalty, Hitler used civil religion as a means to advance nationalistic goals. Less spectacular but none-theless important illustrations of nationalism accompanied by civil religion can be seen in nations in practically every part of the world, including the United States.

In 1967 Robert N. Bellah in an article entitled "Civil Religion in America" stated, "There actually exists alongside of and rather clearly differentiated from the churches an elaborate and well-institutionalized civil religion in America."[2] And Martin Marty writes, "America is not by any means unique in its tendencies to turn the nation into the bearer or the object of religion. But it has special temptations based on its power and the plausibility that goes with its many historic successes."[3]

The doctrines and ethical standards of American civil religion include belief in a democratic social order, the equality of all persons before the law, and the personal rights and freedoms of individuals. The symbols of the faith include the flag, the national anthem, and the Liberty Bell. Among the shrines are the birthplaces and death places of America's leaders, the monuments of Washington, D.C., and the places where significant events took place, such as Plymouth Rock, Independence Hall, and Gettysburg. Pilgrimages are made to these shrines to pay respect to the past and gain inspiration for the future.

The sacred writings of our national religion are dominated by the Declaration of Independence and the Constitution, seen as the inspired and enduring documents on which the nation rests. The saints or holy men are those who founded and preserved the nation, most of them political or military persons. John F. Wilson in "The Status of 'Civil Religion' in America" describes a sort of trinity among the holy men of civil religion: Washington as the father of our country; Lincoln as the propitiating sacrifice to preserve the Union; Kennedy as the spirit of reconciliation between warring religious factions—father, son, and holy spirit.[4]

The ritual of civil religion includes such acts as reciting the pledge of allegiance to the flag, standing or saluting when the flag goes by, and singing the national anthem. Certain days are set aside as holy days for special ceremony—Memorial Day, July 4, Veteran's Day, Labor Day, Columbus Day, and Thanksgiving. Institutions which perpetuate civil religion include government bureaucracies and public schools. These sponsor activities, indoctrinate, and build a common response to symbols of the national faith.

Someone who refuses to participate in the rites of civil religion—such as a Jehovah's Witness who will not salute the flag, a Seventh-Day Adventist who will not eat a hot dog or a hamburger, a Quaker who will not fight a war, or an historian who challenges the popular myths about our founding fathers—is treated as a heretic, a dangerous person to be scorned and isolated, perhaps even imprisoned.

CHRISTIAN ALLEGIANCE

The Christian faith exists side by side with America's civil religion. Baptists in America are expected to embrace both nationalism and Christian allegiance. We Baptists have our own set of religious components—doctrine, ethics, holy men and days, sacred writings, symbols, ritual, shrines, and pilgrimages. Some of these we hold in common with other Christians; a few are distinctive.

Christian allegiance demands that we acknowledge Christ as Lord, not the state. We are to be loyal to him, his way, and his teachings even if they conflict with the laws and policies of the government. "Jesus is Lord!" expressed the early Christian's commitment. The reverse of this statement was implied: "Caesar is *not* Lord."

The situation in the United States has made difficult the task of distinguishing what is Christ's and what is Caesar's. We Baptists have often regarded loyalty to our nation as faithfulness to God. Baptists were practically unanimous in their support of the Revolution, seeing in the new government an expression of biblical truth. During the Civil War Baptists on each side were fiercely loyal to their respective governments because they believed those governments were an expression of God's will. Later the Southern Baptist Convention backed the United States in the war with Spain feeling that it would overthrow oppression and open up new mission fields. Most Baptists saw World War I as a holy crusade against evil and World War II as necessary for God's justice to be done.[5]

On the domestic scene Baptists have also supported nationalistic policy. Few protested the U.S. government's actions against the Indians, Mexicans, or Japanese. In fact, Baptist missionaries accepted federal funds in their work with the Indians, a work viewed by the government as a pacification project.

RELATIONSHIP OF NATIONALISM AND CHRISTIAN ALLEGIANCE

The history of the relationship between nationalism and Christian allegiance in this country is generally marked by friendliness. This fact led Elwyn A. Smith to write in the Foreword of *The Religion of the Republic,* "Why have American religious groups never spawned sedition? Why have they been patriotic to the point of ethical delinquency?"[6] The generally friendly attitude is especially striking in light of the fact there is no official state church or denomination expected to be the religious arm of the government.

Several factors help explain why Christian allegiance and nationalism have seldom been in serious conflict in America. One is the amiable relation between the two in the beginning of our nation. Many who came to these shores left Europe for religious reasons. Here a great many found freedom to express their religious convictions. The governments that were established were not hostile to the Christian faith. In both the northern and southern colonies a close and friendly relation existed between the dominant religious groups and the governments.

The vast majority of early American colonists claimed allegiance to some expression of the Christian faith. They saw the hand of God making and preserving a nation. In his book *Nationalism and Religion in America,*[7] Winthrop S. Hudson provides numerous examples of the close allegiance of Christian expression and national beginnings. Many Christians viewed the United States of America as a product of God's will and supported it as God's instrument for accomplishing his purpose in the world.

The strong Christian statements made by early colonists permeated the rhetoric and writing of the new nation. No rival religion challenged the Christian infusion of national symbols, documents, and pronouncements. The pragmatic formulators of a pluralistic nation realized sectarian expression would be divisive and thus they kept their religious language in the vague middle of the road. "God," "Providence," and "Heaven" were often used. "Jesus," "Christ," "Mary," "Holy Spirit," and "Christian" were almost never used. Each religious group could read its own meaning into the general terms. Some Christians claimed the nation was Christian even though Jesus Christ and the Bible were not referred to in the founding documents.

Although separation of church and state gradually came to be more and more a reality, the separation was friendly, not hostile. Many special favors for organized religion continued even though churches were disestablished—tax exemption, legal enforcement of religious holy days, military exemption for the clergy, and the like.

For the past two hundred years Baptists have generally been supportive of a government which treated them and their institutions well, spoke in religious terms, and aided in missionary endeavors. Church leaders urged Christians to back their government. Some theologians and preachers developed justification for American aggression on the grounds of the special place the United States had in the world. The superiority of America was attributed to the godliness of its people and was cited as justification for forcing the American way on others around the world. Christian leaders hesitated to challenge the exploits of a nation which had a special arrangement with the Deity. Whereas today conservative Christians are known for their super-blue nationalism, in an earlier day the liberals were much more outspoken—men such as Henry Ward Beecher and Walter Rauschenbusch, for example.

Some Christian leaders have seen Christian allegiance in conflict with nationalism, however, and a few have acted on the conviction that allegiance to God takes precedence over loyalty to nation. A number of preachers and lay people challenged the government's policy on slavery, treatment of Indians, war with Mexico, labor unions, business reform, and anti-Communist efforts. Others have spoken out against government action which destroyed racial segregation, removed government sanctioned prayers from the schools, and legalized abortion. Most criticisms, however, have been limited, and most critics have professed continuing loyalty to the nation.[8]

Baptists have been among those who protested when national policy infringed on Christian allegiance. John Leland and Isaac Backus challenged the laws of the state and claimed the right to religious freedom. Harry Emerson Fosdick and Culbert G. Rutenber expressed pacifist sentiments and insisted the state does not have ultimate authority. T. B. Maston and Foy Valentine have warned against blind loyalty to government and called for a responsible challenge to government policy. Martin Luther King, Jr., and Ralph Abernathy boldy refused to obey laws of the state or follow policies of the government which they felt to be immoral. Baptists active in counter-culture movements and writing for journals such as the *Post American* challenge national goals, priorities, and life-styles.

As we move into the third one hundred years as a nation, what should be the relation of Christian allegiance and nationalism? The past should not necessarily fashion the future. "That's the way we've always done it" does not mean "That's the way we should do it."

Briefly, here are our options. One, identify Christian allegiance with American nationalism, national purpose with Christian mission, patriotism with piety, the flag with the cross, the American way with the kingdom of God. Thus the United States is viewed as God's agent in the world, the protector of the innocent against the evil. To paraphrase General Bullmoose, "What is good for the United States is good for the Christian cause." This view essentially holds that there is no basic conflict between nationalism and Christian allegiance and that Christians should work to see that the nation *remains* Christian.

Second, maintain that nationalism and Christian allegiance are two distinct entities, each with a right to exist. Within this position there are several different options: see nationalism as a generally good feature of American life, or a neutral one, or a potentially evil one. Some Baptists do see nationalism as generally good, including the aspect of civil religion. The arguments run something like this: The state is essential for the social order to function. In order to exist, the state must be supported and be able to demand aid in defending itself; taxes, weapons, and warriors are essential. Some national unity is also necessary. Since no single religion has won the allegiance of all the people, civil religion to which all can subscribe aids national unity and stability. Further, civil religion keeps down strife between sects because no one religious group has any chance of becoming the national religion. Also, civil religion is better than no religion at all and at least keeps certain religious symbols before the people.

Other Christians do not view nationalism in such a positive way, although they admit it is valid. They see it as a necessary evil, something to be tolerated. The demands of the state are to be met unless they clearly conflict with Christian principles and beliefs. One tries to go along with government and not create tension unless absolutely necessary. When the state exceeds its rightful sphere, Christians must work to restrict its activities. Foy Valentine wrote in *Citizenship for Christians,* "The state is to be obeyed, the Bible teaches, only so long as it stays within its bounds." He added, "The Christian citizen's foremost obligation is his duty to God. It is the devil's patriotism to say, 'My country right or wrong.'"[9]

Third, consider nationalism a challenge to Christian allegiance and oppose it. The form of opposition advocated varies to some extent with the intensity of the nationalism. Some insist on a passive approach, withdrawing into separate Christian communities and ignoring the state—refusing to serve in armies, work in government, or pay taxes. Some suggest attacking nationalism with its civil religion as idolatry and working to have the Christian faith become the national religion; the goal would be to Christianize the social order. If the goal were achieved, it appears the result would be a blending of nationalism and Christian allegiance—and we would be back to option one.

CONCLUSION

The Bible seems to present models or types of each option. However, the New Testament pattern is primarily a wary coexistence and cooperation with a nationalistic state. When the state exceeded its proper bounds, passive resistance was called for. The Christian was primarily a citizen of the kingdom of God and owed ultimate allegiance to Jesus as Lord. Yet the state had certain legitimate rights, and the Christians were urged to recognize these. There was no thought of "Christianizing" the state or the social order in the sense of having Christianity become the established religion. There was, rather, a desire to bring influence by Christians on all aspects of society.

Perhaps the most disturbing conclusion of this study is that Christian allegiance for most professing Christians takes a back seat to nationalism and civil religion. Whereas thousands have died for their country and the American way, few seem to be willing to sacrifice for the Christian way. If a young person renounces national policy and leaves the country in protest, the nation is highly incensed over his act and reluctant to accept him back. In contrast, if a Christian renounces personal faith, few seem to care; if such a one wants to come back home, that one is welcomed with few if any questions asked. Most people pay whatever taxes are demanded of them, but few give whatever tithes and offerings are asked of them. Nationalism seems a stronger force today by far than Christian allegiance. To put priorities straight may be the biggest challenge facing Baptists in the third one hundred years of this nation.

NOTES

[1] Carlton J. H. Hayes, *Nationalism: A Religion* (New York: The Macmillan Publishing Co., Inc., 1960).

[2] Robert N. Bellah, "Civil Religion in America," *Daedalus,* vol. 96 (Winter, 1967), p. 1.

[3] Martin E. Marty, *The Pro and Con Book of Religious America* (Waco: Word Books, 1975), CON, p. 55.

[4] John F. Wilson, "The Status of 'Civil Religion' in America," *The Religion of the Republic,* ed. Elwyn A. Smith (Philadelphia: Fortress Press, 1971), p. 4.

[5] Foy Valentine, ed., *Peace! Peace!* (Waco: Word Books, 1967), pp. 58-62.

[6] Elwyn A. Smith, ed., "Foreword," *The Religion of the Republic,* p. vii.

[7] Winthrop S. Hudson, *Nationalism and Religion in America* (New York: Harper & Row, Publishers, 1970).

[8] For examples of sermons on these issues, see Clyde E. Fant, Jr., and William M. Pinson, Jr., *Twenty Centuries of Great Preaching* (Waco: Word Books, 1971); Dewitte T. Holland, ed., *Preaching in American History* (Nashville: Abingdon Press, 1969); and *Sermons in American History* (Nashville: Abingdon Press, 1971).

[9] Foy Valentine, *Citizenship for Christians* (Nashville: Broadman Press, 1965), p. 96.

CHAPTER

14

The Church
and
Public Policy:
Rationale

GEORGE W. HILL

Rolf Hochhuth's controversial play, *The Deputy,* was greeted throughout its long post-war run in Europe and America with mingled acclaim and picket lines. The tumultuous public impact of this dramatization was due largely to the fact that it touched the exposed raw nerve of an unresolved problem—the true and proper role of the church in the world. The plot focused on a running battle between those who would call the pope to speak out with all the moral might of his office condemning the Germans for the mass slaughter of Jews in the horror camps of Auschwitz and Buchenwald, and those of his advisers who believed that the Catholic Church must be preserved at any cost—even at the cost of silence in the presence of evil—though all the world should die. In the swirling controversy, Riccardo, the young priest who finally makes the ultimate identification with his doomed Jewish brothers and sisters by pinning the Star of David on his vestments and going with them to the gas chamber, says in a feverishly impassioned word to the Abbot:

> To look on
> idly when tomorrow morning
> our fellow citizens—do not forget,
> the ranks of Jews hold many Catholics too—
> are loaded aboard cattle cars.
> Are *we* to stand by and . . .
> wave our handkerchiefs to them?
> That is, if the kind Germans permit. . . .
> And then—then we go home?
> Confess—what should we confess?

That we have used the name of God in vain!
And sit down to some journal, to read about
the excavations in St. Peter's?
And then on Sunday we ring the bells
and celebrate our Mass—so filled with sacred thoughts,
that nothing, surely, tempts us to consider
those who at that very moment in Auschwitz
are being driven naked into the gas.[1]

Here the battle lines are clearly drawn. Either the whole world is under the judgment and grace of God and the church is to proclaim that universal sovereignty, or by some imperious edict the whole creation has been neatly separated into two mutually exclusive domains, the sacred and the secular, and the church is to proclaim the limited Lordship of Christ over the sacred. This realm is understood to encompass a precariously narrow slice of turf. It includes the interior "spiritual" life of the believer and the pious practices associated with the church. All else, having to do with where people work and play, love and hate, govern and oppress, sweat and starve, belongs to "the world, the flesh, and the devil." The church is seen as a little sacred fortress in a vast secular wilderness, and evangelism, in this view, is, as someone has said, a kind of midnight raid on enemy territory to rescue a few brands from the burning. From this truncated perception of the divine sovereignty and the scope of the gospel flow most of the false dichotomies artificially established between faith and works, religion and ethics, evangelism and social action, individual and corporate sin, private practice and public policy.

Whenever the faith that we profess in private fails to inform our public policy and corporate behavior, and the latter is thereby assumed to flourish in an unprincipled realm where expediency is king, we have all the basic raw materials for a melancholy Watergate tragedy. When the faith that is proclaimed is selectively derived from our biblical inheritance, so that there is no stern prophetic summons to righteousness and justice, no trembling before the awesome majesty of the Lord of all creation who is high and lifted up above us, no sensitizing of conscience, no true and thoroughgoing repentance and no reaching out for the forgiving grace that has already sought us; it matters little whether worship takes place in the controlled atmosphere of the East Room of the White House or in the sanctuary of a church. If the domain of God's sovereignty is so narrowly defined as to exclude the corporate and institutional behavior of the human community because all of this is somehow "secular" and the church is only concerned with "sacred" things, then we have not learned the lessons of our faith or our recent history. When a considerable number of respectable, church-going, "religious" men, some of whom do not drink or smoke as a matter of principle, can mount a deliberate assault on the most cherished institutions of a free society and evidence neither guilt nor remorse when apprehended, it is their tragically dwarfed perception of the role of high religion in personal and public life that stands condemned before the bar of God's judgment.

The problem here is fundamentally theological. We have tended to preach the cross of our Lord Jesus Christ in almost exclusively privatistic terms, as though we had never heard Jesus refer to the moment of his ultimate exaltation as "the judgment of this world" (John 12:31). To appropriate and interpret a cosmic event in exclusively individualistic terms is in some sense to trivialize it and to rob it of a measure of its moral force. Lesslie Newbigin has expressed this concern in positive terms:

> Our faith is that the Word of the Cross is in very truth the power of God unto salvation—not just the rescue of each one of us separately, but the healing, the making whole of the whole creation and the fulfilling of God's whole will. Our faith is that the Cross is in truth the only event in human history which can properly be called the crisis of human history, and that the issue which is raised there for the entire human race is one beside which even the survival of human civilization on earth is a secondary matter.[2]

Before the church is truly free to proclaim the whole gospel to the whole of life, it must deal biblically and theologically with the false dichotomies and lingering dualisms which have plagued and circumscribed the testimony of the faith since the days of the second-century gnostic heresy. It was this deviation from the gospel which sought to pressure believers to affirm their faith in Christ and at the same time to deny the world, as though these realms were mutually exclusive and fundamentally incompatible. And the heresy persists to this day, as though the whole creation were not the handiwork and gift of God, as though his Lordship were limited to a mere narrow segment of his creation, as though we had never heard that "God so loved the world (not the church) that he gave his only Son" (John 3:16). If there is any sense in which the church is the body of Christ, the contemporary embodiment or incarnation of his loving spirit at work in the world, then we are obligated by our very nature and our marching orders to accept and love and serve, to evangelize and reconcile and heal the same world, in all its brokenness and alienation and sin, which he loved and for which he gave his life. As Foy Valentine has written, "Our task is to convert these *modernists,* who have turned away from Moses and the prophets and Paul and John and Peter and James and from Jesus to embrace that wretchedly false and abominably misleading dualism which never ceases to plague the Christian church."[3]

We do not seek safe refuge from this world, but engagement with it for the sake of Jesus Christ and the interests of his kingdom. This, we maintain, is the "worldly" and authentically Christian faith which has successfully exercised the sacred-secular demon and has moved ahead to a biblically mature and faithful religion which seeks a balanced concern for the priestly and the prophetic, grace and judgment, piety and action, the individual and the community. In this biblical and theological context, the church's concern for public policy is not only legitimatized but also it takes its rightful place in the broad spectrum of human concerns which must one day yield to the Lordship of Jesus Christ.

We need to recognize an almost universal human tendency to avoid a difficult issue until it is perceived that one's self-interest is directly involved. This is a common failing among individuals and institutions, including the church. Even Baptists, with an enviable history of courageous action in defense of freedom, have tended to see the problem largely in religious or ecclesiastical terms, and their response is often colored by a generous amount of institutional self-interest. Freedom of worship, church-state relations, issues of religious conscience, taxation or public subsidy of religious institutions—these and kindred matters have ranked much higher on the usual Baptist agenda than the freedom issues associated with oppressed minorities and the unjust attitudes and systems which continue to hold them in bondage.

Return for a moment to the situation with which this essay began—the obscene slaughter of over six million Jews in Adolf Hitler's gas chambers and crematoria during the Second World War. This was probably the most comprehensive act of genocide in the world's long history, and surely the brutal apogee of our "enlightened" twentieth-century orbit. The Holocaust is commonly regarded by the modern Jew as the most inhumane and devastating event in the long and tragic history of a people whose corporate identity and sense of God-given purpose emerged with Abraham, centuries before the earliest biblical writings. Over three decades have passed, but deep scars remain in the Jewish psyche. For many, the crisis was essentially theological and resulted in a partial or complete abdication of faith. To them, no God characterized by power, love, and righteousness would have permitted the Holocaust. All the questions raised by undeserved suffering and death were raised six million times. For other Jews, Western Europe in general had been strongly influenced by the Christian church and its values, and Germany in particular was the home of noted Christian theologians and biblical scholars. It was this culture that turned in venomous attack on the Jews, and the silence of Christians throughout this monstrously obscene chapter in human history was unforgettably and unforgivably deafening. For these Jews, the big questions focused not so much on the love and righteousnes of God as on the love and righteousness of Christians, and the sincerity of their pious professions.

In part, at least, the remarkable silence of the church can be explained by the fact that Christian self-interest did not seem to be threatened by the persecution of the Jews. Indeed, it must be confessed with shame that many Christians actively fanned the flames of anti-Semitism. We had not yet learned the profoundly important lesson that freedom is indivisible, that none of us is truly free unless and until all of us are free, and "us" includes the whole human family. So long as a Jew can be deprived of freedom or life for his or her Jewishness, or a black for the color of his or her skin, or a Communist for political philosophy, or a nonconformist for refusal to follow the crowd, then none of us, even in the white Anglo-Saxon Protestant majority, can claim any real security. Martin Niemöller, the German Lutheran pastor who became a living symbol of heroic and sacrificial resistance to the Nazi tyranny, made a remarkable confession in this regard:

> In 1933, when the Communists were imprisoned, I did not lift up my voice. I did not say to my congregation, "Be on your guard. There is something wrong happening here." And when the feeble-minded were murdered, I said to myself, "Am I to be the guardian of the feeble-minded?" I could not even claim that I was ignorant of the persecution of the Jews, but I did nothing. I only started speaking out when the faith of the Church was persecuted. For this neglect I am greatly to blame. I have sinned.[4]

The issue goes beyond our narrow perceptions of self-interest and the indivisibility of freedom. It is the indivisibility of the human community which is also at stake. Thus the Great Commission is emptied of its moral force if the neighbor that we are enjoined to love is perceived in anything short of universal terms. Any narrowing of neighbor to my kind of person, defined by particularities of race, class, color, religion, nationality, politics, culture, or status, is an act of overt disobedience against the God of the whole human family. Moreover, it constitutes a repudiation of the New Testament goal of Christian mission, "to unite all things in him, things in heaven and things on earth" (Ephesians 1:10). In God's new order of things "there cannot be Greek and Jew, circumcised and uncircumcised, barbarian, Scythian, slave, free man, but Christ is all, and in all" (Colossians 3:11). Thus, in the realms of personal behavior and public policy the obedient church should stand in active opposition to everything that divides, isolates, polarizes, discriminates, and otherwise fractures the human community.

If one is tempted to believe that the church should "stick to the gospel" by an exclusive emphasis upon personal salvation and private virtue, thereby renouncing any effort to influence public policy or to redeem the culture, the lurking dangers of this position are never more clearly illuminated than in the story of the church in Nazi Germany. Paul Tournier makes the lesson unmistakably clear:

> On a number of occasions I have been in Germany . . . at the invitation of the Evangelical Academy of Bad Boll. Here again one could observe that the terrible Nazi flood had produced a perhaps completely unexpected result, namely, that of forcing the church out of its reserve and obliging it again to accept its full responsibility to society. It was there that I was best able to gauge the seriousness of that rift between the church and the world. One of my German colleagues said to me: "One day you may perhaps be thankful to us for having gone through this tragic experience, which had to be gone through in order to understand what this modern dream of building a society detached from its spiritual foundations can lead to."
>
> The Nazi catastrophe was a sign of the bankruptcy of the modern ideal. The church had been shut up in its own chapels. It was tolerated provided that it made no further claim to govern society. Men believed that they could regulate society without any transcendental principle, purely on the basis of a science which proclaimed its moral neutrality. But under these circumstances it was possible for another power to arise which did not hesitate to bend law, medicine, education, and everything else to its pagan ethics.
>
> After the catastrophe the German church, whose most eminent representatives had been the first victims of the regime, understood this very well. There can be a fruitful transformation of the German people only if a new Christian elite is established, consecrated men who in every domain will apply themselves to the reconstruction of a society inspired by Christ.[5]

If the church, through failure of nerve, or preoccupation with the preservation of its own institutional life and the comfort of its constituency, or a limited perception of the range and responsibility of the gospel, fails to speak and incarnate the words of eternal life to a decadent age, it runs the grave risk of participating in the decline of its culture. If it does not stand over against its evil generation in the proclamation of judgment and grace, it has not earned the right to transcend and to outlive the contemporary history which holds it fast and keeps it neutralized. Let us never forget that strangely contemporary church at Laodicea, flawed by internal poverty of spirit and external pretensions to greatness. It represented form without essence, combining arrogant complacency with intellectual, moral, and spiritual destitution. We sense that it was too sophisticated for enthusiasm and too blind to make moral and spiritual distinctions. It succumbed all too easily to our own constant temptation to accept the standards of society as the standards of the church, and it was soon caught in the tender trap of conformity. Like many of us, and like the churches we know, it was neither good enough to be called good, nor bad enough to be called bad. It richly deserved the angelic judgment: "I know your work: you are neither cold nor hot. Would that you were cold or hot! So, because you are lukewarm, and neither cold nor hot, I will spew you out of my mouth. For you say, I am rich, I have prospered, and I need nothing; not knowing that you are wretched, pitiable, poor, blind, and naked " (Revelation 3:15-17). While we remember, and rightfully so, the word of judgment upon the Laodiceans, let us not forget the word of grace: "Behold, I stand at the door and knock; if any one hears my voice and opens the door, I will come in to him and eat with him, and he with me. He who conquers, I will grant him to sit with me on my throne, as I myself conquered and sat down with my Father on his throne" (Revelation 3:20-21).

The search for the appropriate role of the church in relation to public policy will lead to discovery or reaffirmation of our central vocation as responsible disciples of Christ and functional members of his body, the church. To be faithful and obedient in this role means outright rejection of the beguiling temptation to escape involvement with the world which Christ loved and for which he lived and died. As Valentine has said, "If God had wanted to avoid involvement, He would have avoided the incarnation."[6] Christians, if they want to be where Christ is, must be in the thick of the struggle, taking sides and getting involved. Why? Because, as someone has observed, this is the "reassertion of incarnation." Anything else is only partial obedience, or, to put the matter more bluntly, as the Presbyterians have done, "Churches and individual Christians who seek to 'glorify God' only through hymns and prayers and 'living a good life' are sinning against their God."[7] According to a venerable Christian tradition, the sins of omission are just as serious as those of commission, though usually less apparent.

What is our rationale for involvement? In the most fundamental sense it has evolved from our Lord's mandate to go into the world as witnesses to the saving power of God's love, to be like light driving out the darkness, like salt giving zest and flavor to life, like leaven quietly transforming the whole loaf of creation. The arena for this encounter is not within the sheltering walls of the church carefully sequestered from the contaminating influences of the world outside, but precisely in that world to which the Protestant Reformation summoned Christians to return, in which each is to exercise his or her unique ministry, for which our baptism has ordained us all. This is the world where commerce and industry pump lifeblood into the economy, where government functions, where nation takes up sword against nation, where ideas are generated and disseminated, where the vitality of family life ebbs and flows, where birth and growth and death set the limits of our mortal existence. It is to this world that Jesus came as Servant and Savior, and to this world that the church must go.

The love of God and the love of neighbor are coequal in the scale of Christian priorities. We cannot properly pray for and then forget the sick, the undernourished, those whom we call enemies, or the victims of discrimination. A redeemed individual in a redeemed society is the divine intention as represented in the hope for the coming of God's kingdom of right relationships "on earth as it is in heaven." Christians at their courageous best affirm the ancient confession that "Jesus is Lord," rather than Caesar, but they never relinquish their stubborn hope that one day, in God's good time, and with the active participation of the faithful, even Caesar's realm, "the kingdom of the world," shall become "the kingdom of our Lord and of his Christ, and he shall reign for ever and ever" (Revelation 11:15).

In focusing concern upon the church and public policy, there are several important areas in which our effectiveness would be greatly enhanced if we would move in our understanding and practice of the gospel from widely divergent positions on the theological spectrum to a recognition of the new richness to be achieved in a reciprocal movement between the divergent positions. For example, the gap between believing and doing needs to be narrowed. Many a church begins with reflection on a problem and convinces itself that once some clarity of understanding has been achieved, the problem has been dealt with, and it is time to move on to the next item on the agenda. The traditional Race Relations Sunday is a case in point. The consistent emphasis of the Master was on acting out one's beliefs. "Not every one who says to me, 'Lord, Lord,' shall enter the kingdom of heaven, but he who does the will of my Father who is in heaven" (Matthew 7:21). "Whoever does the will of my Father in heaven is my brother, and sister, and mother" (Matthew 12:50). "If you salute only your brethren, what more are you doing than others?" (Matthew 5:47). "Every tree that does not bear good fruit is cut down and thrown into the fire" (Matthew 7:19).

A little girl was hugging her daddy and telling him that she loved him, but she would steal an occasional glance over her father's shoulder at her brother, contort her face, and stick out her tongue at him. Mother soon interrupted this charade by crying out to the little girl, "You can't do that!" Love is to be known more in the doing than the saying, and verbal professions of love for daddy were badly compromised by clear evidence of dislike for another of his children. Love is something we do and which communicates itself easily at the interpersonal level, but is it possible to "do love" at the level of public policy? If we understand justice to be love broadly and equitably distributed, then the diligent quest for justice in the area of public policy becomes for the Christian an important act of believing and doing. Many will content themselves with "doing love" at the interpersonal level, where the rewards and gratifications are more obvious, but the issue here is involvement, sharing with our Lord the heavier burdens of the kingdom.

There is a gap to be narrowed in our divergent understandings of the role of the church. Is it most faithful to its charter when it gives leadership on the "inward journey," or when it prepares us for the "outward journey"? Does it function best and most appropriately as a safe haven from the tumult and temptation of an evil world, or as a training station for the recruits who have volunteered to join with their Leader in the continuing struggle to bring the human community and its institutions under the lordship of Jesus Christ?

Why should one be forced to choose between the inward and the outward journey? Has not the movement between the two been characteristic of the authentic church since earliest days? The community of the faithful is gathered for worship, celebration, spiritual renewal, fellowship in Christ, mutual support and encouragement, and training; it is scattered to witness, to serve, to do battle as Paul says, "against the principalities, against the powers, against the world rulers of this present darkness, against the spiritual hosts of wickedness . . ." (Ephesians 6:12). Are we not called in the church to be both priest and prophet, as Jesus was, offering both grace and judgment? In a recent book, Martin Marty has referred to the two halves of religion as the integrative and the disruptive.[8] This is just another way of speaking of the essential religious task of afflicting the comfortable and comforting the afflicted, the discomforting side of which Paul Tillich refers to as the "protestant principle." This meant no special identification with Protestantism, but was his way of reminding us of the principle that people should never confuse their ways with God's, nor should they try to prevent God from judging not only bad causes, or their neighbors' efforts, but their own good causes as well.

Religion's inward journey needs little defense or recommendation. It is the popular trip. Moreover, it is not the burden of this essay to call it into question, but merely to identify it as an indispensable part of the gospel—not the whole part, by any means, although it is frequently regarded as such. Here we are calling for a full-orbed proclamation of the gospel, giving careful attention to the public and corporate dimensions of life, as well as its personal and individual aspects. The danger of exclusive attention to the inward journey was recognized by the eminent theologian Karl Barth, who summoned the church to

> look and see whether she is not now really, of necessity, compromising herself, i.e., compromising herself with the Devil, to whom no ally is dearer than a Church, so absorbed in caring for her good reputation and clean garments, that she keeps eternal silence, is eternally meditating, eternally discussing, eternally neutral, a Church so troubled about the transcendence of the Kingdom of God—a thing which isn't really so easy to menace!—that she has become a dumb dog. This is just the thing which must not take place . . . today.[9]

The Judeo-Christian concern for the claims of justice in an oppressive society is as old as Moses' cry to Pharaoh to "let my people go." It reaches a dramatic climax in the prophets of the eighth and seventh centuries before Christ, who spoke powerfully to the evils of their day on behalf of a righteous God. Chief among the champions of social justice during this period was Amos, who experienced his God as the Lord of nature and history, calling under judgment all forms of oppression and exploitation, individual and corporate. In vivid language he pictured the righteous God in hot pursuit of unrighteous Israel,

> "as if a man fled from a lion,
> and a bear met him;
> or went into the house and leaned
>   with his hand against the wall,
> and a serpent bit him"
>
> (Amos 5:19).

In an amazingly contemporary way this shepherd of Tekoa confronted the individual and corporate sin of his day, and the modern church would do well to recapture his sense of the sovereignty of God over the whole human community as it seeks to deal with issues of public policy. In an article on the history of the religion of Israel, James Muilenburg has summarized the broad-ranging concerns of Amos:

> He sees the prosperity of the rich and also the grinding poverty of the poor. Houses of hewn stone and ivory, wine from bowls, silken cushions on luxurious couches, choice lambs from the stalls, generosity in tithes and sacrifices, hilarity and excitement at the great festivals witness to the prosperity of the land. But beneath the external show Amos exposes the gross dishonesty of the merchants, the exploitation of the poor, the corruption of justice both in ordinary relations of buying and selling and in the execution of justice in the courts; the gross insensateness of the leaders to "the affliction of Joseph"; the callousness and intemperance of the women—"cows of Bashan" Amos styles them in characteristic bluntness—and the complete unawareness of the deep insecurity that lurks in the shadows of Israel's political and social life. With almost brutal candor Amos exposes the rottenness of Israel's social and economic and religious life, exhibits it to the eyes of all, and goes to the very centers of corruption and entrenched power, the king's sanctuary and the royal palace (7:13), where his message will cut the deepest.[10]

If, as Amos believed, God was fed up with burnt offerings, ceremony, and harp music, and he yearned to have "justice roll down like waters, and righteousness like an ever-flowing stream," would he have remained silent about the Watergate tragedy? Should the church? Is America's double standard of justice—one kind for the rich and influential, another for the poor and helpless—a matter of concern for the church? When our government permits vast sales of surplus grain overseas, with huge corporate profits to a few, and consequent critical reduction in federal food stamp and food supplement programs for the poor, do we remain silent? Is this none of our business? Are we content to leave such matters to the politicians? What would Amos say? Or Jesus? As a matter of fact, we know what Jesus thought and said about the poor. A reading of Luke 16:19-31 and Matthew 25:31-46 speaks to our silence and unconcern in the presence of hungry and helpless people.

One of the first acts of Jesus as he entered into his public ministry following the baptism and temptation experiences was to return to the synagogue in his hometown of Nazareth, and there, by way of establishing the direction of his ministry, to read from the book of the prophet Isaiah.

> "The Spirit of the Lord is upon me,
> because he has anointed me to preach good news to the poor.

He has sent me to proclaim release to the captives
and recovering of sight to the blind,
to set at liberty those who are oppressed,
to proclaim the acceptable year of the Lord." (See Luke 4:18-19.)

If Jesus from earliest times perceived his self-identity and his ministry in the light of Isaiah's great servant song, bringing hope, light, and liberation to the poor, the enslaved, the helpless, and the oppressed, then how can a faithful and obedient servant church in our day neglect this agenda for the sake of catering to its own interests and needs? Much of this agenda simply could not be achieved without knowledgeable participation in the shaping of public policy, for preaching good news to the poor in today's society surely must involve more than a crust of bread, a bowl of soup, and some words about the possibility of a better break in the next world. That has been labeled as "pie in the sky by and by when you die," and the poor of the earth are protesting (as we would), "We want our cut now!" There can be no meaningful and lasting response to the legitimate claims of the poor short of a dynamic commitment on the part of the privileged to a more equitable distribution of education, housing, and employment, coupled with fundamental changes in a social system that tends to perpetuate and widen the gap between the haves and the have-nots. The church that observes the doctrine of "benign neglect" in these matters carries an almost unbearable burden of responsibility to justify its inactivity and unconcern in the light of the gospel.

Faithful Christians must learn to bridge the gap between private morality and public policy, for the problems of justice for the poor and help for the helpless in our society are so massive as to defy successful solution by private and individual means. The church has a long and magnificent tradition of good Samaritanism. We respond fairly well to the immediate needs of individuals, who, as victims of a cruel and impersonal society, find themselves without food or clothing or shelter. But how does the Thanksgiving basket tradition or the relief offering deal in any meaningful way with the estimated 450,000,000 persons, almost half of them young children, who suffer today from acute malnutrition, or with the half of the human race said to be seriously deficient in proteins and other essential nutrients? The caring capacity of the well-intentioned good Samaritan provides a mere pittance in the massive struggle for survival. Unless the lofty ideals and noble sentiments of men and women of goodwill and human concern are translated into public policy, there is little hope for liberation for the world's poor. Legislative and administrative decisions must be made at the highest levels of government, dealing with such matters as trade, assistance, monetary reform, military spending, and all other matters that bear on the hunger problem. The United States is fourteenth in the list of affluent nations in the percentage of its gross national product that is expended in direct assistance and self-help development among the world's poorest people; and those who share our Lord's concern for the lowliest of God's children must rise up and change this. All of this means that Christians must learn how to translate their moral convictions into public policy; and the time is late.

We live in a complex society where good intentions are not enough. Christians, who have been brought up on the notion that "politics is dirty business," must take seriously the need to "politicize" their faith. The good Samaritan story is a case in point. A man is struck down by an automobile in front of the church just as the service is concluding. One may want to help, and the familiar story of the injured man on the Jericho Road comes immediately to mind. Probably, in this day of liability lawsuits, the worst thing one could do would be to take it upon oneself, in the good Samaritan tradition, to provide on-the-spot amateur medical treatment and transportation on the gas-burning "beast" to the "nearest inn." If something were to go wrong, one might be sued for a horrendous sum. Instead, the appropriate twentieth-century Christian response to that situation might well be to anticipate it, to marshal citizen strength to make certain that the appropriate authorities have provided adequate ambulance and hospital service that is immediately available to anyone who needs it. Thus the humanitarianism that is motivated for the Christian by the love of Christ is joined with that of others, possibly coalesced as a vigorous political force to achieve in the public domain that which individual goodwill can no longer accomplish in well-intentioned isolation. This is what is meant by "politicizing" the faith, and Christians have much to learn about the process. In this regard, there is need to develop a long-neglected competence to deal in a preventive and corrective way with those structural and ideological flaws in the system of social arrangements which tend to reproduce victims in every generation. If "an ounce of prevention is worth a pound of cure," Christians might well give thought to a more efficient and humane use of their resources than simply waiting to treat the next victim of an unjust social order. For the church to neglect the domain of public policy is to abdicate a responsibility for the influencing of culture and to turn it over completely to the organized domination of self-interest groups, with the continued victimization of the poor and helpless.

If the church is to fulfill its prophetic and pastoral role in the human community, it must deal with what Helmut Thielicke brands as a "false conservatism":

> False conservatism expresses itself in the inclination to accept world conditions as they are. Under this pseudoconservative banner, a corrupt social order, which keeps part of humanity living at substandard economic levels while allowing another class to exploit and profiteer, is regarded as a matter of divine providence—or visitation—calling for simple acceptance and submission. . . .
>
> It is a terrible judgment on Christianity and on false theology that the decisive social movements of the last hundred years have not originated in any will on the part of the church to play the good Samaritan. The church has not taken the Lord's command to "love thy neighbor" as a concrete commission to change a blatantly unjust social situation. No, the decisive impulses for change have come from within the ranks of the oppressed and humiliated themselves. There has thus been nourished a kind of revolutionary instinct, the terrible symptoms of which may now be seen throughout the world, in their extreme form in Communism.
>
> To be sure, Christians have helped the needy. Think of the church's many works of mercy and of the countless acts of private charity. But these were bound to be regarded as alms, and hence as humiliating to the recipients, a cover-up for the unjust situation, so long as the proletariat was given the impression that the church actually tolerated the unjust situation as a whole—and did so in the name of that evil conservatism which even dared to claim sanction for itself in the will of God.[11]

There was a time in the not-distant past when concerns for social justice and public policy were commonly assumed to be in the special domain of so-called social gospel liberals, and there was always a lingering suspicion among the critics that their social activism was an overcompensation for some deficiency in personal faith. On the other side, evangelical conservatives were frequently accused of escapist pietism and cultural irrelevance. Hopefully, though, both groups are moving away from their polarized positions toward a more biblically and theologically responsible stance in which each group is enriched by the best aspects of the others.

The emerging Christian concern for public policy among conservatives has never received more credibility among its former critics than with the publication of the recent "Chicago Declaration," in which a representative group of evangelicals with impeccable credentials among their peers issued a biblically grounded statement of major consequence on the matter. A writer in *Christian Century* commented, "While the rest of American Protestantism was enjoying the annual festival of orgy and guilt, 40 or so evangelical Christians were making their way to Chicago to take part in marathon discussions which could well change the face of both religion and politics in America." [12] Martin Marty, writing in *Context* for March 15, 1974, added his judgment that "out of this, people might be fed, the law might be rendered justly, and America might relocate itself in the world. One can dream." [13]

Here is the Chicago Declaration, and it deserves careful reading, especially on the part of those who may still have reservations about the role of the church in relation to public policy:

As evangelical Christians committed to the Lord Jesus Christ and the full authority of the Word of God, we affirm that God lays total claim upon the lives of his people. We cannot, therefore, separate our lives in Christ from the situation in which God has placed us in the United States and the world.

We confess that we have not acknowledged the complete claims of God on our lives.

We acknowledge that God requires love. But we have not demonstrated the love of God to those suffering social abuses.

We acknowledge that God requires justice. But we have not proclaimed or demonstrated his justice to an unjust American society. Although the Lord calls us to defend the social and economic rights of the poor and the oppressed, we have mostly remained silent. We deplore the historic involvement of the church in America with racism and the conspicuous responsibility of the evangelical community for perpetuating the personal attitudes and institutional structures that have divided the body of Christ along color lines. Further, we have failed to condemn the exploration of racism at home and abroad by our economic system.

We affirm that God abounds in mercy and that he forgives all who repent and turn from their sins. So we call our fellow evangelical Christians to demonstrate repentance in a Christian discipleship that confronts the social and political injustice of our nation.

We must attack the materialism of our culture and the maldistribution of the nation's wealth and services. We recognize that as a nation we play a crucial role in the imbalance and injustice of international trade and development. Before God and a billion hungry neighbors, we must rethink our values regarding our present standard of living and promote more just acquisition and distribution of the world's resources.

We acknowledge our Christian responsibilities of citizenship. Therefore, we must challenge the misplaced trust of the nation in economic and military might—a proud trust that promotes a national pathology of war and violence which victimizes our neighbors at home and abroad. We must resist the temptation to make the nation and its institutions objects of near-religious loyalty.

We acknowledge that we have encouraged men to prideful domination and women to irresponsible passivity. So we call both men and women to mutual submission and active discipleship.

We proclaim no new gospel, but the Gospel of our Lord Jesus Christ, who, through the power of the Holy Spirit, frees people from sin so that they might praise God through works of righteousness.

By this declaration, we endorse no political ideology or party, but call our nation's leaders and people to that righteousness which exalts a nation.

We make this declaration in the biblical hope that Christ is coming to consummate the Kingdom and we accept his claim on our total discipleship till He comes.[14]

Seeking to translate the lofty human concerns of our Christian faith into effective public policy is tough, frustrating, and seldom successful business. But the effort is an indispensable act of obedience on the part of the church that would live out the moral commitments of its Lord. A sign in a Wyoming restaurant announces: "If you find your steak tough, walk out quietly. This is no place for weaklings." The struggle to make life more human is a tough struggle, and the weaklings may have to walk out quietly, but be assured that the Lord of history is our Leader, and he will lend us his strength.

NOTES

[1] Rolf Hochhuth, *The Deputy,* trans. Richard and Clara Winston (New York: Grove Press, Inc., 1964), p. 155. Copyright © 1964 by Grove Press, Inc. Reprinted by permission of Grove Press, Inc.

[2] Lesslie Newbigin, *Bible Society Record,* February, 1961, p. 19.

[3] Foy Valentine, "Engagement-the Christian's Agenda," in *The Chicago Declaration,* ed. Ronald J. Sider (Carol Stream, Ill.: Creation House, 1974), p. 62.

[4] *Expository Times,* vol. 60, p. 228.

[5] Paul Tournier, *The Whole Person in a Broken World* (New York: Harper & Row, Publishers, 1964), pp. 162-163.

[6] Foy Valentine, "How to Preach on Political Issues," in *Politics: a Guidebook of Christians,* ed. James M. Dunn (Dallas: The Christian Life Commission), p. 74.

[7] *Report of Standing Committee on Social Education and Action, Presbyterian Church in the U.S.A.* (Philadelphia: The Westminster Press, 1955).

[8] Martin E. Marty, *The Pro & Con Book of Religious America: A Bicentennial Argument* (Waco: Word Books, 1975), PRO, 130.

[9] Karl Barth, *The Church and the Political Problem of Our Day* (New York: Charles Scribner's Sons, 1939), p. 21.

[10] James Muilenburg, "The History of the Religion of Israel," in *The Interpreter's Bible,* ed., George A. Buttrick. 12 vols. (Nashville: Abingdon Press, 1952), vol. 1, p. 318.

[11] Helmut Thielicke, *Theological Ethics,* 2 vols. (Philadelphia: Fortress Press, 1969), vol. 2, pp. 627, 628.

[12] Marjorie Hyer, Evangelicals: Tackling the Gut Issues," *Christian Century,* vol. 90 (December 19, 1973), p. 1244.

[13] *Context,* March 15, 1974.

[14] From Ronald J. Sider, *The Chicago Declaration,* Front Cover, pp. 1, 2. Copyright 1974 by Creation House. Used with permission.

The Church
and
Public Policy:
Actions

JOHN W. BAKER*

The concept of a free church in a free state is an essential element of Baptist ecclesiology. Our forefathers were intimately involved in the attempt to achieve this ideal condition through the Constitution generally and especially through the Bill of Rights.[1] However, unlike many of the founding fathers, numerous Baptists today are not acutely aware of the meaning, the imperativeness, the value, or the challenges of a free church in a free state. In the mistaken assumption that the ideal was achieved in the past and that it is self-perpetuating, many religious people, Baptists included, have not fully accepted their individual or corporate responsibility for a stewardship of influence in public affairs.

I

For centuries philosophers have debated the question of the nature and meaning of freedom. No attempt will be made here to resurrect or continue this debate. However, there are truisms about freedom within the context of the free church and the free state which need to be amplified.

*This article first appeared in *Search,* Winter, 1976, Copyright 1975 by the Sunday School Board of the Southern Baptist Convention; it has been revised and reprinted by permission.

"Freedom" and "license" are not synonymous terms. Neither individual nor corporate freedom can be equated with the right to do or say anything at any time.

The free state is one in which there are regularized restraints on the activities of both government and individuals. In the United States these restraints are established by the federal and state constitutions. A denial of a particular power to government may be considered to be a granting of expanded freedom to the people with reference to that power. But both the limits on power and the scope of freedom are themselves limited. For example, the First Amendment denies to Congress the power to infringe on the freedom of speech or religion and thereby expands that freedom. Yet some degree of governmental involvement is not constitutionally proscribed, and a person's freedom to speak or worship may be circumscribed. Justice Oliver W. Holmes asserted that freedom of speech does not permit one to shout "Fire!" in a crowded theater.[2] Similarly the courts have held that government may make monogamy the only legal form of marriage in the United States even though one's religious beliefs may permit or even command a plurality of wives.

Thomas Hobbes, the seventeenth-century English philosopher, held that before there was a society people had complete license and, because of that, the life of man was ". . . solitary, poor, nasty, brutish, and short."[3] People only became free as society and the state were created. The limitations put on individuals by society were essential to their freedom.

Christians are truly free when they are willing to sublimate their human desires and drives into the examples and commands of the Lord. To the extent that they refuse or fall short, Christians are less free.

A New Testament church is both limited and free. The free church concept speaks to the freedom of the church to be the church without interference from the state. It also speaks to the idea that a New Testament church is free only as it adheres to the New Testament.

Freedom for either the church or the state does not require an absolute separation of the two. The church must be free to be the church and the state the state. There are areas of activity which are exclusively the churches' and into which the state must not intrude. The reverse is also true. However, there are broad functional areas in which the church, if it is to remain both free and responsible, must speak to the state. Similarly there are areas in which the state must speak to the churches.

Religion and religious exercises are the exclusive province of the churches. The state has no competence in this area. The preaching and teaching of the gospel, the worship of God, and prayer are all uniquely and exclusively the churches'. If government intrudes—commands what shall be preached or taught, how worship must take place, and where, when, and what shall be prayed—the church is not free. If the churches use their political power to involve government in religion and religious exercises—as some have tried to do with the various proposed amendments to the Constitution dealing with prayer in the public schools[4]—the freedom of the people, the churches, and the state is diminished.

As long as religious bodies are not seeking to use the state to achieve sectarian goals or advantages, they have a right and an obligation to make their views known on public issues. New Testament churches are particularly obliged to speak to government on religious liberty issues, on developing substantive public policy dealing with matters of Christian concern, and on the administration of established policies. They must also be willing and prepared to use the judicial system in every appropriate way to protect the religious liberty and rights of both believers and nonbelievers.

"Separation of church and state" comprehends the idea that the churches must define for themselves their mission and raison d'etre. However, the state may limit religious practices which may harm the health, safety, welfare, or morals of the people. Examples of this limitation of religion by the state are the restrictions which have been put on the snake-handling cults even though their members' participation in snake-handling rites is based on a sincere belief in Mark 16:17-18. Few would question the authority of the government to prohibit human sacrifices in the name of religion.

All of these things can be done without violating the ideals of separation of church and state and of a free church in a free state.

Freedom is a positive as well as a negative concept. Rights are usually defined as limits on the power of the government. The Bill of Rights begins with the limitation that "Congress shall make no law . . ." and the Fourteenth Amendment, which extended much of the Bill of Rights to state activity, begins "No State shall make or enforce any law. . . ." The various levels of government—national, state, and local—are thus prevented from passing or enforcing laws which, among other things, establish a religion or interfere with the free exercise of religion, require a person to testify against himself, deny equal protection of the law to all persons, or fail to give due process of the law.

Such protections of freedom are often viewed in a negative sense.

They say to government, "Thou shalt not!" They are essentially freedoms *from* governmental action.

The limitations on government can be a starting point for the assertion of individual freedom to act where government may not. The state may not establish a religion but people, if they but will, may evangelize the nation and the world. The fact that no government may interfere with the freedom of the press would mean nothing unless people acted and printed newspapers, books, magazines, etc.

So viewed, "freedom" is an affirmation of the capacity of individuals and groups to act in positive and creative ways. Such freedom is freedom *for* action. One area in which people are free to act is in public affairs. If those who uphold the concept of the free church in the free state are unwilling to exercise their freedom for creative action in public affairs, they well may be less free in many substantive ways. The freedom which Christ gives demands that those who have accepted him serve as good stewards of influence in public affairs.

II

"Stewardship" is a word which we know well. To most of us it means the proper giving of money and talents in the local church and, through cooperation between churches, the promotion of home and foreign missions. It does mean this and more. *The Webster's Third New International Dictionary* gives an idea of the breadth of stewardship: "The aspect of the religious life and church administration dealing with the individual's responsibility for sharing systematically and proportionately his time, talent, and material possessions in the service of God and for the benefit of all mankind."

Jesus left no doubt about the obligation of his people to be good stewards in all aspects of their Christian lives. Time, talents, and money must be expended for missions, for evangelism, for education, and for training. They must also be used to help maintain the political and constitutional environment which permits these activities to continue to take place. Time, talents, and money must be made available if individuals, churches, associations, and conventions are to use their influence to protect religious liberty and to achieve the "benefit of all mankind" which is an integral part of stewardship.

Influence may be exerted either individually or collectively. The democratic processes can continue to operate effectively only if a substantial majority of individuals participate in the nomination and election of candidates, the choosing between alternative programs, and the administration of public policies. However, participation in any of these on an uninformed basis undermines the democratic system and falls short of the mark of responsible Christian citizenship. The influence which Baptists can have in public affairs must not be dissipated either by inaction or by the failure to become informed on issues.

Collectively, influence in public affairs must be exerted by the different levels of cooperative alignments of churches. Some Baptist state conventions have separate agencies which attempt to help Baptists better understand their public responsibilities as Christians; they often work directly with state legislators and administrators in an effort to be the kind of "benefit to all mankind" mandated by a Christian stewardship of influence.

The Baptist Joint Committee on Public Affairs, which was established in 1939 to give Baptists a voice in public affairs, brings together eight Baptist conventions of the United States, along with the Baptist Federation of Canada, to perform four basic activities:

1. The Committee is directed to keep Baptist agencies, conventions, and associations informed on the facts of public affairs. This is attempted through news services to denominational and secular publications, and the monthly news journal, *Report from the Capital.*

2. The Committee acts as a source of primary information for individuals, churches, agencies, or conventions in legislative, judicial, or administrative matters. Compilations of data and analyses of a broad range of public affairs issues have been undertaken on request. This service, however, is subject to time and personnel limitations.

3. The Committee is charged with the task of informing government of resolutions on public affairs passed by one of the conventions and of seeing that historic Baptist positions are explained when they are applicable to the formation of public policy. To do this, testimony may be given before congressional committees; discussions may be arranged with appropriate administrators; or amicus curiae briefs, as noted below, may be submitted to the courts.

4. The Committee does not litigate in church-state matters. However, amicus curiae or "friend of the court" briefs serve as a means of communication with the courts on matters of religious liberty. For example, in *Walz* v. *Tax Commissioner,* 397 U.S. 664 (1970), Walz challenged the constitutionality of New York State's exemption of property used for religious purposes from the payment of property taxes. Walz sued the tax commissioner of the City of New York rather than the churches themselves. The commissioner's attorney was the attorney general of New York. Thus, a man holding

a secular post was charged with the responsibility of arguing the churches' case. The only way that the various churches themselves could argue in behalf of their own concept of liberty was through amicus briefs. The Baptist Joint Committee on Public Affairs, in addition to a number of other denominations, filed such a brief.

Court rules require that amicus participation be by groups which have a strong interest in the case rather than by individuals. It should be stressed that such participation in the judicial process by churches is essential for the protection of the principle of religious liberty and in no way violates the concept of separation of church and state.

III

In making input into the formation, administration, and adjudication of public affairs, Baptists must be careful in the selection of goals to seek, circumspect in the methods employed, aware of the limits of possible action, and cautious about the long-range implications of their attempts to be good stewards of influence in public affairs. Therefore, individuals, churches, and conventions need to consider the following guidelines.

There is a need to implement Christian love in the political process. Politics has long been considered a dirty and unwholesome business which is devoid of the elements of Christian love. It is thought to be a system in which winning is the only thing that counts and, consequently, that any means necessary to win must be used.

Such a characterization is a disservice. Politics and the determination of public policy can be—and often is—an arena in which Christian love is quite evident. Where Christian love seems to be absent in dealing with the needs of people, Baptists should use their influence in an effort to implement such love. If they are able to do so, political participation and decision making would more nearly manifest integrity, essential fairness, and a concern for others. Winning in politics will always be vitally important. However, Christian love can add a new dimension to the means utilized to win and to the choice of goals to be achieved through public policy.

Stewardship of influence in public affairs forbids self-oriented pressures on public policy. Baptists, if they are to be good stewards, must be especially concerned that public policy on the local, state, or national levels attempts to aid the needy, the oppressed, the poor, and those who too often find the laws or the system discriminating against them. Public policy which rests on Christian ideals will reflect efforts to protect and expand the religious and civil rights of all people and groups.

Unfortunately many people—and even churches—see in the political arena an opportunity to use their influence to achieve the passage of legislation or the issuance of administrative regulations which protect or enrich selfish, sectarian, or institutional interests rather than the general public interest. The use of influence by churches on legislative bodies ranging from a city council to Congress in order to serve special interests rather than the general public interest should not be condoned.

Pressures for public aid to support parochial schools or for the free use of city personnel, equipment, and materials to pave a church parking lot involve the expenditure of scarce public funds for special rather than public interest projects. Similarly, such activities as influencing a zoning board to give favorable consideration to a church's request for a zoning variance or the use of pressure to secure a modification of off-street parking regulations, while not involving the spending of funds, still serve special interests. Such activities may be legal, but they tend to expend accumulated political power to achieve minor political ends and are self-oriented rather than oriented toward the general public interest.

In the early years of the American Republic, Baptists—who were often an oppressed minority—were active in seeking constitutional amendments and legislation which guaranteed the religious and political rights of minorities. Their zeal for equality did not always include that of blacks or other unpopular minorities. Too often it still does not. Baptist heritage as well as basic Baptist beliefs should impel us to be more effective and less selfish stewards in the public arena.

Public policy which reflects sectarian dogma rather than the protection of the rights and religious liberties of all people usually should be opposed. Sectarian-oriented public policy—whether that public policy reflects an entire religious faith or one of the subgroups which compose it—divides rather than unifies a society. The first example below illustrates how some religious groups seek to maintain existing public policy which has a sectarian bias. The other three illustrate attempts of religious groups to change policies to conform with their sectarian biases. All are divisive. With few exceptions, these and similar attempts should be opposed.

Sunday closing laws or "blue laws" raise particularly sensitive problems. Most Baptists consider Sunday as the sabbath though it is the first day rather than the seventh in our present calendar. As the sabbath, they believe that Sunday should be a day of worship and rest. No one should be required to work on Sunday and, thereby, be denied time to worship and rest. Large numbers of Baptists and allies in other denominations have used their influence to have Sunday closing laws passed, retained, and vigorously enforced. What of the rights of minority religious bodies, such as Seventh Day Baptists, Seventh Day Adventists, or Jews? What of nonbelievers?

Proposed amendments to the Constitution of the United States which would, in essence, put governmental units or their agents into the position of requiring, writing, supervising, and setting the time for prayers in the public school classrooms divide many Christian bodies. The labels "voluntary" or "nondenominational" beg the question. Public school prayers are voluntary only to the extent that a child may participate or leave the classroom, and they are not voluntary in the sense that the student has no input into the content of the prayers or the time or place they are said. In a country with a pluralism of religions there is no way to write a nondenominational prayer that is in any sense a true prayer. The Baptist Joint Committee in 1971 adopted almost unanimously a position opposing such amendments, and yet there is continued substantial pressure on Congress by some Baptists and other religious groups to secure a prayer amendment to the Constitution.

The American Baptist Churches in the U.S.A., the Southern Baptist Convention, and the Baptist Joint Committee on Public Affairs have forthrightly rejected proposed resolutions which would have supported efforts by a coalition led by and composed largely of Roman Catholics to amend the Constitution to forbid abortion for any reason. In both 1973 and 1974, for example, the messengers to the annual meeting of the Southern Baptist Convention adopted by an overwhelming majority resolutions which favored freedom of conscience in determining, under limited conditions, when abortion procedures should be permitted. In these actions the messengers did not endorse abortions. To many who voted for the resolutions, abortion was not a viable personal alternative. However, they saw in the proposed amendment a denial of freedom of conscience and a forcing of sectarian views on all residents of the United States.

Conversely, the so-called "peace churches," supported by individuals, such as Baptists, whose churches do not fit in the "peace" category, in pushing for legislation which would grant amnesty to those who resisted induction into the military during the Vietnam War, are advocating the legitimatizing of freedom of conscience. They are voicing a sectarian theology on war, but they do not seek to force their views on anyone else. They believe that they are attempting to expand freedom. Perhaps because the proposal would expand rather than contract individual freedom of conscience, this push for a sectarian position may be an exception to the rule that such efforts should be opposed.

Churches should provide a forum for a full and open discussion of public issues. An uninformed or misinformed participant in public affairs can only by accident be a good steward of influence in public affairs. Churches have tended to avoid discussion of policy matters as well as partisan political matters. A church should never become a sounding board for partisan issues or endorse or oppose political candidates. Such actions are divisive—and could lead to the removal from the church of the tax-exempt status it now enjoys along with other nonprofit organizations.

Nevertheless, the churches have a responsibility to insure that their people are informed, motivated, and responsible stewards of influence in public affairs. Too often individuals, the mission of the churches, and the cause of religion have been harmed by irresponsible political action based on misinformation or inadequate information.

There are denominational agencies, such as the Baptist Joint Committee on Public Affairs, which have access to reliable facts and whose resources are broad. Churches which do not educate their people on public affairs or do not use the resources available to them through the denomination are failing as stewards of influence.

Politics—which is the lifeblood of public affairs—has been described as the art of the possible. It is not the art of the ideal, and any individual who thinks any person's or church's input into public affairs will produce the ideal is doomed to disappointment. Rather, Baptist stewardship of influence in public affairs must be understood to be a slow, piecemeal, step-by-step process. The pace of positive change on the national and local levels may seem depressing. However, a glance at history shows how far the American society has developed over the past two hundred years. The pace has been slow and relatively steady. There have been few instances of retrogression. A willingness to work on a steady basis within the realm of the possible through churches and denominations and with other denominations affords good prospects for a continued development toward the ideal of a free church within a truly free state.

Churches should insist on responsibility and integrity in all public officials at all levels of public life. The legacy of Watergate should not be a disillusionment with the entire range of public affairs. The young Nixon appointee who appeared before the Senate Watergate Committee was wrong when he advised young people to stay away from politics. Politics is as evil—or as good—as the people who participate in the process. Baptist stewardship of influence demands participation by responsible people in the political process.

However, not all people are capable of or inclined toward personal active participation in day-to-day politics. Yet all persons can insist that those who do participate be persons of integrity who recognize their responsibility to *all* the people who put and maintain them in office.

"Man is born free; and everywhere he is in chains."[5] With these words Jean-Jacques Rousseau opened his treatise on the origin of the state and the human condition within that state. The book, published fourteen years before the American Revolution, had a slight effect on the American scene but provided much of the philosophical underpinning of the French Revolution in 1789.

Neither of these two great revolutions changed the facts that at that time few people were truly free and that most persons were at least figuratively in chains. The chains which burdened Americans in the late eighteenth century included ignorance, oppression, poverty, political and social inequality, isolation, the lack of adequate health services, the establishment of churches in a number of the states, and the very real chains of slavery.

During the two hundred years since the American Revolution, changes have taken place and the burdens of the chains have lightened.

The First Amendment, which Baptists insisted on and worked to get adopted, with its provisions for a separation of church and state effectively prevented the establishment of a national church. This guarantee of religious freedom and inquiry was one of the precipitating elements in the interrelated changes which have taken place in this country.

The establishment, expansion, and improvement of a system of free public schools which has served as a melting pot for an expanding population and as a source of political and social egalitarianism are directly traceable to the development toward a free church in a free state.

The nation, prodded by religious people both North and South, abolished human slavery in its common form. Over the years the churches have led the way in demanding that government assume a major role in lightening the burdens of economic poverty and oppression. The demands for freedom of speech, freedom of movement, freedom to live private lives, and for at least a minimum basis of economic security have been championed by the churches. Churches have joined with others in seeking more adequate health care for all people—a search which may result in the serious beginning of a modified national public health program soon.

During the past two hundred years the United States has evolved into what can at least be classified as a quasi free state in which a free church can develop. Much more must be done before the people, the state, and the churches are truly free. The degree to which Baptists are willing to be good stewards of their influence in public affairs will make a substantial difference in the way this nation and the world will measure up when we face our Tricentennial in 2076.

NOTES

[1]See John W. Baker, ed., *Religious Liberty and the Bill of Rights* (Washington: Baptist Joint Committee, 1972) and the booklet by James E. Wood, Jr., *Religious Liberty and the Bill of Rights* (Washington: Baptist Joint Committee, 1972), available through the Baptist Joint Committee on Public Affairs.

[2]*Schenck* v. *United States,* 249 U.S. 47 (1919).

[3]Thomas Hobbes, *Leviathan* (Cleveland: The World Publishing Company, 1963), p. 143.

[4]See the pamphlet *Religion in the Public School Classroom* (Washington: Baptist Joint Committee, 1974).

[5]Jean-Jacques Rousseau, *The Social Contract,* trans. G. D. H. Cole (New York: E. P. Dutton & Co., Inc., 1947), p. 3.

PART FIVE

Out of Many, One: Baptist Pluralism and Unity

Baptists
of
the North

ROBERT G. TORBET

Baptists, like Americans generally, are asking what their role should be in today's world. The Bicentennial observance of the beginnings of the nation intensified reflection in a broader context than might otherwise have been likely. The reassessment of the American experience in launching a promising and noble experiment in democratic government provided a natural setting in which thoughtful Baptists could reflect upon their contributions to the foundation of that experiment. To what extent has the devotion of Baptists to the principle of a free church in a free state contributed to an effective Christian witness in a pluralistic society? How have Baptists sought to relate freedom and responsibility so as to achieve the strength of unity amidst diversity? To trace briefly the answer to these questions with particular reference to the body now known as American Baptist Churches in the U.S.A. is the purpose of this essay.

As a people who arose in the seventeenth century out of the English Puritans' protest against the compromise and evils which they saw in the Christendom of medieval Europe, Baptists were committed to the restoration of primitive Christianity with its uncompromising devotion to Jesus Christ and his way of life. For them, the expression of a pure church was to be found only in companies of men and women who had been transformed by the power of the Spirit of God. Their claim to the right to be free from civil or ecclesiastical coercion was justified, not as an object in itself, but as a condition necessary for the realization of the Lordship of Christ in their lives as individuals in society and as members of his body.

These early Baptists were, from the outset, confronted by the dilemma of all free churches, namely, how to restore primitive Christianity and yet avoid a narrow sectarianism. They faced an unresolved tension between freedom to obey God and responsibility to the state in which they held citizenship. Theirs was also the problem of finding a balance between an excessive individualism and local church autonomy on the one hand and an unauthorized or unrestrained centralization of authority on the other hand.

VARIOUS SOLUTIONS OF THE DILEMMA IN THE NEW WORLD

When Baptists came to the New World, they hoped for freedom to fulfill their radical obedience to the Lordship of Jesus Christ. At first, they met with the same kind of persecution at the hands of Congregationalists in New England and Anglicans in Virginia as they had met in England. But with the advent of the American Revolution, their free-church goals were caught up in the new society that was emerging under the enlightened leadership of men like Thomas Jefferson and James Madison. They readily joined, therefore, with Quakers and others who shared their devotion to religious liberty in support of the principle of separation of church and state which eventually was embodied in the First Amendment to the Constitution of the United States.

Perhaps the most influential Baptist leaders in this effort were Roger Williams, Isaac Backus, and John Leland. Williams had established the Rhode Island Colony on the basis of complete religious liberty for all people. Isaac Backus, of Massachusetts, fought for over sixty years for an orderly, moral, stable society which should exist without a tax-supported established church. For him, the religious awakening of the 1740s shed "new light" on the question of church-state relations, particularly as it affected the freedom of the individual. By the principle of voluntarism, he sought to protect "the essential rights of Christianity." Backus wrote: "In civil states, particular men are invested [as representatives] with authority to judge for the whole, but in Christ's kingdom each one has equal right to judge for himself."[1] He served as a bridge from the Puritan to the evangelical movement. A current Backus scholar has concluded that "he wrote and worked to exalt the religious liberty of the individual above the church and the state, yet he always asserted the necessity for a Christian state subservient to the ultimate moral authority of God's law."[2]

Less educated and more radically individualistic than Backus was

John Leland of Virginia. Yet, both men were particularly responsive to their own culture. They saw God working in and through the exciting events in American history. As products of the evangelical revivals, they rejected the Puritan covenant theology for the Baptist movement. They affirmed belief in the priesthood of all believers, lay ordination, and lay participation in church and state. The main tenets of what has come to be known as the Backus-Leland Tradition include stress on the individual Christian and that person's freedom, a low view of the church as being local and secondary to conversion in importance, with the minister's authority deriving from the consent of the congregation, and separation of church and state to assure religious liberty. This tradition, with all of its virtue, had the weakness of an excessive individualism and a superficial view of the church as the body of Christ.

The tendency to individualism and an emphasis upon local autonomy was deepened in the years that followed by two other influences: the Wayland influence and the Landmark Tradition, in that order. Francis Wayland, president of Brown University in Providence, Rhode Island, and a staunch supporter of the Baptist mission overseas, wrote a number of books on Baptist polity just before the middle of the nineteenth century. In these, he gave expression to the individualism of the evangelical revivals. In his desire to give free play to the leading of the Holy Spirit, he stressed private interpretation of the Scriptures and the primacy of personal religion over church membership. He asserted that a church is a voluntary association, that "no man joins it, unless he chooses, nor continues in it any longer than he will." [3] For him and other revivalist Baptists, the religion of the heart and the immediacy of the Holy Spirit had little need of creeds, much less a need for systematic and historical theology. Relying upon an oversimplified biblical theology for his views of the church, he refused to recognize visibility of the universal church. He drew a sharp distinction between the authority of the Old Testament and the New Testament. This marked a shift from the older Calvinistic Baptist interpretation of biblical authority which relied upon the whole Bible and stressed the corporate life of the church. For Wayland, the sanction for cooperation between autonomous congregations was purely pragmatic. Accordingly, he resisted any attempt to form out of the missionary organization of Baptists a true denomination.

A second influence to deepen Baptist individualism was a movement to recover the landmarks of primitive Christianity, led chiefly by James R. Graves, editor of the *Tennessee Baptist* from 1846 until his death in 1893. By identifying the marks of the true church with an unbroken succession of local Baptist churches from New Testament times, Graves insisted that all other churches were distortions of true Christianity. Landmarkism, as it has been called, was a sectarian effort to preserve and protect the New Testament pattern of a regenerate society of believers by holding rigidly to close membership, close communion, and an insistence that a local church cannot delegate its authority to anyone.

The movement was reinforced by a number of factors within the social milieu of the nation: the individualism of the frontiersmen, the hostility among local preachers on the frontier to the Eastern clergy and their church organizations, an American devotion to independence and personal freedom, a growing rivalry among denominations following the collapse of the Evangelical United Front (an essentially lay-supported ecumenical movement) after 1837, and the disillusionment of Graves with his early experience of Methodism.

The exclusivism of Landmarkism was dictated by the call to preserve a gospel witness in accordance with the New Testament pattern which was interpreted in purely local terms. The Landmarkers' identification of a Baptist church with the kingdom of God led many to believe that one cannot enter the kingdom without becoming a member of a Baptist church that is faithful to the Landmark tradition. Moreover, the Landmarkers' stress upon an unbroken chain of true gospel churches soon brought to the fore the importance of defining what is a "regular" Baptist church and of eliminating from fellowship those churches which violate the standard in any way.

The influence of Landmarkist teaching has extended far beyond the organization that perpetuates its principles. It has been felt most strongly in the southwestern area of the Southern Baptist Convention and to lesser degrees elsewhere in that body and also in American Baptist territory as population shifts within recent years have extended it into some states of the North.

The consequence of these trends and a general shift in authority during the nineteenth century from the corporate community of faith inherent in Puritanism to the individual experience inherent in American evangelicalism weakened or dissolved the traditional Calvinistic theological base for the church into a pure voluntarism. The church became an option, not a necessity, for the fulfillment of the individual's commitment to Christ. Many argued that it was more important to accept Christ as *personal* Savior than to unite with the church. This was due to a failure to sense that the body of Christ is the church, and to be one with him is to be one with his people. Soul competency, as propounded by E. Y. Mullins, one-time president of Southern Baptist Theological Seminary, became the principle used to support this individualism.

In matters of church order, this individualism was carried out in a stress upon congregational independency, which was expressed in William R. McNutt's *Polity and Practice in Baptist Churches.*[4] Thus the Baptist churchmanship of earlier days was crumbling in the face of individualism and a widespread religious complacency. The complacency was evident in a decline in associational life, in a relaxing of church discipline, in easier admission to church membership, in a disuse of the church covenant, and in a diminished authority of the Bible. Without a high churchmanship, the churches sought cooperation, not on the basis of theology, but of expediency. The Northern Baptist Convention was organized in 1907, not out of a principle of associationalism but out of the expediency of getting the job done, as will be explained in more detail in the next section. Adjustments and compromises were made which have left problems to plague American Baptists. Among these were the authority of the local church versus the authority of the Convention, the autonomy of the national societies, and the relationship of the national body to the emerging ecumenical movement. Continuing efforts have been made to resolve the tensions arising from these issues.

Without an adequate view of the authority of the Bible, American Baptists were ill prepared to deal with the theological currents of the 1890s and the early years of the twentieth century. Accordingly, the rank and file of members remained loyal to a sentimental attachment to the Bible but had little understanding of its content or authority. The more sophisticated were to be found in three camps: liberals or self-styled modernists, fundamentalists, and moderates. Without either an adequate theology or a strong connectionalism, the Northern Baptist Convention was particularly vulnerable to the devastating effects of schism in the 1920s and 1940s over the modernist-fundamentalist issues.[5]

Since 1950 there has been within the American Baptist Convention some effort to reshape the Baptist tradition. This has been due to a renewed interest in theology and Baptist history, to a general dissatisfaction with the inadequacy of the Convention to deal with divisive elements, and to the impact of the ecumenical movement which has pressed Baptists to reappraise their tradition and their relationship to other Christians.

RESHAPING THE BAPTIST TRADITION FOR GREATER UNITY

The advocates of strong denominational unity were never numerous among early Baptists, but they were influential. Among them was Morgan Edwards, for a time pastor of the First Baptist Church in Philadelphia and noted Baptist historian of the late eighteenth century. He proposed a plan whereby new associations might be incorporated into the Philadelphia Association, thereby creating a national solidarity for the churches from Nova Scotia in Canada to Georgia.[6] His plan was defeated by New England Baptists, who feared associational domination of the local congregations.

When Luther Rice came home from India in 1813 to rally Baptist support for the Adoniram Judsons in Burma, the problem posed by the absence of a national organization of Baptists became acute. The means to which he resorted was a common one among Protestants. He set out to create a society of interested people from the churches who would be willing to underwrite the venture. It was not in any sense an organization of churches with a denominational structure. The society thus formed in 1814 was the General Convention of the Baptist Denomination in the United States for Foreign Missions, commonly known as the Triennial Convention from its practice of meeting every three years to conduct business.

It soon became evident to thoughtful Baptists, like Luther Rice, that a more formal connection was needed between the churches if Baptists were to develop into a strong denomination. So the plan was evolved to extend the associational principle "by bringing Associations together in State Conventions, and then linking the State Conventions in a genuine General Convention of the churches."[7]

The first step was to organize state conventions on the basis of existing associations. More than eighteen associations were founded in New York alone by 1820, and at least seventeen in Virginia. The first state conventions formed of delegates from the associations were organized in 1821 in South Carolina and New York.

Rice's plan for a representative convention, which he intended to present to the Triennial Convention in 1826, at first had the backing of Francis Wayland. But it was not long before Wayland changed his entire point of view, and with the support of the delegates from Massachusetts and New York he sabotaged Rice's plan. The publicized reason given by Wayland was that the society method was the best means of securing financial support for missions. The American church historian, Winthrop S. Hudson, has suggested that there were other reasons which reflected the reluctance of individuals to accept a reorganization in which they would have to relinquish control of the Triennial Convention.[8] There may also be reason to infer that the dissent in 1826 against the merger of all Baptist agencies reflected the New England "town meeting" psychology.

The opposition resulted in abandonment of the plan. When the Triennial Convention met in 1826, it was reorganized, not to provide for the needed connectionalism between the churches, but to be devoted exclusively to foreign missionary concerns. The action was buttressed by the argument, advanced by Wayland and others, that the local church cannot delegate authority to a convention.

When the Southerners withdrew from support of the Triennial Convention in 1845, they organized a truly denominational structure in the Southern Baptist Convention. Baptists of the North continued with the society method until 1907 when they organized a national convention.

Organization of the Northern Baptist Convention in 1907 (later named American Baptist Convention in 1950 and American Baptist Churches in the U.S.A. in 1972) was the product of several influences. First was the influence of a strong ecclesiastical connectionalism of Freewill Baptists on Northern Baptists prior to the merger of the two bodies in 1911. A second was a growing insistence of lay people that the national societies unite in a plan that would provide efficient business methods of organizational operation and financial planning. A third was a recovery by many Baptist leaders, caught up in the emerging ecumenical movement, of a concept of the universal church which had been an important aspect of their early ecclesiastical understanding.

The preamble to the Provisional Constitution and By-Laws of the Convention expressed concern for denominational unity, but did not define it theologically. Instead, it sought to achieve a compromise between the "society" and "convention" method of working together. The preamble read as follows:

> We, representatives of Baptist churches in convention assembled, do hereby declare our belief in the independence of the local church, in the advisory and representative nature of the local and state associations, and our loyalty to all our denominational organizations. We do also affirm our conviction that, in view of the growth of our country and denomination, there is further need of a general body that shall serve the common interests of our entire brotherhood, as the individual church, the district and state associations minister to the interests of their several constituencies.[9]

The purpose of the Convention, set forth in the Act of Incorporation, was formally stated as follows: "The objects of the corporation shall be to give expression to the opinions of its constituency upon moral, religious, and denominational matters, and to promote denominational unity and efficiency in efforts for the evangelization of the world." These objectives were not intended to duplicate or to supersede the purpose of the cooperating denominational agencies brought under its umbrella.[10]

Thus was pragmatically described the instrument of the churches that was created to achieve financial unity among the national societies and other enterprises of Baptists in the North. The Northern Baptist Convention united the national societies, the state conventions and city mission societies, and the churches in a Baptist world mission. The cooperating agencies maintained their autonomy, and the Convention was careful to protect the churches from any infringement upon their independence. In retrospect it can be said that a degree of denominational solidarity was achieved through this instrument that surpassed the hopes of its founders.

The variant bases of membership in the Convention that were developed by American Baptists reflect further the lack of a clear theological understanding of this instrument of unity: (1) The most obvious was *church and agency membership,* which has been accepted consistently since the Convention's organization. This was a modification of the individual and organizational membership which has prevailed in the national societies prior to the establishment of the Northern Baptist Convention. (2) Another basis of membership has been *financial support.* This has run throughout the whole history of American Baptist organized work since its inception with the organization of the Triennial Convention. The difference which has come in the years since 1907 has been that the financial support is expected from the churches rather than from individual donors. (3) A third basis of membership which has been considered has been *confessional uniformity.* Only in part has this been accepted within the Convention, and this has been in the definition of its constituency in 1926 in terms of immersed believers. The efforts to prescribe creedal uniformity in 1922 and 1946 were defeated decisively in favor of a general affirmation of commitment to the New Testament as a trustworthy and authoritative rule of faith and practice.

Fundamental to the policy of American Baptists has been the basic Free Church principle "that the local congregation and its membership remain free to hear the Word and proclaim it for others to hear."[11] From this principle flow two corollaries: First, a local congregation, because it needs the guidance of its sister churches in determining the will of God, should enter into associational fellowship and accept the authority of associational discipline. Secondly, churches so united are bound together voluntarily by a covenantal agreement based upon a common faith, purpose, and need mutually accepted when they sought admission.

The association in Baptist polity is unlike a local congregation in two major respects: it cannot excommunicate an individual from the community of faith; and it cannot ordain a minister, although it may examine the standards of ordination of the member churches and withdraw fellowship from any congregations which violate them. In other ways, however, the association is a church in the larger sense of that word. It can preach the Word and seek the mind of Christ for its member churches. Some would grant that it can administer the ordinance of the Lord's Supper since the delegates constitute a part of the body of Christ as truly as does a local congregation. Moreover, the association can discipline any of its member churches which are unwilling to abide by their covenantal agreement.

Although an association or any larger connectional body, such as a national convention, cannot transform itself into a self-perpetuating ecclesiastical organization since such organizations consist of delegates elected by the churches, it can be authorized to speak and act for the churches in matters of denominational concern. The justifying assumption for such authority is that a local association, state convention, or national convention of churches is a representative body.

The fundamental theological premise which undergirds this connectional principle in Free Church polity is succinctly expressed by Ernest A. Payne, church historian and one-time general secretary of the Baptist Union of Great Britain and Ireland, in the following words: "Associations, Synods, Unions and Assemblies of churches are not to be regarded as optional and secondary. They are the necessary expression of Christian fellowship, a necessary manifestation of the Church visible. The local congregation is not truly a church if it lives an entirely separate life." [12] When this premise is not fully accepted, as has been the case among many Baptists, the consideration of the basis for membership of churches within a denominational body is inadequate. This has certainly been true among American Baptists.

Yet, the willingness of American Baptists to move in the direction of a unified denomination that is representative of the churches has enabled them to cope more adequately with the dynamics of rapid societal change since mid-century. This has been evident in a number of ways:

1. *There has been a tacit recognition of the theological diversity within the denomination and a readiness to make room for it in preference to the polarization which led to bitter controversies and secession of churches in the 1930s and 1940s.* Three examples may be cited. The controversial involvement of the denomination in the National Council of Churches was supported by the Convention's actions in 1960 and again in 1965. When sharp division arose in 1966 over an invitation from the Consultation on Church Union to participate in the effort of nine denominations to create a Church of Christ Uniting, polarization was again avoided. The Convention adopted the General Council's recommendation to intensify its ecumenical involvements by establishing a Commission on Christian Unity, in preference to participation in the union talks, but only when amended by a resolution to urge the Commission to give particular attention to a preservation of the Baptist heritage.

2. *American Baptists have sought to update their Christian witness and mission in the midst of tensions and tumultuous change, especially in the ever-widening urban centers of American society.* They have been helped in this effort by the contributions made by black pastors and their lay people within the denomination and by an "associated relationship" with the Progressive National Baptist Convention, Inc., a black denomination. The basic strategies have been to develop new methods of witness and mission, to encourage interracial equality and support for the development of minorities, and to provide a reconciling ministry in metropolitan areas where urban problems and racial conflict were most intense.

3. *The Convention responded to pressures exerted in the troubled sixties by minorities within its membership (Black, Hispanic, Indian-American, Asian-American) for a larger role of participation and decision making.* The initiatives of organized caucuses, which eventually included those of women and youth, were received and given place within the structures of the denomination.

4. *A further indication of American Baptist efforts to adjust with greater unity to the enlarging dimensions of their task in the new era was an intensified program of reorganization which has occupied the attention of the Convention since 1950 when the office of general secretary was created and the four national mission societies (home and foreign) were urged to amalgamate.* In 1953 denominational approval was given for a study by the American Institute of Management of the Convention's business operation and structure. In response to recommendations made in the report of the study, the Convention set in motion a plan for reorganization of its general

structure and selected Valley Forge, Pennsylvania, as the locale for its headquarters.

Reorganization was carried out in two stages: action at the annual meeting in Portland, Oregon, in 1961, making the chief executives of the national program agencies associate general secretaries of the Convention, thereby symbolizing the shift from a loosely united confederacy of national societies in 1907 to a true federation of national agencies with the Convention; and adoption of a more ambitious restructure plan at Denver, Colorado, in 1972, which provided for a new 200-member General Board that would be representative of election districts, strengthened the office of general secretary, and replaced the annual convention with a biennial meeting. The changes were intended to provide a more representative form of church government through a constituency-based, policy-making general board. The national program boards—education, home and foreign missions, pensions—were to be responsible to the General Board. In spite of the centralization thereby achieved, the name of the Convention was changed to "American Baptist Churches in the U.S.A." in preference to an early recommendation of the restructure committee of "American Baptist Church."

Although appreciable progress has been made toward a more mature and unified conduct of church life and mission in a pluralistic society, American Baptists still face a number of unresolved problems. First is the continuance of disunity among Baptist bodies within the United States which embarrasses and thwarts a strong Free Church witness. Second is the lack of agreement concerning the degree to which American Baptists should become more involved in the widening ecumenical movement. Third is the quest for self-identity and for the true meaning of the church and ministry in a rapidly changing society. In some respects American Baptists have come of age; in other respects they stand with uncertainty upon the threshold of a new age.

NOTES

[1] William G. McLoughlin, *Isaac Backus and the American Pietistic Tradition* (Boston: Little, Brown & Co., 1967), p. 31.

[2] William G. McLoughlin, ed., *Isaac Backus on Church, State, and Calvinism* (Cambridge: Harvard University Press, 1968), p. 61.

[3] See Francis Wayland, *Notes on the Principles and Practices of Baptist Churches* (Boston: Gould and Lincoln, 1857); *The Baptist Principle* (ca. 1851); and *Thoughts on the Missionary Organizations of the Baptist Denomination* (New York: Sheldon Blakeman & Co., 1859).

[4] William R. McNutt, *Polity and Practice in Baptist Churches* (Valley Forge: Judson Press, 1935).

[5] Winthrop S. Hudson, ed., *Baptist Concepts of the Church* (Valley Forge: Judson Press, 1959), chap. 8; Winthrop S. Hudson, *The Great Tradition of the American Churches* (New York: Harper & Row, Publishers, 1953), pp. 198-206; John Dillenberger and Claude Welch, *Protestant Christianity Interpreted Through Its Development* (New York: Charles Scribner's Sons, 1954); Norman H. Maring, "Baptists and Changing Views of the Bible, 1865-1918," *Foundations*, vol. 1, nos. 3 & 4 (July and October, 1958), pp. 52-75; 30-61.

[6] Morgan Edwards, *Materials Towards a History of the American Baptists* (Philadelphia, 1770-1792), vol. 1, pp. 121-123; Appendix, pp. i-iv.

[7] Winthrop S. Hudson, "Stumbling into Disorder," *Foundations*, vol. 1 (April, 1958), p. 46.

[8] *Ibid.*, p. 50.

[9] *Annual of the Northern Baptist Convention, 1908* (St. Louis, Mo.: The Freegard Press), p. 3.

[10] W. Hubert Porter, "The Purposes of the American Baptist Convention and Its Agencies as Stated in Their Respective Charters" (mimeographed, 5 pages).

[11] Paul M. Harrison, *Authority and Power in the Free Church Tradition: A Social Case Study of the American Baptist Convention* (Princeton: Princeton University Press, 1959), p. 224.

[12] Ernest A. Payne, *The Fellowship of Believers,* enlarged ed. (London: The Carey Kingsgate Press, Ltd., 1952), p. 31.

Baptists
of
the South

G. HUGH WAMBLE

The Southeast and Southwest are Baptist country. In Virginia, North Carolina, South Carolina, Georgia, Florida, Kentucky, Tennessee, Alabama, Mississippi, Missouri, Arkansas, Louisiana, Oklahoma, and Texas, Baptists are the major religious group. Only in southern Louisiana, southern Texas, central Tennessee, south central Arkansas, southwest Virginia, northwest Missouri, and in and near Missouri's two major metropolitan centers does another religious group, Roman Catholic or Methodist, consistently outnumber Baptists.[1]

Around 88 percent of the churches and 91 percent of members affiliated with the largest evangelical organization (Southern Baptist Convention) in the United States are located in the aforementioned fourteen states plus Maryland and New Mexico. Three of the national Baptist organizations with large constituencies in the South—Southern Baptist and two National Baptist conventions—participate in the Baptist Joint Committee on Public Affairs. These three organizations and, in recent years, the General Association of General Baptists affiliate with the Baptist World Alliance. Several other Southern-bred organizations have structures which maximize the independence of local churches. These include two Landmark groups claiming almost 1.3 million members, Primitive Baptist groups claiming around 1.6 million members, the National Association of Free Will Baptists claiming around 225,000 members, and "independent" Baptist fellowships. In most instances, their Fundamentalist theology and/or Landmark ecclesiology make a virtue out of noncooperation with other Baptist groups, to say nothing of non-Baptist groups.[2]

This study will attempt to show that ideological differences have caused fragmentation and continue to create tensions among Baptists of the South, and that functionalism is the basis of the Southern Baptist Convention's unity. Inasmuch as another chapter in this volume will deal with black Baptists, only limited attention will be given to them.

IDEOLOGICAL DIVERSITY

Southern Baptists, when located on any comprehensive theological spectrum, are conservative in doctrine, but their unity is not the result of ideological uniformity. Efforts to establish and enforce such uniformity have often been disruptive of unity, sometimes resulting in splits.

The first church in the South, First Baptist Church of Charleston, South Carolina, organized by 1696, included both General and Particular Baptists for several decades. Though these two groups agreed on most doctrines, their distinctiveness was due to differences on several subjects: whether sin prevents a person, exercising natural powers, from willing or choosing anything good; whether God unconditionally elects some persons to salvation but leaves others in condemnation; whether Christ died for the elect only; whether an elect person can successfully resist God's will; and whether an elect person can ever fall from grace so as to lose salvation.[3]

Most early Baptists in the Tidewater area of the South seem to have been General Baptists. The earliest Baptists in Virginia and North Carolina held the general theology. Only South Carolina Baptists divided over theology. General Baptist theology virtually disappeared from the South by 1770, and it was not revived until the nineteenth century when Free Will and General Baptist groups won some adherents. Particular theology won out due to various factors. First, being Scotch-Irish and English in background and related to the broad Puritan movement of English origin, most Baptists who moved into the Piedmont area after 1740 shared the anti-Arminian, pro-Calvinistic theology defined by the Synod of Dort (1618–1619).[4] Second, the Philadelphia Baptist Association, whose confession of faith adopted in 1742 and published by Benjamin Franklin in 1743 contained the Calvinistic theology of Particular Baptists, sent evangelists into the South in the mid-1750s.[5] Third, the first Baptist association in the South, Charleston (organized in 1751), followed the pattern of the Philadelphia Association and in 1767 adopted a slightly revised version of the Philadelphia Confession.[6]

Baptists who came into the South from the Middle Colonies became known as Regular Baptists, because they regarded the Philadelphia Confession as their doctrinal rule. Those who came from New England were products of the Great Awakening. Known as Separate Baptists, they objected to the imposition of any doctrinal rule but generally espoused Calvinism; they emphasized experiential religion, fostered by preaching which emphasized sin, grace, repentance, and faith.[7] These Separate Baptists, led by Shubal Stearns who came from Connecticut and settled in northern Virginia in 1754, realized that their brand of religion differed from the brand advocated by Regular Baptists. Though both Separates and Regulars were Calvinistic, their emphases differed. Regulars emphasized doctrinal purity; Separates emphasized personal experience and employed exercises designed to excite personal response.

The Stearns' group moved in 1755 to north central North Carolina and organized the Sandy Creek church in 1756. This church became within seventeen years, as Morgan Edwards of the Philadelphia Association wrote in 1772, "the mother, grandmother, and great-grandmother to 42 churches, from which sprang 125 ministers"—in Virginia, North Carolina, South Carolina, and Georgia.[8] The aggressive evangelism of Separate Baptists, adapted to the constant mobility of the swelling population in the Piedmont, established the foundation of Baptist strength in the South.

The first official action to overcome division between Regulars and Separates occurred in Virginia in 1787 when cooperative effort, mainly in behalf of religious freedom, caused them to agree on a union and to call their churches the "United Baptist Churches of Christ in Virginia." While respecting the Philadelphia Confession as a doctrinal guide which contains "essential truths of the Gospel," United Baptists did not slavishly follow it. They asserted that each Christian ought to believe and each minister ought to maintain "the doctrine of salvation by Christ and free, unmerited grace alone."[9] But beyond this they were not sticklers in respect to theology.

Within a few years differences over the atonement surfaced. Though all agreed that Christ's atonement is the basis of salvation, there was difference over the scope of Christ's atoning work. Some held that Christ died for the elect only; others held that Christ died for all men. During the Frontier Revival in Kentucky in 1801, two associations—one Separate, the other Regular—agreed on a short, eleven-point statement entitled "Terms of Union." The crucial point was "that the preaching *Christ tasted death for every man,* shall be no bar to communion."[10] At least for the time being, division over particular atonement (Christ died only for the elect) and universal atonement (Christ tasted death for every man) ceased being divisive. The name "United Baptists" persisted throughout the pre-Civil War era, but it took on a new emphasis during the "means" controversy.

Doctrinal disagreement surfaced again in the late 1810s and continued for three decades. The occasion of controversy was the missionary movement based on the missionary theology of Andrew Fuller and the missionary practice of William Carey. In the 1780s Fuller, pastor of the Kettering church in England, attacked strict Calvinism which emphasized predestination and particular atonement and opposed invitations to unconverted people. Fuller held that each Christian has an obligation to share the gospel and that each person who hears the gospel, notwithstanding sin's effect, has the power to respond to it. This theology prompted Carey, Fuller's neighboring pastor, to propose the use of "means" in taking the gospel to heathens. In 1792 thirteen persons met in Kettering and organized a Particular Baptist missionary society, with Fuller as secretary. In 1793 Carey went to Serampore, India, as the first missionary of this society.[11] After 1800 some Baptists in America contributed to the English society.

In 1812 Adoniram and Ann Hasseltine Judson and Luther Rice went to Serampore as missionary appointees of a society supported largely by New England Congregationalists. Studying the Bible at sea, the Judsons adopted the principle of believer's baptism by immersion and received baptism at the hands of one of Carey's associates soon after their arrival in Serampore. After vigorously defending infant baptism, Rice soon espoused believer's baptism. Rice and the Judsons offered to serve American Baptists as missionaries. Rice returned to the United States for the purpose of promoting foreign missions. His efforts, enthusiastically supported by several prominent leaders in seaboard states, resulted in the formation in 1814 of the General Missionary Convention of the Baptist Denomination in the United States of America for Foreign Missions, the first national Baptist missionary organization in the country. Rice itinerated in behalf of the new convention, commonly called the "Triennial Convention" because it met every three years. Early responses were favorable. In 1817 the Convention broadened its work to include home missions and collegiate education.[12]

Opposition soon arose in three quarters. First, Daniel Parker, a Virginia-born Tennessean, advocated a new version of predestination under the theme of "two seeds in the Spirit": both good and bad seed are transmitted biologically; the good seed results in salvation for the children of God, and the bad seed results in damnation for the children of the devil.[13] Second, Calvinistic Baptists, led by the venerable John Taylor of Kentucky, emphasized predestination.[14] Third, Alexander Campbell, a Scotch-Irish preacher, broke with Pennsylvania Presbyterians, became a Baptist, rejected Calvinism, and emphasized a restoration of New Testament Christianity; he held that present-day Christians must imitate practices of Apostolic Christianity and reject everything for which there is neither command nor example in the New Testament.[15]

Divisions resulted from each source of opposition to missions. Parker's mobility troubled Baptists in Tennessee, Illinois, Indiana, and Texas, but the "two-seeds-in-the-Spirit" doctrine had less effect. Though a split occurred, Parkerite predestinarians were comparatively few in number. The "two-seed" doctrine won limited support. At present the continuing organization claims only a few churches.

Resurgent predestinarianism caused a deep split between 1820 and 1850. It affected Baptists all the way from seaboard states to Missouri. Viewing predestination as a hard shell which guarantees salvation for the elect but isolates the damned from salvation, these Calvinistic Baptists concluded that missionary efforts, Bible distribution, tract distribution, Sunday schools, colleges, and other means are unnecessary in respect to the elect and ineffectual in respect to the damned.[16] Calling themselves Primitive Baptists, they opposed every means proposed by pro-missioners. In most areas of the South they outnumbered those who favored missions around 1830. For twenty years or so there was conflict between pro-missioners and anti-missioners. In a particular area, however, it often took only a few years for division to occur.[17] Anti-missioners claimed more members at the time of division, but their comparative status declined. Primitive Baptist organizations now claim around 1.6 million members, a small percentage when compared to present organizations which espouse missions.

For several years in the 1820s Alexander Campbell was very popular among Baptists, particularly in the Transappalachian region. His initial popularity was due to advocacy of believer's baptism by immersion when opposing Presbyterians and Methodists. Soon, however, some Baptists opposed Campbell's view that baptism is essential to salvation. Campbell began to attack societies, associations, conventions, colleges, etc., on the ground that the New Testament is silent about them. He advocated the restoration of

Christianity as the New Testament depicts it. By 1830 Baptist churches and associations were dividing over Campbell's "restoration" doctrine. In some places entire churches went with Campbell. By 1835 the Campbell agitation was outside of Baptist organizations.[18]

Missionary theology had a unifying effect among Baptists of the South. It led to the formation of state conventions, Sunday schools, colleges, and national bodies for foreign and home missions and the publication and distribution of religious literature. In the wake of division, pro-means Baptists made the "protracted meeting" an annual affair in most churches. These evangelistic meetings, combining religious and social qualities, became an effective means of ingathering.

Pro-missioners formed the Southern Baptist Convention in 1845. Its origin was due to function, not to doctrine. For eight decades the Southern Baptist Convention had no doctrinal guide. From time to time, however, doctrine became divisive among Southern Baptists.

One system of doctrine which produced tensions among Southern Baptists was Landmarkism, fostered by J. R. Graves, J. M. Pendleton, and A. C. Dayton in the 1850s. The origin of the movement is usually dated in 1851 when the Cotton Grove meeting in western Tennessee affirmed five principles, the effects of which were to reject baptisms and ordinations administered by non-Baptists and to refuse "pulpit affiliation" with non-Baptist preachers. Landmarkism is essentially ecclesiological, not theological.[19] Graves was avowedly anti-Calvinistic; he preferred the confession of the Newport, R.I., Baptist Church because it, according to Graves, does not contain "a scintilla of Calvinism."[20] Neither Calvinistic nor Arminian in his basic theology, Graves was a rationalist who deduced his system from certain premises. A strict logician and effective propagandist, Graves developed an enormous following throughout the Southern Baptist Convention, especially in Transappalachian and Trans-Mississippi areas.

Landmarkism rests on the premise that only Baptist churches are "churches" in the New Testament sense. Local congregations of other denominations are "societies," according to Graves. Not being churches, they cannot validly baptize; therefore, according to Graves, their baptism must be viewed as "alien baptism." During a controversy with R. B. C. Howell, Nashville pastor and president of the Southern Baptist Convention in 1857–1859, Graves contended that only local churches have authority to appoint missionaries; the Foreign Mission Board (SBC), he proposed, should let local churches decide who shall serve as missionaries. Shortly thereafter Graves developed a view called "non-intercommunion," a view which Pendleton did not share; under the practice of non-intercommunion, only members of a local church could commune in the Lord's Supper. Jesus established Baptist churches, according to Graves, and Jesus' statement that "the gates of hell shall not prevail" guarantees that Baptist churches have existed from the first century to the present. The successive perpetuity of Baptist churches became a crucial feature of Landmarkism. However, faith sought facts to back it up; the result was a rendition of Christian history under the theme of "a trail of blood."[21]

Landmark ecclesiology produced controversy among Southern Baptists. In the 1880s T. P. Crawford, applying Landmark principles to foreign missions, contended that missionaries should found churches, not other institutions; that the church, not a missionary board, should be the agency of missions; that missionaries should observe the tent-making principle of self-support; and that the mission board should cease subsidizing natives in foreign countries. For several years Crawfordism agitated Southern Baptists, but the Foreign Mission Board discontinued his appointment in 1892.[22]

Before and after 1900, S. A. Hayden of Texas attacked the Southern Baptist Convention's "board" system and sought to replace it with a "church" system. Specifically, Hayden contended that only a local church could authorize or appoint missionaries; that associations, conventions, and boards should be directly representative of local churches; and that local churches were to determine the conditions of representation in conventions, associations, etc.[23]

Views like those advocated by Crawford and Hayden produced a split from the Southern Baptist Convention in 1905, led by Ben M. Bogard of Arkansas. The specific issue was a question of qualifications of messengers to the Southern Baptist Convention.[24] Bogard and his followers issued an ultimatum that the Convention discontinue the financial basis of representation and agree that messengers are local churches' delegates. When the Convention refused to accede to the ultimatum, Bogardites withdrew and organized a group now known as the American Baptist Association (with offices in Texarkana and now claiming over a million members). In 1950 there was a split in the ABA, the new organization calling itself the North American Baptist Association,[25] now called the Baptist Missionary Association of America (with offices in Little Rock and at present claiming over 200,000 members).

Landmark views have had vocal advocates in the Southern Baptist

Convention, but the Convention has not gone along with strict Landmarkism. For example, in 1963 the Convention defeated an amendment to delete from the proposed Baptist Faith and Message the reference to the New Testament's mention of an invisible church.[26] After the Arkansas state convention refused to seat messengers from four churches which practiced so-called "open communion" and "alien immersion," the Southern Baptist Convention refused in 1966 to disqualify churches from representation in the SBC on such grounds.

Though essentially conservative in theology, Southern Baptists stopped short of a thoroughgoing Fundamentalist position when the Southern Baptist Convention adopted in 1925 its first confession of faith, the Baptist Faith and Message, a revision of the New Hampshire Confession (1830–1833, amended in 1853). Whereas the New Hampshire Confession stated that the Bible is "the supreme standard by which all human conduct, creeds, and opinions should be tried," the 1925 confession said that the Bible is "the supreme standard by which all human conduct, creeds, and *religious* opinions should be tried" (emphasis added). In keeping with some Fundamentalist emphases, the 1925 Confession emphasized God's special activity in creation and the Son's birth from the Virgin Mary, and it added sections on Christ's bodily resurrection and his return. In keeping with some emphases of the so-called "social gospel," against which Fundamentalism was a reaction, the 1925 Confession included new articles on peace and war, education, and social service. In keeping with Southern Baptist emphases and practices, the 1925 Confession included new articles on religious liberty, cooperation, evangelism and missions, and stewardship. The preface to the 1925 Confession on "the historic Baptist conception of the nature and function of confessions of faith" said that a confession is "a consensus of opinion of some Baptist body . . . for the general instruction and guidance of our own people," not an addition to "the simple conditions of salvation revealed in the New Testament"; that confessions are statements which lack "any quality of finality or infallibility"; that any group of Baptists has a right to draft a confession and to publish it to the world at any time; that confessions are "only guides in interpretation [of the Scriptures], having no authority over conscience"; that, being "statements of religious convictions, drawn from the Scriptures," confessions "are not to be used to hamper freedom of thought or investigation in other realms of life."[27]

The 1925 Confession was designed to deal with alleged conflicts between science and supernaturalism in religion. The substance of prefatory statements and certain articles indicate that Southern Baptists refused to make any doctrinal standard, based on Scripture, the test of opinions in nonreligious areas. The article on education affirmed, first, the compatibility of Christian faith with all sound learning and, second, the role of Christian schools as a coordinate of missions and general benevolence.

When one compares the 1925 statement of Southern Baptists with the confession adopted in 1923 by the Baptist Bible Union, a Fundamentalist organization with ties to Northern Baptists, one can more easily discern Southern Baptists' moderate doctrinal position. Concerning the Scriptures, the Union changed the New Hampshire Confession's "divinely inspired" to "supernaturally inspired"; deleted certain phrases from the earlier confession (for example, "a perfect treasure of heavenly instruction," "God for its author, salvation for its end," and "it reveals the principles by which God will judge us"); and added explanatory comments that the Bible, "as originally written, does not contain and convey the word of God, but IS the very Word of God" and that inspiration means supernatural activity of the Holy Spirit which guarantees that the Bible is "free from error, as no other writings have ever been or ever will be. . . ." The Union added articles on the devil (Satan), on the Genesis account of creation, on the Virgin Birth, and on Christ's resurrection and return.[28] The Southern Baptist Convention also stopped short of thoroughgoing Fundamentalism, such as espoused by Landmark (the American Baptist Association and Baptist Missionary Association of America) or other groups.[29]

Nevertheless, Fundamentalist views have enjoyed strong support among Southern Baptists. The popularity of Frank Norris, Fort Worth pastor, was due in part to his Fundamentalist emphasis. Norris succeeded in taking many Southern Baptists with him when he broke with the Southern Baptist Convention. So-called "Independent Baptist" groups have drained off many Southern Baptists who hold Fundamentalist views. The attractiveness of "Independent" movements is due to many factors, some of them being Fundamentalist theology, gifted preachers with forceful personalities, energetic evangelism, Bible-centered teaching in Sunday schools (with pastors often serving as teachers of adults), radio and television ministries, bus ministries, and the like.

In the past fifteen years, doctrine has often been before the Southern Baptist Convention in a controversial manner. The controversy in the early 1960s over Ralph Elliott, professor of Old

Testament at Midwestern Baptist Theological Seminary, revolved around issues which Fundamentalists had highlighted a half century earlier.[30] In 1962 the Convention adopted a motion to reaffirm "the *entire* Bible as the authoritative, authentic, infallible Word of God"; another motion objected to seminary teaching which undermines faith in the Bible's historical accuracy and doctrinal integrity and requested seminary trustees and administrative officers to protect Baptists' historic position on this subject.[31] The 1963 Confession, a revision of the 1925 Confession, contains a preface which both quotes the 1925 preface about the historic role of confessions in Baptist life and asserts that Baptists' emphasis on "the soul's competency before God, freedom in religion, and the priesthood of the believer" does not mean "that there is an absence of certain definite doctrines that Baptists believe, cherish, and with which they have been and are now closely identified." The 1963 revision sets forth "certain teachings which we believe." Of particular significance are two additions to the article on Scriptures and a revision of the article on education. The Bible "is the record of God's revelation of Himself to man," and "[t]he criterion by which the Bible is to be interpreted is Jesus Christ." Concerning education, the 1963 document contains no reference to education's compatibility with sound learning (as in the 1925 document); instead, it states that "there should be a proper balance between academic freedom and academic responsibility," with the freedom of a teacher in a Christian school being limited "by the preeminence of Jesus Christ, by the authoritative nature of the Scriptures, and by the distinct purpose for which the school exists."[32]

Doctrinal controversy among Southern Baptists surfaced again in 1969. When a messenger moved to require seminary professors and writers of literature published by the Sunday School Board to sign annually a statement of "belief in the infallibility of the entire Bible," the president of the Board made a substitute motion, calling attention to the 1963 Confession and urging trustees of agencies to see that programs are consistent with and not contrary to this confession; the SBC adopted the substitute.[33]

In 1970 the Convention ordered the Sunday School Board to recall the first volume of the new *Broadman Bible Commentary,* said to be "out of keeping with the vast majority of Southern Baptist pastors and people," and to have it rewritten with due consideration of the conservative viewpoint.[34] In floor discussion, critics of the commentary on Genesis focused on passages which figured in the Elliott controversy. The Sunday School Board asked the original author, an English Baptist, to revise his text. In 1971 the Convention, by motion, ordered the Sunday School Board to discharge the original writer of Volume 1 of the *Commentary* (actually the commentary on Genesis) and to engage another Old Testament scholar to carry out the 1970 instruction. [35] In 1972 a newly formed organization called the Baptist Faith and Message Fellowship objected to the entire *Commentary* series and announced that it would ask the Convention to order a thorough revision. A 1972 motion called for the Sunday School Board to recall the entire *Broadman Bible Commentary* because "a large segment" of material in it "is out of harmony with the spirit and letter" of the 1963 Confession and to rewrite the *Commentary* "from the point of view that the Bible is truth, without any mixture of error"; the Convention defeated the motion. [36] Opponents of the motion appealed to the doctrine of the priesthood of each believer and asserted the right of each Baptist to interpret the Bible for himself. The Fellowship continued to attack what it regarded as dangerous teachings taught by seminaries or published in Southern Baptist literature. It began to publish the *Southern Baptist Journal,* which has consistently called for doctrinal purity. (The Fellowship cites recent actions of the Lutheran Church-Missouri Synod as illustrative of steps that preserve doctrinal purity and protect against liberalism.) A director of the Fellowship introduced to the 1975 Convention a motion calling for an interpretation of the 1963 article on Scripture, particularly the phrase "truth without mixture of error"; when the motion came up for discussion, the sponsor was absent, and the motion was withdrawn at his request. [37]

The Fellowship has begun to initiate actions on the state convention level. For example, in annual meetings in late 1975 the Georgia convention adopted a motion which affirms faith "in the entire Bible as the authentic, infallible, authoritative word of God"; while accepting the 1963 Confession as the theological guideline for convention employees, the convention defeated other resolutions reportedly inspired by the Fellowship and adopted a resolution affirming each person's "inalienable right and spiritual competence to interpret the Bible for himself, under the guidance of the Holy Spirit, and to freely express his beliefs and convictions." The Maryland convention adopted a resolution against doctrinal subscriptionism which restricts thought and interferes with Christian freedom. [38]

Though Southern Baptists remain conservative in doctrine—when viewed on any comprehensive theological spectrum—they have refused, to date, to establish subscriptionism to a doctrinal statement as proof of orthodoxy. But there is a controversy about this. In the foreseeable future, Southern Baptists will probably feel pressures from the dilemma caused by insistence on doctrinal purity, on the one hand, and assertion of the right of each Christian to interpret Scripture without direction from an ecclesiastical body, on the other hand.

FUNCTIONAL UNITY

The unity of Southern Baptists is functional, not doctrinal. As previously noted, in its first eighty years the Southern Baptist Convention adopted no confession of faith. A confession's authority derives from the consent it enjoys, not from the ecclesiastical body which adopts it. The 1963 Confession, according to its preface, was intended "as information to the churches" and possibly ("may serve") "as guidelines to the various agencies of the Southern Baptist Convention."

The rationale of Baptist associationalism in America, derived from English Baptists, is essentially functional. As affirmed in their *Orthodox Creed* of 1678, English General Baptists believed that "several distinct congregations . . . make up . . . one catholick church"; that representatives of several churches, "being legally convened . . . make but one church, and have lawful right . . . to act in the name of Christ"; that such gathering "is the best means under heaven to preserve unity, to prevent heresy, and superintendency among, or in any congregation whatsoever within its own limits, or jurisdiction"; that a particular church should appeal to such assembly "in case any injustice is done, or heresy, and schism countenanced"; that "the decisive voice in such general assemblies is the major part"; and that such assembly has "lawful power to hear, and determine, as also to excommunicate."[39] As stated in the Second London Confession (1677), Particular Baptists held that messengers of "many Churches holding communion together" may "meet together to consider, and give their advice in, or about that matter in difference"—"matter" includes doctrine, administration, injury to member(s) because of unjust discipline, threat to a church's "peace, union, and edification"—and that assembled messengers "are not entrusted with any Church-power properly so called; or with any jurisdiction over the Churches themselves, to exercise any censures either over any Churches, or Persons: or to impose their determination on the Churches, or Officers."[40] Thus, General Baptists centralized power in the association; Particular Baptists decentralized it.

Though General and Particular Baptists differed over the authority of an association, early associations of both groups served basically functional ends—sending "messengers" (missionaries) to plant new churches, providing ministers to administer ordinances, dealing with special financial needs of a particular church or member, providing "helps" to arbitrate issues which endanger a church, etc. This functional emphasis extended to the New World.

The Philadelphia Association (1707) was formed to protect churches against "strangers" who claimed to be Baptist preachers or members but whose conduct and gifts were unproven and to assist any church which had an internal controversy which it could not resolve.[41] The classic "essay" on the authority of associations, adopted by the Philadelphia Association in 1749, specifies that an association "is not a superior judicature" with power to make decisions binding on a local church, relating to administering ordinances, selecting pastor and officers, admitting and dismissing members, disciplining members, etc. Instead of exercising superintendency over churches, an association is "subservient to the churches." When associating churches consent in doctrine and practice and each church exercises its own power, the association has authority to withdraw from any church or party which deviates from accepted doctrine and practice, to circularize its judgment among confederating churches, and to offer advice about corrective action. An association is desirable for churches' "mutual strength, counsel, and other valuable advantages." These advantages are basically functional. Even an association's consideration of doctrinal matters has functional ends—for example, to assist a troubled church, to guard other churches against an irregularity existing in one church, etc.[42] A cursory reading of associational records will lead one to see that associational meetings served functional ends. For example, in 1755 the Philadelphia Association appointed a preacher to visit North Carolina; in 1755 the Charleston Association recommended that churches contribute funds to help educate preachers, and in 1792 it incorporated a fund for ministerial education; in 1803 some North and South Carolina associations appointed missionaries to the Indians.[43] Associations also provided fellowship and inspiration which colonists and, later, frontiersmen needed and valued.

A major boost to unity among Virginia Baptists was the common struggle for religious liberty before, during, and after the Revolution. As early as 1770 separate groups of Baptists petitioned the government to stop persecution of non-Anglican religionists. In 1775 the General Association stimulated and guided action; in 1777 it appointed a committee to find out which laws discriminated on religious grounds; and in 1778 it appointed a committee to work for changes in offensive laws. In 1784, three years before the term "United Baptist" appeared, Separates and Regulars jointly organized the General Committee to work for religious freedom. For fifteen years this committee gathered information about violations, disseminated it among Baptists and others, originated petition campaigns, addressed public officials, helped to shape public opinion which defeated a proposed bill for taxing all persons to finance teachers of the Christian religion, stirred the legislature to pass Jefferson's bill on liberty of conscience, called for the disestablishment of the Church of England (Episcopalianism), and prompted Madison to propose amendments to the Federal Constitution to guarantee certain rights, the first of which concerns religious liberty. The committee's last act was to recommend that associations effect a plan to promote unity and harmony among churches.[44]

American Baptists have spoken univocally in support of the free exercise of religion and no establishment of religion. The agreement of Southern and Northern Baptists on this point caused the two conventions to hold a joint meeting in Washington, D.C., in 1920 and jointly to establish a church in our nation's capital as a memorial to Baptists' commitment to religious liberty (National Baptist Memorial Church). The Baptist Joint Committee on Public Affairs, the outgrowth of earlier involvement in chaplaincy programs, exists primarily to represent Baptist concerns on matters relating to public policy. The Southern Baptist Convention has adopted numerous resolutions against a U.S. ambassador to the Vatican, against government-compelled religious exercises, against the expenditure of tax funds to finance sectarian education and church-controlled schools, and the like. Convention-adopted positions in this area have never provoked vigorous dissent except, perhaps, in respect to the subject of the Supreme Court's expulsion of compulsory prayers and Bible readings from public schools, with dissenters seemingly failing to consider that the Court ruled against *government-compelled* praying and Bible reading in public schools.

For two centuries religious freedom has been a unifying factor among Baptists of the South. On few other subjects—such as "sin is bad," "grace is good," etc.,—has the consensus been broader than that in behalf of church-state separation. This consensus is breaking down at present, due mainly to government programs of aid to collegiate education and to the activity of many Baptist educators in the South in behalf of government aid.

The missionary function, however, is the major basis of unity among Baptists of the South. Having already dealt with the origin of the mission movement, it now is necessary to indicate how Southern Baptists' manner of dealing with missions has contributed to their unity amidst diversity.

The original pro-missioners in the United States came from seaboard states—from New England to Georgia. The Triennial Convention (1814) first served the cause of foreign missions by "eliciting, combining, and directing the energies of the whole denomination in one sacred effort, for sending the glad tidings of Salvation to the Heathen, and to nations destitute of pure Gospel-light. . . ."[45] From the beginning, however, Richard Furman of Charleston, president of the Triennial Convention, had a larger vision, including serving the "interests of the churches at home," particularly in respect to the educating of "pious youths who are called to the gospel ministry," as soon as finances permitted.[46] At its second meeting (1817), the Convention expanded its powers "to embrace home missions and plans for the encouragement of education." John Mason Peck and James E. Welch—who had received instruction from William Staughton of Philadelphia, a participant in founding the English Baptist missionary society in Kettering in 1792—were appointed to the Western mission.[47] Luther Rice began to promote the establishment of Columbia College in the nation's capital.

Whereas some Baptist leaders in the North (e.g., Francis Wayland)[48] favored a convention structure which comprehends various activities, most favored the one-cause, societal method. One factor behind the return to the societal method was the financial difficulty which Rice experienced in respect to the college. By the mid-1820s the Triennial Convention promoted foreign missions only. In 1824 the American Baptist Publication Society was organized.[49] Originally providing tract and periodical literature, it became a supplier of books in the 1840s and for several generations was the major supplier of Baptist literature among Baptists of the North and South, except where J. R. Graves's influence was strong. In 1832 the American Baptist Home Missionary Society was organized "to promote the preaching of the gospel in North America."[50] The basis of membership in these societies was an annual contribution; a large gift qualified one for life membership.

Statewide organizations—usually called "conventions" or "general associations"—appeared in the 1820s, the first being the Southern Carolina Convention, organized in 1821.[51] In every southern state east of the Mississippi River, except Florida, a state convention appeared before 1840. What distinguished these state conventions from the national societies was their promotion of all missionary, educational, and benevolent causes. In most states a college for the training of youth, especially those preparing for the ministry, appeared within a few years after the organization of a state convention.[52]

The interrelatedness of all causes is easy to document. Promoters of foreign missions also promoted home missions, Sunday Schools, Bible and tract distribution, training of ministers, and the like. They regarded various means as coordinates. Anti-missioners, however, tended to oppose all means, usually on theological and/or financial grounds.[53] Some pro-missioners adapted a United Baptist principle to their purpose—namely, that a difference of opinion should be no bar to fellowship. In 1827, for example, the Concord Association in central Missouri recommended that "the cause of missions be not made a bar to fellowship," a recommendation that evoked from one church a strong declaration of "unfellowship with all the money-begging, hired, pompous missionaries, and hireling priests, with all the societies that stand in connection with them, such as auxiliaries, tract societies, Bible societies, theological seminaries, Sunday-school union, and rag society, etc."[54] Sometimes pro-missioners adapted liberty of conscience to the missionary cause. For example, in 1835 some asked the Mt. Pleasant Association in central Missouri to yield "to all the liberty of conscience upon the subject of missions."[55] When associations granted liberty of conscience in respect to missions or refused to make advocacy of missions a bar to fellowship, Baptists maintained unity amidst diversity; when they censured such advocacy, division usually resulted.

After supporting national societies headquartered in the North, Baptists of the South began in the late 1830s to advocate the formation of Southern agencies. This view intensified in the 1840s, due mainly to feelings generated by the slavery-abolition controversy.[56] Between 1787 and 1791 some Baptist associations in the South condemned slavery as contrary to divine law and civil liberty. Southern attitudes toward slavery changed after the cotton gin (invented in 1793) made slavery far more economically profitable to slaveholders. As late as the 1820s, some Southern Baptist leaders recognized slavery as a questionable institution. During the abolition controversy of the 1830s, however, proslavery sentiment hardened. Some Southern Baptists came to view slavery as a God-established, biblically sanctioned institution. Other Baptists of the South favored gradualism, not immediatism, in ending slavery. Baptist abolitionists, particularly in New England, viewed slavery as sinful—

to be viewed as "ungraduated in the scripture scale of human sins," which scale includes such crimes as "horse-racing, gambling, piracy, the rum-traffick"—and pushed for the immediate eradication of the evil.

Foreign and home mission agencies became the focal points of controversy over slavery. Some Southerners claimed that the Home Mission Society took more money from the South than it spent for missionary work in the South. The American Baptist Anti-Slavery Convention, organized in 1839, advocated immediate emancipation, censured Baptists of the South for condoning slavery, and threatened to renounce fellowship with slaveholders. A Free Mission Society, organized in 1843, conditioned membership on opposition to slavery. In 1841 the Home Mission Society and the Triennial Convention tried to offend neither abolitionists nor slaveholders; these agencies contended that only churches can exercise disciplinary powers, that voluntary societies exist to serve specific objects, and that it would be disruptive to make sentiment for or against slavery a test. These societies' neutrality pleased neither side. In 1844 Georgia Baptists asked the Home Mission Society to appoint as a missionary to Texas a preacher who was a slaveholder; the Society refused to do so, holding that Georgia Baptists were trying to force a test. Also in 1844 the Alabama convention called on the Triennial Convention to state unequivocally that it would appoint slaveholders as missionaries; contending that it had previously regarded neither slaveholding nor nonslaveholding as a condition of appointment, the Convention decided that it would not thereafter appoint anyone who insisted on retaining slaves as property.

Reacting to actions by these national organizations, Virginia Baptists in the spring of 1845 issued a call for a convention to meet in Augusta, Georgia, "to confer on the best means of promoting the Foreign Mission cause, and other interests of the Baptist denomination in the South."

From its formation in 1845, the Southern Baptist Convention had the comprehensive "purpose of carrying into effect the benevolent intentions of our constituents, by organizing a plan for eliciting, combining and directing the energies of the whole denomination in one sacred effort, for the propagation of the Gospel."[57] Its constitution provided that the Convention "shall elect . . . as many Boards of Managers, as in its judgment will be necessary for carrying out the benevolent objects it may determine to promote. . . ."[58]

In 1845 the Convention created two boards—for foreign missions (located in Richmond, Virginia) and domestic missions (located in

Marion, Alabama). Foreign missions received stronger support than did home missions. The Civil War jeopardized both causes. Foreign missions rebounded faster after the Civil War, thanks to the generosity of Baptists in states which suffered least from the war (Maryland, Kentucky, Missouri, and Texas). Home mission work was in jeopardy for four decades.

In 1882 I. T. Tichenor became secretary of the Home Mission Board (so named in 1874) and immediately took actions that established a strong basis for the Board's work. It would be difficult to overstate Tichenor's influence. The Board moved its offices to Atlanta. Tichenor publicized the fact that the American Baptist Home Mission Society had three times as many missionaries in the South as the Board had, and he called on Southerners to support the Board. Within five years the number of general associations or state conventions in the South cooperating with the Board had risen from seven to twenty-one. Though the Society and the Board continued to work together in missionary activities among blacks, Tichenor succeeded in bringing missionaries to whites under the Board's appointment.[59] The most notable exception to Tichenor's success was in Missouri where both the Society and the Board vied for support. So rancorous was the competition that the Missouri Baptist Convention decided in 1889 to keep Society and Board representatives out of the state. Its plan of dual alignment was so distinct that it became known as the "Missouri Plan": the Convention prepared promotional materials and solicited funds for both Northern and Southern agencies. This plan proved to be administratively inefficient. It caused friction among Missouri Baptists. In 1919 the Missouri Convention revoked the plan and established single alignment with the Southern Baptist Convention, a policy that Missouri Baptists have repeatedly reaffirmed and even strengthened in recent years.[60]

Tichenor was also influential in creating a viable publication program among Southern Baptists. The original Southern Baptist Publication Society (1847) was supported by individuals, not by the Southern Convention. It and a voluntary Bible Board (1851) were not successful, due mainly to Landmarkers' domination of the agencies. In 1863 the Southern Convention created a Sunday School Board which did effective work during the Civil War but foundered in the late 1860s. In 1873 the Convention placed Sunday School work under the home mission organization. Tichenor enlarged the Sunday School program and urged churches to procure literature from the Southern agency. The American Baptist Publication Society, for which many Southerners wrote, worked hard to retain its Southern market. In 1890 the Southern Convention voted to create a new Sunday School Board. The new Board began its work in 1891, elected James M. Frost as corresponding secretary (followed in 1893 by Theodore P. Bell, with Frost returning to the position in 1896), and proceeded to promote educational organizations (especially for youth) and to publish a wide range of literature. The Northern Society contested the expansion of the Board's work. Some influential Southerners who had previously supported the Society objected to the Society's efforts to weaken the Board's work. Such reaction secured the Board's position among Southerners. Since 1897 the Board has been a prominent factor in Southern Baptists' unity, despite occasional attacks on some of its publications.[61]

Whereas Northerners and Southerners have been rather successful in effecting comity agreements respecting foreign missions, they have not been so successful in respect to home mission work. In 1894 a joint Northern-Southern conference, meeting at Fortress Monroe, Virginia, had no trouble agreeing on cooperative educational and missionary work among black Baptists. While recognizing that the conference's commission extended only to work among blacks, it proposed that the Southern Home Mission Board and the Northern Home Mission Society recognize the inexpediency of "two different organizations of Baptists to solicit contributions, or to establish missions in the same localities"; it recommended that employees of these two agencies "be instructed to co-operate in all practical ways in the spirit of Christ," with neither agency to open new work in localities already occupied by the other.[62]

For several years this agreement guided home mission work by the two agencies. The breakdown of this agreement was due more to Southern Baptists' mobility than to planned mission work. The outward migration of Baptists from the South put Southern Baptists in areas which the Northern Society had been serving. New Mexico's experience is illustrative. The Northern Society had worked for decades in New Mexico, especially among Indians, but its work was slow. After 1900 increasing numbers of Texans and other Southerners, many of them with Southern Baptist backgrounds, moved into eastern New Mexico. The Northern Society viewed the Southern Board's proposal to serve Southern Baptists in New Mexico as a violation of the Fortress Monroe agreement. Settlers from the South were reluctant to work with the Society. In 1909 a joint Northern-Southern conference noted "the increasing numerical and financial strength of Southern Baptists" in New Mexico and agreed that the Southern Board should take over mission work if the New Mexico convention so requested. From another joint conference in 1911–1912 came the view that "the ideal organization is one association in a given territory and one convention in a given State," subject, of course, to practical problems related to "local conditions" which may prevent "the immediate attainment of the ideal." Until the ideal was attainable, the conference recommended, New Mexico Baptists should support both Southern and Northern conventions, with undesignated funds being distributed according to an agreed-upon formula and designated funds being distributed according to donors' wishes.[63] The report of this joint conference was a factor in the establishment of New Mexico, Oklahoma, and Missouri Baptists' single alignment with the Southern Convention.

The Southern Convention created a Committee on Efficiency in 1913. In 1917 it created an Executive Committee to represent the Convention between annual meetings and to promote coordination of agencies' efforts. Financial difficulties suffered by Southern and state convention agencies in the early 1920s pointed up the need for greater coordination and less competition. In 1925 the Southern Convention established the Cooperative Program to remedy these difficulties, to aid agencies' programs, and to foster Southern Baptists' fellowship. With modifications from time to time, the Cooperative Program has served Southern Baptists for a half century. Under this program, the Southern Convention works with and through each affiliated state convention. The state convention retains a percentage of undesignated funds for its in-state programs and sends the remainder of such funds to the Southern Convention for its programs. Each state convention determines how much undesignated funds it will retain, and it allocates funds for each of its own programs. The Southern Baptist Convention has exclusive power to allocate funds for its programs.[64]

The Depression stimulated an increasing outward migration of Southern Baptists—first, from Oklahoma and Texas to the West Coast and from the Transappalachian area to northern industrial areas; next, due to World War II, from throughout the South to places throughout the country; and next, due to the constant mobility of the American people since World War II, to all parts of the country, especially urban areas. As a result of many factors (cultural, social, theological, etc.), many Southern Baptists refused to unite with Baptist churches outside of the South. In the absence of coordinated work by Southern Baptists, many founded or affiliated with "independent" churches which had no connection with the

Southern Convention. In the late 1930s Southern Baptist churches began to appear in California. Other Southern Baptist churches sprang up outside of the South during and after World War II.

After the Northern Baptist Convention changed its name to the American Baptist Convention (1950), the Southern Convention in 1951 authorized its agencies "to serve as a source of blessing to any community or any people anywhere in the United States." In 1955 the Convention approved the Home Mission Board's policies governing cooperative work in "western and new areas," one policy being the Board's refusal to "solicit or invite Baptist churches already affiliated with some other convention to join [Southern Baptist] associations or [state] conventions." Though some Southern Baptist churches appeared outside of the South and Southwest prior to 1940, the organized expansion of Southern Baptist work occurred after this date—and most of it after 1950.[65]

The chief agencies of Southern Baptists' functional unity are the Foreign Mission Board, the Home Mission Board, the Sunday School Board, the Annuity Board (1918), and six seminaries (Southern, 1859; Southwestern, 1908; New Orleans, 1917/1925; Golden Gate, 1944/1950; Southeastern, 1950; and Midwestern, 1957.)[66]

Of these agencies, the Sunday School Board and the seminaries have drawn the most criticism in the past two decades, due largely, it appears, to their influence in the training of church members and ministers. Recent theological controversies have focused on seminary instruction and on literature published by the Sunday School Board. In recent years the Home Mission Board's emphasis on social ministries has drawn some criticism, but this Board has enlarged its work in this area.

The Southern Convention has other agencies with assigned tasks, chief of which are the commissions (Seminary, Education, Brotherhood, Christian Life, Historical, Radio and Television, and Stewardship), and the Baptist Joint Committee on Public Affairs. The most controversial is the Christian Life Commission, due to its role in addressing social, moral, racial, political, and economic issues, on some of which there is conspicuous diversity of opinion among Southern Baptists.[67] No Convention agency has been under more intense or persistent attack in the past two decades than has this commission. However, it has continued to publish literature, to issue position statements, and to promote discussion on a wide range of controversial subjects. The Radio and Television Commission's reputation is well established in media circles; though some Southern

Baptists object from time to time to some of its innovative communication of the gospel, the commission enjoys a highly visible and deeply appreciated position among most Southern Baptists. The Stewardship Commission takes the lead in promoting stewardship of life, influence, and resources (especially income), a service on which pastors heavily rely. Other commissions touch delineated segments of Southern Baptist life.

CONCLUSION

From a small number at the time of the American Revolution, Baptists have become the largest denominational family in the South. However, Baptists affiliate with various bodies, some of which have little or no contact with other Baptist bodies. The most extensive unity among Baptists of the South is found in the Southern Baptist Convention. Diversity is also present in the Southern Baptist Convention, as evidenced by numerous internal controversies in recent years. Culturally, the constituency of the Convention is less homogeneous now than it was prior to 1940; heterogeneity contributes to diversity. The instinct for cooperative work on the functional level has prevented conspicuous division in recent years. Only time will tell whether Southern Baptists' unity will successfully resist pressures fostered by diversity.

NOTES

[1] See the county-by-county, color-coded religious map of the forty-eight contiguous states, in Edwin S. Gaustad, *Historical Atlas of Religion in America* (New York: Harper & Row, Publishers, 1962), loose map inside back cover.

[2] The two Landmark groups referred to here are the American Baptist Association with 1,003,695 members and the Baptist Missionary Association of America with 203, 903 members. The major "primitive" Baptist group is the National Primitive Baptist Convention; see Constant H. Jacquet, Jr., *Yearbook of American and Canadian Churches, 1975* (Nashville: Abingdon Press, 1975), pp. 26, 34, 73. On Baptist cooperation, see James Leo Garrett, ed., *Baptist Relations with Other Christians* (Valley Forge: Judson Press, 1974), chaps. 7-9, pp. 67-105.

[3] Hugh Wamble, *Through Trial to Triumph* (Nashville: Convention Press, 1958), pp. 4-5, 8; Joe M. King, *A History of South Carolina Baptists* (Columbia: General Board of the South Carolina Baptist Convention, 1964), pp. 13-17.

[4] Henry Bettenson, ed., *Documents of the Christian Church* (New York: Oxford University Press, 1960), pp. 376-377.

[5] Wamble, *Through Trial to Triumph*, p. 10.

[6] William L. Lumpkin, ed., *Baptist Confessions of Faith,* rev. ed. (Valley Forge: Judson Press, 1969), p. 352.

[7] William L. Lumpkin, *Baptist Foundations in the South* (Nashville: Broadman Press, 1961), pp. 20, 153-154. On the origin of Separate Baptists as products of the Great Awakening, see C. C. Goen, *Revivalism and Separatism in New England, 1740–1800* (New Haven: Yale University Press, 1962), pp. 208-210.

[8] Robert A. Baker, ed., *A Baptist Source Book: With Particular Reference to Southern Baptists* (Nashville: Broadman Press, 1966), p. 20. Used by permission.

[9] *Ibid.,* p. 22.

[10] *Ibid.,* p. 24; cf. Lumpkin, *Confessions,* p. 359.

[11] A. C. Underwood, *A History of the English Baptists* (London: Kingsgate Press, 1947), pp. 159-165, 196-198. On Fuller's thought, see James E. Tull, *Shapers of Baptist Thought* (Valley Forge: Judson Press, 1972), pp. 79-100.

[12] Baker, *A Baptist Source Book,* pp. 53-68.

[13] *Ibid.,* pp. 81-82. See Terry E. Miller, "Otter Creek Church, Indiana: Lonely Bastion of Daniel Parker's Two-Seedism," *Foundations,* vol. 18 (October–December, 1975), pp. 358-376.

[14] *Ibid.,* pp. 79-81.

[15] *Ibid.,* pp. 77-78.

[16] Wamble, *Through Trial to Triumph,* pp. 51-52.

[17] In Missouri, for example, most associations resolved the issue within three to seven years, often by splitting.

[18] Wamble, *Through Trial to Triumph,* pp. 50-51. On Campbell's thought, see Tull, *Shapers of Baptist Thought,* pp. 101-127.

[19] Hugh Wamble, "Landmarkism: Doctrinaire Ecclesiology Among Baptists," *Church History,* vol. 33, no. 4 (December, 1964), pp. 429-447; Tull, *Shapers of Baptist Thought,* pp. 129-151.

[20] Graves's editorial note in S. Adlam, *The First Baptist Church in America,* reprint (Texarkana: Baptist Sunday School Committee, 1939), p. 194.

[21] J. R. Graves, *Trilemma* (reprint *Source Book,* ed., Texarkana: Baptist Sunday School Committee, 1928), p. 119; Baker, *A Baptist Source Book,* pp. 142-146. The most widely circulated version of this view of Baptist history is J. M. Carroll, *"The Trail of Blood"* (Lexington, Ky.: Ashland Avenue Baptist Church, 1931).

[22] Baker, *A Baptist Source Book,* pp. 176-180.

[23] *Ibid.,* p. 180.

[24] *Ibid.,* pp. 174-175.

[25] Lumpkin, *Confessions,* pp. 377-381.

[26] *Southern Baptist Convention Annual, 1963,* items 115-119, p. 63; *SBC Annual, 1964,* items 7-8, p. 47.

[27] For introductory information and full text, see Lumpkin, *Confessions,* pp. 390-400.

[28] *Ibid.,* pp. 384-389.

[29] *Ibid.,* pp. 377-381. A "Two Seed" abstract of beliefs affirms that "the scriptures of the Old and New Testaments, as translated under the reign of King James are a revelation from God, inspired by the Holy Ghost. . . ."; cited in Miller, "Otter Creek Church," p. 369.

[30] The controversy centered on Ralph H. Elliott's book, *The Message of Genesis* (Nashville: Broadman Press, 1961). Most criticism focused on Elliott's treatment of the first eleven chapters of Genesis and of Abraham's aborted sacrifice of Isaac.

[31] *SBC Annual, 1962,* items 57, 84-86, pp. 65, 68.

[32] See the 1963 text, in Lumpkin, ed., *Confessions,* pp. 393-400.

[33] *SBC Annual, 1969,* items 48, 162-163, 175, 274, pp. 58-59, 70-72, 81. Also, see *Annual, 1970,* items 90 and 233, pp. 66, 82.

[34] *SBC Annual, 1970,* items 64, 180, 182, and 198, pp. 63, 76, 77-78.

[35] *SBC Annual, 1971,* items 153, 156, 188, and 204, pp. 71, 76, 80.

[36] *SBC Annual, 1972,* items 36, 99, and 100, pp. 55, 71.

[37] *SBC Annual, 1975,* items 102 and 187. pp. 65-66, 79.

[38] Robert O'Brien, "National Wrapup: Conventions Calm amid Sea of Issues," *The Maryland Baptist,* vol. 58 (December 18, 1975), p. 3.

[39] Lumpkin, *Confessions,* pp. 318-319, 327.

[40] *Ibid.,* p. 289.

[41] A. D. Gillette, ed., *Minutes of the Philadelphia Baptist Association from A.D. 1707 to A. D. 1807* (Philadelphia: American Baptist Publication Society, 1851), p. 25.

[42] Baker, *A Baptist Source Book,* pp. 10-11.

[43] *Ibid.,* pp. 11-14, 28-29, 31.

[44] *Ibid.,* pp. 33-40; Wamble, *Through Trial to Triumph,* pp. 25-36; R. B. Semple, *A History of the Rise and Progress of the Baptists in Virginia,* rev. by G. W. Beale (Richmond: Pitt & Dickinson, Publisher, 1894), pp. 29-54, 94-113.

[45] Baker, *A Baptist Source Book,* pp. 62-63.

[46] *Ibid.,* p. 65.

[47] *Ibid.,* pp. 67-68.

[48] *Ibid.,* pp. 68-71.

[49] *Ibid.,* pp. 73-74.

[50] *Ibid.,* p. 74.

[51] *Ibid.,* pp. 75-76.

[52] Wamble, *Through Trial to Triumph,* pp. 52-53.

[53] See examples of John Taylor's, Daniel Parker's, and Primitive Baptists' attacks, in Baker, *A Baptist Source Book,* pp. 79-84.

[54] See documents in R. S. Duncan, *A History of the Baptists in Missouri* (St. Louis: Scammell & Co., Publishers, 1882), pp. 252-253.

[55] Quoted in *ibid.,* p. 165.

[56] See documents related to the controversy over slavery in Baptist mission societies, in Baker, *A Baptist Source Book,* pp. 87-113.

[57] *Ibid.,* p. 116. Quoted words appear in SBC annuals. These words also appear in the 1845 charter conferred by the Georgia legislature with one change—"BAPTIST DENOMINATION OF CHRISTIANS."

[58] *Ibid.,* p. 117.

[59] *Ibid.,* pp. 157-160.

[60] *Missouri Baptist Convention Annual, 1889,* pp. 41-43; *MBC Annual 1919,* pp. 36-38, 87-88, 90-91, 94, 118-119; *MBC Annual, 1959,* p. 28A; *MBC Annual, 1961,* p. 28; *MBC Annual, 1969,* pp. 36-37; *MBC Annual, 1970,* pp. 35, 80; *MBC Annual, 1971,* pp. 42, 89-90; *MBC Annual, 1972,* pp. 46-47, 72-79. The 1975 convention defeated a constitutional amendment that would have discontinued the policy of single alignment policy; *MBC Annual, 1975,* pp. 57-58.

[61] Baker, *A Baptist Source Book,* pp. 127-132, 147-151, 165-168; Robert A. Baker, *The Southern Baptist Convention and Its People, 1607–1972* (Nashville: Broadman Press, 1974), pp. 231-232, 244-246, 273-276, 294-296, 430-432.

[62] Baker, *A Baptist Source Book,* pp. 160-162.

[63] *Ibid.,* pp. 162-165.

[64] *Ibid.,* pp. 181-186, 188, 192-196.

[65] *Ibid.,* pp. 189-192; Baker, *The Southern Baptist Convention,* pp. 363-384.

[66] Baker, *The Southern Baptist Convention,* pp. 426-438.

[67] *Ibid.,* pp. 306-308, 414-416, 439-443.

CHAPTER

18

Black
Baptists

HENRY C. GREGORY III

I

Within a few months in 1963, over one thousand related protest meetings, sit-ins, and marches occurred in the United States of America. They manifested a twentieth-century movement which was directed toward a change of institutional practices and discriminatory behavior which were considered inconsistent with the integrity of the social order. Both the biased practices and the numerous protests were rooted in American history, the former extending back to the inception of the system of slavery and sequential segregation, the latter appearing in slave insurrections, the abolitionist movement, and voluntary associations protective of minority rights. However, requisites for effective organization which were lacking in the past came in the mid-twentieth century in the form of increased education, resourceful leadership, some minimal economic power, and the growing awareness of the cost of discrimination to American society generally.

The social-psychological context of this movement was a relatively severe deprivation among black Americans, a supportive federal government, and a dominant white opinion of gradualism. Black Americans judged their living standards as well as themselves in the cultural terms with which they were primarily familiar, those of the United States and its affluent society. In the final message during the march on Washington, Martin Luther King, Jr., referred to this plight as "an island of poverty in a vast ocean of . . . prosperity."[1] Though this economic disparity was by far the most significant factor in the Freedom Movement, there were also international and regional dimensions to the movement. Driving dissatisfactions were created by proud African nations burgeoning upon the world scene. Blacks in America identified their situation with emerging African nations. From a regional standpoint the heretofore invisible Northern ghettoized blacks became more vocal as they compared their gains in eliminating de facto segregation with those de jure gains of onrushing Southern blacks.

Thus, deprivation at a time of rising expectations was the root basis or underlying condition of the Freedom Movement. Consequently, the movement grew and broadened with increasing urgency. It manifested a shift from limited legislation to a strategy of direct action, from narrow objectives to a full-scale attack on racism, and from pockets of protest to an authentic mass movement cutting across divisions within the black community. The original aim of this movement was to modify, not to overturn, the society which it confronted. It sought to amend, not to ravage. Black Americans were so firmly rooted in and shaped by their land that their united protest attempted to guarantee full participation in the society. In short, they did not wish to deprecate or destroy that which they wished to join.

According to the technical language of social science, the movement was more of a reform than a revolution. Nevertheless, it should be noted in certain culturally isolated and economically deprived sectors—namely, sections in which racism was deeply engrained in the rural ethos—the movement by the same definition should be considered more of a revolution than a reform. Furthermore, to those numerous and more widespread provincial Americans who find racism their pivotal faith, the democratic values of the West were easily transformed by the conflicting requirements of the caste order.

With regard to blacks, they substituted the homogenized mass for the individualistic conceptions of democracy. Freedom was transformed to mean the right to extend private preference into the public domain. It involved independent decision through submission to collectivistic ideological prescriptions based on the subordination and/or elimination of other ethnic groups. Contrary to the original opinion of the participants in the movement, the number of white Americans who adhere to racism in this sense was far larger than anticipated.

In another sense many Americans in varying degrees saw this movement as acting out the country's most cherished values. It dramatized the valuational foundations of American society. It did not offer new values which conflicted with the old as perceived by the racists, but it demanded that old values be inclusively applied. It dramatized the cleavage between democratic ideals and practices as suggested by Gunnar Myrdal:

> The "American dilemma," referred to in the title of this book, is the ever-raging conflict between, on the one hand, the valuations preserved on the general plane which we shall call the "American Creed," where the American thinks, talks, and acts under the influence of high national and Christian precepts, and, on the other hand, the valuations on specific planes of individual and group living, where personal and local interests; economic, social, and sexual jealousies; considerations of community prestige and conformity; group prejudice against particular persons or types of people; and all sorts of miscellaneous wants, impulses, and habits dominate his outlook.[2]

The American creed to which Myrdal referred is that system of human ideals which is the product of the confluence of the Judeo-Christian tradition and Greek philosophical rationalism, further elaborated by recent philosophical and scientific influences. The dynamic concept of democracy contains certain persistent values among which are freedom, equality, justice, and the dignity of the individual which involves self-realization. Democracy, politically, is a form of government by participation and consent. The laws of the state should be equally and universally applied since the individual is the unit of society and since rights inhere inalienably in the individual person. However, the system of racial segregation and discrimination, based on customs and folkways alluding to interest groups and common heritage and based on legal sanctions, has prevented the black American from comparative achievements from the benefits of these values.

In seeking to correct this social condition, the protest movement was not marked by monolithic homogeneity. Rather it consisted of various organizations of differing approaches based on indigenous conceptualizations or angles of particular variants of the undesirable condition. Nevertheless, the polarities within the movement, the heterogeneous groupings and varying ideologies of differing parties, tended to converge when confronted with representatives of discriminatory patterns in intensified clashes in heightened issue areas; and Martin Luther King, Jr., emerged as the leading spokesman of the Freedom Movement. He was considered the leader in the civil rights struggle at this time, and he was a central spokesman in defining and interpreting the purpose and procedure of the movement to the various institutions of society and to the world at large. In short his leadership symbolized the Freedom Movement.

There is another significant sense in which King occupied a central symbolic role in the quest for freedom focused in this movement. As a churchman, he attempted to translate the movement into religious concepts and patterns. He was an active advocate of the interpenetration of the church as an institution in society and the movement.

He was not unaware that organized religion had often assumed a negative and reactionary role in the larger society. He also realized that changes in the institutional patterns of religion were uneven. However, he warned that lags in achieving functions and eliminating dysfunctions in the institutions of religion in relation to the Freedom Movement would destroy the essential efficacy of organized religion.[3]

Focusing on the church, King suggested that it must assume a role of instruction and action. It must clearly state that segregation is morally wrong. It is wrong in the sense that it deprives people of freedom to deliberate and to weigh alternatives, to make decisions and to assume responsibility for them. The church must facilitate the realization of the value of interracial community by exposing the false premises and the rationalizations of racial prejudice in contradistinction to Christian understanding. Furthermore, the white churches must lead in social reform by removing intramural segregation and by taking an active stand against extramural injustices and indignities which blacks and other minorities confront in social institutions. Finally, the church must lead people beyond legalism to love, and instill within its worshipers understanding and a spirit of forgiveness.

With these broad guidelines, the manifest and latent functions of the black Baptist churches in relation to the Freedom Movement may be considered.

Insofar as the black churches had evolved with a variety of responses to their hostile environment, the diverse reactions may be divided into three main categories of activities: toward, against, and away from.[4] Manifest functions of the black churches usually involved intentional movement toward a solution of the social problems confronting the minority group. Wyatt Tee Walker, former secretary of the Southern Christian Leadership Conference, said during an interview, "If there had been no Negro church, there would have been no civil rights movement. . . ."[5] These words may be best understood within the framework of three functions of organized religion for the movement, namely, valuational, structural, and strategical.

Historically black churches have placed a premium on opportunity and community. Opportunity for self-expression and development meant freedom, and community meant identity, ontological and sociological status, as well as fellowship, solidarity, and security. As such the church affirmed the dignity and worth of every person as a human being who is a child of God regardless of the exigencies of individual achievements or one's attitudinal and behavioral patterns stemming from forces of oppression; every person bears an *imago dei* which endows the individual's life with inviolable sacredness. Each person thus has rights which all others are obligated to respect, and the person is obligated to affirm. These include the right to have direct access to God and God's creation and to worship without interference from church, state, and other institutions; and the right to life, liberty, and the pursuit of wholeness without infringement by dehumanizing, brutal, and barbaric societal forces. These rights were upheld and emphasized by black churches. In the same tradition not even God violates our freedom, but rather he allows us to choose which way we will go. Individual and corporate self-determination have always been basic in the value system of black churches.[6]

Inherent in the concern for community are the words of the New Testament, "You are a chosen race, a royal priesthood, a holy nation, God's own people" (1 Peter 2:9). The operational principle of the priesthood of believers led black Baptists to zealously guarded, autonomous congregations functioning by rule of the majority with the hope that the rights of the minority would be scrupulously defended within the community of the faithful.

"Everybody Is Somebody" is the recurring theme of the Lott Cary Baptist Foreign Mission Convention, which was organized in 1897. This is, as Joseph Washington observed, a "convention made up of persons who are 'different'; both the learned and the unlearned walk hand in hand. This is indeed a community of people where men and women take rank according to their love and service."[7] This particular expression is the historical ideal of Baptists' congregational, associational, and conventional life.

II

From their inception, black Baptist churches in varying degrees have existed and striven for increased opportunity and genuine community for the individual not only within the parochial sense but also, and even more so, within the context of larger society.

The black church has been an institution of hope. Its genius has been its capacity to celebrate potential as present reality. Black churchmen have through the years, even in the most dismal days of segregation, looked at their children as future mayors, secretaries of state, presidents, and leaders. Martin Luther King, Jr., once stated that when he boarded a segregated bus in Atlanta to sit in the rear assigned to blacks, he would always make his mind sit in the front seat. His thinking is characteristic of the self-understanding of traditional black churches in relation to God and God's creation. These churches have never been second class or inferior in their own minds. Rather, they have been an avant-garde, seeking a more equitable social order by championing the values of love and justice. Undergirding this role of constituency advancement has been a theocratic view of history. A person was seen as a co-laborer with God, working in history to achieve the benefits of these values for all. The teaching of black churches was supportive of the Freedom Movement because of shared norms and ideals. This was further illustrated by the freedom songs based on spirituals and church hymns rephrased in language relative to the workings of the Freedom Movement, just as the historic spirituals often demonstrated symbolic strivings based on Scripture analogy and developmental identification.

Joseph Washington, in his early and fiery book *Black Religion,* took the position that black religion is an ethical concern with no theology. He suggested that King's faith was syncretistic in that black religion is a folk religion used only for its instrumental value for the advancement of the cause of civil rights.[8] However, not only does Washington fall into the fallacy of negative induction, but he also fails to note the significance of organized religion for King in his own self-understanding and understanding of the Freedom Movement.[9] Every professor of faith in Christ is a theologian. The question is not whether one has a theology, but whether one is a good theologian or a bad theologian. Though King talked about the power of nonviolence as taught by Mahatma Gandhi, when he and his followers protested, marched, demonstrated, and held their rallies, they did so always with the concepts of the God of biblical history, of redemption, regeneration, and sin. At a conference of church people, King said, "The non-violent movement in America has come not from secular forces but from the heart of the Negro church. This movement has done a great deal to revitalize the Negro church and . . . its message [is] . . . deeply rooted in our Judeo-Christian heritage." [10] To King the genius of this movement was an ethical and theological base which was the condition sine qua non to its raison d'être.

Of equal importance was the sharing of these values by the black population. In a *Newsweek* poll in which 96 percent of the respondents professed a faith, 49 percent of them claimed that they attended some form of church service weekly. These people were firmly convinced that their cause of the Freedom Movement would prevail because it was God's road and will.[11]

The second manifest function of black organized religion in relation to the Freedom Movement was structural. The black church began as a response to charismatic leadership. As Dearing E. King has related:

> When black slaves were not allowed to congregate or to communicate in groups, the Negro preacher, who had to keep his identity as a preacher concealed, devised ways of preaching to the slaves. He would tell the water boy to announce the service at a given time by singing through the fields: "Steal Away." All of the slaves knew to go to the swampy forest that night for worship. Another slave would be stationed at the big house to ascertain whether or not acts of worship could be heard. The next morning he went through the fields singing, "Oh, I couldn't hear nobody pray." When the slave preacher gave such a vivid description of Christ, his birth, his life, his death, resurrection and ascension, the Negroes knew that he could not read; so they asked him in the words of the spiritual: "Were you there when they crucified my Lord?"[12]

Black Baptist churches have had a free pulpit. Whereas the priestly function has characterized the white pulpit, black ministers have chiefly exercised a prophetic role, without fear of reprisal from lay leaders in their constituency or their neighborhood. Black preachers have served their communities in pivotal ways which helped the total person. When members of black Baptist churches needed legal counseling, they went to their preacher; when they needed marital, family, drug abuse, and vocational counseling, they went to the church and ultimately to the preacher. When they needed social services, financial counseling, or assistance, they went to the deacons and eventually to the preacher. Even when they needed treatment from a psychiatrist, they often found themselves talking to the preacher. The man of God was the key adviser to a God-centered people.

Though black Baptist churches were in a free-church tradition, with a congregational polity, the pastoral preacher was the undisputed leader as a spokesman for God. With a salary paid by the offerings of his own constituency, he was the freest man in his ethnic group within the context of the larger society. A number of these men were well-educated, like Andrew Marshall, who became pastor of the First Baptist Church in Savannah in 1812.

Many were of more limited formal education, but they, nevertheless, had a genius which catapulted them into prominence.

Typical of such persons was W. W. Brown, at one time pastor of the Metropolitan Baptist Church in New York City. Brown, a native of rural Virginia, never finished elementary school. Yet on the occasion of his death, he was paid many glowing tributes by prominent black Baptists. J. C. Austin, of the Pilgrim Baptist Church in Chicago, characterized Brown as a man not made by schools, but as a man who made schools.

> "Out of his fertile mind were born institutions and out of his character standards and ideals were lifted by which youth might be inspired. He was a sign-post of nobility, with a decisive finger ever pointing toward the highway of righteousness.
> He was a man of piety, prayer, perseverance, personality and power. . . . His equal is found only here and there among the centuries." [13]

Nannie Helen Burroughs in writing about Brown said that no man could write his life.

> "He was unique in his distinction and distinct in his uniqueness. God used him to show us the power of native genius, the beauty of the rough-hewn rock, the challenging influence of a man who is not ashamed to be himself. He was one of those trail blazers who 'come out of Nazareth to teach the world something new.' He took his own ax, went through the woods, felled the trees and built a real highway . . . over which other men have delighted to travel. He had a genius for making churches big. He took the Great Commission seriously and counted in kingdom building. . . . He led Negro Baptist churches that had been giving mites to missions into giving thousands of dollars. He enjoyed his religion and went through the world laughing as he carried his heavy load." [14]

According to William P. Hayes, this man who graduated from "Swamp University," to use Brown's language, was a unique and colorful character. He left a prosperous church in Pittsburgh to take charge of a struggling congregation known as the "Subway Church." In a short time he infused new life into this congregation, and it grew into a large church. A preacher who possessed keen insight into the Scriptures and a great facility in the art of exposition, he contributed greatly to education and missions. He was a friend of humanity and possessed a heart which was both big and warm.[15] He was a colorful man. At the close of his sermon at the National Baptist Convention session in Chicago in 1905, a delegate reported that Brown, in order to create a deeper interest in foreign missions, took from his pocket a solid gold watch costing $110 and placed it on the table to be sold. The money to be used for missions was in addition to a cash contribution already made by Brown at the convention. L. K. Williams noted that in doctrine Brown was a rigid Baptist and a firm believer in all that Baptists stood for. He was interested in every movement for the welfare of his race. But he was this without being a bigot or ever intolerant in his dealings with others.

W. W. Brown to a great extent was typical of the kind of pastor which W. E. Du Bois called "a most unique personality, a leader, a political orator, boss, intriguer and idealist." This pattern or style of leadership has been the model of black Baptist pastors and has largely determined the modus operandi of Baptist associational and conventional groups as well as the Freedom Movement. Leaders of associations and groups or clusters of churches have assumed the role of "pastor" of these larger constituencies. In this sense King, as head of the Freedom Movement and subsequently the Southern Christian Leadership Conference, served as "pastor" with a board of directors consisting mainly of clergymen assuming the function comparable to that of deacons.

Ministers in roles of leadership structured the Movement by determining its priorities, direction, and organization according to their principles. At the same time the church, which historically had been the pivotal institution for the black community, was the direct and/or indirect training ground for these ministers. Through operative principles of reciprocity the ministers led their followers through various programs which motivated and empowered them to seek the elimination of discriminatory practices in the various institutions of society.

A third manifest function of the church was strategical and tactical. The church was the oldest and most prestigious influential institution in the community. Though the precise date of the organization of the first black Baptist church is uncertain, the best available record suggests that it took place between the years 1773–1775 at Silver Buff, South Carolina.

The second Baptist church to be founded by blacks was the First African Baptist Church of Savannah, Georgia. The first minister of this church was George Lisle. Lisle was born in Virginia about 1750 as a slave. During his youth, he moved with his master Henry Sharp, a white Baptist deacon, to Burke County, Georgia. Lisle accompanied Sharp regularly to the local congregation pastored by the Reverend Matthew Moore. Eventually Lisle was converted, baptized, and accepted into membership in the church. When Sharp and Moore recognized his unusual gifts and ministerial potential, they decided to ordain Lisle and allow him latitude to travel up and down the Savannah River to preach to a group of slaves on plantations. Subsequently, Sharp granted Lisle his freedom. However, when Sharp was killed during the Revolutionary War, his heirs attempted to reenslave Lisle. They had him seized and imprisoned in Savannah and would have succeeded in repossessing him had it not been for the intervention of Colonel Kirkland, a British officer in charge of the occupation forces in the city. Kirkland ruled against the heirs, released Lisle from jail, and employed him as his personal servant.

It was during this time that Lisle organized the First African Baptist Church of Savannah. He pastored this church for about four years. The congregation consisted of some fifty members.

In 1783 when the British left Savannah, Colonel Kirkland prepared to go to Jamaica. Because Lisle was still threatened by reenslavement, he offered himself as an indentured servant to Kirkland in exchange for passage to Jamaica for his family. Once in Kingston, Lisle organized the first Baptist church, white or black, in Jamaica.

It is interesting to note that Lisle's departure for foreign mission service predates that of William Carey to India, David Livingstone to Africa, and Adoniram Judson to Burma.[16]

In Jamaica, Lisle preached not only in the city but also far into the rural districts. Within a few years his congregation grew to about five hundred members. In 1790, the congregation in Kingston purchased three acres of land in the east end of town; they built a church in large measure through the labor and skills of the members.

While the work was thriving in Jamaica, the First African Baptist Church in Savannah was growing under the dynamic leadership of Lisle's successor, Andrew Bryan. By 1800, the church had seven hundred members. Within a few years the Second Baptist Church in Savannah was established to accommodate the rapidly growing Baptist population.

Black Baptist churches were established in other cities in the late eighteenth century. Before 1780, the First Baptist Church of Petersburg, Virginia, was founded. In Kentucky, the First Baptist Church of Lexington was founded in 1790. In Georgia, the Springfield Baptist Church of Augusta was founded in 1795.

The Baptist faith took strong roots among black persons in the North from 1800 to 1810. The Joy Street Baptist Church was founded in 1804 in Boston, the Abyssinian Baptist Church in New York City in 1808, and the African Baptist Church in 1809 in Philadelphia.

Two of these three churches were established largely by the efforts of the Reverend Thomas Paul. He was born in Exeter, New Hampshire. There is no record of his having been a slave. He was born on September 3, 1773, baptized in 1789, and ordained in 1804 in Boston. Subsequently, he organized the Joy Street Baptist Church and served as its pastor for twenty-five years.

When black members of the First Baptist Church in New York City wished to withdraw from that mixed congregation to establish an independent congregation, they called upon Rev. Thomas Paul to intercede on their behalf. He persuaded white members of the Gold Street church to grant letters of dismissal to their black brethren to enable them to form their own church; he also helped secure financial aid for the purchase of property for the new church.

On July 5, 1808, four men, twelve women, and three new converts met to begin the Abyssinian Baptist Church of New York City which, more than a century later under the pastorate of the late Adam Clayton Powell, became the largest Baptist congregation in the world.

Other churches were organized in other parts of the nation during the early decades of the nineteenth century. It was also a time of growing interest in foreign missions. Thomas Paul spent six months as a missionary in Haiti.[17] In 1815 the African Baptist Missionary Society was organized in Richmond, Virginia. It made contributions to overseas work through the American Baptist Union. On January 16, 1821, Lott Cary and Collin Teague, an assistant minister and worker of the First African Baptist Church in Richmond, Virginia, departed from Norfolk for Africa on the ship *Nautilus,* thereby becoming the first American missionaries to Africa. They were sent by the African Baptist Missionary Society, and they succeeded in establishing the Providence Baptist Church in Monrovia which was the first Baptist church in Liberia.

The growth of indigenous black Baptist groupings continued. Though from the beginning there were mixed Baptist congregations, both in the North and in the South, the movement toward independent churches steadily gathered momentum. The subtle forces of racism were prohibitive of heterogeneous integrity. Not only was it increasingly difficult for black clergy to function as leaders of black congregations in certain parts of the nations where slavery prevailed, but it also became almost impossible for black ministers to pastor mixed congregations anywhere. White Baptists in the nation were divided on the matter of slavery. In 1845 their division on whether to accept or reject slavery became institutionalized, resulting in the formation of the Southern Baptist Convention. The creation of this convention led to the establishment of many more black congregations.[18]

Associational and state convention life among black Baptists was mainly of post-Civil War origin. The first black Baptist state convention was organized in North Carolina in 1866; the second was organized in Alabama later that same year. The third convention was organized in Virginia in 1867, the fourth in Arkansas in 1868, the fifth in Kentucky in 1869, and the sixth in Georgia in 1870.

On a national scale, the American Baptist Missionary Convention, the first large organization of clusters of churches among blacks, was organized in the Abyssinian Baptist Church in New York City in 1840. The Western and Southern Missionary Baptist Convention was organized in 1864. These two conventions merged in 1866 at Richmond, Virginia, into what was called the American Baptist Missionary Convention. This convention organized direct subgroups called conventions which included, for example, the New England Convention, organized in 1875. Subsequently, these constituent conventions acting independently largely dissipated the strength of the parent body and caused in large measure its demise. In 1880 another missionary convention was organized by the name of the Baptist Foreign Mission Convention of America. This was the foundation group which was later to become the National Baptist Convention. In 1886 the American National Baptist Convention was established with representatives from seventeen states and a delegate constituency inclusive of black professionals, such as lawyers, medical doctors, university professors, and government officials. In 1893 the American National Educational Baptist Convention of the United States of America was organized for the purpose of directing educational policy for the black Baptist population.

The movement for consolidation continued. In 1894 the three national organizations were brought together in Montgomery, Alabama, and thus the National Baptist Convention of America was formed. The first annual session of this new umbrella convention was held on September 24, 1895, in the Friendship Baptist Church of Atlanta, Georgia.

The Lott Cary Foreign Mission Convention was organized at Shiloh Baptist Church of Washington, D.C., in 1897 as a separate missionary outgrowth of the National Baptist Convention of 1894.

In 1915 the National Baptist Convention of the U.S.A., Inc., was organized as the result of educational and legal concerns of certain leaders within the National Baptist Convention of America regarding a publishing house. Although smaller than the new group, the parent body retained the original title.

In 1961 a group of black Baptists founded a third national Baptist convention. The group was led by ministers who were concerned primarily with providing an alternative to the morphological fundamentalism found in the National Baptist Convention, U.S.A.,

Inc. Thus, the Progressive National Baptist Convention of America, Inc., was organized.

These three outgrowths from the National Baptist Convention, organized and consolidated in 1894, emphasized particular thrusts in missions, in education, and in administration. All four, however, though diverse, must be seen in the perspective of a larger unity. Though these four national Baptist bodies are separate and distinct in structure and functions, all possess constituencies who share much in common with one another. Their ethos and style are not as disparate as that between the Southern Baptist Convention and the American Baptist Churches in the U.S.A. These four black Baptist conventions, comprising a combined membership of 11 million in America, share a common tradition that transcends the structures of their existence. They share a common history, a common emphasis on biblical preaching, and a common religious fellowship, style, and language. They all share to some extent the goals of self-determination, of Christian education, foreign and home missions, and goals that seek the eradication of racial discrimination and social and economic injustices. They share a common loyalty to Jesus Christ and a strict adherence to his teachings. They also share a common history of subjection to discrimination and oppression.

III

Historically, the stable and continued existence of the black church in America was in itself a facilitator of the trust necessary to motivate and sustain the interest of blacks in their priorities and concerns for the community. The universe of the church was coterminous in its boundaries with the universe of the black population. The church fostered leaders for many generations, and this in itself was a creative encouragement to black persons who sought to become actors and participants in the liberation and empowerment of their communities. Not only were the presence and the prestige of the church important in determining its strategic role in new and significant movements by the community, but also, and of more importance, the historical agenda, which involved the survival and advancement of members as total persons, was a significant aspect of that role. For instance, during the time of the underground railroad it was the church that often served as the railroad station. During the time of the need for schools, it was the church that preached the gospel of the necessity for education and that shared significantly in directing the formation of black schools and colleges. During the times of the organization of voluntary associations for the social and civil advancement of the black population, it was the church that served as a meeting place and as a facilitator of communication for each substantive organization. During the time that blacks attempted to unite with or without supportive and concerned whites in the cause of human rights during the early development of the National Association for the Advancement of Colored People (NAACP), Sleeping Car Porters, and other such efforts, it was the church that legitimized the cause in the minds of the black population and that furthered that cause, whatever it was, through financial, human, and organizational resources. It was not unexpected then that black churches would have a large role through their freedom, history, prestige, and resources to determine their priorities of direction and action in the Freedom Movement. When the church became interested in suffrage as the major goal of the revolution, many church buildings served as centers for the voter registration drives. When there was a special effort planned for a certain place and time, for a certain cause with a goal in mind, the churches became information and communication stations. In fact, when black leaders in one Southern community were asked to list in the order of importance the main avenues of communication, the church was first, followed by all other agencies, including the NAACP and the Negro press.[19]

The church was the primary meeting place of the Freedom Movement. It has been aptly called its tactical headquarters. The bombings and burnings of black church buildings in the deep South were tacit signs of the recognition by reactionaries of the strategic and tactical role of organized religion in the whole movement. Whereas other organizations in the community meet monthly if not sporadically, the congregation of a church meets at least once a week. Thus a church and its pastor, if deeply committed, can easily stay with a cause in a way which is not possible otherwise. Indeed black churches which were of, by, and for the black population produced the natural strategies for the Freedom Movement.

In addition to valuational, structural, and strategic consequences which were intended and recognized by participants in organized religion, there were other corollaries which were neither intended nor organized but which nonetheless were positive. These were the latent functions of religion.

Organized religion is an important factor in the socialization of the individual. It is a molder of the conscience and compensator for deficiencies. It helps define personal life goals and instills the integrative forces of love, justice, courage, patience, and other moral values in its adherents. It creates a moral awareness by focusing attention on the evils of superimposed segregation and discrimination as well as injustices suffered by minorities.

The church helps individuals to find self-esteem in the midst of undesirable and unavoidable conditions of their environment. Individual deficiencies, failures, and feelings of inferiority are compensated for by a sense of fellowship with God, who is all-powerful and concerned about the oppressed. The church helps persons develop identification with the suffering and dispossessed people in the Bible, who were the chosen of God. The church creates a sympathetic fellowship with others who share the same faith, by providing opportunities in organized religion to give expression to one's inner feelings. Most importantly, the church provides opportunity for persons to participate in church programs on an equitable basis, thus contributing toward developing their stability, personality, and sense of potential worth.

The theocratic teaching of the church leads to the belief that undesirable social conditions can be corrected. It also produces a sense of security and serves to increase courage to take risks in moving toward these conditions.[20] Thus, we find in the words of the old church song, also a rephrased Freedom Song, "We shall overcome. . . . God is on our side."

Thus the black Baptist church has been an agent of socialization which gave identification and status to its constituency. It provided recognition of blacks as human beings of dignity, and more importantly it gave them an opportunity for expression and development of their abilities as they faced humiliating and hostile situations and structures outside their community. That was true especially for newly arrived migrants in urban areas.[21] This sense of identity and worth, along with a sense of what they could accomplish, was important to the willingness of black Baptists to participate in the Freedom Movement.

Another latent function of organized religion was that it was a symbol of solidarity. It was a fellowship for social cohesiveness. It was a major integrative force among a people shorn of their cultural heritage and separated from the larger society. It was the center for social activity, especially in the rural areas. In cities it had this special function for the newcomer to the urban milieu.[22]

Solidarity was promoted by the recreational function of organized religion in the form of spirited singing, colorful speaking, pageantry, and programs [23] involving nonempirical or emotive values which tend to fortify communal groupings.[24] To a certain extent, one might agree with David O. Moberg that "the spontaneity, expressiveness, excitement, rhythm, interest in the dramatic, and love of magic apparent in much Negro religion provide emotional release and escape, but they also mold the group together into an integral whole." [25]

The basis for the fellowship of black Baptists was its service not only as a means of escape and refuge from the hurt of discrimination but also as a springboard for action and wider leadership. The church served as a pivotal institution for "advancing the race." It has tended to promote black businesses and professional services which in turn were related to the church, thus enhancing solidarity. Conversely, ministers were sharply criticized when they did not give preferential support to black businessmen, professionals, and others who were helping the blacks or advancing the cause of desegregation or self-help. [26]

Also the church has served as a springboard for wider leadership. Marian Anderson, James Robinson, Adam Clayton Powell, and others, as well as Martin Luther King, Jr., have entered wider fields of service in the larger society after being nurtured, developed, and supported in the church. Black leaders, sensitive to the influence of the church, often tended to contribute in various ways to the Freedom Movement according to the direction of church opinion. Church functions were adaptive for the individual and for the group.

CONCLUSION

Whereas this approach has attempted to focus on black Baptists in their institutional life and to sketch their positive role in relation to the dynamics of the Freedom Movement, the accentuation of functions does not indicate the absence of dysfunctions. For the Baptist institution is a minority institution, with all the ramifications resulting from minority deprivation and status. From a broader perspective it is best seen as an institution in society. It is interpenetrated with other institutions. It is both a creator and a product of forces within the societal milieu.

There have been dysfunctions stemming from variant worship orientations, class structures, and institutional maintenance patterns obstructive to the cause of freedom. There have been suspicions and conflicts on issues of strategy and normative structures. On occasion there have been hints at heresy in theological stances and statements.

But the miracle is that a massive religious institution in America has emerged, born of mixed and often less than the highest motives and yet is strong in influence, heterogeneous in constituency, diverse in structure, united in objective, and rich in service. Its presence is felt among the significant institutions in every city, village, and hamlet; and wherever this presence is felt, there is a message for America. That message may take on the time and tone of the historical moment, but that message is misread if it is not understood to be prophetic.

It is prophetic like the message of Amos who said, "Let justice roll down like waters, and righteousness like an ever-flowing stream" (Amos 5:24). Like the message of Second Chronicles, "If my people who are called by my name humble themselves, and pray and seek my face, and turn from their wicked ways, then I will hear from heaven, and will forgive their sin and heal their land" (2 Chronicles 7:14). It is prophetic like the message of Micah when he said, "He hath shewed thee, O man, what is good; and what doth the Lord require of thee, but to do justly, and to love mercy, and to walk humbly with thy God?" (Micah 6:8, KJV).

NOTES

[1] Martin Luther King, Jr., *I Have a Dream.* Widely published, this historic address is also available on various commercial recordings.

[2] Gunnar Myrdal, *An American Dilemma: The Negro Problem and Modern Democracy* (New York: Harper & Row, Publishers, 1944), p. xliii.

[3] Martin Luther King, Jr., "A Challenge to the Churches and Synagogues," in *Race: Challenge to Religion,* ed. Mathew Ahmann (Chicago: Henry Regnery Company, 1963).

[4] Thomas F. Pettigrew, *A Profile of the Negro American* (Princeton, N.J.: D. Van Nostrand Company, Inc., 1964), p. 27.

[5] William Brink and Louis Harris, *The Negro Revolution in America* (New York: Simon & Schuster, Inc., 1969), p. 103.

[6] See J. H. Jackson, *Unholy Shadows and Freedom's Holy Light* (Nashville: Townsend Press, 1967), p. 214. See also the writings of Leon Sullivan.

[7] Wendell C. Sommerville, *Lott Cary Mission Annual Report, 1948–1949* (Washington, D.C., 1949).

[8] Joseph R. Washington, Jr., *Black Religion* (Boston: Beacon Press, 1964), pp. 1-30.

[9] Martin Luther King, Jr., *Why We Can't Wait* (New York: Harper & Row, Publishers, 1964).

[10] King, "A Challenge to the Churches and Synagogues," p. 164.

[11] Newsweek editors, "The Negro in America," *Newsweek*, July 29, 1963, p. 26.

[12] Emmanuel McCall, ed., *The Black Christian Experience* (Nashville: Broadman Press, 1972), p. 38. Used by permission.

[13] Porter Phillips, *W. W. Brown Hosts* (New York: Fleming H. Revell, 1941), p. 11.

[14] *Ibid.*, p. 13.

[15] *Ibid.*, pp. 16-17.

[16] See S. S. Hodges, *Black Baptists in America and the Origins of Their Conventions* (Washington, D. C.: Progressive National Baptist Convention, Inc., n.d.), p. 3.

[17] Owen D. Pelt and Ralph Smith, *The Story of the National Baptists* (New York: Vantage Press, 1960), p. 51.

[18] James Tyms, *The Rise of Religious Education Among Negro Baptists* (New York: Exposition Press, 1965), pp. 112-113.

[19] Elaine M. Burgess, *Negro Leadership in a Southern City* (New Haven: Yale University Press, 1953), p. 81.

[20] Martin Luther King, Jr., address delivered in the summer, 1965, in Washington, D.C. "I would have given up . . . the struggle . . . had it not been for prayer. . . ." See also Martin Luther King, Jr., *Stride Toward Freedom: The Montgomery Story* (New York: Harper & Row, Publishers, 1958), which is an account of King's release from jail.

[21] J. Milton Yinger and George Eaton Simpson, *Racial and Cultural Minorities*, 3rd. ed. (New York: Harper & Row, Publishers, 1965), pp. 388-389.

[22] Burgess, *Negro Leadership in a Southern City*, pp. 81f.; and Yinger and Simpson, *Racial and Cultural Minorities*, p. 388.

[23] See St. Clair Drake and Horace R. Cayton, *Black Metropolis: A Study of Negro Life in New York City*, reprint ed. (New York: Harper & Row, Publishers, 1962), p. 423.

[24] Joseph H. Fichter, *Social Relations in the Urban Parish* (Chicago: The University of Chicago Press, 1954), p. 187.

[25] David O. Moberg, *The Church as a Social Institution* (Englewood Cliffs, N.J.: Prentice-Hall Inc., 1962), p. 135.

[26] Drake and Cayton, *Black Metropolis*, pp. 428-429.

Other
Ethnic
Baptists

FRANK H. WOYKE

In the period before the American Revolution, the population of North America, apart from the native Indians and the imported African slaves, was predominantly English. By that time a major sea power, England laid claim to much of the New World. France was the leading power contesting this claim, but its efforts to claim New World territories were largely unsuccessful. The French and Indian Wars determined that Canada was to be a part of the British Empire, and the Louisiana Territory was purchased by the United States during the administration of Thomas Jefferson.

It would be a mistake, however, to conclude that colonial America was settled only by the English and French. German immigrants, for example, came to America almost from the beginning, first individually and later as groups. According to some estimates, about 250 thousand German immigrants had come to America by the time of the Revolutionary War.[1]

Conditions were not conducive to immigration in the years following the Revolutionary War. Europe was troubled by the Napoleonic Wars. The United States situation did not really stabilize until after the War of 1812. Then began a period of mass immigration that lasted, with minor interruptions, until well into the twentieth century. An era of great expansion had begun in America, and the lure of cheap land and unparalleled opportunities proved irresistible to many Europeans. Besides, the potato blight, beginning with the year 1845, caused famine and havoc in Europe, especially in Ireland and Germany. Finally, the abortive and unsuccessful Revolution of

323

1848 in Germany, which many had hoped would bring democracy and freedom, led thousands of intellectuals to come to seek those values in the New World.

The result of all these factors was that a steady stream of immigrants began arriving in the United States in the 1820s and 1830s, a stream that became a veritable flood in the following two decades.

Immigration came to a virtual halt during the Civil War. Within a few years, however, the flow resumed and continued into the twentieth century. Germans came throughout the period, but the peak was reached in the 1880s, when about 250,000 arrived each year.

Swedish immigrants began coming somewhat later than the Germans and also in smaller numbers. Perhaps a total of 100,000 had arrived by the time of the Civil War. The flow continued after the war, cresting in 1882, when 64,607 came.[2] Then a gradual decline set in and dwindled down to a mere trickle by the time of World War I. The great majority of the Swedes settled in the upper Midwest, in such states as Illinois, Minnesota, Iowa, Wisconsin, Nebraska, and Michigan; in the Northeastern states; and in the Pacific Northwest.

Meanwhile many other foreign language groups began arriving. The Germans in Russia had been living there under special privileges granted by Catherine the Great in 1763,[3] but these privileges were suddenly withdrawn in 1871. Soon tens of thousands of Russian-Germans began arriving in the United States, settling largely in such states as Kansas, Nebraska, the Dakotas, Illinois, and Pennsylvania. They continued to come until the First World War, and many of those who survived the war and banishment to Siberia came later. Joining them from Eastern Europe were large numbers of Poles, Russians, Hungarians, and others. Jewish immigrants had been coming from Germany for some time, but in the latter part of the nineteenth century they were joined by great numbers from Russia. The so-called "May Laws" of 1882 brought many restrictions in Russia, among them the exclusion from trade and severe curtailment in admission to the universities. As a result, about two million Jews, most of them virtually penniless, came to the United States during the years from 1881 to 1914.[4]

Italians began arriving in considerable numbers during the latter part of the nineteenth century and continued to come for many decades. Spanish-speaking Americans had been a part of the American scene from the beginning but did not appear in great numbers until after the Mexican War, for at that time many Mexicans remained in the territory taken over by the United States.

They have been joined by many countrymen through the years and are found in large numbers in the Southwest, California, and in the Midwest. Many Spanish-speaking immigrants have also come from Puerto Rico, the Caribbean area, and Central and South America.

Since mass immigration from European countries, with the exception of Italy, was largely finished by 1930, it may be of interest to list some statistics. For the period 1820 to 1930 the total number of immigrants was 37,762,012, with Europe alone contributing 32,276,346. Immigration from some representative countries was as follows:[5]

Germany	5,907,893
United Kingdom	4,990,722
Ireland	4,578,941
Austria-Hungary	4,138,351
Russia	3,338,106
Scandinavian Countries	2,346,069

It should be noted that the figures for Russia and Austria-Hungary undoubtedly include many German-speaking people. Although the Italians began arriving before the turn of the century, only 465,195 had come by the year 1930.

It will be seen that Baptist involvement with minority groups generally followed immigration trends.

INDIAN BAPTISTS

In considering the theme "Other Ethnic Baptists," it becomes obvious immediately that the American Indians occupy a unique place. They were not immigrants; rather, they were the native, original Americans. As such, they had long regarded themselves as owners of the entire continent, supporting themselves by raising small crops and by hunting and fishing.

With the coming of great numbers of immigrants, the Indians soon found themselves in the position of a minority. The white people moved ever westward, often pushing the Indians ahead of them or at least depriving them of their land. For over three centuries the Indian experience has been one of dislocation, injustice, broken treaties, and an overthrow of tribal laws. An example of this treatment is the so-called "Trail of Tears," the forced migration of a number of tribes from the East to the "Indian Territory" west of the Mississippi River in 1838–1839. As one writer has stated, "The story of the coming of the Cherokees, Creeks, Seminoles, Choctaws, and Chickasaws to the Indian Territory is one of the dark chapters of a nation dedicated to brotherhood."[6] The end result was that the Indians eventually found themselves on a series of reservations that were inadequate to provide the hunting and fishing required for their needs. They became wards of the United States government. Since 1955 an effort has been made to close the reservations and to relocate the Indians in towns and cities where they might find employment. Although some have responded by doing so, it has already become clear that this is not the answer for all of them.[7]

Under these circumstances, it is hardly surprising that the Indians have not responded to the appeal of the Christian gospel with great enthusiasm. Nevertheless, Baptists have made an effort to win them almost from the beginning. Early work was largely carried on individually and locally. It is well known that Roger Williams, who insisted on the Indians' right to the land and that it be acquired only by voluntary sale, was a great friend of the Indians. The oldest Indian Baptist Church, organized in 1694, is found at Gay Head on Martha's Vineyard, Massachusetts.[8] The Charleston (S.C.) Association began work among the Catawba Indians in 1802. By 1806 a licensed Indian Baptist preacher was reported living with the Catawbas. Isaac McCoy, who was appointed by the Triennial Convention, began work among the Indians in Indiana and Michigan in 1817. Later he also served in the Oklahoma area, with the result that the first Indian Baptist Church was formed there in 1832 in Muskogee. In 1842, McCoy founded the American Indian Association, which drew most of its support from the South. The work of the association was absorbed by the Southern Baptist Convention's Home Mission Board in 1855.

Most of the work of the Northern Baptists with Indians was under the supervision of the Baptist Missionary Union of Boston until 1865, when it was transferred to the American Baptist Home Mission Society.[9] Even though more than sixty missionaries labored among the Indians prior to the Civil War, the results were rather meager. One report indicates that in 1858 there were fifteen hundred members in Cherokee Baptist churches.[10] Mission work among the Indians was generally not without church-state collaboration.[11]

Following the interruption caused by the Civil War, the work more or less had to start all over again. The Northern Baptists were fortunate in enlisting the services of Almon C. Bacone, an Indian who had studied at Rochester University. He had gone to the Indian Territory as a teacher in 1878 and "two years later was appointed principal of the Indian Normal and Theological School at Tahlequah," the capital.[12] When the Creek Council later donated 160 acres to the Home Mission Society for a school near Muskogee, the school was moved there in 1885. This was the beginning of Bacone

Junior College, a coed institution serving both Indian and white students. It was also the start of an emphasis on Indian Baptist workers. A children's home was started by missionary J. S. Murrow at Unchuka. Named the Murrow Children's Home, it was moved in 1910 to a location near Bacone College. This institution, with several fine buildings and some cottages, still serves the Indian community.[13] American Baptists also support three Christian Centers located at Reno, Nevada; Clovis, California; and Anadarko, Oklahoma. American Baptist Churches sponsor work with Indians in the following states: Arizona, California, Montana, Nevada, New York, Oklahoma, and Wisconsin.

Meanwhile Southern Baptists also intensified their efforts following the Civil War. Henry F. Buckner was one of their most dedicated missionaries to the Indians. The early missionaries were usually employed by the Home Mission Board and carried on their ministry in a paternalistic spirit. In later years the emphasis has been on entrusting the work to Indian ministers, the missionaries serving primarily in supportive roles. This has been especially the case in the Cherokee, Chickasaw, Choctaw, Creek, and Seminole tribes. That this approach is much more effective is shown by the fact that of the estimated twenty thousand Indian Baptists that are members of Indian churches related to Southern Baptists, twelve thousand are to be found in these five tribes.[14] Today there is also more emphasis on missions and less on church buildings.

In spite of what is often considered slow progress in Indian Baptist work, the results are nevertheless promising. In addition to the institutional work, American Baptists report thirteen churches among eight tribes.[15] Related to the Southern Baptists there are 126 workers and 325 congregations with twenty thousand members.[16] What is most encouraging is that the work is at last becoming indigenous and that the "melting pot" pressure is fading. One writer has put it in these words: "Indian Americans bring a rich cultural heritage to American life and they have a right to interpret it and express themselves through it. Baptists must acknowledge these rights, even while they offer to many a new Way and continue to help with specific problems."[17]

GERMAN BAPTISTS

The Beginnings, 1839–1865

Konrad A. Fleischmann is generally regarded as having been the first German Baptist preacher in America.[18] Born in Nuremburg,

Germany, in 1812, he was confirmed in the Lutheran faith and remained there until he was eighteen. Then he went to Switzerland, where he committed his life to Christ and united with a Separatist church in Geneva. He was baptized by immersion in Basel at the age of twenty-three and soon afterwards went to Bern to study under Carl von Rodt, a Separatist leader. For three years he served as a pastor and an evangelist, at times having his clothes torn and being stoned by state church mobs. After returning to Nuremburg in 1838, he made his way to America a year later via England, arriving in New York in March, 1839.

His preaching that year, mostly in Newark, at first met with some success, but many people turned against him when he refused to practice infant baptism. Before he left Newark, he baptized three converts, a Mr. and Mrs. Albert and David Felsberg. These were the first German Baptists in America. On his advice, they united with an American Baptist church in Newark. On the invitation of American Baptists, he then moved to Reading, Pennsylvania, and reluctantly agreed to accept twenty dollars per month as a missionary among German immigrants in the state. In accordance with Swiss Separatist practice, he felt that ministers should depend on the Lord to provide, and thus he hesitated to accept a regular salary. For three years he served as a missionary, the best results coming in Lycoming County, where about two hundred were baptized after a series of revivals in 1840. In 1842 he moved to Philadelphia, and a year later the first German Baptist church was organized. This church, now called the Fleischmann Memorial Baptist Church, is still carrying on a productive ministry at its present location, Ninth and Luzerne Streets.

In succeeding years numerous other German churches began appearing in such places as New York City, Buffalo, Rochester, Williamsburg (now Brooklyn), and Albany, New York; Newark, New Jersey; St. Louis and Pin Oak Creek, Missouri; Chicago and Peoria, Illinois; Milwaukee, Watertown, Racine, and Manitowoc, Wisconsin; Pittsburgh and Lycoming County, Pennsylvania; and Dayton, Ohio.

The first German Baptist Conference was held at Fleischmann's church in Philadelphia in the fall of 1851, with five pastors and three co-workers as delegates. Though small in number, the delegates considered such weighty matters as a hymnal, a German confession of faith, a German periodical, and a ministerial training program. The first three matters were discussed with the leadership of the American Baptist Publication Society with a view to receiving financial aid. The Society was ready to help finance the printing of a statement of faith as well as a hymnal but felt that a periodical was not yet warranted. In January, 1853, a periodical named *Der Sendbote des Evangeliums* ("The Messenger of the Gospel") was launched and edited by Konrad A. Fleischmann. A fine hymnal, prepared primarily by August Rauschenbusch, appeared several years later. As far as ministerial training was concerned, German students began attending Rochester Seminary the following year, and in the fall of 1858 August Rauschenbusch began heading a German Department under appointment of the seminary.

The German work grew steadily during this period. Whereas there were eight churches and 405 members in 1851, the number had grown to about sixty churches and 3,300 members by 1865. Most of the new churches were formed in the West as the population expanded relentlessly in that direction.

What were some of the growing pains? One problem that arose almost immediately concerned the retention of the German language. Many of the German immigrants were free thinkers who opposed the Sunday blue laws and agitated for open beer halls. This was one of the factors that led to the formation of a strong nativist movement composed of people who were anti-immigrant. Feeling that such people were a threat to the American way of life, they condemned the use of the German language as well as the perpetuation of German culture. The German church leaders argued that use of the German language and expansion of the German work was absolutely essential, as this was the best possible way of Americanizing the immigrants. Another issue that caused some difficulty in the beginning was the matter of open communion. Fleischmann and several others believed in open communion, while the majority practiced closed communion for Baptist church members only, which was the position taken at that time by most American Baptists. The dissension that arose led to division in both Buffalo and Philadelphia. As more and more churches were organized in the West, there was increasing agitation for a division into two conferences. It was generally agreed that the distances were great and that many churches could not affort to send delegates to the annual conferences. The division actually took place in 1859, when the conference was held in Cincinnati, where Philip W. Bickel, an aggressive and talented young graduate of Rochester Seminary, was pastor. Most of the Eastern leaders, including Fleischmann, had opposed the division as being premature.

To make matters worse, young Bickel almost immediately, with the approval of the Western Conference, launched a second periodical, which he called *Die Biene Auf Dem Missionsfelde* ("The Bee on the Mission Field"). Fleischman was disturbed by this move, feeling that a second paper was unnecessary and would lead to disunity. Bickel countered that there was room for both and that besides, his paper would major on missionary news, an area that, Bickel maintained, Fleischmann was not covering adequately. Fleischmann resigned as editor several years later, and arrangements were made for the Eastern Conference to take over publication of *Der Sendbote*. Although the new editor, Andreas Henrich of Lycoming County, Pennsylvania, was conciliatory, the controversy continued. By 1864 both Conferences were agreed that a General Conference should be arranged in an effort to resolve the problem. Such a General Conference was held in Wilmot, Ontario, in the fall of 1865. It was there decided that sessions of the General Conference were to be held triennially in the future; that a publication society responsible to the General Conference be organized; that the two papers be combined into one, the name to be *Der Sendbote*; and that Philip W. Bickel would be the full-time editor and Konrad A. Fleischmann the part-time associate editor. This paper continued in its own right through the 1960s when it became an optional supplement of *The Baptist Herald,* the official English organ of the Conference.

Although generally an insignificant minority in the communities where they were located, these immigrant churches did take positions on moral and social issues. They opposed as being harmful to the cause of Christ such things as membership in secret societies, attendance at theater performances, and the excessive use of cosmetics. Coming from a country where drinking a glass of beer or wine, usually in connection with a meal, was almost universally approved, they could hardly be expected to espouse total abstinence; but they did resolutely champion the cause of temperance. They were almost unanimous in their opposition to slavery. The 1862 "Message to the Churches," written by Professor August Rauschenbusch with the approval of the Eastern Conference, consisted entirely of an impassioned denunciation of slavery as unscriptural and unchristian. This conviction naturally led also to the general support of the Union cause in the Civil War.

It should be noted that the group was generously assisted by English-speaking Baptists from the beginning. Local groups were aided by neighboring churches and state conventions as well as by the Home Mission Society. The Rochester Seminary defrayed the major part of the expenses of the German Department, including the entire salary of Professor Rauschenbusch, thus aiding ministerial training.

Sustained Growth and Institutional Development, 1865–1919

A long period of growth followed the Civil War. There was no dearth of prospects, for mass German immigration continued throughout the next fifty years, the crest coming in the 1880s. To meet the challenge, a cooperative effort with the American Baptist Home Mission Society was developed. Each German conference had a mission committee that made recommendations concerning new fields and workers to staff them. In response, the Home Mission Society agreed to assist the program by matching every dollar raised by the German churches with a dollar of its own. This spurred the growing German fellowship on to greater effort, with the result that the Home Mission Society soon felt it necessary to set a maximum, usually about seven thousand dollars per year.

By 1880 the Western Conference had grown to the point where it was felt wise to divide and form three conferences—the Central, Northwestern, and Southwestern. Three years later the General Missionary Society, with a General Committee and a General Secretary, was organized in order to coordinate the work. J. C. Grimmell, a popular preacher and pastor of the First German Church of Brooklyn, was elected General Secretary and served until he became editor of *Der Sendbote* in 1892. His successor was G. A. Schulte, able pastor of the First German Church of New York City, who served until his death in 1916. The General Missionary Society took over more and more responsibility, and by 1919 the German Conference had become self-supporting. How well the program succeeded is shown by the fact that in 1895 there were 224 churches with 20,772 members and in 1919 the report showed 292 churches with 32,103 members.

The use of the German language continued to be a problem. German leaders were adamant in keeping their churches entirely German, arguing that only in this way could the German immigrants be evangelized. The Home Mission Society was also interested in evangelizing the immigrants; but they were equally concerned about Americanizing them.[19] A crisis of considerable proportions developed when the United States entered the war against Germany in 1917. A wave of anti-German feeling swept the country, making German Baptist work very difficult. Fortunately the animosity disappeared soon after the war came to an end.

Meanwhile, the institutions of the Conference were also being strengthened. Mention has already been made of the formation of the

General Missionary Society. Under the aggressive leadership of Philip W. Bickel, the Publication Society was moved from Cincinnati to Cleveland in 1870. Eight years later a fine new building on Payne Avenue was dedicated, which provided the Society excellent facilities for many years. The seminary program was strengthened with the addition of a second professor, H. M. Schaeffer of New York, in 1872 and a third professor, J. S. Gubelmann, of Philadelphia, in 1883. The Tracy Institute building at Alexander and Tracy streets in Rochester was purchased in 1874. A new building was erected in 1890 at the same corner. When Professor August Rauschenbusch retired in 1889, two able young men, A. J. Ramaker and Lewis Kaiser, joined the faculty and were destined to serve with distinction for over forty years. A Children's Home, started in Louisville in 1871, was later moved to a more central location in St. Joseph, Michigan. Homes for the aged in Philadelphia and Chicago served their constituencies well—and still do.

It was during this period that the German group contributed its most famous son, Walter Rauschenbusch, to the American scene. He developed his social gospel views while he was pastor of the Second German Baptist Church of New York. The fellowship held him in high esteem, asking him to succeed his father at the seminary in 1889 and offering him the position of editor of the denominational periodical in 1892. Although he declined both offers, he did succeed Professor H. M. Schaeffer at the seminary a few years later. He became known nationally and internationally as the founder and prophet of the social gospel movement after he transferred to the English Department of the seminary. His writings remain a major legacy to American Christianity.

Language Transition and Further Growth, 1920–1946

Until this time leaders of the German Conference had always assumed, with the concurrence of the Home Mission Society, that their fellowship had only one mission: to preach the gospel to German-Americans. Those individuals and churches that preferred the English language were simply advised to leave, which many of them did.

Now that German immigrants were no longer coming in large numbers, a decision had to be made. The older generation was inclined toward maintaining the German language, whereas the young people were all for changing to English. Although the Conference made no decision in the matter, the younger generation gradually carried the day. The English language youth paper, *The*

Baptist Herald, began appearing in 1923 and eventually became the official organ of the denomination. In 1940 the General Conference overwhelmingly voted not to become an "associated organization" of the Northern Baptist Convention. William Kuhn served as General Missionary Secretary during this entire period.

Developing a Denominational Program, 1947–1975

The Conference now proceeded to develop a complete denominational organization. The General Council was made more representative. A revolving loan fund to assist churches with building programs was created. The seminary was moved from Rochester, New York, to Sioux Falls, South Dakota, in the fall of 1949, where it has since become a fully accredited graduate theological school. In 1954 a highly successful church extension program was launched. Among other projects were the publication of an English hymnal, strengthening the Ministers' Pension Fund, and the development of a college and theological school in Edmonton, Alberta.

Since 1944 known as the North American Baptist General Conference, the membership of the fellowship now stands at about fifty-five thousand. The Conference participates in the work of the Baptist World Alliance, the Baptist Joint Committee on Public Affairs, and the American Bible Society. Among its members in recent years who have gone on to serve a larger fellowship, the following should be mentioned: Conrad H. Moehlmann, William B. Lipphard, Fred Meyer, Althea Kose, Harold E. Stassen, Reuben P. Jeschke, William A. Mueller, and Ralph Rott.

The Conference has also been active in foreign missions. Prior to World War I, the missionaries served under the American Baptist Foreign Missionary Society, and gifts were channeled through that organization. Among the missionaries who served during this period were Miss Emma Rauschenbusch (later Mrs. John E. Clough), Jacob Heinrichs, Jacob Speicher, Samuel Hamel, Bruno Luebeck, and many others. Between the two World Wars the General Missionary Society supported and supervised missions in a number of East European countries. Since 1944 successful work has been developed in the Cameroon Republic, West Africa, Japan, and Brazil.

SWEDISH BAPTISTS

The Pioneer Period, 1852–1871

In the early period, Swedish Baptists in America were closely related to the Baptists in Sweden.[20] This is clearly evident when one considers the early Swedish preachers. A Swedish sea captain, G. W. Schroeder, was converted in America and baptized by Ira K. Steward, pastor of the Mariners' Baptist Church in New York on November 3, 1844. He returned to Sweden the following year and met F. O. Nilsson, also a former sailor, who had been converted in New York in 1834 and was at the time a missionary of the American Seaman's Friends Society. Nilsson became convinced of believer's baptism and later went to Hamburg, Germany, where he was baptized by J. G. Oncken, the German Baptist leader on August 1, 1847. Returning to Sweden, he became the first Baptist pastor there. He baptized the first five converts, four men and a woman, in the Vallersvik, a bay of the Kattegatt, and together with them formed the first Baptist church in Sweden. Persecution by pastors of the state church soon followed, with the result that he was summoned to the Supreme Court and banished in February, 1850. First fleeing to Denmark, he accompanied a group of followers to America in the spring of 1853. The group first went to Rock Island, Illinois, though some members moved to Houston, Minnesota, and organized a Baptist church there in August of that year. Nilsson preached to Swedish immigrants in Illinois and Iowa until 1860, when he returned to Sweden, where he had meanwhile received a pardon from the king. He served as pastor of the Gothenburg Baptist Church for eight years, after which he moved to Houston, Minnesota. He made his home there until his death in 1881. During these years his ministry was rendered ineffective among many Baptists because of his leanings toward Unitarianism.

Anders Wiberg, a state church minister in Sweden, left his church in 1850 because of doubts about giving communion to unbelievers. On his way to the United States, he stopped off at Copenhagen and was baptized there in the Baltic Sea at midnight on July 23, 1852, by F. O. Nilsson. He worked among Swedish immigrants for a number of years, preaching and writing. In September, 1855, he returned to Sweden and became a beloved Baptist leader there. His book *Who Should Be Baptized? And What Is Baptism?* greatly influenced Swedish Baptist work, both in Sweden and the United States.

Another Swedish Baptist pioneer, Gustav Palmquist, came from the Laesare Movement, a group within the state church of Sweden that emphasized spiritual commitment and service. After years of service as a teacher at the Normal School in Stockholm he came to Rock Island, Illinois, in the summer of 1851. Hearing of a revival at the American Baptist Church of Galesburg, Illinois, he went there in the spring of 1852 and was baptized there on June 27. Ordained by the

Galesburg church a month later, he returned to Rock Island where, forty-seven days after his baptism, he organized the first Swedish Baptist Church in America on August 13, 1852. Employed by the Home Mission Society, he first served as a traveling missionary and from 1855 to 1857 divided his time between Rock Island and Chicago. He then returned to Sweden to spend the rest of his life there.

The Swedish Baptist movement grew slowly during the first twenty years. The most capable leaders came from Sweden and had a tendency to return there. Lutheran pastors offered strong opposition wherever Swedish Baptist churches were launched. Immigration from Sweden was also slow during these years. In spite of these obstacles, the work did not stand still. Although most of the new churches were to be found in Illinois, Minnesota, and Iowa, missions were also started in South Dakota, Nebraska, Kansas, Wisconsin, and New York City. By the year 1871 there were twenty-three Swedish churches with fifteen hundred members in our country.

Era of Expansion, 1871–1902

The next thirty years witnessed an era of rapid growth. There were at least three factors involved in this development. First of all, Swedish immigration reached its climax during these years. A second factor was the beginning of a ministerial training program, thanks to John Alexis Edgren. Here was another Swedish sea captain who found faith in Christ in New York and was baptized by Ira K. Steward of the Mariners' Baptist Church on April 29, 1858. In a storm at sea he later promised God to serve only the gospel if his life would be saved. After studying at Princeton and the Hamilton Theological Seminary, he was ordained in 1867 by the Mariners' Baptist Church. He returned to Sweden and helped found Bethel Baptist Seminary in Stockholm but in 1871 responded favorably to a call from the First Swedish Baptist Church in Chicago. Soon after arriving he began plans to start a school in the basement of his church. Hearing of his plan, the Baptist Union Theological Seminary invited him to organize a Swedish Department. In 1877 the Department was moved to Morgan Park, twelve miles farther south. By 1884 Edgren, as well as others, felt a desire for an independent seminary. During the next four years the school moved three times, first to St. Paul, Minnesota, then to Stromburg, Nebraska, and finally back to Morgan Park. Edgren himself, in poor health, moved to California. The important thing was, however, that the churches were now being supplied with trained ministers. The third factor that helped to build the fellowship during these years was the publication of a paper, also begun by Edgren. The first attempt was *Zions Woektare* ("The Watchman of Zion"). After several changes in name, Eric Wingren came from Sweden as an assistant in editing the *Evangelisk Tidskrift* ("Evangelical Journal"). By 1885 the monthly had become a weekly. The name later changed to *Nya Wecko-Posten.* This independent periodical served the churches well until 1918 when it was taken over by the denomination.

With a challenging field, a seminary, and a periodical assured, the Swedish churches began spreading out beyond the upper Middle West to the East and to the far West. In 1879 there were 65 churches and 3,000 members; by 1894 this had grown to 238 churches and 17,223 members. When the Fifty Year Jubilee was celebrated in 1902, the Conference had 324 churches with 21,769 members.

Institutional Development, 1902–1927

Important changes took place during this period in the area of institutional development. Although the General Conference had been organized in 1880, the program had thus far not been much of a challenge. Home mission efforts had been almost entirely the responsibility of the local conferences. All foreign missionaries were serving under appointment of the American Baptist Foreign Mission Society. The Seminary had been operating comfortably as a department of the Divinity School of the University of Chicago ever since 1888, with the Conference being responsible only for the salary of one of the three professors there. The denominational paper, *Nya Wecko-Posten,* was a private undertaking serving the churches, but it was not an official organ of the Conference.

Many projects were now to be developed. In 1902 the Fridhem Home for the Aged was founded in Morgan Park. The Klingberg Home for Children was started in New Britain, Connecticut, a year later. Bethel Academy began its program at Elim Church in Minneapolis. The Conference chose its first Mission Secretary in 1906 in the person of G. Arvid Hagstrom. While this position was not filled continuously, a precedent had been set. The American Baptist Publication Society had provided literature with a "Swedish Department." This arrangement was terminated in 1909 when the Conference started its own publishing house. In January, 1911, the first issue of the *Svenska Standaret* ("Swedish Standard") appeared, and in 1918 the *Nya Wecko-Posten* was absorbed. A tremendous challenge confronted the Conference in 1910 when the University of Chicago gave notice that the Swedish Department of the Divinity

School would no longer be maintained. The Conference in Chicago in 1912 was unable to reach agreement with regard to a seminary of its own. In 1913 the annual meeting, termed "The Peace Conference," voted to locate the Conference seminary in St. Paul, Minnesota, and to merge it with Bethel Academy, effective in 1914.

When the Seventy-fifth Jubilee Conference was held at the Moody Memorial Church in 1927, with 2,225 delegates registered, the statistics showed 333 churches with a membership of 33,830.

Language Transition and Further Growth, 1928–1975

Beginning with 1900 some of the churches had become bilingual. The complete transition from the Swedish language took about forty years. By the time the Conference adopted the new name "Baptist General Conference of America," the Swedish language had all but disappeared.

The Conference reached a momentous decision in 1944 when it voted to terminate its cooperation with the American Baptist Foreign Mission Society. The immediate cause of this action was a lack of enthusiasm for the "inclusive policy" of the Society, although there had long been a general feeling that much more would be accomplished if the Conference had a program of its own. The cooperative program had worked well prior to 1930, with scores of Conference missionaries serving under the Society, but after that an increasing number of young people began enlisting under so-called "Faith Missions." The Conference foreign missionary program has been greatly expanded since 1944.

The educational program of Bethel College and Bethel Seminary has also been tremendously strengthened. The Academy was gradually phased out, and the Junior College was created. This led to a four-year college in 1949. Today both Bethel College and Bethel Seminary are fully accredited institutions. Carl H. Lundquist serves as president of Bethel.

Meanwhile the membership of the Conference has also grown rapidly. In 1952 the membership had grown to fifty thousand, and today it stands at well over one hundred thousand.

The Baptist General Conference of America is today making a major contribution to the life of the nation. Among its sons and daughters who have gone on to render outstanding service in the larger Baptist fellowship we mention two, although many more could be named: Reuben Nelson, the late General Secretary of the American Baptist Convention, and C. Emanuel Carlson, former Executive Director of the Baptist Joint Committee on Public Affairs.

ITALIAN BAPTISTS

A number of factors have strongly affected Baptist involvement with Italian immigrants. First, they did not begin coming in large numbers until the latter part of the nineteenth century. By 1930 only 465,195 had arrived, whereas German and Scandinavian immigration was virtually finished. Second, almost all of them were at least nominally Roman Catholic. This would not have made much difference if they had come a hundred years earlier, for through most of the nineteenth century Baptists considered Catholics an object of intensive missionary activity. Their actual coming, however, coincided with the development of a strong ecumenical movement in America, with the result that the effort to win them for the Baptist cause was much less aggressive than it would have been earlier.

Nevertheless, the American Baptist Home Mission Society did launch a missionary effort in 1894. At that time a mission was started in Buffalo, New York, with Ariel B. Bellondi as the missionary. During the next few years missions were started in various cities of Connecticut, where many Italians settled, as well as in New York City, New Jersey, Massachusetts, and Vermont.[21] For fellowship purposes, the group of small churches organized the Italian Baptist Association in 1898. The Italian Baptist Convention was organized the following year. The organization apparently reached its high point in 1920 with 3,265 members.

Antonio Mangano, a graduate of Union Theological Seminary, was an outstanding leader during this period. First appointed a general evangelist in 1903, he later headed the Italian Department of Colgate Seminary, located in Brooklyn. In 1911 a chapel and church house were opened in Brooklyn.[22]

The Italian churches in the North gradually went through a language transition and remained essentially a part of the Northern Baptist Convention. An example of this process is seen in Meriden, Connecticut, where the Liberty Street Baptist Church, formerly German, merged with the Italian Baptist Church to form Grace Baptist, a church affiliated with the American Baptist Churches.

The Southern Baptist Home Mission Board began work with Italians in Tampa, Florida, in 1908. Today two Baptist churches minister principally to Italians. Work among Italians was begun in Birmingham, Alabama, in 1922 and continued through the Immanuel Baptist Church there and the Good Will Center. Self-sustaining Italian Baptist churches resulted from the Board's efforts in Illinois. The Board in recent years has supported missions in California, Florida, the Great Lakes area, and the Northeast.

SPANISH-AMERICAN CHURCHES

The Spanish-Americans in the United States are a varied group. Mexicans and those of Mexican ancestry have resided in this country in large numbers ever since territory was lost by Mexico to the United States. In recent decades increasing numbers of Mexicans have been entering the country, both legally and illegally. These have been joined by immigrants from Central and South America. Puerto Ricans, who are of course United States citizens, have been coming to the mainland in increasingly large numbers, especially since 1940. Many thousands of Cubans have found homes in the United States since Fidel Castro came to power. It is estimated that there are more than five million people in this country with at least one parent born in Latin America. Of these, about one million are found in Texas, another million in Arizona and California, and still another million, mostly Puerto Ricans, in metropolitan New York.[23]

Although Baptists worked among Spanish-speaking people, especially in Texas and New Mexico, prior to the Civil War, the work was then interrupted and not seriously resumed until 1880. There was slow progress until after 1910.

With the appointment of the Reverend and Mrs. Troyer in 1911 to serve in Southern California, the work took on new life. The Troyers, who had previously ministered in Puerto Rico, were accepted by the Spanish-Americans and within three years had seven missions and an evening school with industrial classes in operation. In 1921 the Spanish-American Seminary was opened in Los Angeles as a branch of the International Seminary in New Jersey.[24] With new buildings dedicated in 1930, this institution was training fifty resident students by 1931. The school has continued its ministry, becoming independent after the International Seminary was closed. Among its outstanding graduates are Benjamin R. Morales and Robert Porras Meynes.

In later years Spanish-American churches arose in the Middle West as well as in the East. By 1962 there were over one hundred Spanish-American churches related to the American Baptist Convention, although there were many others also that were not so related. A number of Spanish-American conventions have been organized. Since Spanish-speaking people are continuing to come to this country, use of the Spanish language will no doubt continue for years to come. In recent years there has also been a widespread interest in welcoming Spanish departments or congregations in established Baptist churches. An example of this is found in the First Baptist Church in Bridgeport, Connecticut, where the services of the

Spanish Department are as well attended as those of the English-speaking group, and where leadership for the church is drawn from both groups.

There have been Spanish-speaking churches related to the Southern Baptist Convention in Texas and Florida for many years, but the outreach to other areas did not come until the 1940s. Since the 1940s missions have been developed in Colorado, California, the Great Lakes area, and New England.[25] In 1947 the Valley Baptist Academy in Harlingen, Texas, was opened as a training institution for Spanish-speaking people. The Mexican Baptist Bible Institute was established the same year in San Antonio. Literature for Spanish-Americans is supplied by the Spanish Baptist Publishing House in El Paso, a large and modern facility operated by the Southern Baptist Foreign Mission Board. During the 1960s the Mexican Baptist Convention of Texas merged with the Texas Baptist General Convention.

Baptist work among Latin or Spanish Americans has grown rapidly. By 1967 there were 695 missionaries serving among Spanish-Americans under support of the Southern Baptist Home Mission Board. That the progress has been substantial is evident from the fact that more than five hundred predominantly Spanish-speaking churches are today affiliated with the Southern Baptist Convention. In addition, there are many other Spanish-American Baptist churches not so related, as well as Spanish departments and Spanish-speaking congregations in English-speaking Baptist churches throughout the nation.

It should be noted that the North American Baptist General Conference also sponsors a number of Spanish-language churches in the San Luis Valley of Colorado and the Rio Grande Valley of Texas, as do other national Baptist bodies in other parts of the country.

OTHER ETHNIC GROUPS

What shall one say about the many smaller ethnic groups? Space will unfortunately permit only a brief mention.

Oriental Baptists

The ministry among Oriental-Americans has been hampered in a number of ways. For many years such people were considered unassimilable, an attitude that contributed to the rise of various "Chinatowns" and to the evacuation of 112,000 Japanese during World War II, of whom 71,000 were native-born Americans.[26] To say that such an attitude has not been conducive to the spread of the

Christian gospel among them would be an understatement.

In spite of the handicaps, some work has been developed in such areas as California and New York. The Chung Mei Home for Chinese Boys, in San Francisco, sponsored by the American Baptist Home Mission Society, served the community well from 1923 to 1954. The Southern Baptist ministry among Orientals, which began in California in 1854, has also brought good results, a late report showing 32 Chinese-American churches and 13 Japanese-American churches.[27] In recent years, Korean Baptist congregations have also begun to appear. Jitsuo Morikawa, a prominent American Baptist leader of Japanese descent, has risen to give outstanding service not only within the Baptist communion but also in the entire Christian community of this country.

French Baptists

During the Civil War period, many French Canadians came to New England and other parts of our country. French Baptist groups were formed, especially in New England, and a French Department was established at the Newton Theological Seminary.[28] The churches never became firmly rooted, as services were held either in homes or in English-speaking churches. By 1931 only seven groups with 380 members were reported and these have largely disappeared into American Baptist churches. The mission among French-Americans in the South has had its center in Louisiana.[29] There are about 150 French-language Baptist churches related to the Southern Baptist Convention.[30]

Norwegian and Danish Baptists

The first Norwegian Baptist church in the United States was formed at Indian Creek, Illinois, in 1848. As immigration continued, additional Norwegian and Danish churches were organized. Each group formed a conference of its own in 1910. The maximum strength was apparently reached in 1920 when the Danish Baptist Conference numbered 46 churches and missions with 4,038 members and the Norwegian Baptist Conference 43 churches and missions with 1,849 members. Dr. P. Stiansen was an important leader, serving as Dean of the Norwegian Seminary, in Chicago, for many years.[31] Both groups have since been absorbed by the American Baptist Convention.

East European Baptists

Since the turn of the century, immigrants from many East European countries, among them Russians, Ukrainians, Poles,

Hungarians, Czechoslavakians, and Rumanians, also formed Baptist churches in various parts of the country.[32] Although they remained modest in size, a number of the groups organized conferences in the second decade of this century. Their number has declined somewhat with waning immigration. Following World War II some of these groups looked to the Southern Baptist Home Mission Board for guidance. Related to the Board are two Ukrainian, one Hungarian, and thirteen Polish congregations.[33] Elias Golonka has been a prominent leader as director of the Polish work on behalf of the Board. The Russian-Ukrainian Union still operates a Conference Center and a Home for the Aged, north of Hartford, Connecticut.

SOME GENERAL OBSERVATIONS

How have the ethnic groups participated in the American experience of the past two hundred years? We venture to make only a few general observations.

1. All of the groups have encountered serious problems in adjusting to the American scene as it has developed. The American Indians as the native and original Americans occupy a unique place in this respect. Gradually deprived of the hunting and fishing grounds they had long owned, and possessing an ancient culture that clashed sharply with the emerging American way of life, they are still struggling to maintain their identity while trying to find their proper place in our country. Though the difficulties of the other minorities have been less severe, they also have found it necessary to give up their native language and to sacrifice much of their cultural heritage. Only those who have experienced it really know how traumatic such a process can be.

2. In spite of problems of cultural accommodation, virtually all of the groups have made many adjustments and have become loyal Americans. They have become practically indistinguishable, except perhaps for the sound of their names, from the average Anglo-Saxon American. The fears of the nativists of a hundred years ago have thus proved largely without foundation.

3. As they were being gradually assimilated, the minority groups have contributed greatly to changes in the American experience itself. It is not possible here to enumerate the contributions each group has made. Apart from this, however, the very attitude of Americans toward ethnic variety has undergone a marked change. The old "melting pot" idea is giving way to a new appreciation of the

contribution that each minority group can make. One writer is at least partly right when he states:

There is no melting pot. Never has been. The whole thing was a schoolboy myth. Oh, it sounded good in the textbooks—a nice Madison Avenue slogan that no one ever took time to question until a few years ago. Then people began to realize that the concept had never become concrete—the United States was not a "melting pot." . . . The concept that's emerging is based on the idea that different isn't bad; it recognizes strength in diversity, beauty in dissimilarity.[34]

Today we recognize that there has been both good and bad in the American experience of the past two centuries, and that many of our noble goals as a nation have not been achieved. This has also been true of Baptist churches. Yet we should not dissipate our energies in lamenting past failures, but rather we must look to new opportunities and resolve to build a better tomorrow for the churches and the nation as a whole.

NOTES

[1] Richard O'Connor, *The German-Americans* (Boston: Little, Brown and Company, 1968), pp. 35, 67.

[2] Adolf Olson, *A Centenary History* (Chicago: Baptist Conference Press, 1952), p. 18.

[3] Reinhold J. Kerstan, "Historical Factors in the Formation of Ethnically Oriented North American Baptist General Conference" (Ph. D. diss., Northwestern University, 1971), pp. 15-43.

[4] O'Connor, *The German-Americans,* pp. 258-259.

[5] Charles L. White, *A Century of Faith, Centenary Volume* (Valley Forge: Judson Press, 1932), pp. 127-128.

[6] Dorothy O. Bucklin, *Strong Hearts for God* (Valley Forge: Judson Press, 1955), p. 16.

[7] *Ibid.,* p. 110.

[8] *Ibid.,* p. 7.

[9] Louise A. Cattan and Helen C. Schmitz, *One Mark of Greatness* (Valley Forge: Judson Press, 1961), p. 114.

[10] White, *A Century of Faith,* p. 83.

[11] An intimate partnership existed between church and state in America in the work of Christian missions among the Indians. Federal funds were accepted for Indian mission

work by virtually all the denominations, including Baptists. See R. Pierce Beaver, *Church, State, and the American Indians: Two and a Half Centuries of Partnership Between Protestant Churches and Government* (St. Louis: Concordia Publishing House, 1966). Based upon the Joseph M. Dawson Lectures on Church and State delivered at Baylor University, the author provides a detailed, factual account of the U.S. government and the churches' making "common cause in civilizing and Christianizing of the Indians for two and a half centuries."

[12] White, *A Century of Faith*, p. 84.

[13] *Ibid.*, pp. 85-86.

[14] Wendell H. Belew, *Missions in the Mosaic* (Atlanta: Home Mission Board, n. d.), p. 24. See also "Home Missions to Indians," *Encyclopedia of Southern Baptists* (Nashville: Broadman Press, 1959), vol. 1, pp. 682-684.

[15] Bucklin, *Strong Hearts for God*, p. 19.

[16] *Ministering to Language Friends* (Atlanta: Southern Baptist Home Mission Board, n.d.).

[17] Cattan and Schmitz, *One Mark of Greatness*, p. 118.

[18] Unless otherwise noted, the material in this section is based on the Annual Conference Minutes and *Der Sendbote*, the Conference periodical.

[19] Eric Henry Ohlmann, "The American Baptist Mission to German-Americans" (Th.D. diss., Faculty of the Graduate Theological Union, Berkeley, California, 1975), pp. 49 ff.

[20] Adolf Olson, *A Centenary History* (Chicago: Baptist Conference Press, 1952), p. 5. Unless otherwise noted, this section is based largely on this exhaustive study.

[21] White, *A Century of Faith*, pp. 141-145.

[22] *Ibid.*, p. 142.

[23] Adam Morales, *American Baptists with a Spanish Accent* (Valley Forge: Judson Press, 1964), p. 16.

[24] White, *A Century of Faith*, pp. 147-148.

[25] Arthur B. Rutledge, *Mission to America: A Century and a Quarter of Southern Baptist Home Missions* (Nashville: Broadman Press, 1969), p. 156.

[26] G. Pitt Beers, *Ministering to Turbulent America* (Valley Forge: Judson Press, 1957), pp. 70-73.

[27] See *Ministering to Language Friends*.

[28] White, *A Century of Faith*, pp. 140-141.

[29] Rutledge, *Mission to America*, p. 150.

[30] See *Ministering to Language Friends*.

31 White, *A Century of Faith,* pp. 138-139.

32 *Ibid.,* pp. 151-156.

33 *Ministering to Language Friends.* For a perceptive study of ethnicity in America, see Nathan Glazer and Daniel Patrick Moynihan, *Beyond the Melting Pot: The Negroes, Puerto Ricans, Jews, Italians and Irish of New York City* (Cambridge: Massachusetts Institute of Technology, 1963).

34 "From Melting Pot to Mosaic . . .," *Home Missions,* vol. 48 (January, 1975), p. 3.

Baptist
Pluralism
and
Unity

PENROSE ST. AMANT

The motto on the obverse side of the Great Seal of the United States—*E Pluribus Unum* (out of many, one)—sets forth an important element in our heritage as Americans and Baptists. It testifies to the belief that diversity and unity are compatible. Indeed, one could argue that diversity and unity are not merely compatible but can be mutually supportive and even mutually enriching.

UNITY AND DIVERSITY

There is, of course, a unity, coerced and monolithic, which crushes diversity, and a diversity, diffusive and without direction, which shatters unity. There is a unity forged from the top down that provides great rewards for conformity and severe punishment for independence. The heavy hand at the top may be military might or police power or ideology, political or religious. There is a diversity that recognizes no loyalties beyond the passing whims of individuals who make an idol of nonconformity as if freedom were an absolute value.

Unity without diversity means tyranny, the tyranny of an elite by whom the political, social, or theological rules are made and enforced. Diversity without unity means anarchy, the anarchy of an individualism that rejects political or theological guidelines. Tyranny places an absolute value upon conformity, and anarchy makes a god of dissent. The unity forged by autocratic leadership in church or state levels life in the interest of keeping things under control. Such leadership is (or pretends to be) so sure of itself that it can provide prescriptions for the regulation of those who dissent from the required consensus. The tyrant, whether on a throne bedecked in the finery of a king, promulgating decrees in stentorian tones, or behind a desk dressed in a business suit, issuing orders in a quiet voice, is (or pretends to be) utterly certain as to what is best for everybody. The anarchist, whether an iconoclast in the streets who spends his time on a soapbox denouncing all forms of authority or an intellectual who believes in nothing because he believes everything is relative, is (or pretends to be) skeptical about the political and religious loyalties which unify life. The tyrant is corrupted by power and the anarchist by certainty, the certainty that there is no certainty. Thus, there is danger in unity or diversity carried to the extreme.

History is replete with examples of enforced conformity and the high price exacted by authoritarian regimes. Nero, Louis XIV, Hitler, Stalin, and Franco are well known. Others not as well known in church and state have made repression of dissent a policy relentlessly pursued, sometimes without pity, because of absolute devotion to limited and self-serving ends. No less frequent are examples of anarchy and the consequences that followed in societies which lacked a common core of loyalty. A drift of this sort is evident in the contemporary world. Within a period of three days in mid-October, 1975, three comments in the *International Herald Tribune* pinpointed this phenomenon. "The only clarity in Portugal now," wrote Flora Lewis, "is that things remain uncertain, that stability is elusive because people are being polarized and no group is about to give up. The majority is in-between but . . . the extremists set the tone."[1] Dr. Donald Coggan, the Archbishop of Canterbury, launched "a major spiritual initiative" at a press conference, in which he condemned "greed and materialism in British society" and called for a new national commitment to discipline and responsibility to stop the country's "drift toward chaos."[2] Daniel Bell, lamenting the absence of "common purpose or common faith" in America and sensing "only bewilderment," declared: "There is no longer a manifest destiny or mission. We have not been immune to the corruption of power. We have not been the exception. Our mortality now lies before us."[3]

A tendency of this sort is not surprising in times of historical transition, when the old is dying and the new is striving to be born. We are now living in such a time when this tendency is especially evident in the lives of people like Abbie Hoffman, who wrote *Revolution for the Hell of It,* and Janis Joplin, "the White Queen of the Blues," who, a few months before her untimely death in a pathetic quest for freedom, told a friend that she was working on a new tune.

"I'm gonna call it," she confided, "I Just Made Love to 25,000 People But I'm Goin' Home Alone."[4]

Thus far, three possible relationships between unity and diversity have been noted. The first is a mutually supportive relationship. The second is a coerced unity that crushes diversity. The third is a diversity that shatters unity. Of course, to speak of three disparate relationships between unity and diversity is an oversimplification, but I am trying to describe a dynamic process that can seldom be clearly delineated. A monolithic church or state may tolerate a limited diversity as a matter of practical policy to create an impression of flexibility and not because of a belief in the dignity of the individual or the right of dissent. An institution committed to a pluralistic philosophy may exhibit a rhetorical unity to placate those who equate dissent with heresy or disloyalty. As for the idea that unity and diversity are compatible, what is envisaged involves shifting degrees of emphasis, now upon unity, now upon diversity, now both simultaneously. Decisions are required repeatedly as to what continuities need to be sustained in the midst of the discontinuities that flow out of diversity. Nevertheless, for the purpose of analysis at least, three historical processes may be cited: unity that is imposed arbitrarily; diversity in which objective norms are rejected; and unity and diversity that are mutually supportive.

Caricatures of these three tendencies are, of course, commonplace. A "conservative" attitude, which stresses continuities with the past based on tested experience, can be caricatured to mean an intransigence inspired by self-interest in sustaining a status quo in which its exponents have a stake. That can be a correct estimate, but it also can be an undiscriminating judgment based on doctrinaire considerations. What appears to some as excessive police power designed to suppress legitimate dissent may be to others a necessary restriction of civil rights required to protect our democratic society against revolutionaries. The "liberal" attitude, which stresses discontinuities with the past based on a genuine need for change, can be caricatured to mean a view that favors change due to a desire to destroy our democratic system. That can be a correct estimate, but it can also be an undiscriminating judgment based on doctrinaire considerations. What appears to some as heresy where traditional values are concerned may be to others an openness necessary to preserve our democratic society. The "mediating" attitude, in which continuity and change are seen as mutually supportive, can be caricatured to mean a view that vacillates back and forth for reasons of expediency. That can be a correct estimate, but it can be a partisan criticism of a genuine effort to achieve a creative balance between conservation and change.

Daniel Bell believes we can rebuild faith in the future of our country by realizing that such a balance is required and by working to achieve it. He reminds us of our "unique history, a history of constitutionalism and comity." Constitutionalism means respect for the framework of law and acceptance of the outcomes of due process. Comity means mutual regard in the midst of our differences.[5]

HISTORICAL PERSPECTIVE

Among those who came to these shores from Europe in the seventeenth century were many who came as dissenters from political and religious establishments. Of course their motives were mixed. The desire to improve their lot in life and the lure of adventure as well as a search for freedom sent them to the new world. And yet an important ingredient in this movement was the spur of a more open and flexible life. Dissent was in their blood. Even the Puritans in Massachusetts and Connecticut, who refused to grant to others the freedom they found for themselves, quickly turned away from their "dear mother," the Church of England, and became Congregationalists. Puritans in Rhode Island forged forms of faith that undercut the idea of an established church.

People of various religious traditions poured into the middle colonies, which became havens of religious freedom. Governor Thomas Dongan of New York in his report of 1687 described the religious complexion of the colony, where "the most prevailing opinion" was that of the Dutch Calvinists, by noting that "here bee not many of the Church of England; few Roman Catholicks; [an] abundance of Quaker preachers, men and Women especially; Singing Quakers; Ranting Quakers; Sabbatarians; Anti-Sabbatarians; some Anabaptists; some Jews: in short, of all sorts of opinions there are some. . . ."[6]

The third provision of the "Act Concerning Religion," passed by the Maryland Assembly in 1649, provides a picture of the great variety of religious groups in the colony. Severe punishment was promised for any person who "in a reproachful manner" called any person within the province a "heritick, Scismatick, Idolator, puritan, Independant, Prespiterian, popish prest, Jesuite, Jesuited papist, Lutheran, Calvenist, Anabaptist, Brownist, Antinomian, Barrowist, Roundhead, Sepatist, or any other name. . . ."[7]

The diversity manifested geographically (in space) was matched by a chronological diversity (in time). What was orthodoxy strenuously defended in one generation became a lightly held faith in another. Beliefs regarded with suspicion and even horror at one time became the accepted doctrines of another time.

Edwin S. Gaustad has taken up this theme in his recent book, *Dissent in American Religion,* in which he describes the "wild diversity" in space and the "unsettling instability" in time in the colonies:

> What was doctrinal sobriety in Pennsylvania was intolerable "enthusiasm" in Connecticut; what was proper churchmanship in Rhode Island was arrogant pretension almost everywhere else. . . . What was theological terror for one generation was for the next a vaguely disquieting dream. That which one age was willing to die for another age was not willing to live for.[8]

With the adoption of the First Amendment in 1791 and consequent church disestablishment, the categories of theological and cultural distinctions were further compounded.

Out of these changing conditions came the principle of pluralism as a way of life. It became clear that the stability of American society could be sustained without the sacral conception of society and state and, therefore, without the cement of an established church and thus without common creedal norms. The national Constitution provided an adequate core of doctrine to insure the unity of the new nation without the support of an official religious establishment. Thomas Jefferson put the point succinctly in a letter written in 1808 to a group of Baptists: "Freedom of religion is compatible with order in government and obedience to the laws." This was a radical idea against the background of the state churches in Europe. In the old world, it was widely assumed that religious liberty would threaten the solidarity of the state. Never in their wildest dreams did Martin Luther and John Calvin believe in a free church in a free state, especially in the sense in which Baptists espoused it and as it was eventually realized in the United States.

Baptists were conspicuous in their contribution to religious liberty and none more than Isaac Backus (1724–1826). In his *Appeal to the Public for Religious Liberty Against the Oppressions of the Present Day* (1773), Backus noted the irony of the struggle for civil liberty that was being carried on by the colonists, especially in New England, who supported the repression of religious liberty. The tax on tea was far less pernicious than the ecclesiastical tax. After all, Backus argued, the former could be avoided by not drinking tea whereas the latter was mandatory. In 1774, he wrote, "We are determined not to pay either [tax] not only upon your principle of not being taxed where we are not represented, but also because we dare not render that homage to any earthly power which I and many of my brethren are fully convinced belongs only to God."[9] He sought liberty of conscience and insisted upon the competence of the soul before God. What Backus stood for had been strongly supported by Baptists from the beginning in both England and America and eventually spread throughout the new nation. The point here is only a reminder that the right to be different is an essential element in our heritage. This meant the right to differ with this or that religious and political establishment. This also means the right to differ among ourselves. Freedom of conscience and the competency of the soul before God mean the right to diversity within the nation and within the church. It would be strange indeed for a Baptist to insist upon religious liberty and its implications for everyone except fellow Baptists. Our Baptist forefathers frequently pointed out the importance of a certain openness to alternatives within the context of their heritage. In the quaint words of the time in a "circular letter" sent to a Kentucky Association in 1802, the "Dear Brethren" were warned to "watch against a spirit of dogmatical Arrogance and Bigotry; remember," the letter continued, "you are far from infallibility or perfection in Knowledge; and others have an equal right of private Judgment with yourselves."[10] A committee of the Elkhorn Baptist Association of Kentucky in 1793 issued a warning against permitting a Confession of Faith to become "a tiranical power over the Consciences of any, we do not mean that every person is to be bound to the strict observance of every thing therein Contained."[11]

One of the bonds of our unity is our freedom to question bureaucratic, institutional, and theological unities imposed from above, even when this is done with the best of intentions. Historically Baptists have stressed both the sanctity and the sinfulness of all men, including Baptists! Our philosophy of diversity, rooted in a basic respect for the individual conscience and in the recognition of the taint of self-interest in our judgments of what is just and true,[12] is one of the threads that paradoxically binds us together. This unity in diversity is a dynamic process that does not lend itself to precise historical analysis. The levels of unity and the degrees of diversity are constantly changing. Historians especially have a responsibility to wrestle with this process not only to clarify our past but also to make resources available for the tasks of today and tomorrow.

BAPTIST UNITY AND DIVERSITY

As has been indicated, unity and diversity seem antithetical. Unity is unity and diversity is diversity, and never the twain shall meet would appear at first glance to be true. At least superficially, unity appears to threaten diversity and diversity seems to threaten unity. It is not surprising that authoritarian regimes almost automatically take the view that unity requires the suppression of dissent and that proponents of pluralism frequently tend to be suspicious of strong legal prescriptions designed to support ecclesiastical or civil order. However, democracy requires the delicate balance between the freedom which makes diversity possible and a unifying core of values which provides a creative order. Such a balance is fragile and requires constant nurture. Vigilance is the price of both liberty and community.

What does this comment about unity and diversity have to do with Baptists? It suggests an important issue for us because our heritage is marked by two basic tendencies: the unity that flows from our belief that God has spoken and speaks in his Word and the diversity that flows from our freedom to listen, to read, and to implement what we hear. God speaks in his Word, and every Baptist has the freedom to respond according to his or her conscience.

Of course, there are sociological sources for our unities and our diversities. We see the things we hold in common and the things on which we differ through a variety of "spectacles," and what we see is colored by what we look through. There is a Baptist heritage we hold in common, but within this heritage are specific heritages rooted in where we grew up, the churches we have attended, the people we have admired, the sections of the country from which we have come, our personal interests, our educational backgrounds, our political and economic views, our particular talents, our insecurities, our temperaments, our responsibilities, and our institutional involvements. The list is almost endless. In other words, each of our lives is imbedded in a particular history as well as in the larger historical stream of which each of us is also a part. Our identities are drawn from both. Our historical memories are specific as well as general and actuate processes of unity and diversity, sometimes simultaneously.

In addition to the heritages on which we draw, the contemporary contexts within which we carry on our tasks in America should be noted. Baptists have spread throughout the land and into all segments of society. As a consequence, social customs and prejudices on a broad scale are intertwined with the religious beliefs of the people. The ethos of Baptists in a small rural church in a southern state is quite different from what is expressed in a large church in an eastern metropolitan center.

There is, of course, a sense in which we possess a common heritage because of our common humanity, and yet the humanity in which we all share is conditioned by specific cultures. There is a unity based upon our common humanity. There are diversities growing out of our involvement in specific cultures. A. R. Tippett has suggested that "every man, anthropologically speaking, has two identities—one as a member of the human race [which means theologically, that he is one for whom Christ died] and the other as a member of some specific culture, from which he derives his habits, his language and his outlook on life." [13] It is possible for us to be aware of our common human identity and sadly oblivious of our diverse cultural identities. The former means that every person is made in God's image, is precious, is a sinner prone to self-interest, and needs the gospel. The latter involves languages, vocabularies within languages, forms in which the message of redemption is communicated, the manner in which the new life in Christ is nurtured, and the life-styles through which it is expressed. Thus within our common human identity there are certain diverse cultural identities. Such diversity within limits is significant and should be preserved. The idea of a "melting pot" in which our diversities as Baptists are neutralized is a mistake. Of course, cultural pluralism and the differing visions of our Baptist life it inspires can actuate chaos, but it can also have a positive value. The canceling out of our differences, even if this were possible, in the interest of an abstract model of unity would not be desirable. This might solve some problems, but such a result would deprive us of significant sources of wisdom and vision and remove a reservoir of diversity and alternatives we cannot afford to lose. Baptist identity cannot be given a precise definition because it involves a dialectic between the need for continuity and the need for experimentation, the need for unity, and the need for diversity.

Of course, there is little danger that Baptists will agree on everything or will become alike! If we did, we would cease to be Baptists. What we need to do is to learn from our differences. The true meaning of unity lies in discovering how blacks and whites, middle-class folk and those of the counterculture, professional people and unskilled workers, men and women, young and old can work together and learn from each other without giving up their basic cultural identities. It is to be hoped that increased intercultural dialogue will contribute to our unity by excising some irrelevant differences among us, by modifying others, and by helping us to appreciate, or at least understand, differences that seem important to us.

Perhaps a clearer focus on this issue can be gained by examining more closely Baptist unity, Baptist diversity, and Baptist unity in diversity.

There is a conception of unity grounded in this or that alleged Baptist "orthodoxy," deviations from which are labeled "liberal" or "heretical" or what not. Exponents of this view tend to define what Baptists believe, theologically and otherwise, in their own propositional terms and sometimes imply that those who do not share their outlook are subverting Christian truth. Unity is based on conformity to this or that alleged objective criterion. Such an approach is exclusivist-because it uses a strict measuring rod to separate the "true believers" from those who wear the name "Baptist" without the substance of what is regarded as Baptist belief. "Liberal" is a frequent label applied to those who are open to theological and ecclesiological alternatives and for whom Christian truth is a category pointing beyond itself to mysteries more to be experienced than explained. It can be a code word used pejoratively to describe those who deviate from a certain theological or ecclesiological line. From this perspective, diversity which goes beyond the confines of very specific guidelines is suspect and suggests a lack of "conviction" on or a deficient "understanding" of this or that issue.

There is the conception of diversity grounded in a largely relativist theological outlook, which finds little basis for unity beyond the tolerance of diversity. In other words, there are those who take the view that since we cannot be really sure of anything, we should hold our diverse and tentative beliefs lightly and try to live together tolerantly. Such a conception is inclusivist because it defines Baptists so broadly that a Baptist can be almost anyone who wants to assume the name. "Conservative" can be a convenient tag applied to those who find specific biblical, theological, and historical guidelines viable. It can be a code word used pejoratively to describe those who find specific Baptist traditions meaningful. From this perspective, a unified theological perspective held with "conviction" is suspect and is symbolic of those who are afraid to subject faith to critical scrutiny.

These descriptions of unity and diversity among us are deliberately somewhat extreme in order to focus the central concern of this chapter. On the one side is unity with a minimum of diversity; on the other side is diversity with a minimum of unity. Is there a third alternative that is viable? Is there a possible interplay between unity and diversity that takes both seriously? The history of democracy in general and Baptists in particular suggests an alternative that can be described as unity in diversity or diversity in unity. Continuities that undergo little or no change tend to become institutionalized and rigid; changes without some underlying continuities tend to become a diffused process.

We cannot take our cue from the Baptist posture in any one cultural tradition, sectional perspective, or theological temper in our pluralistic land. Within our general Baptist heritage, let us glean those elements which characterize specific heritages among us, explore the continuities that unite and the discontinuities that divide, and seek to understand our underlying faith in the light of the varying nuances in that faith. One of the most important contributions of bringing Baptists together from a variety of perspectives, theological and otherwise, as in the Baptist Joint Committee on Public Affairs and the Baptist World Alliance, may lie at this point. It opens up the opportunity for rapport that could broaden and deepen our understanding of ourselves and our mission in today's world. A case in point is black Baptists. They do not come empty-handed seeking equality; they come with their values and perceptions forged in the fires of oppression and offer precious gifts that we deeply need. Their hearts and their hands are full of treasures too long buried by a sometimes overt and a sometimes covert racism.

Pluralism that is simply a polite tolerance of diversity may ease our consciences, but this is not the kind of pluralism we are talking about when we speak of Baptist pluralism and unity. Pluralism that merely tolerates differences is little more than a life-style designed to mollify tensions and sustain the status quo. It can be a device to keep things neatly in place in a world where creative change is required. Productive, enriching, meaningful pluralism means genuine dialogue not merely of words with words but of life with life. A pluralism that is merely tolerant but not open to new insights from those who share in it is like alleged dialogue where the participants do not really listen to each other and are set against any possible change. Such so-called dialogue is only polite conversation among people who agree to disagree. Though this is more desirable than impolite conversation among people who disagree disagreeably, it is not the creative pluralism that involves an open mind and not merely an open mouth. For creative pluralism, pluralism which leads to unity, means a willingness to learn from one another when differences arise in areas of belief, practice, and policy and not merely a pluralism which makes it possible to tell others how we see this or that. Pluralism used as a weapon to manipulate others can forge only the appearance of unity, only a facade which on close inspection is devoid of substance, and frequently foments artificial diversities in which we are more concerned with scoring historical and theological points than with what we can learn from each other. Games people play because they are free to speak their minds have little to do with the purpose of true pluralism.

CONCLUSION

I have no easy answers to the many questions posed by the theme of this chapter. It is easier to speak of pluralism and unity as mutually supportive and enriching than to carry it through in the actual life of Baptists. Our secular society with its technological values tends to push pluralism toward an atomism in which people are isolated and alienated. Creative community is a rather rare commodity whether we speak of the family, the church, the civic club, or the nation. Perhaps this is why we see such frantic and pitiful pursuits of synthetic unity. Janis Joplin was an exaggerated symbol of a widespread tendency. Twentieth-century dictators offered an ersatz community that appealed to millions. The disintegration of authority in contemporary Western society is accompanied by a cultivation of naked power that moves toward military and paramilitary forms, threatening an atomized citizenry with despotism and dictatorship. Pluralism that flies apart because it lacks any meaning other than "we do as we please" is often the prelude to arbitrary unities, for people cannot long live by liberty alone. The radical skepticism that leads to a complete relativism is often the prelude to an idolatrous credulity, which inspires worship of the state, the nation, this or that class, this or that human vitality. An unbelieving epoch like ours is the cradle of new superstitions. In the face of the breakdown of human communities, the futility of synthetic unities, and the idolatries spawned thereby, Baptists believe in a gathered community, a community of grace, a *koinonia,* in which human freedom and dignity are preserved.

Though we frequently fall short of it, Baptist understanding of community involves a sense of unity in which our freedom is preserved and a sense of freedom in which unity is sought. Our Baptist heritage at its best involves a blend of loyalty and liberty. This is our cue, our model. In this context, we must strive to bridge the gaps between our schools and churches, our theology and the secular mentality, our professors and laymen, our pastors and people, our Christian faith and culture, between Baptists and Baptists, and between Baptists and those of other traditions.

This raises the question of leadership. We need neither Men of Destiny who think they know all the answers nor Caspar

Milquetoasts who cannot make up their minds. We must stay in touch with the people, but this need not mean an opportunism that capitalizes on the superficialities of mass culture. In our search for Baptist unity, the prophetic voice must not be muted where war and poverty and racism and political chicanery are concerned. Serious moral conviction and Christian truth sometimes exact a price precisely because they stand against a popular consensus. Such a stance sometimes elicits serious opposition and in certain situations may exact sacrifices which appear mindless to the majority. Baptist unity purchased at the price of expediency costs too much. Baptist freedom sacrificed on the altar of peace at any price is simply a surrender. We must bear witness to what we believe to be true. We will not make much progress toward creative pluralism if we constantly look over our shoulders to see what our neighbors are doing and then follow suit. What is called for is not confrontation but conciliation, not rigidity but flexibility, not doctrinaire demands but love, not division but reconciliation, not exclusion but inclusion, not ostracism but what Gabriel Marcel has called "a kind of spiritual welcoming." Such a welcoming spirit we sense sometimes in quiet moments, in worship, in the dark, sleepless solitudes of night, when we forget our quarrels and vanities and forgive and understand others and ourselves, as we forgive and understand the quarrels of little children. Of course, this is only one side of it, for quarrels with what we feel is false and wrong are sometimes required; but we also need to be reminded that our vision of what is true and right is human and partial and needs the corrective of competing visions.

Baptist pluralism and unity go hand in hand. In a sense, we cannot have one without the other. Pluralism without unity means fragmentation, bitter debate, and proliferating division. It means a corrosion of commitment to common ends, a contraction of interest in missionary concerns, and a dwindling of financial resources. Unity without pluralism means bureaucratic structures which feed on themselves, unimaginative institutionalism, and the loss of initiative and zest. It means a smothering of innovation, a "displacement of goals" [14] so that the means served by the bureaucracy tend to become ends, the subordination of people to policy that is placed on a level just short of sanctity, and the rise of what has been called, albeit with some exaggeration, "the iron law of oligarchy," by which representative structures are changed into a hierarchy of authority. [15]

"Faith," "freedom," and "fraternal love" are words that run through every chapter of Baptist history. Only when we have permitted one or another of them to slip out of focus have our ranks been broken and our strength dissipated. Paul pinpointed these elements in his letter to the Galatians: "You are sons of God through *faith in Jesus Christ.* . . . You, my friends, were called for *freedom;* only use not your freedom as an occasion for the flesh, but through *love* be servants one to another" (see Galatians 3:6 and 5:13). Faith alone means a creed to which all must conform; freedom alone means a centrifugal force that dissipates unity; fraternal love means a sense of belonging together in both faith and freedom, a spirit that magnifies our agreements and seeks to learn from our differences. Such a spirit of magnanimity means not only that we shall try harder to manifest fraternal love, especially in "sticky" situations, but, above all, that we shall sustain our confidence in the Holy Spirit at work, lifting our hearts, dispelling gloom, and shedding joy.

E Pluribus Unum (out of many, one) is not a static goal toward which we strive but a dynamic process that goes on and on. This motto does not pose a problem we hope one day to solve. For Baptists, it is a way of life.

NOTES

[1] Flora Lewis, "Close-up of a Revolution: Urgent Confusion in Portugal," *International Herald Tribune,* October 14, 1975. According to Joao Ribiero Coelho, a police official in Portugal, "there has been a loss of authority and nothing has filled up the vacuum. Maintaining public order has become very difficult. Before the revolution people were frankly afraid of the police. It's not that way now." Cited in John Vinocur, "Portugal Revolution Marked by Crime, Police Laxity," *International Herald Tribune,* October 21, 1975.

[2] Donald Coggan, "Anglican Head Starts Campaign to Redress United Kingdom," *International Herald Tribune,* October 16, 1975.

[3] Daniel Bell, "The End of American Exceptionalism," in *The Public Interest,* the Bicentennial number, cited in Anthony Lewis, "The American Dream," *International Herald Tribune,* October 14, 1975.

[4] *Time,* "Alone with the Blues," August 27, 1973. "Liberty on its own essence becomes destructive," says Will Durant, "when it becomes complete. And as it approaches completion, we resign ourselves unwillingly to order, to commandments, to discipline because we perceive that without a restoration of order in the moral sphere, we will lose the stability of character and purpose and courage—even of life—that is necessary for existence." "The Life and 'Civilization' of the Durants," *The Stars and Stripes,* November 16, 1975.

[5] Daniel Bell, "The End of American Exceptionalism, *International Herald Tribune,* October 14, 1975. See comment by Karl Jaspers, which is applicable here, in *The Perennial Scope of Philosophy,* trans. Ralph Manheim (Hamden, Conn.: Archon Books, 1968), p. 14: "We must become concerned with the historically different without becoming untrue to our own historicity."

[6]Thomas Dongan, cited in Clifton E. Olmstead, *History of Religion in the United States* (Englewood Cliffs, N.J.: Prentice-Hall, Inc., 1960), p. 127.

[7]"Act Concerning Religion," cited in Olmstead, *History of Religion in the United States,* p. 96.

[8]Edwin S. Gaustad, *Dissent in American Religion* (Chicago: The University of Chicago Press, 1973), p. 3.

[9]Isaac Backus, cited in Gaustad, *Dissent in American Religion,* p. 12.

[10]William Taylor, "Circular Letter: To the Churches with Whom We Are in Union," cited in William Warren Sweet, ed., *Religion on the American Frontier: The Baptists, 1783–1830* (New York: Henry Holt and Company, Inc., 1931), p. 623.

[11]"Minutes of the Elkhorn Baptist Association," cited in Sweet, *Religion on the American Frontier: The Baptists,* p. 459.

[12]An English historian once said, "Modern democracy rests upon the insight that what I think to be just [and true] is tainted by my own self-interest. I have just enough residual virtue to know that it *is* tainted, and that someone has to stand against me, and declare his different conviction." Cited in Reinhold Niebuhr, *Justice and Mercy,* ed. Ursula M. Niebuhr (New York: Harper & Row, Publishers, 1974), p. 44.

[13]A. R. Tippett, "Conceptual Dyads in the Ethnotheology of 'Salvation Today,'" *International Review of Missions,* vol. 61 (July, 1972), p. 246.

[14]Peter M. Blau, *The Dynamics of Bureaucracy* (Chicago: University of Chicago Press, 1955). See E. H. Lurkings, "Bureaucracy and Moral Order," *The Expository Times* (October, 1975), especially p. 20.

[15]Robert Michels, *Political Parties: A Sociological Study of the Oligarchical Tendencies of Modern Democracy,* trans. Eden and Cedar Paul (New York: Collier Books, 1962). See Lurkings, "Bureaucracy and Moral Order," p. 20.

A Selected
and Annotated
Bibliography
on Baptists in America

JAMES E. WOOD, JR.

Adams, C. C., and Talley, Marshall A., *Negro Baptists and Foreign Missions*. Philadelphia: The Foreign Mission Board of the National Baptist Convention, U.S.A., Inc., 1944. Of limited value.

Adams, James L., *The Growing Church Lobby in Washington*. Grand Rapids, Mich.: Wm. B. Eerdmans Publishing Company, 1970. Although there is much good factual material in this book, it is seriously inadequate at many points; plays down the role of Baptists.

Ahlstrom, Sidney E., *A Religious History of the American People*. New Haven: Yale University Press, 1972. The most comprehensive volume on the subject; a definitive and reliable study.

The American Baptist Bill of Rights. Washington, D.C.: Associated Committees on Public Relations, 1940.

Backus, Isaac, *A History of New England with Particular Reference to the Denominations of Christians Called Baptists*. Newton Mass.: Backus Historical Society, 1871. Reprint (2 vols. in 1). A major history of Baptists with valuable documentary material.

Bailey, G. S., *The Trials and Victories of Religious Liberty in America*. Philadelphia: American Baptist Publication Society, 1876. Published as a "Centennial Memorial."

361

Baker, Robert A., *A Baptist Source Book*. Nashville: Broadman Press, 1966. A collection of primary or original documents produced by people who made Baptist history from 1682 to 1966, with particular reference to Southern Baptists.

———, *Relations Between Northern and Southern Baptists*. 2nd ed., rev. Fort Worth: Marvin D. Evans Printing Co., 1954. A scholarly analysis, originally written as a doctoral dissertation.

———, *The Southern Baptist Convention and Its People, 1607-1972*. Nashville: Broadman Press, 1974. The most comprehensive and up-to-date history of the Southern Baptist Convention to appear; more encyclopedic than interpretative.

Baptist Home Missions in North America: Including a Full Report of the Proceedings and Addresses of the Jubilee Meeting and a Historical Sketch of the American Baptist Home Mission Society, Historical Tables, etc., 1832-1882. New York: Baptist Home Mission Board, 1883.

Barnes, Lemuel Call, et al., *Pioneers of Light: The First Century of the American Baptist Publication Society, 1824-1924*. Philadelphia: American Baptist Publication Society, n.d.

Barnes, William Wright, *The Southern Baptist Convention, 1845-1953*. Nashville: Broadman Press, 1954. A significant study.

———, *The Southern Baptist Convention: A Study in the Development of Ecclesiology*. Seminary Hill: The author, 1934. A valuable contribution.

———, "Why the Southern Baptist Convention Was Formed," *Review and Expositor,* vol. 41 (January, 1944), pp. 3-17.

Baxter, Norman A., *History of the Freewill Baptists: A Study in New England Separatism*. Rochester: American Baptist Historical Society, 1957.

Beers, George P., *Ministry to Turbulent America: A History of the American Baptist Home Mission Society, 1932-1957*. Valley Forge: Judson Press, 1957.

Bellah, Robert N., *The Broken Covenant: American Civil Religion in Time of Trial.* New York: The Seabury Press, Inc., 1975.

Benedict, David, *A General History of the Baptist Denomination in America.* 2 vols, 1813. Reprint (2 vols. in 1). New York: Lewis Colby and Co., 1848. See Chapters 7-29. A major early history of Baptists, particularly in America.

Bodo, John Ranier, *The Protestant Clergy and Public Issues, 1812-1848.* Princeton: Princeton University Press, 1954. A scholarly and thoroughly reliable study of the period, with frequent references to Baptists.

Bond, A. J. C., *Seventh Day Baptist Beliefs.* Plainfield, N.J.: American Sabbath Tract Society, 1941.

Boyd, Jesse L., *A History of Baptists in America Prior to 1845.* New York: American Press, 1957.

Boyd, R. H., *A Story of the National Baptist Publishing Board.* Nashville: National Baptist Publishing Board, 1924.

Brawley, E. M., *The Negro Baptist Pulpit.* Philadelphia: American Baptist Publication Society, 1890.

Brimm, Hugh A., "The Social Consciousness of Southern Baptists in Relation to Some Regional Problems, 1910–1935." Th.D. dissertation, Southern Baptist Theological Seminary, 1944.

Cathcart, William, *The Baptists and the American Revolution.* Philadelphia: S. A. George & Co., 1876. Published as "A Centennial Offering."

————, ed., *The Baptist Encyclopedia.* 2 vols. Philadelphia: Louis H. Everts, 1881.

Carlson, C. Emanuel, and Garrett, W. Barry, *Religious Liberty: Case Studies in Current Church-State Issues.* Nashville: Convention Press, 1964.

Cauthen, Baker J., et al., *Advance: A History of Southern Baptist Foreign Missions.* Nashville: Broadman Press, 1970. Not a definitive history, but attempts to provide an account of institutions, personnel, and trends in Southern Baptist world mission enterprise.

Christian, John T., *A History of the Baptists of the United States from the First Settlement of the Country to the Year 1845.* 2 vols. Nashville: Broadman Press, 1926. Contains valuable documentary sources.

Cox, Harvey, "A Baptist Intellectual's View of Catholicism," *Harper's Magazine,* vol. 225 (December, 1962), pp. 47-50.

————, *The Secular City: Secularization and Urbanization in Theological Perspective.* New York: Macmillan Publishing Co., Inc., 1965. A major study by a leading contemporary Baptist theologian.

Crook, Roger H., "Ethical Emphases of the Editors of Baptist Journals Published in the Southeastern Region of the United States up to 1865." Th.D. dissertation, Southern Baptist Theological Seminary, 1947.

Dawson, Joseph M., *America's Way in Church, State, and Society.* New York: Macmillan Publishing Co., Inc., 1953. Written by the first Executive Director of the Baptist Joint Committee on Public Affairs.

————, *Baptists and the American Republic.* Nashville: Broadman Press, 1956. A valuable study.

————, *Christ and Social Change.* Valley Forge: Judson Press, 1937.

————, *Separate Church and State Now.* New York: R. R. Smith, 1948.

Ebersole, Luke, *Church Lobbying in the Nation's Capital.* New York: Macmillan Publishing Co., Inc., 1951. An important pioneer study; limited by the fact that it was published twenty-five years ago.

Edwards, Morgan, *Materials Toward a History of the American Baptists.* Philadelphia, 1770-1792. Of the twelve-volume work projected, only a few have been published. Copies of these are in the New York Public Library and the American Baptist Historical Society Library, Rochester, New York, and on microfilm at the Southern Baptist Historical Commission, Nashville, Tennessee.

Eighmy, John L., *Churches in Cultural Captivity.* Knoxville: University of Tennessee Press, 1972. A valuable analysis and interpretation by a Southern Baptist historian.

Encyclopedia of Southern Baptists. 3 vols. Nashville: Broadman Press, 1958, 1971. Volume 3 published as a "Supplement" in 1971. Reliable.

English, Carl Dean, "The Ethical Emphases of the Editors of Baptist Journals Published in the Southeastern Region of the United States, 1865–1915." Th.D. dissertation, Southern Baptist Theological Seminary, 1948.

Estep, William R., *Baptists and Christian Unity.* Nashville: Broadman Press, 1967. A historical study, with attention given to the differences among Baptists in the United States, as well as in other countries, toward contemporary ecumenism.

Foundations. Rochester: American Baptist Historical Society. A quarterly of Baptist history and theology published since 1958 as successor to *The Chronicle.*

Gaddy, J. Welton, "The Christian Life Commission of the Southern Baptist Convention: A Critical Evaluation," Th.D. dissertation, Southern Baptist Theological Seminary, 1970.

Garrett, James Leo, ed., *Baptist Relations with Other Christians.* Valley Forge: Judson Press, 1974. A collection of essays prepared for the Baptist World Alliance Commission on Cooperative Christianity.

Gaustad, Edwin Scott, *Dissent in American Religion.* Chicago: University of Chicago Press, 1973.

_____, *The Great Awakening in New England.* New York: Harper & Row, Publishers, 1957. A definitive study.

————, *Historical Atlas of Religion in America.* New York: Harper & Row, Publishers, Revised Edition, 1976. An original and valuable contribution. Illustrated by maps and charts.

————, *A Religious History of America.* New York: Harper & Row, Publishers, 1966. A comprehensive and reliable history, well illustrated.

Goen, C. C., *Revivalism and Separatism in New England, 1740–1800.* New York: Yale University Press, 1962. A useful study of strict Congregationalists and Separate Baptists in the Great Awakening; originally written as a doctoral dissertation.

Greene, L. F., ed., *The Writings of John Leland.* 1845. Reprint. New York: Arno Press, Inc., 1969.

Handy, Robert T., *A Christian America: Protestant Hopes and Historical Realities.* New York: Oxford University Press, Inc., 1971.

————, *Religion in the American Experience: The Pluralistic Style.* New York: Harper & Row, Publishers, 1972.

Harrison, Paul M., *Authority and Power in the Free Church Tradition: A Social Case Study of the American Baptist Convention.* Princeton: Princeton University Press, 1959. A valuable contribution.

————, ed., *Memoir of John Mason Peck.* Carbondale, Ill.: University of Southern Illinois Press, 1965. The memoirs of a major Baptist pioneer missionary in the West who lived from 1789 to 1858.

Haselden, Kyle B., *The Racial Problem in Christian Perspective.* New York: Harper & Row, Publishers, 1964. Written by a Baptist editor and journalist.

Hastey, Stanley L., "A History of the Baptist Joint Committee on Public Affairs." Th.D. dissertation, Southern Baptist Theological Seminary, 1973.

Hays, Brooks, *A Southern Moderate Speaks.* Chapel Hill: University of North Carolina Press, 1959. Written by a former member of

Congress and former president of the Southern Baptist Convention.

Hays, Brooks, and Steely, John E., *The Baptist Way of Life*. Englewood Cliffs, N.J.: Prentice-Hall, Inc., 1963.

Heimert, Alan, *Religion and the American Mind: From the Great Awakening to the Revolution*. Cambridge: Harvard University Press, 1966. A significant study for understanding the background of a formative period of American Baptists.

Hill, Patrick H., "The Ethical Emphases of the Baptist Editors in the Southeastern Region of the United States, 1915–1940." Th.D. dissertation, Southern Baptist Theological Seminary, 1949.

Hill, Samuel J., Jr., and Torbet, Robert G., *Baptists North and South*. Valley Forge: Judson Press, 1964. An examination of the factors which divide Baptists of the North and South. From the perspectives of two authors, one from the North and one from the South.

Hill, Samuel S., Jr., *Southern Churches in Crisis*. New York: Holt, Rinehart, and Winston, Inc., 1967. A valuable study.

Historical Commission of the Southern Baptist Convention. *Index of Graduate Theses in Baptist Theological Seminaries, 1894–1975*. Nashville: Southern Baptist Historical Commission, 1963-1975.

Hodges, S. S., *Black Baptists in America and the Origins of their Conventions*. Washington, D.C.: Progressive National Baptist Convention, Inc., n.d.

Hopkins, Charles Howard, *The Rise of the Social Gospel in American Protestantism, 1865–1915*. New Haven: Yale University Press, 1940. A comprehensive and scholarly study by a Baptist scholar.

Hudson, Winthrop S., *American Protestantism*. Chicago: University of Chicago Press, 1961.

———, *The Great Tradition of the American Churches*. New York: Harper & Row, Publishers, 1953. A fresh and perceptive analysis of the American tradition of religious voluntaryism and the freedom of the churches through church-state separation.

————, *Religion in America*. New York: Charles Scribner's Sons, 1965. Portrays "the religious life of the American people in interaction with other dimensions of their experience," both the unity it exhibits and its particularities.

Johnson, Charles Price, "Southern Baptists and the Social Gospel Movement." Th.D. dissertation, Southwestern Baptist Theological Seminary, 1948.

Joiner, Edward Earl, "Southern Baptists and Church-State Relations, 1845–1954." Th.D. dissertation, Southern Baptist Theological Seminary, 1959.

Jordan, Lewis G., *Negro Baptist History, U.S.A., 1750–1930*. Nashville: The Sunday School Publishing Board, National Baptist Convention, 1930.

Kelley, Dean M., *Why Conservative Churches Are Growing: A Study in Sociology of Religion*. New York: Harper & Row, Publishers, 1972. An important and provocative study of particular interest to Baptists in America.

Kelsey, George D., *Social Ethics Among Southern Baptists, 1917–1969*. Metuchen, N.J.: American Theological Library Association, 1973. Originally written as a doctoral dissertation. The author is a Baptist professor of Social Ethics.

Kersten, R. J., "Historical Factors in the Formation of the Ethnically Oriented North American Baptist General Conference." Ph.D. dissertation, Northwestern University, 1971.

Keucher, William F., *Main Street and the Mind of God*. Valley Forge: Judson Press, 1974.

King, Martin Luther, Jr., *Stride Toward Freedom: The Montgomery Story*. New York: Harper & Row, Publishers, 1964. Written by the most articulate and most influential leader for human rights in recent American history.

_____, *The Trumpet of Conscience.* New York: Harper & Row, Publishers, 1968.

_____, *Where Do We Go from Here: Chaos or Community?* Boston: Beacon Press, 1968.

_____, *Why We Can't Wait.* New York: Harper & Row, Publishers, 1964.

Knight, Richard, *History of the General Six-Principle Baptists.* Providence: Smith & Parmenter, 1827. A basic study.

Kuhn, William, et al., *These Glorious Years.* Forest Park, Ill.: Roger Williams Press, 1943.

Latourette, Kenneth Scott, *A History of Christianity.* New York: Harper & Row, Publishers, 1953. A valuable history for background by Baptists' most renowned historian.

Littell, Franklin H., *From State Church to Pluralism: A Protestant Interpretation of Religion in American History,* Revised edition. Garden City, N.Y.: Doubleday & Company, Inc., 1971. An important study, with many fresh insights.

Locke, Harvey James, "A History and Critical Interpretation of the Social Gospel of Northern Baptists in the United States." Ph.D. dissertation, University of Chicago, 1930.

Lumpkin, William L., *Baptist Confessions of Faith.* Rev. ed. Valley Forge: Judson Press, 1969. A valuable collection of Baptist statements of faith.

McCall, Duke K., ed., *What Is the Church? A Symposium of Baptist Thought.* Nashville: Broadman Press, 1958. A helpful collection of essays.

McCall, Emmanuel L., *The Black Christian Experience.* Nashville: Broadman Press, 1972. A brief and helpful introduction by a black Southern Baptist denominational executive.

McCoy, Isaac, *History of Baptist Indian Missions.* Washington, D.C.: W. M. Morrison, 1840. Written by a renowned Baptist missionary among the Indians.

McLoughlin, William G., *Isaac Backus and the American Pietistic Tradition*. Boston: Little, Brown and Company, 1967. An admirable study.

————, ed., *Isaac Backus on Church, State, and Calvinism: Pamphlets, 1754–1789*. Cambridge: Harvard University Press, 1968. A valuable collection.

————, *Modern Revivalism: Charles Grandison Finney to Billy Graham*. New York: The Ronald Press, Inc., 1959.

————, *New England Dissent, 1630–1833: The Baptists and the Separation of Church and State*. 3 vols. Cambridge: Harvard University Press, 1971.

Maring, Norman H., *American Baptists—Whence and Whither*. Valley Forge: Judson Press, 1968. Focuses on the present and future of the American Baptist Churches, U.S.A.

————, and Hudson, Winthrop S., *A Baptist Manual of Polity and Practice*. Valley Forge: Judson Press, 1963. A valuable study which attempts to "bring together traditional Baptist positions and practices and the modifications adopted over the years by Baptists in local churches and larger groupings."

Maston, Thomas B., *Isaac Backus: Pioneer of Religious Liberty*. New York: American Baptist Historical Society, 1962. Backus is generally acknowledged to be, with the exception of Roger Williams, America's foremost champion of religious liberty.

Mays, Benjamin E., *Disturbed About Man*. Richmond: John Knox Press, 1969. The thinking of a major black Baptist educator and leader.

————, *Seeking to Be Christian in Race Relations*. New York: Friendship Press, 1957.

————, and Nicholson, Joseph W., *The Negro's Church*. New York: Institute of Social and Religious Research, 1933.

Mead, Sidney E., *The Nation with the Soul of a Church*. New York: Harper & Row, Publishers, 1975. A provocative collection of essays helpful as background in interpreting Baptists in the light of the American experience.

Meyer, Donald, *The Protestant Search for Political Realism, 1919–1941*. Berkeley: University of California Press, 1960.

Miller, Glenn T., *Religious Liberty in America: History and Prospects*. Philadelphia: The Westminster Press, 1976. An examination of America's developing history of religious liberty from colonial times to the present, including insights for dealing with critical issues today.

Miller, Robert Moats, *American Protestantism and Social Issues, 1919–1939*. Chapel Hill: University of North Carolina Press, 1958. A major contribution.

———, "Social Attitudes of American Baptists," *Chronicle,* vol. 19 (July, 1956), pp. 100-114.

Morales, Adam, *American Baptists with a Spanish Accent*. Valley Forge: Judson Press, 1964.

Moss, Lemuel, ed., *The Baptists and the National Centenary: A Record of Christian Work, 1776–1876*. Philadelphia: American Baptist Publication Society, 1876.

Mullins, Edgar Y., *Axioms of Religion: A New Interpretation of the Baptist Faith*. Philadelphia: American Baptist Publication Society, 1908.

Newman, Albert H., ed., *A Century of Baptist Achievement*. Philadelphia: American Baptist Publication Society, 1901.

———, *A History of the Baptist Churches in the United States*. Philadelphia: American Baptist Publication Society, 1898.

Ohlmann, Eric Henry, "The American Baptist Mission to German Americans." Th.D. dissertation, Faculty of the Graduate Theological Union, Berkeley, California, 1975.

Olson, Adolf, *A Centenary History as Related to the Baptist General Conference of America*. Chicago: Baptist Conference Press, 1952.

Pelt, Owen C., and Smith, Ralph Lee, *The Story of the National Baptists*. New York: Vantage Press, 1960.

Pinson, William Meredith, Jr., "Contemporary Southern Baptist Involvement with the State." Th.D. dissertation, Southwestern Baptist Theological Seminary, 1963.

Posey, Walter B., *The Baptist Church in the Lower Mississippi Valley, 1776-1845*. Lexington: University of Kentucky Press, 1957. An excellent study.

Putnam, Mary B., *The Baptists and Slavery, 1840-1845*. Ann Arbor, Mich.: George Wahr, Publisher, 1913. A scholarly study.

Randolph, Corliss F., *Seventh Day Baptists in Europe and America*. 2 vols. Plainfield, N.J.: American Sabbath Tract Society, 1910.

Rankin, Charles Hays, "The Rise of Negro Baptist Churches in the South Through the Reconstruction Period." Th.M. thesis, New Orleans Baptist Theological Seminary, 1955.

Rankin, M. Theron, et al., *Light for the Whole World*. Nashville: Broadman Press, 1948. Reflects Southern Baptist thought concerning the Christian world mission at the end of World War II.

Rauschenbusch, Walter, *Christianizing the Social Order*. New York: Macmillan Publishing Co., Inc., 1912. A major work by a Baptist who became widely acknowledged as the foremost prophet of social Christianity in America.

Report from the Capital. Washington, D.C.: Baptist Joint Committee on Public Affairs. A monthly periodical registering Baptist concerns in public affairs; published since 1946.

Review and Expositor. Louisville: Southern Baptist Theological Seminary. A quarterly journal published since 1904, it is the oldest Baptist scholarly journal published in the Americas.

Riley, Benjamin Franklin, *A History of the Baptists in the Southern States East of the Mississippi*. Philadelphia: American Baptist Publication Society, 1898.

Rogers, Albert N., *Seventh Day Baptists in Europe and America,* vol. 3. Plainfield, N.J.: Seventh Day Baptist Historical Society, 1972.

Rutledge, Arthur B., *Mission to America: A Century and a Quarter of Southern Baptist Home Missions.* Nashville: Broadman Press, 1969. Well documented, this volume is the most complete history of Southern Baptist home missions available.

Semple, Robert B., *A History of the Rise and Progress of the Baptists in Virginia.* Rev. ed. Richmond: Pitt and Dickinson, 1894. Revised and enlarged by G. W. Beale.

Shelley, Bruce L., *Conservative Baptists: A Story of Twentieth-Century Dissent.* Denver: Conservative Baptist Theological Seminary, 1960.

Smith, W. Earle, *Foundations for Freedom: A Consideration of Baptists, Their Heritage and Contribution to American Life.* Valley Forge: Judson Press, 1952.

Southwestern Journal of Theology. Fort Worth, Tex.: Southwestern Baptist Theological Seminary. A Baptist journal, published semiannually since 1958. A successor to an earlier journal with the same title published 1917–1924.

Spain, Rufus B., *At Ease in Zion: A Social History of Southern Baptists, 1865–1900.* Nashville: Vanderbilt University Press, 1961. An admirable study.

Starr, Edward C., ed., *A Baptist Bibliography: Being a Register of Printed Material By and About Baptists; Including Works Written Against the Baptists.* Rochester: American Baptist Historical Society, 1947–1976. Twenty-three volumes published to date. To be completed during the next year or two.

Stillman, Karl G., *Seventh Day Baptists—New England, 1671–1971.* Plainfield, N.J.: The Seventh Day Baptist Historical Society, 1971. A tricentennial publication of early Seventh Day Baptists in New England.

Stokes, Anson Phelps, *Church and State in the United States,* 3 vols. New York: Harper & Row, Publishers, 1950. The definitive work on the subject, with important references to the role of Baptists.

_____, and Pfeffer, Leo, *Church and State in the United States*. 2nd ed. rev. New York: Harper & Row, Publishers, 1964.

Sweet, William Warren, *Religion in Colonial America*. New York: Charles Scribner's Sons, 1942. A standard work.

_____, *Religion on the American Frontier, the Baptists, 1783-1830: A Collection of Source Material*. 1931. Reprint. New York: Cooper Square Publishers, Inc., 1964. Contains valuable source materials.

_____, *Religion in the Development of American Culture, 1765-1840*. New York: Charles Scribner's Sons, 1952.

Taylor, Raymond Hargus, "The Triennial Convention, 1814-1845: A Study in Baptist Co-operation and Conflict." Th.D. dissertation, Southern Baptist Theological Seminary, 1960.

Thom, William T., *The Struggle for Religious Freedom in Virginia: The Baptists*. Baltimore: Johns Hopkins University Press, 1900.

Torbet, Robert G., "Baptists and the Ecumenical Movement," *The Chronicle,* vol. 18 (April, 1955), pp. 86-95.

_____, *A History of the Baptists*. Rev. ed. Valley Forge: Judson Press, 1973.

_____, *Venture of Faith: The Story of the American Baptist Foreign Mission Society*. Valley Forge: Judson Press, 1955.

Trotter, Donald F., "A Study of Authority and Power in the Structure and Dynamics of the Southern Baptist Convention." D.R.E. dissertation, Southern Baptist Theological Seminary, 1962.

Tull, James E., *Shapers of Baptist Thought*. Valley Forge: Judson Press, 1972. With but two exceptions the focus of this volume is on seven figures who profoundly influenced American Baptist thought—from Roger Williams to Martin Luther King, Jr.

Tupper, Henry A., *A Decade of Foreign Missions, 1880–1890.* Richmond, Va.: Foreign Mission Board of the Southern Baptist Convention, 1891.

———, *The Foreign Missions of the Southern Baptist Convention.* Philadelphia and Richmond: American Baptist Publication Society and Foreign Mission Board of the Southern Baptist Convention, 1880. A comprehensive study.

Vail, Albert L., *The Morning Hour of American Baptist Missions.* Philadelphia: American Baptist Publication Society, 1907. Excellent.

Valentine, Foy Dan, "A Historical Study of Southern Baptists and Race Relations, 1917–1947." Th.D. dissertation, Southwestern Baptist Theological Seminary, 1949.

Vedder, Henry C., *The Gospel of Jesus and the Problems of Democracy.* New York: The Macmillan Co., Inc., 1914.

———, *A Short History of Baptist Missions.* Valley Forge: Judson Press, 1927.

———, *A Short History of the Baptists.* Rev. ed. Philadelphia: American Baptist Publication Society, 1907.

Wamble, G. Hugh, *Through Trial to Triumph.* Nashville: Convention Press, 1958. An account of the Southern Baptist Convention.

Washington, Joseph, *Black Religion.* Boston: Beacon Press, 1964.

Weaver, Rufus Washington, *Champions of Religious Liberty.* Nashville: Sunday School Board of the Southern Baptist Convention, 1946.

———, *The Christian Faith at the Nation's Capital.* Valley Forge: Judson Press, 1936.

———, *The Road to the Freedom of Religion.* Washington, D.C.: Joint Conference Committee on Public Relations, 1944. The first publication of the Joint Conference Committee on Public Relations, which later became the Baptist Joint Committee on Public Affairs.

White, Charles L., *A Century of Faith: Centenary Volume of the American Baptist Home Mission Society.* Valley Forge: Judson Press, 1932.

Whitted, J. A., *A History of the Negro Baptists in North Carolina.* Raleigh: Broughton, 1908.

Wood, James E., Jr., "Baptists and Religious Liberty." *Southwestern Journal of Theology,* vol. 6 (April, 1964), pp. 38-59.

_____, "The Church and Politics in Historical Perspective." *Review and Expositor,* vol. 65 (Summer, 1968), pp. 267–282.

_____, *The Problem of Nationalism in Church-State Relationships.* Scottdale, Pa.: Herald Press, 1969.

Woodson, Carter G., *The History of the Negro Church.* 2nd ed. Washington, D.C.: The Associated Publishers, 1945.

Woolley, Davis C., ed., *Baptist Advance: The Achievements of the Baptists of North America for a Century and a Half.* Nashville: Broadman Press, 1964. An excellent collection of essays, written from a variety of denominational perspectives.

Wright, Mary Emily, *The Missionary Work of the Southern Baptist Convention.* Philadelphia: American Baptist Publishing Society, 1902.

Biographical Notes

CHARLES G. ADAMS graduated from the University of Michigan, B.A.; and Harvard Divinity School (Rockefeller Fellow) S.T.B. He was born in Michigan in 1936. Formerly a teacher at Andover Newton Theological School and Lecturer at the School of Theology of Boston University, he is presently Senior Pastor of Hartford Avenue Baptist Church in Detroit, Michigan. He is Editor of *Baptist Progress*, a denominational journal of the Progressive National Baptist Convention, and a member of the Baptist Joint Committee on Public Affairs.

O. CARROLL ARNOLD was born in Illinois in 1914. He has studied at Wheaton College, A.B.; University of Pennsylvania, M.A.; Eastern Baptist Theological Seminary, B.D.; and Harvard Divinity School (Merrill Fellow). He served as editor in the American Baptist Publication Society from 1950 to 1954. Pastor of the First Baptist Church of Ann Arbor, Michigan, since 1969, he has published articles in the *Christian Century, Christian Herald,* and *Baptist Leader.*

JOHN W. BAKER is Associate Director in Charge of Research Services, Baptist Joint Committee on Public Affairs. Born in Texas in 1920, he received his B.A. from the University of Texas and his Ph.D. in Political Science from the University of California, Berkeley. Formerly Professor of Political Science at the College of Wooster (1958–1969), he is co-author of *Member of the House* and has contributed to various denominational and professional journals.

C. EMANUEL CARLSON (1906–1976), born in Canada, received his B.A. from the University of Alberta, Edmonton (Canada), and his M.A. and Ph.D. in History and Education from the University of Minnesota. Professor of History and Social Science at Bethel College from 1932 to 1945 and Dean of Bethel College from 1945 to 1953, he served as Executive Director of the Baptist Joint Committee on Public Affairs from 1954 until his retirement in 1971. He was co-author of *Religious Liberty: Case Studies in Current Church-State Issues.*

C. WELTON GADDY was born in Tennessee in 1941. He was educated at Union University, B.A.; and Southern Baptist Theological Seminary, B.D., Th.M., and Ph.D. Director of Christian Citizenship Development of the Christian Life Commission of the Southern Baptist Convention, he is author of *Profile of a Christian Citizen, Proclaim Liberty,* and *Under God—A New Birth of Freedom.*

EDWIN SCOTT GAUSTAD is Professor of History at the University of California, Riverside. Born in Iowa in 1923, he received his B.A. from Baylor University and his M.A. and Ph.D. in History of Religion from Brown University. A member of the Baptist Joint Committee on Public Affairs, he is a contributor to numerous journals. His major publications include *A Great Awakening in New England, Historical Atlas of America, A Religious History of America,* and *Dissent in American Religion.*

HENRY C. GREGORY III was born in New York City. A fourth generation Baptist minister, he is Senior Minister at the Shiloh Baptist Church of Washington, D.C. He holds degrees from Howard University, Drew University, and Harvard University, and has done further graduate study at Oxford University. Chairman of the Theological Commission of the National Baptist Convention, U.S.A., Inc., he is currently compiling a book of theological position papers on *National Baptist Churches and the Holy Spirit.*

GEORGE W. HILL is Pastor of the Calvary Baptist Church of Washington, D.C. A native of California, he graduated from the University of Southern California, B.S.; Colgate-Rochester Divinity

School, B.D.; and received the honorary L.H.D. from the California College of Medicine. Former Chairman of the Division of Christian Social Concerns of the American Baptist Churches, U.S.A., he is presently Chairman of the Ecumenical Task Force of the Greater Washington Council of Churches and a member of the Baptist Joint Committee on Public Affairs.

WINTHROP S. HUDSON is Colgate Professor of the History of Christianity at Colgate Rochester Divinity School/Bexley Hall/Crozer Theological Seminary in Rochester, New York. Born in 1911 in Michigan, he received his Ph.D. in Church History from the University of Chicago. He has served as President of the American Society of Church History and the American Baptist Historical Society. Founding Editor of *Foundations* and the author of numerous publications, his books include *The Great Tradition of the American Churches, Baptist Concepts of the Church, Religion in America,* and *Nationalism and Religion in America.*

WILLIAM F. KEUCHER is Senior Minister of the Covenant Baptist Church of Detroit, Michigan. A graduate of Eastern Baptist College and Eastern Baptist Theological Seminary, he has served as Vice-President of the Central Baptist Theological Seminary. From 1952 to 1970 he served as Executive Minister of the Kansas Baptist Convention, during which time he was editor of the *Kansas Baptist.* A frequent contributor to various publications his books include *An Exodus for the Church, Main Street and the Mind of God,* and *Good News People in Action.* He is a member of the Baptist Joint Committee on Public Affairs.

GLENN T. MILLER is Assistant Professor of Church History at Southeastern Baptist Theological Seminary. He formerly taught at Union Theological Seminary in New York City and St. Mary's Seminary in Baltimore, Maryland. He was born in Virginia in 1942. A graduate of the University of Richmond, B.A.; Andover-Newton Theological School, B.D.; and Union Theological Seminary in New York, Th.D. in American Christianity, he is the author of *Religious Liberty in America: History and Prospects.*

W. MORGAN PATTERSON, Dean of Golden Gate Baptist Theological Seminary, was previously Professor of Church History at the Southern Baptist Theological Seminary. Born in Louisiana in 1925, he received his education at Stetson University, B.A.; New

Orleans Baptist Seminary, B.D. and Th.D. in Church History; and did advanced study at Oxford University. A contributor to numerous periodicals and professional journals, he is author of *Baptist Successionism: A Critical View* and co-editor of *Professor in the Pulpit.*

WALFRED PETERSON is a native of Minnesota and received his education at the University of Minnesota, B.A., M.A., and Ph.D. in Political Science. For fifteen years a Professor at Bethel College, he formerly served as Director of Research Services, Baptist Joint Committee on Public Affairs. He presently serves as Professor of Political Science at Washington State University. He is the author of numerous articles on religious liberty and church-state relations in professional journals and denominational magazines.

WILLIAM M. PINSON, JR., was born in Texas in 1934. He is a graduate of North Texas State University, B.A.; Southwestern Seminary, B.D., M. Div., and Th.D. in Christian Ethics. Formerly Professor of Christian Ethics at Southwestern Baptist Theological Seminary (1963–1975), he is presently Pastor of the First Baptist Church of Wichita Falls, Texas. He is the author of several books, including *How to Deal with Controversial Issues, Resource Guide to Current Social Issues, The Local Church in Ministry,* and co-editor of *Twenty Centuries of Great Preaching* (13 volumes).

C. PENROSE ST. AMANT is President of the Baptist Theological Seminary, Ruschlikon, Switzerland. Born in Louisiana in 1915 he graduated from Louisiana College, B.A.; Louisiana State University, M.A.; New Orleans Baptist Theological Seminary, Th.M. and Th.D.; and University of Edinburgh, Ph.D. in Church History. Formerly Professor of Church History at the New Orleans Baptist Theological Seminary and the Southern Baptist Theological Seminary, he is the author of *A Short History of Louisiana Baptists, The New Church History, Baptists in a Revolutionary Age,* and *Baptists and the Human Heritage.*

JAMES R. SCALES is President of Wake Forest University. A native of Oklahoma, born in 1919, he received his B.A. from Oklahoma Baptist University and his M.A. and Ph.D. from the University of Oklahoma. He has done post-graduate work at the University of Chicago and the London School of Economics. Formerly Professor of Political Science at Oklahoma Baptist

University, which he served as President from 1961 through 1965, he was also Professor of Political Science and Dean at Oklahoma State University.

GARDNER C. TAYLOR was born in Louisiana in 1918. He was graduated from Leland College, A.B., and the Oberlin Graduate School of Theology, B.D. He has served as Pastor of the Concord Baptist Church of Christ in Brooklyn, New York, since 1948. Lecturer on Preaching at Colgate Rochester Divinity School (1968–1974), Union Theological Seminary, New York, and Harvard Divinity School, he delivered the Yale Lyman Beecher Lectures in 1976. He has served as President of the New York City Council of Churches, the Urban League of New York City, and the Progressive National Baptist Convention.

ROBERT G. TORBET was born in Spokane, Washington. He is a graduate of Wheaton College, A.B.; Eastern Baptist Theological Seminary, B.D.; and the University of Pennsylvania, M.A. and Ph.D. in History. Assistant General Secretary for Ecumenical Relations of American Baptist Churches in the U.S.A. and a member of the Baptist Joint Committee on Public Affairs, he was formerly Dean and Professor of Church History at Central Baptist Theological Seminary. Among his numerous publications are *A History of the Baptists; Venture of Faith: The Story of American Baptist Foreign Missions, 1814–1954; Ecumenism: Free Church Dilemma;* and co-author of *Baptists North and South.*

G. HUGH WAMBLE is Professor of Church History at Midwestern Baptist Theological Seminary. Born in Georgia in 1923, he graduated from Mercer University, B.A.; University of Missouri, M.A.; and Southern Baptist Theological Seminary, B.D. and Ph.D. in Church History. He is President of the Missouri Baptist Convention and a member of the Baptist Joint Committee on Public Affairs. A contributor to various journals, he is the author of *Through Trial to Triumph* and *The Shape of Faith.*

JAMES E. WOOD, JR., is Executive Director of the Baptist Joint Committee on Public Affairs. Born in Virginia in 1922, he was educated at Carson-Newman College, A.B.; Columbia University, M.A.; Southern Baptist Theological Seminary, B.D., Th.M., and Ph.D.; Yale University; and the Naganuma School of Japanese Studies (Tokyo). Founding Editor of *Journal of Church and*

State (1959–1973) and Professor of Religion at Baylor University (1955–1972), he is author of *The Problem of Nationalism,* co-author of *Church and State in Scripture, History and Constitutional Law,* and editor of and contributor to *Jewish-Christian Relations in Today's World.*

FRANK H. WOYKE was born in Russia in 1905 of German parents. He received his education at Wesleyan University, B.A.; the Hartford Theological Seminary, B.D.; Yale University, Ph.D.; North American Baptist Theological Seminary; and Marburg University. He taught at the North American Baptist Theological Seminary from 1936 to 1943 and served as Executive Secretary, North American Baptist General Conference (1946–1968) and Associate Secretary of the Baptist World Alliance from 1968 until his retirement in 1972. He is presently writing an official history of the North American Baptist Conference.

Index

383